The Life of Cicero

Philip Kay-Bujak is a former GSA Headmaster and Associate of The Royal Historical Society. He taught English and European History at Langley School in Norfolk and was Headmaster at Stover School for Girls, was Chief Executive of Montessori and is a Koestler Literary Award winner. Other publications include articles on British history and books on The Great War.

Other books by Philip Kay-Bujak

Norfolk and Suffolk in the Great War
Attleborough: the evolution of a town
Undefeated
Around the World in 100 Years
The Bravest Man in the British Army
My Heart is in the Highlands: The Life and Work of Archibald Kay

The Life of Cicero

Lessons for Today from the Greatest Orator of the Roman Republic

Philip Kay-Bujak

PEN & SWORD
HISTORY

First published in Great Britain in 2023 by
Pen & Sword History
An imprint of Pen & Sword Books Limited
Yorkshire – Philadelphia

Copyright © Philip Kay-Bujak 2023

ISBN 978 1 39909 741 3

Typeset by Mac Style
Printed in the UK by CPI Group (UK) Ltd, Croydon, CR0 4YY.

FSC
www.fsc.org
MIX
Paper | Supporting
responsible forestry
FSC® C013604

Pen & Sword Books Limited incorporates the imprints of After
the Battle, Atlas, Archaeology, Aviation, Discovery, Family History,
Fiction, History, Maritime, Military, Military Classics, Politics,
Select, Transport, True Crime, Air World, Frontline Publishing, Leo
Cooper, Remember When, Seaforth Publishing, The Praetorian Press,
Wharncliffe Local History, Wharncliffe Transport, Wharncliffe True
Crime and White Owl.

For a complete list of Pen & Sword titles please contact

PEN & SWORD BOOKS LIMITED
47 Church Street, Barnsley, South Yorkshire, S70 2AS, England
E-mail: enquiries@pen-and-sword.co.uk
Website: www.pen-and-sword.co.uk
or
PEN AND SWORD BOOKS
1950 Lawrence Rd, Havertown, PA 19083, USA
E-mail: Uspen-and-sword@casematepublishers.com
Website: www.penandswordbooks.com

For my mother and brother

Contents

A Note on Sources

Where extracts from the letters of Cicero have been included in the text, these have been taken from '*Cicero, Selected Letters*', part of the Penguin Classics series and translated by D. R. Shackleton Bailey. Where Roman names are used, a more user-friendly version has been included, also in the index, for those new readers of Roman history, which hopefully will assist in the identification of key individuals. References to Plutarch are to his *Life of Cicero*. Where key texts or research articles have been accessed these can be found in the footnotes, which have deliberately been kept to a minimum.

A Roman bore his *clan* name (*gens*), the *nomen* usually ending in -*ius*, which is then followed by a *cognomen* – for first name at the end. Slaves only had one name eg. Tiro, although these were added to if they managed to achieve the status of freedman, as Tiro did; he took the name of his former owner, becoming Marcus Tullius Tiro.

Acknowledgements

Any work on the life of a statesman is a risky undertaking as so many talented authors have learnt before and I could not have attempted this work without the advice and guidance of numerous individuals and to all of them I offer my sincere gratitude. Any errors in my work are entirely my own. Thank you most especially to Dr Frank Millard, Dr Edward Bujak, Jason Georgini, Professor James Whitwell and @decimusclaudius on Instagram for access to his fabulous library of images. My interpretation of the personality traits displayed by Cicero in his letters are formed from discussions from Dr. Caroline Green, a behavioural psychologist, and are a preliminary effort at an historical psychological study. I am also indebted to JSTOR for their invaluable work collating their incredible archive of academic research.

To Pen & Sword Books, and especially Philip Sidnell, for having confidence that such a work was possible and for his support during the period of Covid which restricted so many deadlines from being met, and to Alan Dorrington for his skilled work and artistry in the hand drawn illustrations he created.

Finally, to my wife Helena and my children Skye and Cameron for their understanding and patience while they waited for me to arrive late for dinner so many times.

Part I

Early Life and Influences

Chapter 1

Home, Heritage and Patriotism

We cannot always build the future for our youth but we can build the youth for our future.

Franklin D. Roosevelt

A note on dates: The calendar that we use is called the Gregorian, named after Pope Gregory XIII, which was introduced in 1582 CE and was a reform of the Julian calendar created by Julius Caesar in 45 BCE.[1] The Gregorian calendar recognises 365 days of the year, divided into twelve months, and weeks of seven days. It established the Roman year of 648 as the year zero, i.e. the year that Jesus is presumed to have been born and counted each year thereafter starting at 1 AD (Anno Domini – the year of our Lord). Dates before that were referred to as BC (the sacred phrase Before Christ). With the global acceptance of the Gregorian calendar in our secular world and the recognition that the world does not wholly accept Jesus Christ, or necessarily religion, the alternative BCE and CE (Before the Common Era and Common Era) are now commonplace and will be used in this book.[2] All dates within the text are BCE unless otherwise specified.

Father & *Familias*

The Cicero family home was located near Arpinum, and today Arpino is still the beautiful Italian town clustered high on a hillside that it always was. The exact location of what would have been a substantial villa outside of the main town is unknown – erased by 2,000 years of history and the environment – but we can still imagine a striking complex of white walls, bright red *tegulae* and *imbrices* (plural for the terracotta fired clay *tegula* and *imbrex* overlapping tiles), roofs sloping in all angular directions, entrance arches, mosaic floors, stables and green lush trees and vegetation all suited to impress the visitor. The family had a fine local reputation. Around, the complex fields would have been peppered with olive trees and groves all watered from the small River Liris which flowed through the valleys around the town. The walk up to the hilltop community would have been steep, and tall poplar and alder trees also drank from the river, offering shade from the scorching summer heat to walkers moving up the hill, or simply strolling down to a rural home and having deep conversations. Livestock would appear in fields across the valley, perhaps goats and sheep, and orchards and vegetables would be tended closer to the main house with its retinue of servants and slaves.

Situated 100 km, or 62 miles, south of Rome, Arpinum was captured by Roman troops, who were extending the reach of the embryonic nation state in 305 and granted the right of Roman citizenship – except the right to vote – described in Latin as *civitas sine suffragio*. As time passed, this right was also extended to the inhabitants of the town in 188 – and it finally received recognition as a Roman town in 90 after the coming Social War. The Cicero family would have seen this latest event at first hand.

As it remains today so it was in Cicero's grandfather's time. Marcus Tullius Cicero (senior) was a successful local administrator keen to play his part on a local level perhaps with an office in the town itself, he built a reputation for being a fair and just man and administer to the town on a local political level. We know of his talents and localism through part of a letter to him from a Roman statesman of his time: *'With your courage and ability, Marcus Cicero, I wish you had preferred to be active at the political centre rather than at the municipal level.*[3] This Marcus Cicero had two sons, one of which, another Marcus Tullius Cicero, was to be father to our own Marcus.

The Roman calendar at the time of our Marcus' birth on the estate, was very unlike our own and, much like the Roman state itself, had evolved over the hundreds of years from the supposed founding of the city by Romulus around 753. The original Roman calendar calculated a year divided into ten months and covered 300 days, with the additional sixty-five that we are used to just scattered unevenly amongst those months. The addition of January and February by a Roman ruler named Numa Pompilius brought the year almost up to 365 days.

According to that calendar then, and as far as we currently know, our Marcus Tullius Cicero was born in the year 106 (what was the Roman year of 648 i.e. 648 years after the founding of Rome) and 106 years before the birth of Christ according to our Gregorian calendar. His actual birthday is generally agreed as being between 3 and 6 Janus – the month we know as January. This was an auspicious month. Janus was an ancient God to the Romans and it was he that was the god of all doorways, openings and therefore by implication, opportunities – a very popular god, especially for the ambitious.

What little we know of Cicero's mother Helvia has invariably been taken from Plutarch. Piecing together an accurate picture of Roman history has always been a challenge for historians, even more so when it comes to the lives of Republican women, but at least with Plutarch, a Greek Platonist philosopher and historian who lived from 46 CE until at least 119 CE, we have a respected and prolific essayist who wrote only a matter of years after many of his subjects and their exploits. Plutarch's essay, The Life of Cicero, is one of the extant texts from his series of biographies, *Parallel Lives*; he tells us that Cicero was born to Helvia *'without travail or pain'* and that *'she was well born and lived an honourable life'*. While it is dangerous to assume much more than this scrap, we also have a reference to Helvia in a letter from her second son Quintus to Tiro, the tireless secretary, telling history that she was a careful and thrifty woman always remembering to keep the lids on wine jars – lest they been seen as empty. Not much to go on, but would it be reasonable to assume that Marcus benefited from a steadfast and caring mother in his early years? Evidence to support this in the later mass of letters from Cicero is, however, almost non-existent and remarkable by its absence. A man devoted to his mother, or even having a devoted mother, would surely be something that would find its way into correspondence in some way, but the words are not there, no loving phrases, no admiration or any reference to his mother exists. Dangerous though it is to extend this thought too far, one could offer for the prosecution of this suggestion the following:

Central to the traits identified in men with 'maternal issues' or the 'mummy wound' can be emotional instability – more specifically, erratic relationships. This is because the emotional connections between people were never taught, observed or felt as one was growing up. If Helvia was indeed a dutiful but emotionally unattached mother then this would explain why Cicero himself often fell out with friends, made friends of his enemies, vilified enemies only to befriend them, became estranged from those closest to him and failed to recognize his mother as having any part in his life.

Additionally, the 'mummy wound' often displays itself in men of little sincerity of emotion – those who say they are sentimental, but are in fact unable to feel sentimentality. He chose the academic path because of its certainty, the law because of its objectivity and he wrote with a scholarly, rather than a Shakespearian, pen. Far easier to talk of facts and figures than people and emotions.

The penultimate giveaway here could be that the lack of a mother's love often creates a need to prove oneself. Men with maternal issues or a lack of affection shown by their mothers, drive themselves harder than the rest, no achievement is the final one, there have to always be new goals, more money, more power. There is never any moment of marked self-esteem or finality as it is not possible and the drive and feeling of lack of achievement can last throughout life and show itself as a cold, brittle personality, often self-pitying and angry – unable to accept being corrected or able to admit fault. Almost from when he could first stand, Cicero embarked on a journey of self-flagellation through work, career and political success – all of which ended with his horrible death, but which never proved enough for a mother's (or indeed a wife's) love in return. His letters often betray his true feelings of self-pity, a resistance to criticism, a self-belief bordering on mental illness – all a cry for help that no one could hear.

Finally, resistance towards intimacy drives the man with 'maternal issues' towards the younger woman – she at least will not challenge him emotionally like an older woman. A younger woman, by and large, has yet to experience the emotions that life will throw at her, which gives the emotionally lacking man a distinct advantage. Older women threaten his emotional strong box, offer the potential to explore feelings and expose frailties. Cicero married twice. At the age of 27 he married Terentia – an 18 year old and, although they were together for over thirty years, their relationship ended in divorce and, at the age of 60, he then married Publilia who was aged just 15. This is not to suggest Cicero felt the same way about his wives as he did about his mother – indeed there are some references in his later letters of 58 that praise the virtues of his wife Terentia – if not his love for her –

> *To think that a woman of your virtue, fidelity, uprightness and kindness should have fallen into such troubles on my account!*

Whatever we might try to deduce and infer from the available evidence, the young Cicero took into his adolescent and adult life a fragile mix of traditional ideas and emotions built in his early childhood and fashioned by what he saw and heard from his father. His wavering emotional attitudes are betrayed in his later actions as he tried to measure up to what his father expected of him and possibly what he hoped his mother would love about him. We might say the same of Donald Trump, whose parental issues are well documented, but with Cicero there was the added chemistry of a sharp, agile mind that could see his efforts were always going to be insufficient.

Patrocinium – Patronage

> *The client-patron relationship system called patronage built the social and cultural infrastructure of the Roman Empire.*

The young Cicero would of course have heard stories about his grandfather. As he walked across the beautiful mosaic floors of the villa, around the atrium or entrance hall and into his father's office or *tablinum*, no doubt there were images of his grandfather, either sat on columns of marble or set into the walls to impress visitors and the family – a constant reminder of service and ambitions. In many homes of the upper middle classes, a corner would be set aside specifically to locate the various images of past relatives of note – this household shrine was called the *lararium*. However, the teenage Cicero would have seen far more of his father the local official – and due to his poor health and probable disability – the work from home administrator. Unlike our mode of living today, although Covid has started to adjust this, the typical well to do and professional Roman father spent a great deal of time at home regularly welcoming guests from the earliest morning hours into his home, furnishing refreshments and conducting business in his office space, reciprocating or receiving favours, advice or strategy.

Marcus Cicero Senior would no doubt have worked very long hours and instilled in both his sons the necessity of working as much as one could, and both Marcus and Quintus would have become familiar with the regular comings and goings – usually at the start of the day – from their home. Personal status and reputation, or *dignitas*, were fundamental foundations of Roman society. The entire social construct rested on both private and public displays of acknowledged and recognized dignity and respect underpinned by open inequality, which was celebrated and reinforced by the very visible layers of the Roman class system.

The salutation was the morning greeting when clients gathered in the atria of their patron, or perhaps outside in the street in order to have a meeting in his *tablinum*. The more clients the greater the social and political standing of the patron. Marcus and Quintus would watch clients arrive in their best togas

A villa complex of the Republican period – rustic grandeur prior to Augustan extravagance.

and see their father, in his toga displaying a higher status, receive, refresh and meet a regular flow of clients. Patronage relationships could be built up over succeeding generations, rather like solicitors' clients in our time, and they dealt with issues such as advice or even protection, advancement and recognition, favours such as posts for members of the family and, commonly, legal advice. Although business was conducted privately, it was vital that everyone knew it was happening.

The opposite to the private exercise of patronage was the public. In Republican Rome it was equally fundamental to the acquisition of power and social standing to display one's ability to bestow patronage. In this case bestowing gifts on the community or public eulogizing (*laudationes*) by the patron or for the patron was commonplace, as was publicly accompanying a client in the street or to the Forum or the law courts and, in so doing, flagging up your support and endorsement of an individual. In either respect, the rituals of patronage stemmed from the male world and in return, the patron expected loyalty (a fragile expectation), deference in public, and public support in pursuit of political ambition. These were the rules of the game in Republican Rome and would have been of pivotal significance for the young Cicero boys as they assimilated how the world around them worked.

In line with the central theme of this book, one might ask how much has really changed? One hundred years before the birth of Christ, and 2,200 years after, as I write, patronage is still the 'grease that keeps the wheels of the economy, society and politics turning'. What does this tell us about our own age and what might we learn from the world that Marcus was about to enter? Contemporary societies, everywhere, are dependent on patronage and nowhere more than in the United Kingdom or the United States. However, we can see that there is a key contrast with our own age in that our political elites try to hide the patronage they give and receive, whereas in Republican Rome they were at least open about the reality of what was needed for personal success.

Newspaper and social media reports displayed faux outrage against something that they knew existed and indeed they had benefited from. When Boris Johnson was savaged by the press in 2022 for giving a seat in the House of Lords to Evgeny Lebedev we saw a mirror image of Roman *patrocinium* in action. This would not be lost on the Prime Minister – himself a writer on Roman history – and perhaps he enjoyed being able to exercise the same degree of authority that his Roman heroes had done. Despite being advised that Mr Lebedev, the son of a KGB spy, was an unwise choice for the award of this senatorial rank, Mr Johnson pressed on, giving his personal and public endorsement, just as if he were walking beside Mr Lebedev on their way to a meeting at the Forum in central Rome. Of course, Mr Lebedev had already supplied his patron with a great many examples of *salutatio* with numerous parties and effusive hospitality at his own expense. Additionally, the Prime Minister had received the public backing of Mr Lebedev through, the now Lord Lebedev's, *Evening Standard* newspaper when he was Lord Mayor. In 2020, Mr Johnson had first tried to reward Mr Lebedev by nominating him for a peerage for his services to philanthropy and the media – it was only from his position as Prime Minister however that he was able to push this through as his personal patron.

Under Donald Trump *patrocinium* reached even higher levels. As Politico reported in 2016, seventy-three donors contributed more than $1.7 million to Donald Trump personally and $57.3 million to the Republican party. In return, Trump gave official posts and overseas diplomatic posts to nearly 40 per cent of those donors. The contrast with Republican Rome again comes in the form of Trump's attempts to pretend this was not the case and for statements such as *'By self-funding my campaign, I am not controlled by my donors, special interests or lobbyists'* and calling political opponents 'puppets' for accepting large donations. At least in Republican Rome the senators were open about bribery being a fundamental part of the political process – rather than covering their tracks with leaves of lies. In so doing, patronage in both the UK and the USA has declined from a laudable, openly practised and almost honourable activity to become part of the subterfuge of political power, a dirty word and something to be avoided in public – something to be done behind closed doors. Later in Cicero's life he would comment on the start of this decline in Roman society and it being part of the road to ruin and despair for the Republic – is this also perhaps going to be the case for our own modern democratic western liberalism and, if so, does it begin with the degradation of moral values within established political, social and moral norms as the corruption of patronage began in Republican Rome? Western liberal society is under attack from many directions and a failure to respond to 'sleaze' is a sure sign that it has reached and already poisoned the top.

Iconography and imagery

Central to the journey through the Cicero household would be the images of their forbears. Unlike the Greeks or the earlier Etruscans – whom the Romans eclipsed after the sixth century – iconography in the Roman home, at any level, was less to do with art and much more to do with capturing a sense of place and achievement – a retrospective archive or service. In the case of an ancestor, especially a successful or notable one, the potential collateral prestige for the Cicero family was immense. In contrast to the Greek idealized forms of body and face, Republican Roman statues were meant to be as close to the original as possible. In what is now referred to as the 'veristic style', head and shoulder busts were especially realistic and the closer the resemblance to the original person the better, regardless of wrinkles, warts, or the ravages of time. Imperfections of the skin all added to the heroism of the subject. His (we must remember that it was mostly *his* until the arrival of the Principate when the role of women became more prominent and they were rewarded with their own statues) service to the state and the people, or his bravery in extending or defending Roman rule were enshrined in these images which we can see today.

The Romans worshipped their history as they sought to preserve their heritage and memory and pass responsibility for stability and growth onto future generations. In the second and first centuries, this cultural clash with the Greek influences over art, literature and philosophy had gone too far. In her excellent and very readable book *SPQR*, Mary Beard particularly draws on Cato (the Elder) as a noisy bastion of what it was to be Roman:

> *Some of the most outspoken voices of the third and second centuries* BCE *became famous for attacking the corrupting influence on traditional Roman behaviours and morals of foreign culture in general, and Greek culture in particular; their targets ranged from literature and philosophy to naked exercise, fancy food and depilation…. (the Elder) Cato warned that Roman power could be brought down by the passion for Greek literature (and)…once remarked that pretty boys now cost more than fields, jars of pickled fish more than ploughmen.*[4]

We can reflect on these concerns about what it meant to be Roman and what levels of dilution were occurring in second century Rome as we live through our own experience of renewed national consciousness. The first twenty years of the twenty-first century in the UK, and in many other countries around the world, were marked by increasing sensitivity over what was seen as unregulated immigration. A fundamental source of energy behind Brexit was created by the Conservative elements in society who voiced anger and concern for decades, even founding their own party, which some might remember was called UKIP. In the United States of America, Donald Trump, a figure who will feature throughout this book, took aim at the Mexican border and began to build a wall along it. When Donald Trump stated, '*The security of the US is imperilled by a drastic surge in illegal activity on the southern border*' he was echoing Cato (the Elder) in his fear for the future stability of the nation in the face of immigration and cultural appropriation. What difference is there between Nigel Farage's statement, '*Immigration is good for the rich because it's cheaper nannies and cheaper chauffeurs and cheaper gardeners but its bad news for ordinary Britons…it has left the white working class effectively as an underclass and I think that's a disaster for our society*' and Cato's '*pickled fish and ploughmen*'?

In the iconographic world therefore that surrounded the young Cicero there was already an increased sense of danger for the survival of the Republic and he was not born into the later age of Imperial stability.

It was only later under Imperial rule, after the Republic had fallen, that we witness the standardization of message, and of worship of one man becoming more fundamental – and hence the Greek style of mass-produced beauty re-emerges as a way of establishing a single unifying image. However, this was all in the future and the young Cicero grew up in an environment surrounded by expectations and reminders of service as well as portents and dangers to the stability of the Republic and its centuries old 'democratic' foundations. Similarly in the British Royal family, there is little escape from the marble stare of the forbear who expects you to ensure that the monarchy survives at a time of ever-increasing questions of relevance. The centrality of the notion of service inside the House of Windsor has dominated the lives of King Charles and Prince William and is doing the same to Prince George, Princess Charlotte and Prince Louis, but it is also now accompanied by a real sense of danger ahead.

This environmental impact of iconography on the young is an increasing preoccupation for those whose mortality beckons and their desire to ensure continuity presses on them more acutely each day. One could argue that there is no difference between the current British monarchy in this sense and the Roman Republicans – except of course one is currently attempting to preserve the concept of monarchy and the other was trying to resist it – totally opposite ideals, but identical use of propaganda. So, we can try to imagine the Marcus born in 106 as a young child becoming conscious of the funereal images of his grandfather and older family members situated in the atrium or entrance hall and being made aware by stories from his father of the concept of service to the state and a life devoted to the people and not himself. When Cicero entered public life as a young man in his twenties, it was this notion of public service and the public good that went with him and was accompanied by an increasing sense of the need to fight for the Republic against growing threats from inside and outside Rome. It was his turn and what sort of statues and busts would be created to mark and preserve the service he was to give to Rome and the state?

Loyalty to the *Provincia* vs the lure of the urban City *(Urbs)*

We would do well to note at this point the tremendous difference between the iconography of the provincial home and that of the city. In the most recent book on this subject, Sarah Lepinski and Vanessa Rousseau examine the contrasts between the grandeur of Republican Rome (as opposed to that of the Imperial age) and the provincial attempts to replicate this.[5]

We all live in provinces and in that, as in so many respects we, again, are no different from the Romans. *Provinciae* (pl.) were and are territorial subdivisions of any country – or empire. We might call them Counties, the Germans and Americans call them States, and in Finland they are *Pirkanmaa*, but they all serve the same function and are subdivisions for government, taxation and law and order. *Provincia* in the Roman Republican era provided the centre with food, supplies, manpower, and occasionally problems and States, Counties and *Pirkanmaa* do the same today. In reverse the centre or capital city – what we could refer to as the metropolitan power within a nation – builds a relationship with the provinces. The established view on the Romanization of the *Provinciae* in the time of Cicero, during the first century tended to support the view of Francis Haverfield, a British scholar of the early twentieth century. In 1905 Haverfield argued that 'Romanization' in Italy was the simple process by which provincial elites adopted the symbols and cultural developments of Rome itself. Thus, we could assume that in the Cicero household from 106 onwards – say to his 16th birthday in 90 – changes in the domestic design mirrored what they saw as civilised developments in Rome. Consequently, men and women's fashions would change, the haircut would take on a new look and even the layout of the home or *domus* would take on changes in city chic.

A good comparison to Rome is how London influences the shires. Those who have lived and worked in London and then relocated to the country have an advantage in being able to see this relationship from both sides. The Heverfield position would see the last 1,500 years of London's history as a one-way process where the melting pot of cultural and political changes that boiled in London have simply fed out to the shires, which have then mimicked the centre. So, when a young person arrives in London, they are awe struck by the power, wealth, fashion, noise, landmarks, buildings, talent, pace and metabolism of the *civitas*. However, there is a push back argument that suggests cultural appropriation is and was a two-way street. Described as Creolization, this theory is based on the sociological study of Caribbean identity and suggests that through city and provincial mixing, groups imitate each other. An example of the need to replicate the countryside in the city can be found in the prevalent presence of four-wheel drives, or Chelsea tractors, on the|streets of cities all over the United Kingdom. Thus, Rome too must have assimilated certain aspects of provincial life – those that moved to the *civitas* could bring with them aspects of country living – such as the four x four chariot.

In the same way as might a young person today arriving from the provinces to Moscow, Quebec, Nairobi or Pnom Penh, the young boy Marcus Cicero must have felt overawed when he made his first trip to Rome sometime around 90, travelling with his father and no doubt a small retinue, including his mother, as he made a decision to purchase a small home in Rome:

While the exact date cannot be fixed it is certain that Cicero's father, moved by the desire to give his sons opportunities for education not to be had in the provincial town, purchased a house at Rome in the street called Carinae, a fashionable quarter between the Coclian and Esquiline mount where the family resided each year, at least during the period between October and June.[6]

While we cannot be certain what drove this decision, it is very likely that Marcus Cicero (the elder) saw that the time had come to introduce his sons to Rome and the opportunities for advancement that this would give and we can only imagine the awe and wonder with which the two boys took in their surroundings as they recognised that a new era in their lives had begun.

All children enjoy overhearing the conversations of adults. You and I have both shared in this desire when we were young and, depending on what you hear, your view of the world is shaped to a large extent by the 'secrets' that you uncover. Consider then for a moment overhearing, at a young age, conversations between powerful and influential figures. Perhaps Sasha Obama overheard the conversation regarding whether or not to kill Osama Bin Laden, maybe William Wallace Lincoln was passing his father's office listening to him discussing how to defeat the South in the American Civil War, or consider the son of Gaius Octavius (a contemporary and, ultimately, the nemesis of Marcus Cicero) in hearing stories of how to survive in the political turmoil of Rome. The point here is that the environment of one's upbringing was as relevant then as it is now. Marcus may have seen the relics of past service in his home, but it would not be until he reached Rome that his real education in political survival would begin. So it is true today. Boris Johnson would have learnt much about social survival at Eton College, but until he made it to London, he would be only a minor part of what he needed to succeed at the very top. With this in mind, we might ask ourselves to what extent the political mistakes made by Donald Trump were, in part, a function of never having served in political office? His life had been spent solely in the 'art of the deal' so what chance did he have in understanding the tactics of political power and survival. This mismatch between background, education and upbringing has never been any different and Marcus Tullius Cicero (the elder) knew this as well as Stanley Johnson 2,000 years later.

Notes

1. It was not until the Roman calendar became hopelessly muddled that Julius Caesar introduced the Julian Calendar in 45.
2. Many nations still also maintain their ancient religious calendars alongside the Gregorian such as in Islamic and Jewish states.
3. Everitt, A., *Cicero: A Turbulent Life* (John Murray. 2001)
4. Beard, Mary, *SPQR, A History of Ancient Rome*, (Profile Books, 2016, pp. 204–205)
5. Lepinski, S. & Rousseau, V., *The Oxford Handbook of Roman Imagery & Iconography* (OUP, 2002)
6. Willis Jones, V., 'The Family Life of Marcus Tullius Cicero.' (Masters Thesis, 1926)

Chapter 2

From Arpinum to Rome

The education of Cicero c. 98–91

The foundation of every state is the education of its youth.
Diogenes (412–323)

Situated some seventy miles from Rome, Arpinum is today still close enough to be affected by events in the capital city but also far enough away to maintain its own singular country way of life. One could, as far as one wanted, be involved in the life of Rome – a two to three days journey away – or imagine that it did not exist. From the early years, it was clear that Marcus was a bright child and he needed the best education. As today, this was unlikely to exist in the countryside – tutors needed to earn a living like anyone else and they needed clients, so it would have to be Rome where they moved – to live in the right postcode for their son's education.

We do not know the exact date that Marcus Cicero (elder) moved his family to Rome for the future summers, but we can estimate somewhere around 98 when the young Marcus was around 8 years old. According to Plutarch, Cicero was a brilliant pupil with an outstanding memory – something that was a crucial natural gift for someone to enter a career in rhetoric and oratory. The Roman curriculum in the late Republican period was challenging and varied. Hours would be spent each day studying and learning by heart Latin poetry and the plays of the Greeks. In later years Cicero would often use phrases he learnt in his youth to illustrate his love and patriotic empathy with the earliest dramatists and writers and we have him to thank, through his surviving speeches and letters, for many of the phrases otherwise lost to history. His earliest teachers used the Greek poet Archias as the exemplar for his study of rhetoric and the Greek rhetorician Apollonius. Cicero also absorbed as much philosophy as he could locate and it is said that in 87, Philo of Larissa, head of the Academy of Plato, some 300 years old by then, arrived in Rome and at his feet sat Marcus Tullius Cicero inspired and inspiring.

Being from a semi noble or equestrian family – a Knight from the Shires with enough money to mix at the lower end of the best social circles – Marcus was also blessed to be given openings through his father's contacts and the exhilaration of building his social diary drove him on. Among those he met very early on in Rome was the statesman and heroic figure Lucius Licinius Crassus – orator, man of letters, hugely wealthy, successful politician at the very top of his powers and Roman celebrity. Once accepted or recognized by Crassus, many more doors would open including, in all likelihood, access to Crassus' own home on the celebrated Palatine Hill. Titus Pomponius (later called Atticus), a little older than Cicero quickly became what was to be his lifelong friend, mentor, conscience and ultimately keeper of the Cicero flame in history. In the same whirlwind his father did him one more great service by introducing the young, impressionable and dashing Cicero to Crassus' father-in-law, Quintus Mucius Scaevola the Augur – greatly admired with nationwide *dignitas* and a legal expert who was around 80 years old. He may have even met at a gathering or party for young nobles Gnaeus Pompeius Magnus (known to history as Pompey the Great), whose life began in the same year as Marcus Tullius in 106 – although to the far northeast near modern day Ancona. From Arpinum and its provincial tranquillity, known faces and predictable routines, young Marcus Cicero now threw himself into the cyclone of Roman social and political life, armed with the expectations and precepts of home.

It was through social mixing that the various elites of Roman society sifted through the available talent and marked out those destined for office and even high office. Cicero's father made the most of his contacts and as Scaevola aged so Marcus was passed on to an older student named Marcus Pupius Piso, who became a minder and mentor to the young Cicero. In future years, the historian Sallust tried to suggest a homosexual relationship developed between Piso and Cicero – nothing unusual in the Roman Republic and nothing that Cicero could not deal with. We know that Cicero was a sincere if not serious child, delighting in learning and reading and shunning physically aggressive sports and pastimes. 'The time which others spend in advancing their own personal affairs, taking holidays, and attending games, indulging in pleasures of various kinds or even enjoying mental relaxation and bodily recreation, the time they spend on protracted parties and gambling and playing ball, proves in my case to have been taken up with returning over and over again to...literary pursuits.' By the age of 14 in 92, Cicero had already composed his first poetry. Although lost to us now, references state that one poem, 'Pontius Glaucus', was the story of a fisherman who, upon eating a magic herb, becomes a sea god able to tell the future. Already able to use his words for the persuasion of others, Cicero showed himself to be a quick writer and translator, good with words and acquiring a larger than usual vocabulary – this, however, did not make him a poet of the stature of others like Catullus, but it marked his love for using words rather than steel as weapons.

Class in the last century of the Roman Republic

The social structure of Roman society was fixed and there was little blurring of the edges as there is now in our own time. We find it hard now to identify who is a genuine member of what was once called the working class as we did one hundred years ago and even harder now is to subdivide middle class into lower, middle and upper. Access to the once easily identifiable upper class is not an issue, as no one can really identify what it is any longer. This was not the case in Republican Rome.

At the very top was the senatorial (*senatores*) class. This was a political grouping of men who had served as senators, but also included all their family – the *dignitas* afforded to the rank flowed forwards into future members of the family, but also backwards into long dead relations and the *familias* become bestowed with the upper-class distinction. Within this upper ruling group were also the nobles (*nobiles*) or aristocracy of Republican Rome – families whose ancestors included at least one consul – one of the two ruling men chosen for a year of service leading the whole state. While it was often the case that senators and consuls were drawn from the same collection of noble families, it was sometimes possible for a man from the next class down, the equestrians, to achieve the status of a senator or even consul and he was referred to as the 'new man' (*novus homo*). The small hilltop town of Arpinum was to produce two such new men – Gaius Marius who was consul seven times in his lifetime between 157–86 and Marcus Tullius Cicero who was to rise to the rank of consul in 63.

A case in point is that during his earliest years in Rome in the late 80s, Marcus Tullius would have met Gnaeus Pompey, his exact equal in age, but the son of exactly such a man – his father Gnaeus Pompeius Strabo – was the first in his family to reach the rank of senator in Rome and thus was a prime example of a *novus homo*. Pompey's father very quickly acquired a reputation for greed and double dealing as well as ruthlessness, and his son moved through the younger circles of Roman society as a model for Marcus Tullius and very likely a good friend. At the age of 20 in 86, when both he and Cicero were finding their feet in Rome, although at very different levels, Strabo died and the very young Pompey inherited all his father's estates and great wealth – he was indeed a rising star in the Roman firmament and Cicero would have been close to his orbit.

Arriving in Rome as a member of the equestrian class meant a number of things: there would already be a good network of social and business connections, support and patronage would flow in terms of opportunities to network and meet influential people and, most importantly, the immediacy of changing events would be felt far more keenly than in Arpinum. The Romans are famed for their communication systems, especially their road network that expanded where their influence was dominant, and with that came a well-run postal system carrying private messages between individuals as well as tremendous amounts of civil management and government communications. Along every road we can imagine a range of scenes, carts and horses passing on their ways to all sorts of places across Italy and beyond, military units marching, cavalry units trotting, horses being watered at wayside troughs, funerals for those who died whilst on their journey – which in some cases could take weeks or even months – roadside markets and of course stopping points with small temples to offer thanks or request salvation from the gods. Behind all the communications were scribes working full time for government officials or departments, sellers of parchment, ink and wax tablets – as well as sealing wax for signet rings to seal off the communications. Of course, there were also many dangers. Any sort of illness or injury was unlikely to receive much or any treatment, unless you happened to be near to a settlement of some kind, and along every route there were bandits waiting for night to fall and for weak targets. *Pax Romanum*, or the peace that came with Romans, dealt severely with any sort of crime, but the road distances were long, vagrants and escaped criminals in gangs fed off the transportation networks so giving thought to personal safety and security was an essential part of any travel plan.

In Rome, however, it was the tongue that was the main method of transporting information. The immediate availability of information was essential when events were moving quickly, and often critical when needing to run to save one's life, or vital when an opportunity arose to make another personal link and build another bridge towards success. So, a melting pot of conversation, gossip and babble accompanied the dust, smell, noise and smoke of any walk around the busy streets of Rome or the highways of the Empire. The *viae* or *strata* in the city would be annotated by wooden signs with their names or painted onto corner walls much as today and the Cicero of his 20s would gradually build up his knowledge of how to get from A to B either the quickest or safest way or via a stopover at a friend or contact. In Arpinum most roads would not have been paved, but in Rome many were, although the rapidly expanding late Republican city often had to digest more people than it could either feed or maintain. Being seen in a fashionable street was essential to old values thus there existed an ongoing battle to fill potholes (forgive me if this sounds familiar) or raise the standards of the roads. Possibly the following phrase would have often been used in district meetings:

There is an urgent need to remake the level of the street, of the neighbourhood or of the great agglomerative dwellings – the social fabric whereby man may be able to develop the needs of his personality.

Est ergo necessarium illam restitui socialis viate contextam rationem, que quisque humanae personae iutis appetitionbus possit satisfacere, ac quidem qoud pertinent ad urbis via, ad regionas, ad civum universtatem.

Or – the streets need to be improved – how can a man make a statement about his skills and potential when the streets look so poor, the neighbourhood is so urgently in need of improvement and his status cannot be displayed adequately.

These things mattered to a member of the equestrian class – a class built not on political status, but economic potential. As the Republic blossomed and an empire expanded, these men could become fabulously wealthy (the bourgeoisie of the French Revolution or the MPs of the shire in the reign of Charles I), but had absolutely no influence on the direction of government or taxation. They needed good streets, elegant courtyards and places to display their wealth and if they were to invite a person of influence to their suburban home, how could they bring them by the most prestigious route? Equestrians were Knights (originally descended from mounted cavalry far earlier in Republican history) and it was they who could swell the ranks of the senatorial class either by marriage (bringing their fortunes with them) or, less commonly, by their skills.

Under the two most influential classes came a variety of other groups largely separated by whether they were entitled to or held Roman citizenship – this was the most important base currency for the lower classes. Those freeborn Romans were entitled to all the freedoms, protections and privileges that full citizenship offered, these were the Commons or plebs, the true people of Rome about whom we know so little. Our history of the Republican period relies heavily on the stories of great men, heroic deeds and the papers of a very few intellectuals that have survived. Digging, literally, beneath the surface, archaeologists are now more concerned with the everyday life of the plebs – how they saw Rome, what their concerns were and how they were able to influence or be influenced by events. The evidence is fragile and not prolific, but through research and the dedication of our modern experts, the picture is becoming clearer. Indeed the Roman citizen was a citizen of the known world and that known world was expanding rapidly.

Our Bible classes at school may well come to mind when we consider how St Paul was a Roman citizen. Even his Roman commander told Paul (Acts 22:28) that he had had to buy his citizenship (probably after years of service and saving his pay in the army). Paul tells us he was born a Roman citizen (Acts 16:37) and it was a gift and privilege that protected him even as a rebel in the eyes of the Romans and helped him throughout his life, especially on his epic missionary journeys across the Mediterranean. Indeed there is a link between the later St Paul and Cicero himself. Tarsus, his home town in Cilicia, was made a Roman province by Cicero's friend, by then a great General in the army, Gnaeus Pompey, in 64. Paul escaped flogging (Acts 22:25–27) and was able to appeal for a hearing before Emperor Nero (Acts 25:10–11) all because of the power of his citizenship, but was martyred in 66 CE – just over 100 years after the foundation of Tarsus.

Below the freeborn citizen of Rome came the Latins (the *Latini*) – the people of Italy not under Roman control, although they too were all granted citizenship in 89. Foreigners (*peregrini*) were the freeborn peoples of Roman territories, but they were rarely granted full citizenship and had to wait for another 200 years. Lastly came the *liberti* or freed people – men and women who had bought their freedom from slavery and the slaves themselves. No one knows how large this class of people was, but certainly Rome and the growing empire relied heavily on both of these groups to till the fields, grow crops, provide the labour for buildings and cheer in the political gatherings that made or broke their heroes. It was into this rich tapestry of city life that Marcus Tullius Cicero stepped, the talented young man with the agile intellect, the good breeding, the loyalty to the state and public service that would help him to go far – all under the watchful gaze of his ancestors.

Part II

The Law, Forum and the Republic

Chapter 3

The Innate Instability of the Republic

Political seizures in Rome 91–87

Rome was already undergoing the first tremors and aftershocks of sustained political and economic growth well before Cicero arrived in Rome. His life was coterminous with a century of substantial change and there are echoes of this in our world today; whereas Rome was a nation state dealing with the world events they themselves were creating, today's levels of change and instability are global. In the same way, however, the challenges the world faces in the twenty-first century have their roots in the twentieth and the looming problems and challenges facing Rome in the first century had their roots at least one hundred years previously in the second.

There is a scene in Ridley Scott's Roman epic *Gladiator* where the now sadly deceased, David Hemmings plays the part of Cassius introducing and trying to inspire the crowd and the young Emperor Commodus about the forthcoming battle in the Colosseum. He booms out in his best rounded English Shakespearean tones that what they are about to watch is the Battle of Zama. It was at this battle in 202 that Rome's greatest rival at that time – Carthage – was defeated and, along with the army, their general Hannibal. The subsequent period laid the foundations of Rome's expanding hold over trade in the Mediterranean and as such, was a crucial event. The leader of the Roman forces was Scipio Aemilianus Africanus, an icon of Roman Republican history, and his victory drove a decisive nail into the coffin of Carthaginian civilisation, but the main impact was to launch Rome forward as the dominant and expansive trading power in the Mediterranean. With Scipio's victory came massive financial benefits, the growth of the merchant classes, wider horizons, greater ambitions, further responsibilities and greater opportunities.

De Republica and Somnium Scipionis

Much like our own cataclysmic event of climate change, the great victory over Carthage also heralded an era of social upheaval and change, mass migrations, changing roles, poverty and rural upheaval. We are seeing the impacts of climate change all around us and, in the same way, the Roman Republic witnessed major social shifts of population and problems of poverty and famine, which fed into the destabilizing impact of political change and challenges to the stability and authority of the constitution. With his keen interest in the history of the Republic, Cicero idolized Scipio even to the extent that in later life he would give him the central role in his dialogue *De Republica* (On the Republic). Written in 54–51, this work was a major attempt by the then famous Cicero to explain how the constitution of the Republic had developed and why it needed protection from attack. Carefully placing the debate into the hands of legendary Romans long since dead, Cicero avoided direct criticism as it read like a dialogue – or even a piece of fiction. Only small sections of the six-part work survive, but one segment that does is named *Somnium Scipionis*, or Scipio's Dream. Here, in what is the conclusion to the work, Cicero uses the venerated reputation of Scipio as a catalyst for delivering a rebuke to Julius Caesar, who increasingly challenged the foundations of the Republic in his quest to return to Kingship. Today we might imagine a critic of the decay in British politics being challenged by an MP using a conversation or dream by Winston Churchill to criticise Boris Johnson – a literary device probably beyond the talents of many Members of Parliament today. This work, however, does tell us how Cicero appreciated the achievements of the past and attempted to use history to re-educate his contemporaries and admire what had gone before – just as he had been bred to do as a young child.

So it was that, many years later in 137, a grandson of the great Scipio, Tiberius Gracchus, was riding northwards on a journey to Spain where he was due to join a legion. On his travels he mused at what was happening to the traditional Roman country farmer: their lot was changing, with the ever growing number of slaves being brought in as free labour and driving the small farmer into poverty. What developed was a precursor to a series of growing pains for the Roman state with conservative and short-sighted senators convinced that restrictions of power and citizenship were essential to maintaining the elitism of their position versus the inexorable demand for access to Rome and its power from allied tribes across the Italian peninsula. When the Gracchi brothers were fighting for the greater rights of citizens, they were reflecting the early demands for libertarian growth that would inevitably follow in later years.

At nearly 16 years of age, the teenage Cicero enjoyed the patronage and no doubt the home of Crassus and his studies with Piso and Archias, the municipal way of life, joined parties, accumulated a large address list and made contacts; Marcus Livius Drusus was tribune at this time. The office of tribune was one of the steps that a man of talent, money or connections had to fulfil on his way up the 'greasy pole' of power. The *cursus honorum* or 'ladder of offices' had various grades of responsibility and authority, and each post was either civil or military in nature with a defined age for each rung on the ladder – the ultimate prize being to become consul. The key offices in order were: military tribune/ quaestor, aedile, praetor and consul. However, 300 years before Cicero's arrival in Rome in the late 90s, the power of the people had already made itself felt and, well in advance of other civilisations, an influential and powerful political post of tribune of the plebs had been created. Unlike the other offices of state, this position was open to men of plebeian, or common, rank and the role was specific – to protect the right of the common man and to prevent exploitation by the upper or senatorial classes. Such a role needed brave men – they were often set on a direct collision course with the patronage and power of the governing classes. As such they were vulnerable to attack, hence tribunes of the plebs were accorded powerful authority and sacrosanctity – a right to be protected from physical harm. They had the power to veto acts by magistrates, they could even convene the Senate and veto their acts, and they could order capital punishment on anyone preventing them from performing their duties. They were never allowed to live more than a day's journey from Rome and their houses were to be open to visitors day and night. Perhaps the first major exposure for Cicero to political tensions in Rome would have been the growing clash between Drusus as tribune of the plebs and the upper classes.

The social decay and need for reform the Gracchi brothers had witnessed, and in fact died for, had only grown worse and by 91 social tension was evident throughout Rome and its provinces. Whether Cicero had met Drusus early on in his time in Rome is unknown, but he would certainly have been aware of his complex and wide-ranging proposals in 91 to try to solve everything at once. Republican Rome had begun a series of convulsions, each triggered by the growing tensions within a changing society and world. Trying to maintain a hold on these competing forces by relying on historical political principles would ultimately prove impossible, but Drusus is marked in history as triggering one of the most momentous of these seizures.

In conclusion we could ask what the relevance of these events is, when Cicero himself barely refers to them in any of his almost 1,000 surviving documents, speeches, letters, books and essays? The best answer comes from Cicero himself, speaking to us across the centuries and onto this page when he wrote:

Nescire autem quid ante quam natus sis acciderit, id est semper esse puerum. Quid enim est aetas hominis, nisi ea memoria rerum veterum cum superiorum aetate contexitur ?

Not to know what happened before you were born is to be a child forever. For what is the time of man, except it be interwoven with that memory of ancient things of a superior age?

We must always try to remember that Cicero was more a reflection and product of his age rather than a creator of it. Like a nineteenth century Bismarck, he less created events but learnt how to swim with the current, applying his many gifts and skills to navigating the waterfalls, rapids and rocks of the late Republican period. To do this well he needed a knowledge of the past in order to place events in the context of their time, and we would be wise to do the same in our own age and learn from what Cicero is telling us down the centuries.

The Social War 91–87

The extent to which young Cicero became personally involved in the civil war which erupted in 91 is unknown, but he would have been affected. The development of his studies in Rome would have been disrupted, and at 16 years old he was, in Roman terms, eligible to don a uniform, pick a side and to fight. Not for the first time his fellow students invited their parents to come and watch and listen to the childhood prodigy, but as 91 progressed, other more pressing matters took their attention as another great test for the Republic unfolded.

Cicero would have sensed new dimensions in the game of power and the importance of either picking the winning side – or being prepared to lose everything – there was little or no middle ground in Roman power struggles. Rome was more than a city on the river Tiber, it was already a political behemoth not just in the peninsula where neighbouring states saw the benefits of being Roman, felt Roman and wanted to be Roman. But the world was changing fast – and faster than we might imagine. Social institutions and classes were threatened – some expanding, others feeling their positions of long-held privilege ebbing away. Whatever the rights or wrongs of the reforms put forward by Marcus Livius Drusus, they came at a time of increasing tension where the social dynamics of change had never been experienced before. The challenges were novel and, just like in our current world, a new word was in the air – narcissism.

Not only were the equestrian order (the newly enriched commercial class) determined to have a greater political role in the running of the state, but the senatorial order (the established political elite) was determined to oppose them. In both groups, ambitious men who broke rules were coming to the fore and old men, who played by old rules, were increasingly on the back foot. In addition, many states across the Latin peninsula now wanted access to Roman citizenship, which neither of these classes or the new men wanted to give. Much of what Drusus tried to do was a sensible reaction to the new social pressures on Rome brought on by its own success, but with these problems, and the solutions he proposed, came opportunity for conservative opposition in the Senate, either to protect long established positions of authority, or for ambitious, narcissistic men, both inside and outside the Senate to make new names for themselves.

History teaches time and again that a close compatriot of chaos is opportunity. The past is littered with examples of instances where enterprising and ambitious individuals have seized on chaotic moments to make their move. Some enjoy adding to the chaos and even creating it. In our own times we have seen the rise of the Republican right in the USA fanned by fear of uncontrolled liberalism and woke philosophy. In the period between 2014 and 2020 predictions of chaos needed to come true and unscrupulous, power crazed individuals such as Donald Trump thrived on chaos, creating their own instability and feeding off the resultant fears and discontent. In the run up to 2016, Boris Johnson, and others who should not be forgotten, seized on Brexit as their chance to stoke the fires of anti-European feeling among the right and left in the United Kingdom, dividing society and at the same time feeding off the xenophobic frenzy that they created. Both men created Social Wars – the embers of which are still warm and ready to ignite again.

For a young Cicero, the events of his own Social War (in effect a class war) shattered the marble and stone images of a stable Roman state, a class structure set in stone and the assumptions young men have about their place in the new world. Cicero would have witnessed the power of ambitious men, the duplicity of weaker men, and the impact of a social civil war on a society ostensibly dedicated to maintaining strong yet democratic rule.

Early on, the war came very close to Cicero with the untimely death of his patron Lucius Licinius Crassus. A titan of the Republic in the 90s, Cicero would have been in awe of the oratorical skills of Crassus and perhaps, along with his guide and mentor in Rome, Piso, he may have witnessed the great man in action and seen the power of speeches and what a difference words can have on people. When Cicero was born in 106, Crassus had already been protecting the Republic for years, long engaged in the Senate battling to prevent the outbreak of war, passing laws to end a growing monopoly on juries by the equestrian classes. Ten years later in 95 he had risen up the *cursus honorum* to become consul of Rome and by the time of his friendship with Cicero in 91, Crassus was a key ally of Drusus and his reforms. Cicero, although young, was in the very centre of things able to stand outside rooms and listen to conversations just as he had done in his father's villa in Arpinum. On 13 September 91, Crassus gave what Cicero later described as his swan song speech, but his tremendously exhausting efforts in defending Drusus from the verbal attacks of the Senate, left him drawn and debilitated, he fell ill soon afterwards and died, leaving Cicero, his mentor Piso, and other students of the great man without their patron. Shortly after this, the second pillar of the establishment's effort to control events, Drusus, was stabbed in the side with a workman's knife by an unknown assassin at a meeting in his own home and bled and died on the floor of his own Atrium – the first political murder that Cicero would have seen – a rapacious, murderous and vengeful civil war began.

This was not the first civil war that the Republic had to endure and it would sadly not be the last. In his affection for the grammarian and antiquarian Lucius Aelius Stilo, Cicero had already acquired a good knowledge of the history of the Republic – fulfilling his later statements on the need for context. The fact that one so young was able to place these events into context was just one more skill that made Cicero an exceptional child – one who cared about context and who was willing to see the present in relation to the larger picture and within history, as opposed to a simple reflex of actions reacting to events and dismissing the past to the trashcan of history. In his later life Cicero used every opportunity to relate and record the history of the Republic – partly no doubt in the hope that future generations would learn from the mistakes being made, but also to educate the uneducated.

But history does not always contain an answer or an example. As we view the continuous attacks on the stability of the American Republic and western democracy it is less a case of the lessons of history not being recognised and understood, but more that they are absent in the minds of men and women in power because they have rarely, or never, occurred before. In the United Kingdom the moral debasement of political life has had its catalyst in the premiership of Boris Johnson. This has been an indicator of dry rot within our democracy and, as anyone with wooden timbers holding up their house knows only too well, dry rot never fully leaves the building alone. Once it is there it is always there.

The same challenges were ever present within the Republic of Cicero's lifetime. What they faced as lawmakers was new, the opponents the Republic faced used new weapons to attack democracy – weapons that had not been used before – the attraction of the mistruth. In America, they have already endured one 'Social War' with the clash in the American Civil War of the 1860s – we may be 150 years on from that event, but it sowed the seeds of discord almost exactly as the Social War of the Roman republic was to do. The dry rot hidden within American society lingers on. It may be an inconvenient truth, but history does change and despite what Francis Fukuyama has written, it is not over. In a nation where the lie becomes the popular metaphor for living, anything is possible – even the creation of a totally new nation state and form of democracy.

The Social War was bloodthirsty, rapacious in terms of burnt cities, settling old disputes and cruelty – the worst kind of war, as all civil wars are. It ended after four dreadful years and many battles up and down the peninsula; Rome was militarily victorious, but politically defeated. Italy emerged united under Rome and home to the Latin people, a process that was probably inevitable and where partial integration had already been well established. As Mary Beard comments:

Whatever the causes of the Social War, the effects of the legislation of 90 and 89 that extended full citizenship to most of the peninsula were dramatic. Italy was now the closest thing to a nation state that the classical world ever knew, and the principle…that Romans could have dual citizenship and two civic identities, that of Rome and that of their home town, became the norm.

But this period of unrest and slaughter was not yet over and a reaction was soon to follow – not enough to cure Rome of the dry rot, but enough to add some radical treatment to stop the spread.

Sulpicius, Marius and Sulla

Towards the end of the Social War in 89, the provincial town of Pompeii was under siege from Roman troops. Lucius Cornelius Sulla Felix (meaning fortunate or lucky) was 49 at the time of the siege, having been born in 138. Sulla brought with him an impressive reputation of military success, but also personal battles – he was a proven military leader and tactician, but his family had lost their fortune in previous generations and he had struggled for political recognition. His route up the *cursus honorum* had been beset by disappointment, despite significant military success in the previous ten years. His command of Roman legions in the Social War was marked by further tactical success on the battlefield – accompanied by a reputation for harsh discipline and punishment of the defeated enemy. Cicero was close by at Pompeii as a young officer on the staff of Strabo, although whether he met the great Sulla is unknown. The colourful, busy and impressive city of Pompeii fell to Sulla that summer and recent archaeological research has identified damage from catapult shots in the city walls probably from this period as well as graffiti naming Sulla in some of the streets – this latter evidence, however, might be linked to the period after 89, given that Sulla stationed a garrison of his veterans in the city, many of whom decided to retire there.

Prior to the Social War, Sulla had fought alongside Gaius Marius – fellow resident of Arpinum. Ambitious from the start, Marius, similarly to Cicero, hailed from the equestrian class but unlike Sulla, his political successes had been startling. Where Sulla was aligned to the elite or *optimates* (best ones or aristocratic) class in his defence of the Republic and its values, Marius was more aligned with the popular causes (the *populares*) and therein an inevitable clash was likely. Marius had managed to secure a fine marriage to Julia, aunt of the young Julius Caesar and made himself a fortune as governor of Hispania. He was the very model of an ambitious man and Roman general – indeed he had all the advantages that Sulla lacked.

Although not born until 86, the historian Sallust recorded the events of the Jugurthine War which had been fought between Rome and the King Jugurtha of Numidia (located along the north African coast and modern-day Algeria) between 112 and 106. This was an ugly, complicated, brutal, and costly exercise in the subjugation of a part of the empire constantly niggling at the Senate. Although it had been rumbling for years, it was Marius and Sulla that eventually brought the war to an end, humiliating King Jugurtha by parading him through Rome and adding to the glory of the great general Marius at his Triumph in 104. However, in his monograph Jugurthine War (*Bellum Jurgurthinum*) Sallust was able to expose the already advanced decline in Roman Republican ethics that accompanied the bribery, corruption, double dealing and thirst for power displayed amongst senators keen to exploit the war and the weakness of another kingdom. In his new translation of Sallust's texts, William Batstone wrote:

> In the struggle for power, wealth played an important, if not determinate, role. Those who had money and land used the electoral process to protect it; those who did not have money and land used political institutions to acquire it. According to Sallust, wealth promoted both luxury and greed, avarice and sloth. It weakened the power, but not the arrogance, of old aristocratic families.

Sulla was to become one of these men for whom success in war brought success on the *cursus honorum* and Marius added to his already monumental list of honours. But Batstone continued by saying:

> it (wealth) raised to prominence and pre-eminence men who had no investment in the traditional power base of the Senate. Elections could secure...political

influence. At Rome, everything was for sale; such is the refrain of Sallust's Jugurthine War.

So, the Republic was already in deep trouble and distress at the time of the birth of Cicero in 106. The growth of empire and military opportunity created ambitious men who had no interest in the history or perpetuation of political institutions. With wealth came ambition for something more – power – and with power came whole generations of men intent on the exploitation of institutions and processes that had taken hundreds of years to build and maintain. It was true then and it is true now. In our own age, few people are able to rise to the very top of political power without immense wealth – either their own or by attracting the investment of others. Capitalism therefore has brought to politics across the world people with often no political experience or merit, running political parties like their own businesses, ignorant of how delicate political stability is and determined to overturn anything that hinders their rise to the top.

One set of changes that accompanied Marius in his later career and that had both benefits and warnings for Rome were his adjustments to the Roman Army. By the last century of the Republic, the Army had become a major weapon for the Roman state – they had, after all, had plenty of opportunity to fight, but also to incur significant losses. The traditional format of raising an army was for the two consuls in any one year to levy troops with an appeal in either a particular region for a particular fight, lead the army themselves – or appoint a commander to lead them, whom the usually rural poor recruits had never heard of – and then hope for victory – taking a Triumph and vast plunder for themselves if they were victorious, anointing and further promoting the general if he was successful, destroying his reputation if he wasn't and disbanding the legion or army either way. Recruitment was across all social classes but dependent on property holding status, as each man had to supply his own equipment and there was little or no pay, which restricted the numbers of available recruits and the subsequent disbandment meant that there was never a hard core of veterans with military experience on hand when needed and all the experience of campaigning was lost each year.

With the growth of lands occupied by the Republic and increasing numbers of uprisings, the demand for troops had become so large that Marius could see no way he could even fight Jugurtha when he was put in command after his own first consulship in 107. Thus, the Marian Reforms completely restructured the military by opening up recruitment to the masses and legions were now 'counted by the head'. The state therefore took on the cost of supplying the arms and large contracts were issued for our equivalent today of arms dealers and the members of the new army were also to be paid, creating the profession of soldier – with the promise of a bonus from victory on campaign. These reforms laid the basis of the numerous legions of the Imperial period and, with enlistment now for a period of sixteen years, vastly enlarged the size of the standing army at a cost, of course, for the state. Standardizing the equipment helped enormously and the legionary now became the backbone of the Roman army, which offered a career, advancement and retirement with a pension to the common man.

It was not long before a concomitant concern accompanied these reforms in so far as the fortunes of the legionary were inextricably tied to both the quality and the ambitions of their general. Soldiers had a direct financial incentive to fight for a general who was going places, advancing to new territories, destroying an enemy and making a name for himself. Less able commanders could sometimes suffer accidents in battle in order that they were replaced, or even less diplomatic ends to their careers. This form of loyalty grew in intensity as the volume of gold and silver looted from newly conquered provinces rose and subsequently meant that commanders such as Marius, Sulla, Lepidus and later Julius Caesar effectively had their own private army of profiteering soldiers and could be used to march on Rome itself.

Sulla may not have reaped the glory that Marius did, but he had still made his fortune in the Jugurthine War and followed this with his successful general-ship in the Social War – for this he finally reached the top and, returning to Rome a hero, was elected consul in 88. Feeding on the glory and adoration, on another command from the Senate he was preparing his army, camped outside Rome, to leave to campaign again along the Black Sea coast in 87. At this juncture another series of convulsions struck the Republic as ambitious men seized their chance to expunge their jealousy – the 70-year-old Marius reappeared on the central stage, persuaded the tribune of the plebs, Publius Sulpicius Rufus, to agitate for the removal of Sulla's command, deprive him of a continuation of his authority and pass it to Marius for one more foray into heroic adoration. In his utter humiliation and anger, Sulla escaped Rome to Nola, but then rode to his camp, roused his legions and ordered them to march on Rome itself. Street fighting lasted only hours, the aging Marius was spirited away in the night and made it to Africa, but Sulpicius was found in a villa at Laurentum southwest of Rome and was executed. His head was taken to Sulla, who ordered that it be placed in the forum for all to see.

For the young Cicero this was another shock, a further example of the brutality that jealousy could create and more proof if he needed it, of the power of words to build or destroy. We know from one of his later books *Brutus (De Claris Oratoribus)* – a work on the qualities of oratory – that Cicero had sat, watched and listened to Sulpicius on numerous occasions. Written sometime in 46 when Cicero was 60 years of age, it takes the form of a dialogue mostly spoken by Cicero, but with comments from his close friend Atticus, and Marcus Brutus who, two years later, was to be one of those stabbing Julius Caesar to death. In the book, Cicero talks about the qualities needed for good oratory *'there are two classes of good orators (for we have no concern with any others)'* and describes in great detail all the leading Greek and Roman orators in recorded history up to that time. *Brutus* was a vehicle for Cicero to explain his views on what made a good orator, how the orator contributed to peace and decision making and to ultimately defend the qualities of his own oratory – at a time of intense violence for those in the public eye he needed all the defences he could muster.

On Sulpicius, Cicero tells us that:

> *Sulpicius was really the most striking, and, if I may be allowed the expression, the most radical orator I ever heard – his voice was strong and sonorous, and yet sweet, and flowing – his gesture, and the sway of his body, was graceful and ornamental, but in such a style as to appear to have been formed for the forum, and not for the stage – and his language, though rapid and voluble, was neither loose nor exuberant. He was a professed imitator of Crassus.[1]*

Cicero uses Brutus to illustrate the time in which he is writing – in effect criticising the Republican world of the 40s, but at the same time trying not to draw the fire of his rivals and enemies. He points out the role of the orator as highly honourable, a man who can change history and in legal terms manipulate the outcome of any prosecution or defence – even above the facts. He also pointed out delicately that there were not as many legal trials for treason in the earlier days (perhaps hoping this might encourage those in authority to apply the brakes) and that the abundance of so-called orators speaking in trials – the new custom being to have numerous men giving speeches on behalf of their clients – rather than the old ways of reliance just one – such as himself. We can only wonder what the effect of the ruthless murder of Sulpicius had on Cicero in his formative years.

Reactions to the corruption of democracy

As for Sulla, ordering the death of Sulpicius was just the start of a new methodology in dealing both with internal enemies of the state and the creeping decay of the Republic. Sulla had changed history. His army had marched into Rome and in so doing shown that the loyalty of a soldier was no longer to the state but to their general and this new precedent – with Sulla facing no consequences or punishment from the Senate – was a new fixture in the armoury of the ambitious man. Feeling that Rome was under his control and stable, he left for his expedition. No sooner had he began his three-year campaign, than Marius returned. The consul for 87, Lucius Cornelius Cinna, seemingly had no control over the sick and weak Marius, whose troops went on a five-day rampage through the city and when Marius died in 86, Cinna ruled for two years as consul, but with a dictatorial style. As a *popularis*, this was a dangerous time to be exposed as an enemy of the people and Cicero may have fled the city along with thousands of others. But a victorious Sulla returned in 83. Landing in Brundisium, a crossroads port between Rome and the rest of the world, he closed in on Rome like Michael, the archangel of the Old Testament God. He appointed himself Dictator – a post rarely used, but part of the Republic's distant history – and set about restoring and reforming the Republic. A slaughter of the men of the *populares* followed – Marius had killed many of the senatorial class, so now the tables were turned. The streets were filled with the cries of those cut to pieces by Sulla's legionaries and the screams of their families and children. To control the executions, armed men were ordered to act only against those whose names appeared on white tablets displayed in the forum – this was known as the proscription (*proscriptio*). To see your name on the list, or more usually to hear the frantic footsteps of a friend or slave arrive at your door to tell you your name had been listed, meant that you were an enemy of the state, that anyone could legally kill you or anyone defending you, that your property was forfeit to the state and a reward could be claimed for presenting your severed head. One would literally have minutes to escape or see your family dragged into the street to watch.

Cicero, despite his connections, was not proscribed, but his cousin Marcus Marius Gratidianus was; his name was entered on the list by Catulus, whose father had been forced into suicide by Marius. Mere implication was enough for the armed mob and there are numerous accounts of his murder among the works of Plutarch, Sallust and Livy. It seems that Gratidianus was flogged through the streets to the tomb of the Catulus clan and there his arms and legs were smashed with rods, his ears cut off, his tongue wrenched out, his eyes gouged out and finally he was beheaded. The story continues that an army officer was so repulsed by what he saw that he fainted and he too was executed for disloyalty. Cicero also refers to this particularly gory event in his speech *In Toga Candida*, which was given just before the consular elections in 64. Although the entire speech does not survive, in the extant portion, Cicero tells us that the head was indeed cut off by Catiline and carried in his arms through the streets of Rome to the Temple of Apollo at one end of the forum – apparently still full of life and breath – and placed before Sulla.

Cicero would have been 24, his friend Atticus 27 and Julius Caesar, also now a young man in Rome, 18 at the time of these events and he would have seen upwards of 2,000 to 9,000 executions – we cannot be certain. The Senate lost many of its most noble members, families were exiled never to return, houses were looted, and over 1,500 members of the equestrian class were also brutally murdered by the mob. This then was how Sulla reacted to the internal political rivalries among the noble families all jockeying for increased power and position and willing to destroy democracy in the process. Cicero would have witnessed these struggles among the elite class played out in the speeches in the Senate, in elections and speeches in the forum and in the criminal courts where justice was often not based on the facts. There was frequently nothing wrong with the policies being debated, it was all about the prestige and ambitions of individuals. Sulla also acted to try to deal with the other half of the problems facing the Republic – economic and social change which, since the time of the Gracchi, had never been stable, nor could they be. Rome was changing. But apart from Sulla, what of the other witnesses to this history? According to Anthony Everitt, three very different conclusions were drawn from these events by three young men – Cicero became hardened in his belief, like Sulla, that the Republic needed defending. Julius Caesar on the other hand become convinced the Republic needed reforming, if not ending. Finally for Cicero's closest friend Titus Pomponius Atticus, the shock of what he saw in the streets of Rome to the men and women of his equestrian class was too tormenting – instead he opted to withdraw permanently from public life altogether; it is through his eyes and his letters to and from Cicero that we can watch the Republic fall.

Donald Trump and Boris Johnson 2020

Those of us in the developed world not having to survive each day enduring wars or starvation are socially, culturally and economically very privileged. But we are also privileged to have a ring-side seat to watch, in our laps if we wish, the real-time challenges to democracy in our own existence. On Wednesday, 6 January 2020, I watched the events of the Capitol riot unfold in real time, as did millions of others around the world – we did not have to wait for news three days after the event, as would a Roman farmer in Parma in the north of Italy or five days if we happened to be in a Roman colony in north Africa, or even nine days if we were in a legion serving in modern day Turkey. We were there, albeit remotely, able to watch a demagogue in action, inciting an armed mob to hang the Vice President of the United States of America.

Even now, two years after the event, it is hard to take in that this toxic far right attack on democracy took place – it would have been exactly the same for the ordinary men and women of Rome, but far more extreme as they witnessed daily bloodshed for weeks afterwards. Events in Washington on 6 January may not have ended with the savagery of a Sullan counter reaction, but it was close. Five people died, but many more could have been killed, maybe as part of an alcohol and drug fuelled execution; had the senate house been packed when the rioters broke through the doors – who knows what they would have done with Mike Pence, whether President Trump would have used this paralysis to call in the army and then, maybe then, he would have turned into Sulla – using the forces of democracy to end democracy, sacrificing his followers on the altar of his own ambitions, imprisoning enemies of the state by implication and then proclaiming himself dictator to 'save' the nation and preserve his version of democracy. It was close.

For modern day democracy, the lessons of the gradual decline of the Roman Republic do not end there. As the hearings into the Capitol Riot unfolded so we saw modern day Ciceros at work, trying to protect the Republic he so cherished. With 45 per cent of Americans believing the 'Great Lie' that democracy was subverted and Trump deprived of victory by election fraud, so Senator Liz Cheney, Senator Jamie Raskin and former CIA Director General David Buckley tired to make history repeat itself and, using due process, expose the homicidal aims of Trump and his extremist followers, prevent him from being able to (legally) run for office again and protect the future by securing the powers of the state against an elected leader who does not wish to give up their power. In this way they echo the efforts of Sulla and what was left of the senatorial class when he had purged it, the shoring up of democracy in the Roman Republic – but not with oak but pine. They also mirror Cicero in their reactions to the corruption of democracy in their efforts to protect what is there for the future and their fears that America will continue to fight for new democracy abroad but not be strong enough to protect old democracy at home.

There are also the Caesareans – those for whom the events of the attack on the Republic in 82 and Washington in 2020 signalled that democracy was and is no longer fit for purpose. Two years before the attempted coup on 6 January, the Centre for Strategic and International Studies (CSIS) published a report on the growth of right-wing extremism in the United States.[2] Between 2016 and 2017 alone, the number of right-wing politically motivated attacks quadrupled across America – in other words – Donald Trump was seeding and feeding the feelings of discord well before the 2019 election, as if a coup d'état would be his insurance policy in the event of him losing. In fact, the threat from al-Qaeda was far smaller than that of the anti-democratic terror groups from inside America. Thus, the events of 6 January were far from a dramatic series of consequences unfolding by accident – they were carefully planned, funded and orchestrated to maintain Trump's grip on power and, if necessary, would provide the cannon fodder he needed in order to maintain the pretence of protecting democracy. This is why the Great Lie began being disseminated well before the election even took place. This is not to suggest that America is alone in facing this resurgence of the right – the UK has threats from such groups to deal with and the French and German Ministries of the Interior are hard at work every day monitoring their own right-wing threats.

Another Trumpian moment has just passed in the United Kingdom. In the middle of June 2022, the premiership of Boris Johnson yet again came under attack from inside democracy. The continual evidence of his unfit nature to lead the country finally came to a head, as expected, this was through his own hand and, as expected, he was brought down by his own supporters. Rishi Sunak and Sajid Javid may not have wielded knives, but their resignations were designed to seal the fate of their leader. In the final days, Boris Johnson exhibited a set of characteristics not confined to his own loss of power, but common to all dictators in democratic clothing – a determination to resist the obvious, anger at perceived treachery, a vision of the future if they could only hold their nerve – everything but the reality that had brought this upon themselves, made mistakes and had to pay the price at last. It was somewhat ironic that, for a leader who had characteristically portrayed himself as a rebel against the commonly held principles of respect and process within the civil service and Whitehall, Johnson should be bowled middle stump and fall flat on his face by a simple letter from a former senior civil servant, Sir Simon McDonald. The impact of this piece of paper quietly but succinctly put in train the events that Johnson could not stop. But it was Johnson's determination not to leave his post that increasingly concerned those around him – not for decades has a Prime Minister risked, by staying in post, unrest and demonstrations in the streets. The mood of the country was heating up and democracy again was threatened and another Trump moment came and went as Johnson finally decided to leave.

In their attempts to outmanoeuvre democracy, both Trump and Johnson used the democratic mandates that they had, or felt they had, been given as an excuse for taking dictatorial power into their own hands. As both departed, they attempted to end the careers of potential future leaders of their cause and laid the groundwork for their own returns – either in person or as clandestine composers of chaos. Interestingly, Sulla had faced the same issue when he was deciding the fate of hundreds of potential future leaders of the Republic. As he acted to protect the future of the Republic, he unwittingly ensured its collapse. Among the slaughter were future leaders of consequence with all the right motives to maintain and protect democracy, he murdered talent, executed experience and allowed revenge a higher priority than prudence. He also made mistakes. Among the pleadings for mercy was one group agitating for the removal of the name of the young Julius Caesar from the proscription list. Against his better judgement, Sulla eventually agreed and Caesar, by now having escaped Rome into exile, was spared the arrival of Sulla's troops to end his life. The historian Suetonius recorded for us that when he agreed to spare Caesar, he warned those around him that this was a mistake, predicting that he would one day bring down the Republic; Sulla spoke 'In this Caesar, there are many Mariuses.' The sentences handed out by the US Justice Department were totemic, they neither repulsed the attacks on democracy nor ended them. Heroes are often created inadvertently and just as Rome did and was to do again in Cicero's lifetime, America is good at creating heroes – interestingly however, no one in America has emerged as a hero protecting democracy. Even the Vice President Mike Pence is seen as being tainted for not giving in to Trump – as if he maintained the decay, not protected the future.

Notes

1. Sulpicius left no written speeches, Cicero stated that he had told him he was unable to write down a speech in advance but just had to deliver his thoughts. Those that bear his name were written after the event by Publius Canutius.
2. CSIS Brief, 7 November 2018, Seth G. Jones.

Chapter 4

The Legal Profession in Republican Rome

When you have no basis for an argument, abuse the plaintiff.
Marcus Tullius Cicero

In fourth or third century Greece, or more specifically Athens, it was not easy being a lawyer. In strict democratic terms, being a specialist of any kind was seen as elitist and, at its most extreme, anti-democratic. There was no profession as such, no official grouping or honourable calling and in reality, lawyers were disrespected and often, mirroring their shortcomings, disreputable.

Not so in Rome. The oft quoted phrase 'the grandeur of Rome' could be argued in fact to be the grandeur of Roman Law. It was not that the average Roman citizen admired the law particularly or that he or she was litigiously minded, it was more a case that lawyers were admired and therefore so was the law. This admiration stemmed partly from the long history of Rome as a city-state that was marked apart from many others. The fact was that by the time that Cicero began his legal work in the 80s, the traditions of the Republic were already some 500 years old. Although difficult to achieve a consistently robust narrative on the exact development, archaeology tells us that the first cremations in the forum, the epicentre of Roman civilisation and history, date from 1000, the first cottages or huts on the Palatine Hill (eventually to become the Mayfair and Knightsbridge of late Republican Rome) date to around 700, and by 500, a thriving urban and trading community lived either side of the Tiber with an identifiable and established democratic order in place. Apart from a long history we are also tied to the vivid myths and stories surrounding Romulus and Remus, the openness with which the early city welcomed foreigners, the rituals that survived over hundreds of years right into the final century of the Republic and the long-established way that things were done. For all these to have survived over 500 years points to well-developed mechanisms for preventing radical change, preserving heritage and history and wrapping everything around with the 'law'.

For the first 400 years of Roman history, there was no Republican tradition – it was monarchy and kingship that ruled. Rome and the Republican history that Cicero knew so well first appears in the years after the rape of Lucretia

– who resisted a Roman King only to commit suicide rather than admit any shame – and the erection of the great temple of Castor and Pollux in the Roman Forum – both dating to the 490s. It was in this era that the birth of liberty began and the formulation of laws took shape; Lucretia's husband, Collatinus, became one of the first two consuls of Rome. Henceforth the title 'King' or *rex* became a term of disgust among Romans. But it was the conceptualization of the Twelve Tables that gave the legal aspect of Roman society the greatest momentum. Deciding to put together a definitive pronouncement of the laws and indeed customs (for that is what most law was based upon) of Rome opened a long period where two groups of ten men (the *decemviri*) spent years consulting, debating and researching what should be written. Some scholars believe that these boards (the *decemvirates*) visited Greece for guidance while others suggest it was a purely Italian exercise, but Livy concludes the year of publication as 449. Etched into large bronze tablets and after a session of the plebs to force the Senate to accept them, they were placed on walls in the forum for all to read, understand and communicate.

Yet as we well know even today, interpretation of the law can still cause many twists and painful experiences in the courts and so it was, only on a far more exaggerated scale, with the Twelve Tables. With writing and expression still in its infancy, the delicacies of language could not be captured on bronze and these 'laws', despite a valiant attempt to codify understanding of how things were, created vast windows of opportunity for men like Cicero to base their entire lives and careers upon their interpretation. The new regulations probably created more questions than they answered, but they did at least imply shared responsibility and commitments to certain obligations and actions. The creation of the Tables reflected the changing nature of Republican society with the law being used to a far greater extent in cases of financial irregularity and land ownership with increasingly wealthy patrons for lawyers. But matters of custom and practice also inherent in the tables are well expressed by Mary Beard when she states –

For the most part, the Twelve Tables confront domestic problems, with a heavy focus on family life, troublesome neighbours, private property and death. They lay down procedures for the abandonment or killing of deformed babies, for inheritance and for the proper conduct of funerals. Particular clauses prohibit women from tearing their cheeks in mourning, funeral pyres being built too close to someone's house and the burial of gold – except dental gold – with the body.[1]

To begin with, there was an unbreakable bond between men who presided over the law and priests. The office of state priest of a temple, or any temple official were high status roles taken on by wealthy individuals of independent means in return for high social rank. Presiding over legal matters was also part of their function as they were trusted to guard religion and therefore should be trusted to maintain the law – or custom. They would have acquired a large experience in public life and therefore a strong understanding of the law and it meant that the guardianship and ownership of the law, as inherited from the Twelve Tables, was largely in the hands of the aristocracy. It would be very hard for a *novus homo* to break into that level of authority, for not only would he need either exemplary service to the state as a precondition for being accepted into a particular 'college' of priests, but he would also need to be expert on religious as well as secular law, given that the main job was not to argue the case for or against, but simply – or complicatedly – to explain what the law was. It was assumed that the information provided was factually correct – quite a departure from the courts of today. However, it was in the issuing of responses (*responsa*) that the next major development occurred. This moved the priest-lawyer into the new area of giving an opinion on the merits of the case even over what the verdict should be. Given his high status – the highest of all being the *Pontifex Maximus* (the chief high priest of the College of Pontiff (*Collegium Pontificum*) in Rome – it was unusual to argue against the decision or response of a state priest, aware of the law as he was. But he was not a judge and if matters did proceed to court, then the *juris consultis* came to the fore.

The relationship between patron and client was, as we know, an essential bond between men of established or aspiring ambitions. Thus, as more legal cases arose because of a larger empire, greater population, expanding wealth and more ambitious men, it was a necessary step to hand legal cases on to other patrons interested, or skilled, in the law – most importantly able to speak with gravitas and authority on behalf of their client. This became the *patronus causarum* – someone who believed in a legal cause and was willing to help, advise and speak in court on their behalf. It is this relationship between status, authority and experience that set Roman jurists apart from their despised Greek counterparts. The dignity of office came from their skills and experience outside, not inside the law. It very quickly became, along with service in the Army, a position of dignity to serve the state as a lawyer-jurist and as the stakes and the legal cases grew more important, so the role merited the skills of the most able and intelligent, as well as the necessary aristocratic background. As time moved on, and certainly by the first century, the jurist-lawyer had been supplanted by a new level of professional, the 'forensic orator' and he, especially if successful in pleading in public, became perhaps one of the most respected men in Roman society. As Cicero's own mentor and patron Quintus Mucius Scaevola once observed, 'it was a shameful thing for a patrician and nobleman…to be ignorant of the law under which he lived', and Cicero himself once observed that young boys, as part of their education, were still learning parts of the Twelve Tables off by heart some 400 years after they had been written.

By the time of the Sullan proscriptions in 83 and 82, Caesar had to regroup, remain and decide when to return from exile and Pomponius (from now on referred to as Atticus) had fled to Greece – with his newly inherited fortune – and intended to stay there until matters in Rome clarified themselves. In fact, Atticus had the misfortune of bumping into Sulla in Athens. Atticus had become quite the wealthy celebrity, fluent in Greek, a successful businessman and patron of the arts and so it was hard to hide when the general called in on Athens on his way back to Rome. He invited Atticus to come with him – we can only imagine his horror and suspicion as to what such an invitation meant in reality – but in a moment of heroic desperation he is supposed to have replied, 'No, please, I beg you. I left Italy to avoid fighting you alongside those who you want to lead me against.' Sulla may have scoffed but in any event, he let the matter pass without comment and Atticus survived. Cicero on the other hand had learnt at first hand the savagery and brutality of war and decided a soldier's life was definitely not for him. He had also watched, at almost too close a distance, the work and words of Scaevola and Sulpicius and their sacrifice and death in the purges. For Cicero the protection of the state and Republic, with all its history and traditions, was to become his strategic objective, excelling in the high dignity of rhetoric and oratory as his weapons, a career as a forensic jurist his tactical plan and the forum, an area little more than the size of a modern-day football pitch, his lifelong battlefield.

Becoming aware of his audience

The post Sullan world of the 70s was very uncertain. Rome was still reeling from the tragic slaughter seen on its streets, in its beautiful homes and on the steps of its temples. The severed heads of the dead rotted, nailed to walls in the forum for months on end, until reluctantly taken down by local officials or stolen back by loving relatives and friends in the dead of night. Rome was severely traumatized and struggled to get back to any sort of normal life. Sulla had decreed that the sons and grandsons of those he had proscribed could never hold office and as such he further deprived Rome of whole swathes of talented and influential, though no longer wealthy, supporters of the Republic.

Like the impact of the Great War on British governing society where so many suitable and experienced members of the liberal and conservative elites were slaughtered within four years, the ongoing impact of those events, it could be argued, not only affected the post war period, but went on affecting British history and the effects are still being felt. So it was for late Republican Rome. Just because we know so little about the poorer classes it does not mean that we cannot empathise with what they saw and felt. Like right wing radicals today, there would have been many who no doubt cheered the murders of so many in their own quarters while others would have recoiled at the power of the mob and the inability of the Senate to regain control from a dictator. Cicero would have seen and felt these events too.

In his 1998 book *The Crowd in the Late Republic*, Fergus Millar sees the decade of the 70s as a continual clash between the newly reconstituted Sullan Senate and the Roman urban crowd. It is important here to remember that the Roman crowd was not typical of the whole of Italy. The urban mob was educated in political movements, they felt part of the changes, they were able to influence change – this was part of the privilege of living in the poorer quarters of Rome and of being so close to the centre of events. It was also the city middle classes that were the first to sense new problems and difficulties and therefore also the first to vote – and complain. Through their tribunes they could change policy, legislate, make a difference. They could hold up or push through legislation and were active and quickly activated. Not so in the countryside. Of course, that took far longer and the immediacy of action in the face of events was absent. A popular rural swell could take months to build, whereas the Roman crowd could conduct a revolution overnight. Millar was right to emphasise the theatre of crowd sponsored change – 'control the Forum and you controlled Rome' – but it was possible to control the forum and still not depend on the crowd. The electoral changes introduced during the Social War and the far larger voting blocks that now existed meant that old power balances would inevitably change, and Cicero was in a position to absorb and reflect on all this as he studied and prepared to launch his career. He would need skills of oratory that spoke to the Senate and the common man, that appealed to the intelligent wit of the intellectual and the passionate zeal of the *popularis* reformer and he needed to be able to perform on the stage of the rostra in the forum and the gladiatorial area of the senate house – for Millar and for Cicero, Rome was a fully functioning democracy and we can view it from a distance with confidence that events that unfolded there could, and do, unfold in our own world today.

The perspective of the Roman Republic as being fully fledged by the time of Cicero is disputed. The laws of the Twelve Tablets were still in place, there was much that needed to be done to improve and refine the Republic if it was to survive, and maybe in the power of the crowd we are given some clues as to why the Republic fell in the 40s. An unrefined or unmodernized political structure based on age-old principles cannot be sustained in the face of multiple modern challenges. Democracy has to evolve with the changes. Cicero embarked on salvaging something unsalvageable without substantial change. A system of government based on readings and a sense of what had always been done was archaic and not fit for purpose in a modern nation state so to set out to defend a changing political, social and economic universe by adhering only to what had gone before was doomed to fail.

We hear echoes of this situation in the United States today where the Constitution is consistently under threat from all sides. This has recently reached a new high point with the Trumpian Supreme Court willingly interpreting the articles of the American constitution through the eyes of eighteenth-century merchants and politicians. Is their constitution fit for purpose – has America modernized its democracy and is it 'fully fledged'? The answer might be that as long as the government is in the hands of men and women pledged to defend it then it works perfectly well, the founding fathers could barely conceive of anyone wishing to end the independence of the people just as the defenders of the Roman Republic failed to interpret radical social change as a need to adapt and evolve their own attitudes to government in a new age. The arrival of a contemptuous and charismatic leader at a crucial geopolitical time is a gun to the head for democracy at that stage of development. The interpretative measures being taken by the US Supreme Court seem to be based on interpreting what a certain part of the nation wants rather than defending what the whole nation needs and therein lies the real danger. So it was for Cicero.

Note
1. Beard p. 144.

Chapter 5

All the World is a Stage – *The Forum Romanum*

The limelight for Cicero was to be at the very centre of Rome, indeed the very heart, the forum. A visit there today presents a very different image to that of Cicero's Day. The jumble of remaining pillars, entrances, thousands of steps, flagstones all seem incredibly cramped and this is because the remains of the forum today are largely those of the new buildings ordered by Caesar and his successor Augustus after the Republic had fallen. Each new build was a monument to some other aspect of success and iconic immortalization of parts of the lives of the various emperors and each of course wanted their building to be as close to the original forum as possible.

In the earliest days, this area in between the seven hills of Rome was a marsh where the women and men of the tribes living on the surrounding hills came down to collect water and to converse, discuss and ultimately start joining together to create a small town. This boggy, grassy area was where legend states that Romulus met with his brother Remus between their two collections of buildings and wooden stockades on each of the Palatine and Capitoline hills before the formal foundation of the city in 753. Over time, the huge main drain or 'Greatest Sewer', the Cloaca Maxima, was excavated and built, both draining the land and starting to take away the sewerage from the streets – just as it still does in parts. Thus, over hundreds of years the forum became the main market place, a place for meetings, speeches, proclamations and court cases – the latter always heard in the open air. By Cicero's time, the forum already contained many Republican buildings and temples and had transformed itself into the spiritual heart of the Roman people – a place even more sacred than the city itself.

Not much larger than a football field orientated northwest to southeast, by the time Cicero strode out to make his first public speech in 81, the forum was surrounded by great white marble temples and red brick public buildings and sites of spiritual and historical significance. To the northwest, sitting at the foot of the steep face of the Capitoline, was the Tabularium and it was here that all the public records of the city and associated provinces were stored and also where many of the public officials and servants of the state copied letters, sent out decrees, tabulated statistics and recorded the work of the Senate. A robustly designed building, it looked down over the forum stretching out below and above the affairs of Rome, as if keeping a watchful eye over events and reminding all in the forum of the importance of the past and its records. The previous building on this site had been destroyed in a fire in 83 during the city riots and it was Sulla who had ordered its reconstruction in 78. It remains one of the oldest and best-preserved buildings of this final century of the Republic.

Just in front of the Tabularium at the northwestern end and again looking down on events in the forum were the Temple of Concord (dedicated to the Roman goddess Concordia) and the Temple of Saturn – this latter building was also used as the state treasury – region and state business being indivisible in the Roman mind. The Temple of Concord was well known to Cicero, who often climbed its still extant steps for occasional meetings of the Senate, and in whose great hall he gave one of his most memorable speeches (the fourth Catilinarian). To the northern side of the forum, Cicero would see the senate house or Curia (*Curia Hostilia*). Situated on the original site for the previous 600 years and named after its supposed founder King Tullus Hostilius, it was this small building, where so many vital and momentous events took place,

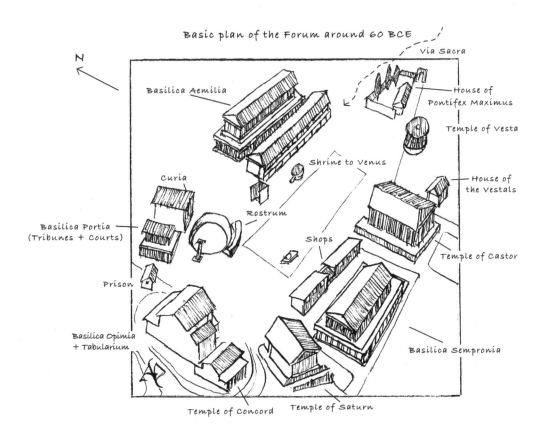

Basic plan of the Forum around 60 BCE

Via Sacra

N

Basilica Aemilia

House of Pontifex Maximus

Temple of Vesta

Shrine to Venus

Curia

House of the Vestals

Rostrum

Basilica Portia (Tribunes + Courts)

Shops

Temple of Castor

Prison

Basilica Opimia + Tabularium

Basilica Sempronia

Temple of Concord   Temple of Saturn

that affected the lives of everyone across the known world; it also looked down over the forum below as if keeping watch on the people of Rome.

Between the forum itself and the Curia was the Comitium – a circular orifice dug down into the ground like a small amphitheatre and it was here that, to one side and opposite the senate house, Cicero would have stood to give his first of many speeches, legal defences and orations. All around the edges of the Comitium, the six huge prows of ships, or *rostra* in Latin, captured in past battles had been set into the walls pointing inwards like a giant clock. Standing high on a raised section of the steps at 5pm on this clockface Cicero would have taken his turn, in the same place where thousands across centuries had stood before and others would stand again – every time we ourselves stand on a rostrum or stage, it is Cicero we are imitating from 2,000 years ago. This was his stage, a place he knew intimately, where he knew how to carry his voice, project his emotions northwards towards the great Curia, and where he knew his audience. To his front and on the rostra itself sat the senators and around the circular layers of steps sat everyone else hoping to hear and watch the legal and political dramas and theatre played out there. At times, it was possible for the speaker or group of speakers to call to the forum below from the roof of the rostrum if they wished for a large audience. The comitium and rostra was also of course where the severed head of Gnaeus Octavius, the consul who lost Rome to Marius, was displayed – nailed to the wood of a ship's prow. It was also the place where Sulla ordered the heads of his most notable enemies in his proscription to be displayed for all to visit and see. From the forum below people could look up and gaze at the power of men and the price of attacking democracy – as well as choosing the wrong side. Specific to this story, the rostra, where Cicero made his name and spellbound the world with his rhetoric, was to have particular meaning, as the very rostra that he had sat between and upon for the majority of life was eventually to be the place where his own severed head and indeed hands were nailed. But that is still a long way ahead.

Moving eastwards along the northern and southern sides of the forum were various shrines and parallel rows of shops to entertain and entice the large volumes of people passing through or visiting the forum every day. Like a modern-day Dubai Mall, Burlington Arcade or Fifth Avenue, the large Basilica on either of the parallel sides mimic the lower levels of the shopping malls surrounding the Louvre in Paris with their consecutive Roman arches to shield onlookers from the sun, creating galleries to gossip, lure and plot whatever was needed on that day. One can imagine the type of businesses that thrived here – only the Republican equivalents of modern-day shops in Old Bond Street or Knightsbridge in London would have been able to afford

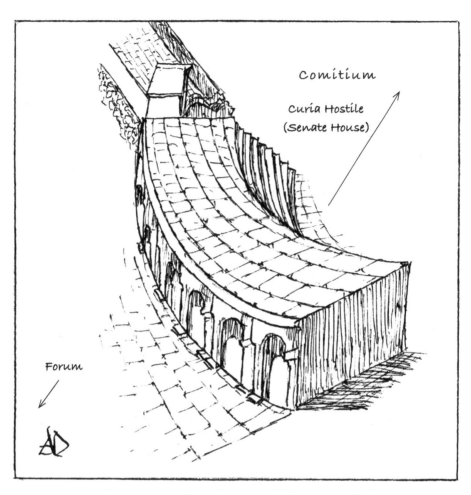

Comitium

Curia Hostile
(Senate House)

Forum

The Rostra in the Republican period.

the rents in this quarter of the inner city. As one strolled southeast along the southern arcade of the Basilica Sempronia, sheltered from the oppressive sun and gazing into the shops to one's right, through the throng of crowds bustling in both directions, suddenly one would arrive at the side of the Temple of Castor and Pollux. Almost at the far end now of the forum, it had taken maybe only two minutes to stroll along the length of the forum to be met by a sun-soaked blast of white stone, marble and gold leaf. Even today the three remaining columns of the Temple of Castor and Pollux stand imposingly alongside the forum. Originally with eight tall Corinthian columns on the short sides and eleven on the long, and standing on a platform 100 ft x 162 ft, the temple was dedicated in 484 by the son of Aulus Postumius Albus Regillensis – dictator of Rome – for his victory in battle after which, the legend states, the Dioscuri appeared and watered their horses near the forum. Twin brothers in Greek and Roman mythology, they were supposed to have been members of the crew of the Argo with Jason. Their presence in Rome through the power of their temple and the cult that would have worshipped them, gave pride but also confidence in the military ability of Romans and many a soldier gave thanks to them both for victory or survival in the field of battle.

Having passed the steps up to the temple, a group of smaller religious buildings lay in front. Chief among these was the circular Temple of Vesta. As goddess of the hearth, Vesta was worshipped in most Roman homes as the deity most responsible for the home and family. Her festival in June each year was one of the most celebrated public holidays and entry to her temple was restricted only to her priestesses, the Vestal Virgins, who guarded sacred objects inside and kept her eternal flame alive – as long as the flame burned, Rome's future was assured. The virgins were selected between the ages of 6 and 10 and they served for thirty years in chastity – if discovered having broken this vow then punishment was severe: being buried alive outside the city boundary while their lover was whipped to death. Next door to the temple was a house for the Chief Pontiff (Pontifex Maximus). He led the highest religious council and was a revered personality within the *cursus honorum*. The College of Pontiffs declared when public holidays would run, oversaw the complicated calendar of events and regulated relations between men and the gods. They interacted with the augurs, the traditionally revered soothsayers of Republican history, in order to set dates at the most auspicious time and often after the augurs had carried out their observations of animals and all manner of indications. The home of the Pontifex was known as the State House (*domus publica*) and he was ceremonially married to the Vestal Virgins. The title of Pontifex Maximus is now held by the Pope.

This counterpoint of secular savagery and sacred religious devotion maybe a heady mix for us to comprehend, but for Romans it was quite understood. To break the most sacred of laws reduced the offender to the most basic of social class, it was all about class, and the lower one's social standing, the harsher and more obscene the sentence would be. Each crime and each legal case required the class of the perpetrator from the very beginning and this started the framework of judicial savagery and punishments that might be employed at the end. To stroll around the forum therefore, Cicero would constantly have been reminded of the glory of success and the gory nature of failure.

Part III

Changing Times

Chapter 6

First Cases First Risks

The risk of a wrong decision is preferable to the terror of indecision.
Maimonides

As far as we are aware, Cicero took to the legal stage in 80–79. His initial roles suited his youthful disposition in so far as he was seen to be a penetrating prosecutor, however, early success was to be a double-edged sword and in taking on a potentially difficult defence case, his career could have faltered before it had really begun. Cicero must have felt he was ready after all he had studied, practised, prepared and, combined with the impenetrable arrogance of youth, now had his chance to impact the national stage.

Although his work was beginning to build, it was to be some overzealous Sullan proscriptions in various parts of Italy, even after the bloodletting had died down in Rome, that provided his first breakthrough in 79.

A successful merchant with his name on a local proscription list had been legitimately (under the terms of Sulla's decrees) murdered, but it was rumoured and then proven that his name had only been entered on the list so that a contact of Sulla could buy his confiscated property for very little. The affair went viral by local Roman standards and, to evade prosecution, the supposed criminals decided to accuse the rightful son and heir, Sextus Roscius, of the murder. However, the young Roscius was not without his own network of local influence and he resisted these charges. Word would have reached Rome within two or three days and the matter was seized upon by some members of the Senate as an opportunity to illustrate to Sulla what was now being done in his name. Whoever took on the case to defend Roscius would have to evaluate the serious element of concomitant risk in respect to how Sulla and his lieutenants might react and so stepped forward the youthful Cicero, enthusiastic, confident, exuberant and with the taste of opportunity in his mouth and an interesting attitude to risk. Given that in the Roman Republic rhetorical skill was an essential skill for advancement and that a key element of rhetoric was the performance, it is safe to say that Cicero, indeed all orators, loved to act.

Cicero was at the very start of his acting career – regarded in history as a great orator, defender of democracy and skilled writer and philosopher and indeed he was all these things, but he was also a great actor, a thespian, a dramatist and as such he needed that audience and that risk, it was what ignited his passions. It is the American acoustic guitarist Leo Kottke who said 'The principal element in performance is risk and if you are losing interest then by scaring yourself to death the audience will feel it and boy it'll wake them up.' In this way Cicero took on the case of defending Roscius to wake up the senatorial audience and indeed the great heroic general Sulla himself with the risks associated with failure, providing the inspiration Cicero needed to make that performance. As Kottke describes so well, the audience would be only too familiar with the risk he was taking, become awakened by his fear and feel part of his journey on the stage with him – in that way Cicero had won the case before it had even started.

Some consider his concluding speech as one the best of his career. Chrysogonus, the Sullan profiteer, is shown to be exploiting and perverting the political reprisals that Sulla's followers had been enacting and Cicero tiptoes around any blame for the dictator himself by shrouding him in a cloak of dedicated hard work for the cause. At the age of 26, he was a success, congratulated and from then on, in great demand, but the emotional energy required of a great orator, like any great performer, came at a cost and he was close to collapse right at the start. Looking back at these events of 81 in *Brutus* (46) Cicero informs us:

At that time I was very thin and physically weak, with a long slender neck – a bodily habit and appearance that is generally associated with critical danger to health, if accompanied by hard work and severe strain to the lungs. Those who cared for me were all the more concerned because I always used to speak at full pitch, never relaxing and straining my voice and whole body to the limit.

Whether it was stress, a nervous breakdown or a cover story to escape Rome because there was such a reaction against his success, we do not know, but Cicero left for Greece and specifically Athens and did not return to Rome for two years. After what would have been a road, river and sea trip of 1,500 kms lasting around twelve days, Cicero met up with his old friend Atticus and was able to depend on him for a long relaxation and journeyed across the area. He visited Sparta in the north, joined by his younger brother Quintus (perhaps further evidence of the need to exit Rome) he travelled on to Asia Minor, Rhodes and rekindled his relationship with the teacher of rhetoric Apollonius Molon, whom he had earlier studied under in Rome.

Terentia, marriage and political ambitions

Having restored his strength, survived exhaustion, and arrived back in Rome, Cicero was ready to take on numerous new cases and, according to his later writings, due to his workload he was soon 'somewhat smelling of midnight oil'. His brilliant victory over Roscius' enemies now marked him as a known man in Rome and a talented orator. The way he had built his oration showed tactical skill as well as bravery and a talent for showmanship, as he did not shy away from criticizing the excesses and indulgent behaviours of those supported by Sulla – who by now was about to retire from public life himself. For some in the Senate, this courage marked him out as a new man of the Republic, a defender of the established order and, potentially, a future consul. The next step, however, was to secure his profile as a potential political heavyweight, thus at some point in 77 he also had time, in between his legal submissions and orations, to take a wife, and he married Terentia.

With an established reputation and portentous future, he had already fulfilled the main prerequisites for a young Roman man of status to look for a wife – namely that he had served in the military or overseas on behalf of the Republic and he had pleaded cases in the civil courts. Brides for these young men in their mid to late 20s were almost always much younger. In her scholarly examination of Julia Augusti, only daughter of later Emperor Augustus, Elaine Fantham points out that the main age for a woman of status to marry was between 15 and 20. Families could not see the need to risk the further education of an eligible daughter as time was not felt to be on their side and beauty was thought to fade. Protecting a young girl's chastity was also vital and at risk the longer marriage was delayed and of course childbirth was a very dangerous experience and the younger the bride, post puberty, so it was thought, the better chance of survival:

> betrothal tended to follow as soon as possible after puberty, even when the girl's physique suggested postponement of consummation in marriage, because she seemed insufficiently developed to carry a healthy pregnancy or survive the high risks of childbirth.

Although we do not know the exact age of Terentia we can confidently assume that she was around ten years younger than Cicero and aged 17 or 18. The young Terentia brought with her a dowry of 400,000 sestertii and this strongly suggests that she was from a rather wealthy middle class, and perhaps noble, background – it may be quite by chance that this was the exact fortune required for a young man's entry into the equestrian order and thus subsequently to be able to run for the Senate – all in all then a very good match indeed for Cicero. As an only child, Terentia inherited her father's fortune on his death so in addition to her dowry in coin, she is recorded as owning two blocks of tenements in Rome, a plot of woods in the suburbs of the city and a large farm in the country, thus her independent additional annual income would have been considerable. There is also a mention in one of Cicero's later letters in 58, in respect to Terentia owning a village which she was planning to sell to assist Cicero in what were to become serious troubles for him at that time.

Given that Cicero was still subject to the wishes of his own father as head of the family, *pater familias* (the oldest living male in the household was able to exercise authority over his entire family), he needed funds to kickstart his political career until his father died. Evidence that Terentia was no fool and a woman of strong character is that she entered her partnership with Cicero in a *sine manu* marriage. There were two forms of marriage (*manus*) at this stage of the Republic – *cum manu* where the wife was moved into the legal control of her husband and her future was thus in his hands and had the same rights of inheritance as his children or after the children. The wife in *cum manu* held no property, as everything she owned would become the property of her husband. Over time, however, the *sine manu* union became more widely popular; in this type of marriage, a wife legally and ritually remained a part of her father's family and, when he died, which was usually before her new husband, she retained her independent property and that which she might inherit. This was a major step in improving the position of women in the Roman household and there is plenty of evidence that in the case of certain women, they would only consent to a *sine manu* marriage and this may have been the case with Cicero and Terentia in so far as she remained a woman of considerable means in her own right, sitting behind her husband's career, but not dependent on its success.

The ceremony would have been both ritualistic and practical and we do not know whether it was Terentia's parents who sought out Marcus Tullius as a good prospect for their daughter or vice versa. In any event, marriage provided a change of gear and an opportunity for political ambitions and realignments for them both. It is likely that from this time onwards, Terentia and her new husband would have the typical two home structure of a well situated, but not yet impressive, home in a favourable suburb of Rome and a rural home to which to travel when the family needed time away from the hot, often dirty, smelly, and dusty city – a smaller estate or attractive farm perhaps near Tusculum where Cicero was to live outside of Rome for the rest of his life.

Marriage was, as it used to be in the history of our own western civilisation, a lifetime commitment but it is worth noting here that it was also used indiscriminately by men of extensive power and ambition as simply a useful tool for joining forces with another family, another fortune or another political promotion. Two already famous contemporaries of Cicero were the slightly younger Julius Caesar and a man who was to become a titan of Republican history at this stage – Gnaeus Pompeius Magnus (known to us as Pompey the Great) – the latter also born in the same year as Cicero of 106. By the time of Cicero's marriage to Terentia in 79, Pompey had already been married three times and the tragedy of his first wife, Antistia, whom he married in 86, illustrates where women, be they wives or daughters, lay in the esteem of some great men.

In his, yet again, essential history *Parallel Lives*, Plutarch refers to an incident where the young Pompey was accused of retaining property once looted by his father in the Social War from the town of Asculum. The events surrounding his trial provide us with a valuable window into the position of women, but also paint a clear picture of the social and political rivals of Cicero's generation.

In the civil court case – as we know held in public – Pompey defended himself impressively and displayed a rhetorical skill rivalling that of Cicero. The judge and praetor Antistius, was so impressed that, according to Plutarch, he offered Pompey his daughter in marriage. Clearly there was far more to this offer than admiration, as Pompey was already a well-known young general and a man going places with a considerable fortune to inherit. Consequently, despite many embarrassing moments when the judge spoke out to help Pompey in the case, Pompey was acquitted – to the sarcastic cheers of the crowd – and a few days later he indeed married Antistia. But the story does not end there nor well for this ill-fated young bride. Only three years later and having achieved such great victories with heroic leadership and displaying a contempt for the process that Sulla admired, Sulla and his wife Metella agreed that it would be prescient to bring Pompey into the family, lest he become a rival to the dictator. Thus they persuaded Pompey to divorce the hapless Antistia and she was sent away in disgrace, allowing Pompey to marry Aemilia, the stepdaughter of Sulla and Metella. As if these machinations were not tawdry enough, Aemilia was already married and pregnant, but that mattered not to Sulla nor, it seems, Pompey. As for poor Antistia, her pain and suffering continued – her father was murdered in the senate house, probably as a precaution against his causing embarrassment to Pompey by trying to oppose what had been done to his daughter, and then Antistia's mother reacted to this disgrace and the destruction of their family reputation by committing suicide. As if the augurs had seen the very worst signs in the skies, Plutarch then tells us:

Aemilia had scarcely entered Pompey's house before she succumbed to the pains of childbirth.

Sulla had tried the same strategy with Caesar, another young arrivistic who was now firmly on the centre stage of politics and another talented military leader. Caesar, however, had flatly refused to divorce his first wife and become controlled by Sulla – despite the obvious personal risks this entailed. The jury may not be out given Pompey's acquittal, but it certainly is in terms of his decisions in marriage. In her 1985 article 'The Five Wives of Pompey the Great', Shelley Hayley is in no doubt that it was just 'pure cold-blooded ambition' that was the driving force behind his marriages and women were incidental pawns in his strategy.[1] For the sake of completeness, in the same year that Cicero and Terentia were married, Pompey took his third wife Mucia. Cicero would have been well acquainted with the young Mucia, as she was the daughter of his great legal mentor and friend Mucius Scaevola who, as we have seen, had been murdered in 82 during the city riots of the Social War. Her noble connections would have been strong until 62, this was to be the longest lasting of his five marriages and the only one to provide him with children: a daughter Pompeia and two boys Gnaeus and Sextus.

Watching how Pompey behaved in his strategic and pragmatic attitudes towards women would have demonstrated to Cicero what men were prepared to do to reach the top and attract power.

Note
1. Hayley. Shelley P. 'The Five Wives of Pompey the Great.' *The Journal of Greece & Rome*. Vol 32, No.1 (April, 1985). CUP

Joining the political stage

Only those who will risk going too far can possibly find out how far we can go.
T.S. Eliot

The grand tour went well. It was a time of reflection and calm for Cicero, he was feeling refreshed and perhaps safer in 77. Plutarch records that Cicero held back from a full-on legal career in advocacy and began to think of running for official office. In his defence speech for Roscius he had used the phrase 'I have not yet entered politics', which to any politician suggests that this career was on his mind and at 29 he began his campaign for a quaestorship. The office of quaestor or 'investigator' was the first step on the greasy pole of the *cursus honorum* and was a position used to provide the Republic with free or low paid administrative work either in audits or logistics in Rome or the growing empire and in return the officiant got to see the world, rubbed shoulders with other families also on their way up the ladder and, hopefully, added to their reputation as a future senator. All posts were filled via election and appointment by the Senate, thus between 77 and 75 Cicero had to get out into Rome and canvass for support and see his name brought, again, to the attention of the Senate.

His election went well and Cicero was posted to assist the Roman governor of Western Sicily. With plenty of history to see and grain contracts to organize to relieve starvation in Rome, Cicero enjoyed his time there and even carried out his own archaeological excavations as we can sense from his *Tusculan Disputations* written during 45:

> But from Dionysius's own city of Syracuse I will summon up from the dust – where his measuring rod once traced its lines – an obscure little man who lived many years later, Archimedes. When I was quaestor in Sicily I managed to track down his grave. The Syracusans knew nothing about it, and indeed denied that any such thing existed. But there it was, completely surrounded and hidden by bushes of brambles and thorns. I remembered having heard of some simple lines of verse which had been inscribed on his tomb, referring to a sphere and a cylinder modelled in stone on top of the grave. And so I took a good look round all the numerous tombs that stand beside the Agrigentine Gate. Finally I noted a little column just visible above the scrub: it was surmounted by a sphere and a cylinder. I immediately said to the Syracusans, some of whose leading citizens were with me at the time, that I believed this was the very object I had been looking for. Men were sent in with sickles to clear the site, and when a path had been opened, we walked right up to it. And the verses were still visible, though approximately the second half of each line had been worn away.... So one of the most famous cities in the Greek world, and in former days a great centre of learning as well, would have remained in total ignorance of the tomb of the most brilliant citizen it had ever produced, had a man from Arpinum not come and pointed it out!

Conscious then as he was of his humble origins it came as a shock on his return to Rome to realize that few had noticed that he had even gone. In his examination of Cicero, Shackleton Bailey picks out one apposite quotation to illustrate the point. Later in his life when he had risen to the high rank of proconsul (a man of authority acting on behalf of a consul) he wrote to a young pretender as he had once been:

Stick to Rome my dear fellow, and live in the limelight! Residence abroad of any sort, as I have thought from my youth upwards, is squalid obscurity for those whose efforts can win lustre in the capital.

This is not to say that Cicero did not know the value of overseas postings, for it was soon clear that only at a high level of office where power was practically unlimited, as one acted on behalf of the Senate, was the availability of financial gain equally so. A talented or lucky man or general could return from a period in the empire both very famous and very wealthy, setting his next stage of momentum in train. The Tusculan Disputations are so called as they are supposed to have been written by Cicero at his villa in Tusculum. They cover five books on Greek Philosophy including Contempt of Death, On pain, On grief, On emotional disturbance and whether Virtue is enough for a happy life. His daughter had recently died and is supposed to have stimulated his writing at this time.

The time of Pompey and Crassus

Two men who had already inherited and reaped the rewards the Roman state had to offer were Marcus Licinius Crassus and Gnaeus Pompeius Magnus. Both were already major figures of the Republic and both had amassed considerable prestige and fortunes and, as a result, power. While Cicero had been away in Sicily partly gaining considerable praise from the Governor in whose service he worked, and also discovering the lost tombs of famous Greeks, events in Rome had been changing at some pace. A new alliance had been formed between Crassus and Pompey, which made them a formidable force within the Senate and the marble and ornate corridors of power around the forum.

M. Licinius Crassus was slightly older than Cicero, having been born nearly ten years earlier in 115 and a member of the *Licinia* family – a far older and more noble line compared to that of Cicero. As the second of three sons born to another hero of the state Publius Licinius Crassus, who had been both consul in 97 and censor in 89, he had the misfortune to see both his father and two brothers die early in his life. His father and younger brother were either killed or committed suicide as they were hunted down by supporters of Marius in the civil wars of 87–86, and this tragedy followed on from his elder brother having died before that war began. This left Crassus alone and the beneficiary of an already considerable family fortune as well as reputation. It is worthy of note that within his family line was Lucius Licinius Crassus, one of the greatest Roman orators of the second century Republic – indeed Cicero saw him as a childhood hero and model.

Unlike others whose families had perished in the proscriptions, Crassus actually benefitted. Like his father and brother, he had supported Sulla from the outset and, despite having a period of exile in Spain in order to protect himself from assassins, he returned and become one of Sulla's greatest recipients of favour. Later to be called the richest man in Rome, his fortunes were not just based on inheritance as he was a ruthless businessman in his own right. In the periods of proscription, Crassus was the renowned expert at expropriating the lands, houses and estates of the murdered – and at knock down prices. He was also a key employer of talented slave labour – talented because he looked for carpenters, stone masons and artists to rebuild the often-destroyed homes of those whose names appeared on Sulla's lists – he even leased the properties back to their original owners – if they had survived. With his political heritage, combined with an immense fortune and ambition, Crassus had to be at the front or the back of any man attempting to become consul of Rome.

Pompey on the other hand had something that Crassus did not – military majesty. As we have already seen, Pompey was the great general, the vanquisher of the Republic's foes, the protector of right and used might to do the job. Crassus could well be forgiven for feeling that his rising star was constantly in the shadow of a Pompeiian eclipse, but that was something he had to deal with, control and, naturally, manipulate: Crassus always had in mind effecting his own military victory to match or even eclipse Pompey but when his chance came it was to end in disaster.

While Cicero had been winning his first major case with the defence of Roscius in 80, Pompey had just completed an eighteen-month incursion into Sicily and North Africa, chasing down and killing enemies of Sulla who had fled with their soldiers from the Italian mainland. During the battles in Africa his own troops proclaimed him *Imperator*. The distinction of *imperium*, the legal power to command an army or a province, was much sought after by those intent on getting to the top. Normally conferred by the Senate and usually for the right reasons, A.H.M. Jones described *imperium* as 'the power vested by the state in a person to do what he considers to be in the best interests of the state'.[1] Holding *imperium* normally meant a badge of office in the form of an ivory baton with the golden eagle of Rome at the top. The equivalent of a magistrate on the *cursus honorum*, he was also accompanied by his own body of lictors, a mixture of bodyguard and assistant, and the number of lictors in attendance with the magistrate was commensurate with the seniority of his office so:

Aediles had two lictors

A Praetor was accompanied by six lictors

Consuls had twelve lictors each and after the fall of the Republic, a dictator was followed by twenty-four lictors.

Each lictor carried the well-known symbol of the power of the Senate – the fasces. This was a bundle of wooden rods bound together by straps and, outside the pomerium, the official boundary of the city of Rome, a shining sharpened axe was held in the centre of the rods with the blade for all to see protruding at the top. The fasces were of course a symbolic representation that power from the Senate, and its use in the protection of democracy and law, now rested in the magistrate acting on its behalf. Offenders of the law could be flogged by the rods – or decapitated by the axe. In his analysis of the retinue of the magistrate, David Braund enables us to see the fine detail with which the Romans of this period valued the idea of the entourage to glorify the status of the official.[2]

Although in the earliest days of the Republic this was how law was dispensed, the Twelve Tables ended summary execution without trial in the fifth century. However, the iconography of this particular symbol of Roman Republican power lives on in our world today and illustrates just how close the marriage between democracy and dictatorship has always been. Mussolini used the fasces as a key symbol of his dictatorial powers, illustrating his perverted dream of the glory of the popularism of Rome with the murderous intent of total control of the state like a modern-day Sulla. In France, throughout Europe and even in Russia, the fasces can be seen in military and state iconography – again stirring memories of what leaders want to believe Republican Rome stood for, stealing the images of democracy and perverting them for the use of power over the people. Even in America, where the fasces sit under the right hand of Abraham Lincoln in the Statue of Emancipation, they are used to symbolize the power of the state in the perceived, service of the people. At the base of the Seal of the Senate of the United States of America are two crossed fasces – the branches upon which the eagle stands – and yet the United States of America sits perilously close to seeing the power of the state abused to murder democracy. A recent quotation from Eric Trump resonates with echoes of how Sulla persecuted and murdered his senatorial opponents:

Last night my father killed another political dynasty, that's the Cheneys. He first killed the Bushes, then he killed the Clintons and last night he killed the Cheneys. He's been rhino hunting ever since he got into politics, and last night he was successful again.

Replace the names of those United States political dynasties with the four consuls and their families who had opposed Sulla – Norbanus and Scipio Asiagenes (consuls in 83) and Carbo and Marius (consuls in 82) and we are witnessing today a similar killing of the opposition by Donald Trump and his many followers.

> *Sulla immediately proscribed 80 persons without communicating with any magistrate. As this caused a general murmur, he let one day pass, and then proscribed 220 more, and again on the third day as many. In a harangue to the people, he said, with reference to these measures, that he had proscribed all he could think of, and as to those who now escaped his memory, he would proscribe them at some future time.*[3]

Is it too far a step of the imagination to think that, should Trump return to power in the USA in 2024, many of his opponents would find themselves proscribed in a modern sense? Sulla allowed unrestrained vengeance on his enemies or opponents, and the Capitol Riots in Washington on 6 January 2020 came within a doorway of unfolding in the same way, with threats to hang the Vice President and kill Democrats. Is it too much to envision the day after Donald Trump is signed into office that his own lists of un-American opponents is issued? Aurelius was reading a proscription list in the forum when he suddenly saw his own name. In horror he tried to run back to his family, but was murdered on the way. Gnaeus Papirus Carbo, who led many of the forces of Marius in the civil war against Sulla, escaped from Rome, but only as far as Sicily where he was chased down by Pompey who 'treated Carbo in his misfortunes with an unnatural insolence', taking him in fetters to a tribunal he presided over, examining him closely 'to the distress and vexation of the audience' and finally sentencing him to death. Carbo was beheaded – a onetime ally of Pompey, he had once defended him in a trial. Can we imagine a scenario where the forces of law in the United States of America, modern day lictors with their badges of office containing images of the fasces, use the unrestrained power vested in them by the state to arrest, detain and vilify enemies and opponents of Donald Trump? They may not be beheaded, but they could end up in very different circumstances from their lives today.

Thus, although too young for high office and always away from Rome when elections were called, Pompey failed to take on any official political role. Again, there is a contemporary analogy with Donald Trump – why bother to climb the *cursus honorum* when celebrity, wealth and charisma are all the credentials one needs to aim for the top straight away? Why marry once for love when one could marry numerous times for money? Pompey's magnitude as a hero and celebrity brought him close to Crassus as a candidate for the highest position of all – Consul of Rome.

So it was that between 75 and 70, as Cicero quietly but carefully cultivated his own political position, Pompey and Crassus felt that their time had come and aimed at the consulship together in 70.

SPARTACUS 73

There was one other factor that helped these two apprentices of Sulla, as if they needed assistance, and that was the revolt of the slaves under Spartacus in 73. Not only was Spartacus a Thracian and thus well trained in the art of war, he was also reputed to have been well educated, charismatic and physically aggressive – the perfect leader of a revolt doomed to fail. Initially the trouble began in Padua to the west of Venice and it would only have taken two to three days – at most – for news to arrive in the centre of Rome by military riders. Cicero, now in his early thirties, would have seen how the Senate reacted, heard the speeches, the passion and the fears in the many speeches in the Curia, in short he was able to assimilate the way the Senators acted when under violent threat; furthermore, Cicero was able to weave the threat that Spartacus represented into many a warning and speech to the people and senate in future years.

The Senate convened immediately and, over the coming months, at least four expeditions were sent out to crush the revolt, but it was finally Crassus who defeated Spartacus, much to the annoyance of Pompey who was fighting in Spain, and it was Crassus who crucified 6,000 of the followers of Spartacus along the Appian Way from Capua to Rome. To the chagrin of Crassus, Pompey arrived just in time, his armed forces marched hard all the way and mopped up any remaining opposition and still managed to claim an equal share of the credit – Pompey had the ability to attract applause with his radiant personality – the anthesis of the emotionless and brutal Crassus.

Notes
1. Best known for his work on the later Roman Empire, Hugo Jones was a key twentieth century scholar of classical history. His work was published between 1937 and 1972.
2. Braund, D.C. Cohors. 'The Governor and his Entourage in the self-image of the Roman Republic'. In *Cultural Identity* R. Lawrence & J. Berry (Ed). London, pp. 10–24.
3. Book 1 of the Second Pleading by Cicero sections 64–75.

Chapter 7

Political Aspirations and The Trial of Verres

To win without risk is to triumph without glory.

Pierre Concille

B asking in the glory of another victory, Pompey was awarded a Triumph through Rome. Standing in his chariot, drums and trumpets heralding the arrival of his soldiers in their best uniforms, gleaming gold and tens of thousands of ordinary Romans on the streets to party the day away; Crassus received instead an *ovatio* – he walked in full gleaming armour with his own train of troops and cavalry, waving as plaudits were read out to the crowds. One can imagine the irritation Crassus must have felt and he still lacked that crushing imperial victory that he so craved to equal Pompey.

The election campaign was a grand affair. Both Pompey and Crassus had an endless supply of funds to promote their causes, Pompey had an army at his disposal which would certainly have focussed the minds of the Senate, and Crassus could buy what he didn't have. Promises are always cheap and are of little value and both men made many of them. In a Rome bathed in sunshine there was nothing else to talk about except the imminent coming to power of two of its greatest names, combining the two most glorious attributes that every Roman admired – money and military conquest. What could be better for the Republic than the election of these two men? So what if the law stated that Pompey was six years too young for office, that he had never placed even a toe on the *cursus honorum* and that he was not even a senator – in even the recent past such disqualifications would have been sacrosanct, but in a world turned upside down by Sulla and where civil war was still a painful memory the last thing people wanted was to stop the candidacy of such popular heroes – to do so was to sign one's own political suicide note (cf. Elizabeth Cheney and the 6 January hearings). Roman democracy was in a state of change – one step away from chaos and the Senate recognized the expediency of granting Pompey dispensations, and in so doing signalled not just the weakness of their own judgement, but also their willingness to see democracy fail. And this is the key point – if democracy does fail in a nation, then it has to be by general consent that it does. Either through fear (Nazi Germany), malaise (Republican France in the 1940s) or lack of leadership and crippling use of conspiracy theories (the United States of America today). In each case, consent to collapse is an integral part of the process of democratic decay.

Once dispensation had been granted it was plain sailing, both were elected as consuls for the year 70 and both displayed the full power of their place in Roman society. In a display of *amicitia* – a bond of mutual respect, apparent friendship and sometimes dependency between individuals or states – Pompey launched a series of games in the capital while Crassus tried to outshine him by donating 10 per cent of his fortune to temples and the god Hercules. Despite their testing relationship, both recognized the advantages of working together and no doubt over many a meeting both day and night thrashed out a strategy for granting popularist measures to the people.

First on this list was to restore the power of the tribunate which Sulla, in his efforts to maintain control of the state in the hands of the conservative block, had done so much to destroy. A *popularis* measure, but one that would also play into their hands later on. In addition, they went about reforming the courts and, during their year of office, Cicero would have been especially interested to see that the Sullan decree of senatorial control over courts was set to be repealed. Not only did this pave the way for fairer representation on juries, but for Cicero, this move opened a new door with which he, as a minor member of the nobility, as an *equites*, could open further to force his way in to the top and his chance came in the very same year. But before the new measures could be passed, Cicero had a new and massive case to deal with and one in which he would be able to plead to the senatorial jury how important it was going to be to make the right decision against one of their own.

In Verrem

Without the trial of Verres it is quite possible that Cicero's name would have disappeared into the mists of anonymity in Roman history, furthermore, the story surrounding the case could not have been more meaningful even if it were scripted. Against a backdrop of years of excessive murders, excessive wars, excessive social pain and excessive wealth came a case of excessive greed and extortion and where better than in Sicily, a place where Cicero had already won a reputation for being fair and honest as quaestor, and where he could already count on a number of influential and good friends. Some of these old contacts and *amici* travelled to Rome to see him at some point during 71.

The normal period for a Roman magistrate to serve in his appointed office was a year, however, the recent slave troubles in Italy had given Caius Verres three years as Governor of Sicily while he waited for his successor to arrive.

Perhaps it was his natural way to exploit his office, or maybe he felt forgotten and master for life of his island, but in any event he became hated and unpopular as he bled the island white with his thirst for money and valuables. Indeed, it was his desire for a particularly fine statue from a so-called friend, Sthenius, that triggered the chain of events that soon led to Cicero's door. Sthenius had already given a large part of his art collection to Verres when the latter further asked for a Greek statue that belonged to the people of Thermae. Stirred on by Sthenius, the local council refused and, in his rage, Verres constructed false charges of forgery against Sthenius who, sensibly, left with his family for exile. Despite a huge 500,000 sestertii fine against him, Verres' anger was still not assuaged and, despite Sthenius appearing in Rome to plead his case, Verres had him condemned to death. It was this that prompted a delegation from Sicily to travel the four days north by bumpy and dusty road to Rome and to make representations to the new consul elect, Pompeius. While they were lodging with good friends in the city, they also sent a message that they wished to meet with their old friend Cicero – the rising star of the legal profession and all they had to do was persuade him to act for the prosecution rather than his preferred defence.

What we know about Caius Verres comes mostly from the speeches of Cicero, which were the result of his acceptance of the case and the construction of his forensic arguments and speeches which were then later published and have survived. As such, we have to treat his descriptions of Verres with the caution of anyone who has faced a prosecution counsel – their aims are not to present a fair and balanced legal view of what happened, or to rely on evidence, but to tar and feather the person in the dock in the eyes of the judge and jury, to mercilessly paint a picture of guilt and/or a character intent on crime – they are paid for getting convictions, not for uncovering the truth. This was something that Cicero was proving to be particularly good at – despite his love for the defence – what we would call spin was written by a man who was possibly the best prose writer ever to write in Latin. Cicero was to end Verres' career: during the trial, Verres left for voluntary exile (an option for the most powerful in the state) until his death in 43 either by his own hand, or by those of soldiers sent to murder him which, coincidentally, is exactly what happened to Cicero and in the very same year. Thus, there was a symmetry in their lives at this moment in 70 – both had made their way up the *cursus honorum*, both had served the state in Sicily, and both were to die in the same year, probably in the same way, murdered by the state. The main difference was that Verres was a consummate criminal, extortionist and murderer, while Cicero achieved similar ends through the courts.

Because a Roman official was immune from prosecution whilst in office (echoes again of the Presidency of Donald Trump) this could only begin once Verres had become a private citizen. In accepting the case, Cicero knew well that he would again, just as he had in the defence of Sextus Roscius, run the risks of failure in front of the Senate. Verres, despite his criminal activities, corruption and stealing from the state, had powerful friends, and lined up for the defence against Cicero was the most prominent man in the Roman judiciary, Quintus Hortensius Hortalus (known to history as Hortensius). Already elected as consul for 69, Hortensius chose delay and obfuscation to try to get the trial postponed to the following year where he would be able to influence the result, so it was pressure of time that influenced the strategy of both sides. Cicero proceeded into the *postulatio* phase, applying for permission to prosecute the case and postulating the basis of the attack, but as a first stalling tactic, a supporter of Verres, Caecilius Niger, was encouraged by Hortensius also to apply for permission to prosecute the case. This meant a *divination*, or preliminary hearing before a jury and praetor as magistrate and, miraculously, Cicero's complete speech *Divinatio in Caecilium* survives. Part I gives a snapshot of the tone and delivery that Cicero employed:

Si quis vestrum, iudices, aut eorum qui adsunt, forte miratur me, qui tot annos in caisis iudiciisque publicis ita sim versatus ut defenderim multos, laeserim neminem, subito nunc mutata voluntate ad accusandum descendere, is, si mei consili causam rationemque cognoverit, ujna et id qoud facio probabit, et in hac causa profecto neminem praeponendum mihi esse actorem putabit.

If any one of you, O judges, or of these who are present here, marvels perhaps at me, that I, who have for so many years been occupied in public causes and trials in such a manner that I have defended many men but have prosecuted no one could now on a sudden change my usual purpose, and descend to act as accuser – he, if he becomes acquainted with the cause and reason of my present intention, will both approve of what I am doing, and will think, I am sure, that no one ought to be preferred to me as manager of this cause.

Cicero used this additional requirement to speak as a valuable opportunity. Not only did he largely ignore the facts of the case, only referencing them in passing, but he used the speech to explain to Caecilius the profound importance of this case, its vital nature, not just to the people of Sicily, but also to the Republic. He asked Caecilius whether he really felt qualified enough to deal with a case of such importance and whether he had the necessary oratorial skills to do it justice. What Cicero was really doing was showboating his own knowledge, skills and substance to an audience that knew about such things. He was not boasting so much as he was teaching, and he cleverly allows his audience to recognize his genius, using phrasing which appealed to a circle of talented and educated men and thereby presenting Caecilius as being outside this group; naturally Cicero won this first round handsomely.

With the *divinatio* out of the way, Cicero quickly followed up with the formal charges in the *nominis delatio* which was accepted and Verres now knew what he was up against. To get his case together, Cicero asked for 110 days to visit Sicily and gather evidence and depositions. Cicero referred to this period in his two later speeches – one given and the other not necessary, as Verres, seeing he had no chance even with Hortensius on his side, fled Rome. Cicero referred to the period he was given as 'astonishingly brief' (Ver.1.6: *dies perexigua)* and was very pleased with 'the speed of his return' from Sicily (Ver.2.1.16 *celeritas reditionis)* – he spent sixty of the allotted 110 days travelling to and from Sicily and travelling around the island. Verres and his acolytes had spent time bribing Sicilians not to give evidence and threatening others if they did, so it was a hard task for Cicero and his team, but by the time of the trial which began in the second half of July 70, he was ready for its two phases – *actio prima* and *actio secunda.* To save time, Cicero rather wrong footed Hortensius and instead of a first act of lengthy condemnation and many witnesses, he just gave a summary of what he was planning to give in great and damaging detail in the second – these are known as *In Verrem* I and *In Verrem* II. The accusations ranged from extortion of vast sums of money from notable Sicilian families and farmers in return for favours, corruption and fraud in charging the Roman treasury for costs no longer required, not executing pirates, but keeping the good looking ones for his own sexual pleasures (Cicero did not hold back from exploiting the well-known homosexuality of Verres and one of his sons) and executing instead (with bags over their heads to avoid identification) Roman slaves from local quarries, pocketing the plunder seized from pirates, murder of numerous men who stood up against him and the crucifixion of Roman citizens who were exempt from this particular form of punishment. One of many accounts of a man who stood up to Verres was noted in detail in Book One of the eventual five books of the *actio secunda* (which were never delivered by Cicero), that of Philodamus.

The only thing that equalled Verres' lust for art was his lust for sexual pleasure with both men and women. At the town of Lampsacus Verres paused and asked his 'dogs' to search the area for any virgins worthy of his attentions and Rubrius, a specialist it seems in such matters, brought to his notice the name of a young girl – the daughter of Philodamus, who was one of the town's most prominent citizens and was noted for his generosity of spirit – *Philodamus, uir aliis prouincialibus semper multo hospitalior amiciorque* (Philodamus, a man (who was) always much more welcoming and friendlier than the other provincials). Noting this welcoming character and having no choice in the matter, Philodamus was forced to have Rubrius stay with him while Verres lodged nearby and Philodamus, possibly to try to create a positive relationship, foolishly invited Rubrius to a banquet at his home and told him to bring any guests he wished. At the end of the evening, Rubrius asked that Philodamus have his daughter join them, a request which her father refused at which point the whole atmosphere changed and Rubrius ordered his slaves to bar the door and guard the house. Philodamus knew exactly what the plan was and ordered his own servants to protect his daughter and to tell his son who came running. A nasty fight ensued, during which Philodamus was badly scalded with boiling water. The townspeople arrived with Philodamus' son and many of Verres' slaves were wounded and one of his lictors Cornelius was killed. Disaster. Verres was the townspeople's next target and he quickly fled. Days later and in rage at not having his way, Verres successfully had charges laid against Philodamus and his son for the murder of his lictor. The jury was stacked and both Philodamus and his son were executed on the town square of Laodicea – their crime was defending the honour of this young girl. Verres ensured that the trial execution was hundreds of miles away from Sicily, in fact Laodicea was a thriving Roman city to the east of Ephesus in Turkey, the impressive ruins of which are still evident today, as is the location of the market square. We do not know if any of the townspeople travelled there to support Philodamus and his son, or whether their friends even knew of their location and we can only imagine the grief of the daughter, the wife and family or the conversations had between father and son before they were murdered. Interestingly in one of his later letters to Atticus, Cicero records holding assizes in the city some twenty years later in 50 – one can only wonder if he walked through the city market place and remembered the trials of Philodamus.

Although a horrific story which no doubt would have appalled many in the Senate, the power that Verres wielded was by no means unique. This account was used by Cicero to open the eyes of the senators to how the authority they dispensed was being abused and that they must act to clean up the actions of their magistrates across the growing empire. The attack on Verres was also an attack on all abuses of power and in so doing Cicero showed himself to be a *popularis*, a man determined to pursue morality and justice in his legal career – but in return he obviously marked himself down as something of a pious troublemaker for those intent on the abuse of power.

Looting from the Sicilian port of Syracuse was ordered by Verres on an industrial scale, and Cicero also intended to detail the case of C. Servilius, a well-respected trader who had the courage to speak out against the actions of Verres. The lictors, the dispensers of 'justice' whose authority came from the Senate itself, took out their rods from their bundles and beat Servilius in public so hard that he was blinded from blows across the face and died a few days later from his injuries. Let no one in the modern world be under any illusions that power is often used unjustly; how often in the history of nations has power dispensed justly been used unjustly? Today flogging with canes remains a punishment in, for example, Brunei, Singapore and Saudi Arabia, while Sharia Law uses this punishment liberally for any overheard possible criticism of the prophet. Who is to say that these judgements are fair or how many Verres figures there are dispensing it.

Finally, Cicero made all the current senators think carefully on their verdict, given the disrepute into which Verres had dragged his high office. By defending Verres, Hortensius was accepting a degree of affinity with the man and the Senate too, should they find Verres innocent or acquit him, were also risking being seen as corrupt as Verres. *In Verrem* I Cicero aimed at them all when he said:

> *Is it not enough to stir any man's indignation to see how you (Hortensius) and our other grandees admit this worthless scoundrel to your friendship in preference to the honest merit of any one of us? You and your peers find the activity of new men (Cicero) distasteful; you despise their sober habits and sense of decency, you would like to see their ability and energy permanently kept under. But you love Verres!... He is so popular with your butlers and footmen, such a favourite with your freedmen and slaves – of both sexes! When he arrives, he is ushered in out of turn, admitted all on his own, while the doors are closed to all other callers, very worthy people often enough. It may be inferred that you make your favourites out of people whose survival in the community depends on your protection.*

The reference to keeping the doors shut on worthy callers was in fact a sideways attack on all the aristocracy. Cicero was always to be conscious of his relatively modest *equites* background compared to the sacred families of Rome, despite holding the highest of offices. He was never going to be one of 'them', but he could use the actions of Verres as a battering ram to show the Republican nobility that times were changing. There had always been *novi homines*, but now there were more of them. The empire was growing, population growth and wealth were accelerating, pressures from the changes in Roman society had to be accommodated and toleration of actions such as those of Verres had to come to an end. Cicero had adopted a form of *narratio*, but not that rhetorical theory as he had been taught; this was due to the pressure of time, the need to employ less of a speech detailing the crimes forensically and instead contextualize Verres as a man bad for Rome and the times in which they were living.[1]

One might have thought that Hortensius and Verres must have spent many an hour discussing over midnight oil the impact that Cicero would bring to *In Verrem* II, however, as Anthony Everitt concluded, 'Hortensius was appalled by what he heard and his sense of being ambushed by Cicero magnified the impact of the evidence. He withdrew from the case.' In addition, Cicero had really won the case before it had really begun, such was his genius for the direction of his attack. Verres decided to quickly pack all his loot and leave for exile before the second part was needed – taking a fortune of millions of sesterces with him by baggage train.

Achieving this crushing victory over a powerful senator catapulted Cicero to fame across Italy. He had achieved this just days before an official break would have had to have been taken for the public holidays surrounding Pompeius' games to celebrate his election as consul. A victory of sorts for Cicero, but for an actor of his quality and need for attention and affirmation, he felt robbed. The days spent fashioning *In Verrem* II had been hard labour indeed and now there was no need to perform. Congratulations flowed of course, the Senate heeded his warnings of needing to get the answer right which, by implication was a test case against all of them and Verres was found guilty, but Cicero went further and, thankfully for future generations and world history, decided to publish in full all the work he had prepared for the trial of Verres. Some might say that the Verrine orations are the outstanding publication of his entire career – they are certainly the largest single enterprise – and no doubt his desire to cement his place in the judicial system as the most prestigious orator will have played some part in his determination to publish all three speeches. They show Cicero at his best, already a master of the rhetorical question that promotes disquiet and self-guilt among his audience – pathos as we know it – he entertains, drops in calculated jokes at others' expense, displays his detailed knowledge of Greek and uses language to grip the attention, and hits his adversaries hard below the belt – in all, a study of his speeches beginning with the Verrine Orations take us deep into the minds and realities of late Republican Rome and the attitudes they held.

One footnote to the content and context of the Verrine Orations comes in the shape of Cicero's attitude towards the theft of property undertaken by Verres. It was commonplace enough, though not always wise, for victorious generals to strip an area of booty. The Romans were no different from modern day looters such as Putin in the Ukraine, the British throughout their

An imagined bird's-eye view over the roof of the Senate House looking down on a speech from the Rostra into a huge crowd both in the Comitium and covering the entire Forum.

eighteenth and nineteenth century empires, or the French in colonial Africa. The Roman Senate was no different from modern day governments in that they decided when a riot became a rebellion or taking became looting. This is self-evident when we look, for example, at Gaza, Syria and Iraq – when government troops seize private property it is to protect themselves, when local people seize the same property, it is looting and so it was in Republican Rome. The exception here is that Cicero devoted much of *In Verrem* II to the issue of looting and the legacy of these statements shaped modern European thought in the eighteenth century through to our own day. When Cicero described, with great pathos, how Verres looted everywhere he touched, he of course generated indignation among the senatorial audience – but most of them had precisely such property in their own homes – rank hypocrisy was a readily available commodity in Rome. However, when Verres displayed these plundered items in Rome, Cicero further explained how often visitors and officials from towns across Sicily were appalled to see their art looted and yet displayed in front of them. In this way, Cicero was both accusing Verres of his disreputable attacks on the *virtus* of the Republic, and promoting a better understanding of why art was sacred to the people who created it; Verres was in fact looting from Roman citizens in one part of the empire to grandstand his power and wealth in another part.

Cicero goes further in *In Verrem* II by pointing out that art should be seen in different classifications – public and private and where Verres seized property from temples to adorn his own home crossed the lines of morality and right behaviours for a magistrate of Rome. Cicero himself became a great collector of – especially Greek – art, and the actions of Verres touched a raw nerve with him. In her book, *Art as Plunder*, Margaret Miles highlights how Cicero accepted that plunder was taken in war as remuneration for costs or punishment and that this could be displayed in Triumphs through the streets of Rome, but this was not what Verres did. Communal art looted in peacetime was a clear violation of the Roman ideal and Verres was the worst example of such practice and distinctions needed to be made. The legacy of these thoughtful commentaries by Cicero have resounded down the ages and been the platform for modern interpretations of the value and ownership of art.[2]

Notes

1. For a far more thorough examination of Cicero's narratives see Levine, D.S. *Cicero the Advocate*, Oxford pp. 117–146.
2. Miles, Margeret M. *Art as plunder: the ancient origins of debate about cultural property*, New York & CUP (2008).

Chapter 8

Domestic Life and the Tides Change

If there was a year in the life of Cicero where all seemed to be going well, it was 69. Free from the exertions of the trial of Verres, basking in the glory of being one of the leading figures in Rome and with his first child, a new daughter he adored, named Tullia, all that was left was to find the time to pursue his next political step – that of being elected aedile. The position of aedile was not a formal requirement on the *cursus*, but it was a useful role to hold, as it showed a willingness to work for the civic good and public service. Given that the four aediles in any one year were responsible for the repair of public buildings, the overseeing of regulations on traffic, weights and measures, public decency and organizing the main festivals in the Roman celebratory calendar, an aedile could earn considerable popularity among the ordinary people of Rome. A wealthy, ambitious man could splash out a lot of his private money in supporting these festivals and thus cement his reputation with the city masses. Each year two pairs were elected – two by the plebeians and two by the patricians – this latter group hopeful that the need for personal wealth to pay for games and feast days would ensure that only men of noble birth rose to the office of aedile and further.

Having been elected in the summer of 70, Cicero began his role in the January of 69 and found himself now part of the social and political whirl of the centre of the city of Rome and, with much to comment on, had probably been writing to Atticus for some months or years. However, our first extant letters date to the following year and this is where we open our window into the most detailed life of any Roman in history.

Titus Pomponius Atticus

Every man can tell how many goats and sheep he possesses but not how many friends.

Marcus Tullius Cicero

Titus Pomponius was neutral both in character and in policy. Perhaps this was his natural disposition or maybe it was the enduring fear and threat that he had experienced during the violent Sullan proscriptions, but whatever the cause, Cicero saw Atticus as trusted, fair minded and safe – and in Republican Rome these were rare and highly valuable commodities. The cognomen 'Atticus' was a personal title that he used reflecting the twenty or so years that he spent in Athens – Atticus – the Athenian. Largely friends with everyone, this was less due to any emotional need for a social network and more to do with an intellectual interest in Epicureanism as a philosophy and his engaging personality. As important as anything was that he maintained a position where he was a threat to no one. It was due to his travels away from Rome, a place he visited, but rarely stayed for any length of time, that we owe Cicero's letters, tracking Atticus down in his various pursuits or homes as he moved around the growing Roman world, watching events from a safe distance and doing his own share of writing about Roman history, how to manage a large fortune and his Epicurean philosophy. Central to Epicureanism was, and is, the pursuit of pleasure and the avoidance of pain. For the Greek philosopher Epicurus, who founded his teachings around 300, the essence of this world view is summed up in a short poem by one of his followers Philodemus –

> *Four part cure :*
> *Don't fear God,*
> *Don't worry about death;*
> *What is good is easy to get, and*
> *What is terrible is easy to endure*

This was not membership of a philosophy devoted to a hedonistic lifestyle – far from it – it was more a value judgement in everyday life about avoiding those things that bring pain and suffering and instead realizing the true meaning of life, which is to enjoy the opportunity, therefore, the relevance for us of what Atticus felt and believed shaped his relationship with Cicero and thus permeated his responses to Cicero's letters. Often Cicero read with frustration what seemed like childlike innocence on the part of Atticus when compared to the daggers and cuts of political life in Rome, and responded tussling with Atticus over his advice and sometimes showing his irritation that he did not see things his way. But, despite occasional friction, the letters show their close emotional relationship – something that had begun when they were schoolboys and Cicero knew well what depth Atticus had as a person. The 1901 edition of the correspondence of Cicero by Robert Tyrell and Louis Purser captures succinctly why it would be a mistake to view Atticus as someone without a real presence. 'It is easy to be less than fair to a man who made so bland a success of safe living in troubled times and who, unlike Montaigne, has left no self-portrait to engage posterity in his favour. There was more in Atticus than "the quintessence of prudent mediocrity".[1] We should remember that, while Cicero has naturally always been the main focus, just as the nearly 900 letters of Cicero provide us with an invaluable insight into the life of a key Roman figure of the Republic – so the responses of Atticus tell us a huge amount about an observer of the events in Rome and life in the Republic. Of the total number of Cicero's letters that have survived, 416 were to Atticus, and a further 419 to one or other of the 94 different friends, contacts or enemies that are immortalized in his correspondence. We have no idea of how many further letters Cicero drafted in his lifetime – undoubtedly thousands which are now lost to history. Through those that we have it is possible to hear Cicero's voice dictating to his various *scribae* – no doubt each specializing in their own types of letters and each trustworthy with the messages he was sending so privately. It is very possible, with time and peace to reflect, to sense the complex nature of his character and personality, his humour, intellectual capacity, political astuteness, fears and his underlying softness – perhaps feet of clay in a world of granite majesty.

The erosion of the *mos maiorum*

Cicero also displays the aspects so dear to him and all conservative Romans of the *mos maiorum* – the founding and guiding principles of what it meant to be a Roman. Translated literally as 'the ways of our ancestors', it is a recurring theme for Cicero to lament the slow erosion of Republican morals and values through his letters; through his speeches and books shines his commitment to fidelity, *fides;* piety and devotion towards the gods, *pietas;* proper performance of rituals and customs, *cultus;* self-control and self-discipline, *disciplina;* virtue and knowing what is right and what is evil, *virtus;* dignity, honour and esteem shown in service to the state, *dignitas and auctoritas.* These are the values of a society that had developed over a 600 year period and that generations of Romans had died to protect and lived their lives by. We might well ask what a modern day *mos maiorum* looks like and whether the young are taught the history and duties of citizenship well and are standing the tests of our own times.

But the letters, as well as his other many works, can also be tense, lashing out at rivals, fearful of making the wrong decision – they show us how vulnerable success made a person in the Republic – exposed to jealousy with only one direction to travel to avoid obscurity.

Given the initial impetus for this book, it only seems right to use the Shackleton Bailey translation *Cicero Selected Letters* published by Penguin in 1982. There are of course many other translations, but this one remains a constant in studies of Cicero.

A day at the office with the *scribae*

The upper-class Roman was a letter writer. As he spent time at home after a day listening in the Senate, at work in some profession or other, on his country estate or in his humble home in the provinces, he thought of friends and family, and this was the only way to communicate his thoughts and messages. Wax tablets in a wooden frame were the staple form of recording and these could be re-used over and over again – hence we have few examples in the world today. However, anything could be used to write on, as recent wonderful and ongoing excavations at Vindolanda reveal with their collection of postcard-sized thin wooden tablets. Parchment was available and sent in scrolls, but again few survive from the millions that would have been written.

Although there was no official postal system, there were private companies that rented out carriers by horse if the letter was important enough, or the scribes themselves could be sent on long or short journeys helping to fill the Roman road and river system with a flow of communications across Europe and Asia. An alternative was to pay or ask a friend or business traveller to deliver the letters as another way of getting information moving around. Even this could be tricky and risky –

Cicero to Atticus
Rome, 67

I get letters from you far too seldom considering that you can much more easily find people starting for Rome than I to Athens…it is owing to this uncertainty (of where you are) on my part that this very letter is somewhat short, because not being sure where you are, I don't choose my confidential talk to fall into strange hands.

Official government business was carried in all manner of ways and the masses of movement orders from the *legates* to their legions, requests for information from merchants (*mercatores*) on the arrival of their goods in ports, taxation demands from *scribae* in the public treasury (the *aerarium*), reprimands from the Senate to their provincial governors and the like would all find their way along the roads, rivers, sea lanes and pathways of the empire. Roman legionaries who could write, would send their letters home from all parts of the empire on the backs of mules and supply trains or in the hands of another soldier going on leave. They tell of their enjoyment at seeing the world, send good wishes to families and the gods and how they missed each other. Like blood pumping around a body, communications of all sorts made their way every day and night around the Roman Republic. The news of personal sadness and loss also had to take its chances and time making its way along the roads at night and day –

Cicero to Atticus in Athens
January 66

I have to inform you of the death of your grandmother from pining at your long absence, and at the same time because she was afraid that the Latin towns would revolt.

Here we can see what is probably an example of rather cold humour. The old lady was possibly still anxious over the events of the Social War back in 89 and sensing a danger no longer there and it is not absolutely certain that she was dead at all. It would be down to Atticus to sense the true meaning from his friend.

To support his increasing workload, Cicero would have needed a team of scribes, working from rooms within his home such as the *tablinum*, where most family records would be stored, or in rooms in the city and this would all be duplicated – the team would follow with him, along with any hard earned lictors, to his country homes, to visits to friends and on official business. Terentia and little Tullia would always be there, but the increasing demand that a great man of Rome would spend time meeting his clientele – just as he had watched his father do back in the early days in Arpinum – or dictating letters, notes, speeches to his well trained and loyal group of writers, meant that their time together was limited.

The *scribae* were therefore crucial to the success of any one man and to the entire state. They had in fact been important for hundreds of years – without them the Republic could not have functioned, nor coped with the significant stresses of imperial expansion. For Cicero the selection of the men who would work alongside him in the most critical aspect of his work was a vital exercise.

There were four main layers in the hierarchy of the *apparitores*, the civil servants that kept the masses of parchments, scrolls and wooden and wax tablets flowing across the Roman world. Working in the treasury or the other offices of state, these men and occasionally women, came from an educated background and developed a considerable knowledge of their areas of expertise, including the law. They were well paid, but could also earn an extra income by copying long documents (such as the Verrine Orations), or through the bribery and corruption endemic in the state at that time. Backgrounds could vary greatly, from freedmen – slaves released from their bond – from any part of the empire, to educated Roman men, and even members of the *equites* who had developed a love of writing and learning, and for whom a career in the civil service was the ideal role. We have the admission in the opening of the first book by Horace, the renowned poet of the later Augustan period, that he was a freedman, civil servant and *scriba quaestorius* – clerk to the quaestors in the public treasury.

In a society that regarded status as so important, it is perhaps not surprising that the *scribae* saw themselves as socially mobile and the profession as a passport to higher status and, in so doing, they invalidated the purely economic view of class held by Marx – showing that 'cultural capital' was every bit as important as financial capital. In his excellent book *The Scribes of Rome*,[2] Benjamin Hartman opens our eyes to the value of knowledge and writing skills as a way of determining class at this time – a pure synthesis at last of the value of education. While status derived from birth was and is the easiest or often most accentuated form of class – take for example the Brahmins in India, or the east coast Bostonian elite – status can also be bought by wealth, over time, and cultural capital, which takes even longer to 'arrive'. In Rome, the phenomenal growth of empire in that final century created a concomitant demand for more *scribae* and civil servants. Thus, opportunity was created for thousands of new educated people across the Mediterranean, while those working at the very centre of power saw their cultural capital rapidly enlarge and, as a result, their status. The integrity of the record keeping became even more important, the levels of confidentiality required of them even more acute and dependency by the Senate on this very select group of men became pronounced.

But as with all things, power brings with it corruption and the Senate of Rome reminds one of a quotation from Theodore Roosevelt: 'When they answer the roll call in the Senate, the senators do not know whether to answer "Present" or "Not guilty".' It was natural therefore that some of the biggest crooks had to be members of the *scribae*, covering up lies, re-writing texts, melting wax and starting fires. Some gained great wealth and public notoriety, such as Horatius Flaccus (known to history as Horace) and Maevius, the personal scribe to Verres in Sicily. We also know the names of over 300 scribes in Roman history although only fifty or so in the Republican era. When M. Porcius Cato Uticensis (Cato the Younger) enters our story shortly, he does so insisting that he could not take office as quaestor in 64 unless he spent time watching the scribes do their work in order to understand where error could lay. This was a man who knew the true value of a comma in a statement.

Both Cicero and Atticus would have relied on finding and keeping *scribae* to sustain their flow of communications and, over time, they would have developed a close bond knowing the writing speed of each, their individual technical proficiency, nuances of tone, humour and advise each other on how not to get the delicate phrasing misinterpreted. In his work, Hartmann illustrates – in a society where only a very small fraction of people were literate – just what a vital role these people had in the life of the Roman Republic and empire and just what special place they held – closest of all to great men and events, making history happen as they wrote as they were instructed. We do not know where Cicero found his team of scribes, but we do know that he most depended on Tiro, an almost lifelong support to him and it is to Tiro that we owe much because of his efforts to see the life and achievements of his master, and later friend, preserved for posterity. In many of his letters, Cicero mentions Tiro and exposes to us that he was younger than his master, referring to him as an 'excellent young man' (*adulescentem probum*) in 50. It is possible that Tiro was a homegrown slave or *verna*, although Cicero may have come across him somewhere in some other capacity, we do not know, but he tells us that Tiro carried out many tasks including taking dictation, deciphering Cicero's handwriting, managing his garden and financial affairs. Indeed Tiro was so important to Cicero that he was freed in 53 and became a Roman citizen in a great celebration, taking the name Marcus Tullius Tiro.

Against the background of his very busy year in office in Rome, a constantly moving political landscape now that Pompey and Crassus had finally arrived on the same stage, and his growing family commitments, Cicero not only found time to start his correspondence in depth with Atticus, but also carry on with his litigation briefs and his office of *scribae* must have been hard at it all day long.

Between 69 and his next major challenge as the central legal figure in Rome in a coming battle with Catiline six years later in 63, Cicero wrote, delivered and published a number of legal speeches. In 69 alone, Cicero produced three extensive speeches – *Pro Tullio* (On behalf of Tullius), *Pro Fonteio* (on behalf of Marcus Fonteius) and *Pro Caecina* (on behalf of Aulus Caecina). His correspondence with Atticus takes off from November 68 and we begin to sense and feel the world around Cicero on an almost daily basis as these extracts portray:

Cicero to Atticus
Rome, November 68

Knowing me as well as you do, you can appreciate better than most how deeply my cousin Lucius' death has grieved me, and what a loss it means to me both in public and in private life. All the pleasure that one human being's kindness and charm can give another I had from him.

You write to me of your sister. She will tell you herself how anxious I have been that my brother Quintus should feel towards her as husband ought. Thinking that he was rather out of temper I sent him a letter designed to mollify him as a brother, advise him as my junior, and scold him as a man on the wrong track.

I am glad that you are pleased with your purchase in Epirus. Yes do please look after my commissions and anything else that may strike you as suitable to my place in Tusculum, so far as you can without putting yourself to too much trouble. It is the one place where I rest from all troubles and toils.

We are expecting Quintus back any day. Terentia has had a bad attack of rheumatism. She is very fond of you and of your sister and mother, and sends her best love as does my darling little Tullia. Take care of yourself and your affection for me; and be sure of my brotherly affection in return.

Within these lines then written late on in 68, Cicero, the great legal name in Rome, reaches out to his friend Atticus on a level that we can all appreciate. The loss of a close friend upsets him, the behaviour of his brother towards his wife Pomponia, sister of Atticus, concerns him and he asks for help in fitting out his new home in Tusculum just a day's journey southeast from Rome. Both men in fact had new homes to talk about – while Cicero purchased a magnificent villa in a sort of Hollywood area of the beautiful high and green Alban Hills noted for its thirty plus villas of the rich and famous, Atticus chose Epirus in modern day Albania – rural, high and mountainous and just on the Ionian Sea – and far enough away from trouble. Already, Cicero sees Tusculum as his retreat from pressures in Rome and looks for help from Atticus to furnish it. Cicero is always on the lookout for property acquisitions both for himself and his friend.

Cicero to Atticus
Rome, December 68

I won't give you any excuse hereafter for accusing me of neglecting to write. It is you that must take care that with all your leisure you keep up with me.

Rabirius' house at Naples for the improvement of which you have designs drawn out and completed in imagination, has been bought by M. Fonteius for 130,000 sesterces. I wished you to know this in case you were still hankering after it.

Clearly Cicero's financial position had been enhanced considerably not only by his marriage to Terentia, but also his legal work – money would have flowed as water in gratitude for advice, support for political campaigning and victorious cases won. The request for help fitting out Tusculum indicated that this was a relatively new acquisition and in keeping with Cicero's lightning rise – rubbing shoulders as in Malibu, Beverly Hills or Monaco with the very wealthiest and most influential of families. We know that Cicero also owned a very grand villa in Rome situated on the much sought after and ancient Palatine Hill just to the south of and overlooking the forum and this was probably acquired at around the same time. Land was already especially scarce and prices of property the highest in all of Italy and yet Terentia and Cicero lived their city life right in the centre of an equivalent of Mayfair in London, a Greenwich Village in Manhattan or Beijing's Haidan district. Although it was destroyed only ten years from the date of these letters, archaeologists have still been able to pin down exactly where parts of Cicero's home remain. It was therefore not to be a long residence on the Palatine. Lest we should think that Cicero stayed in only two homes, Cicero owned another villa further to the south and again on the lavish and beautiful Lazio coastal strip also popular with wealthy Republican nobility for hundreds of years. Situated halfway between Rome and Naples, Formia was an ancient city overlooking the Mediterranean. Local archaeology and reputation states that Cicero's Villa had two *nymphaeums* – rock monuments dedicated to spirits and nymphs – richly decorated with Doric topped columns, vaulted ceilings and marble water fountains – Cicero refers to this place as Formianum and its existence is reinforced by Seneca, who tells us that it was here Cicero would eventually meet his end.

If we accept that 69–68 was a frantically busy time with the responsibilities of an aedile, organising events and feasts, writing legal orations and speeches and travelling between his three homes then the following year Cicero's mind was on becoming elected as praetor, the final step required before the consulship. That his attention was taken up by this we can read in this extract to Atticus:

Cicero to Atticus
Rome, August 67

When you wrote in one of your letters that you supposed I was already elected you little knew of the worries of a candidate in Rome at the present time, with all kinds of injustices to plague him. No one knows when the elections will take place. But you will hear all this from Philadelphus.

It is likely that Philadelphus delivered this letter in person and was able to explain many things to Atticus after his long journey – not just that Cicero was still embroiled in the necessary intrigues required to become elected as praetor against some heavily supported opposition – but also what was going on in Rome or, to be exact, the rapidly changing times for the political future of the Republic.

How to swim across changing tides

A nation can survive its fools, even the ambitious. But it cannot survive treason from within...for the traitor appears not to be a traitor...he rots the soul of a nation...he infects the body politic so that it can no longer resist.

Marcus Tullius Cicero

It was hardly likely that Crassus and Pompey the Great felt that they had achieved the pinnacle of their success. The joint consulship had shown that, despite their differences and irritations with each other, they could work together and the question now was what would they want next? Rome was a melting pot of societal change, population growth, imperial ambitions, expanding wealth and of course, ambition, and within all of this, Cicero was fighting for his space, his spotlight and his political position. Success now was dependent on where one stood in relation to the two great men – without one it was still possible to be a success, but without either, any sort of political achievement would be impossible. There were a growing number of senators who were more than concerned about the new balance of powers and these fears gained traction during the mid-60s as the changes impacting on the Republic grew in intensity.

When Cicero wrote to Atticus in 67 it was against a backdrop of new threats to the balance of the Roman universe from the ever-vacillating Pompey. Pirates had become a growing pest around the coasts of the Mediterranean. Verres had had his own way of dealing with them – doing deals, killing some, bedding others, and always pocketing their treasures, but that was hardly a campaign designed to rid the Republic of the disruption they caused to trade and therefore the economy. As the pirates impacted upon the pockets of merchants, so pressure grew to eradicate the threat, and when the islands of Crete and Delos were attacked, the matter became a scandal. Hortensius, as consul in 69, had been unable to solve the problem and early in 67, the senator Aulus Gabinius, against great opposition, proposed that a special law be passed that contradicted all of Sulla's past efforts of avoiding the concentration of power in one man's hands. Sulla's laws on age qualification had already been broken by Pompey as had his intention that men of power should have climbed the appropriate ladder – Pompey had ignored this too. Now Gabinius demanded that someone (clearly Pompey was the man of the hour) be given extraordinary powers to raise both a huge army, build a massive fleet of ships and be given absolute command of the entire Mediterranean fifty miles from any coastal area – in essence be given command over the empire ostensibly to deal with the pirates. This proposal undermined every principle both of the constitution of the Republic enshrined in law for hundreds of years and devalued the whole point of Sulla's actions in the civil war. Cicero records that Hortensius gave a lengthy, authoritative and brilliant speech in the Senate against this offer of proconsular *imperium* for three years. Rome was tense and aggressive with threats from both sides – the consul for 67, Calpurnius Piso was threatened with lynching by the Roman *populus* for stating his opposition and even the *augurs* spoke when a Roscius tried to argue that the command should be shared and received such a roar of disapproval from the crowd that a raven flying over the forum fell dead into the crowd – who in the Senate could argue with that. Pompey feigned disinterest while of course his acolytes did all the work for him and he was given the command when the *Lex Gabinius*, named after his most prominent supporter, was passed.

Whether it was Pompey's brilliance, an undercover agreement with the pirates, or the problem was not as acute as had been stated, the pirate issue was solved within three months – but the lasting impact for the reputation of Pompey is inestimable. Pompey's legions rapidly cleared Roman ports of pirates and their ships, executions were commonplace and the threat was ended. Cicero, who had not opposed the proposal, tied his colours to Pompey by praising him for restoring security to the empire – but at what cost? Modern contemporary history is littered almost on a daily basis with politicians having to make value judgements where their own moral values and beliefs grapple with their thirst for power. The power of the internet and social media means that their vocabularic gymnastics are there to be tested and judged with an immediacy that Cicero would probably not comprehend. He had the advantage of time on his side where modern generations of politicians do not. Their loyalty is tested in public in front of millions and their ability to avoid committing themselves either way is finely tuned – the more we watch the more we see these people manifest themselves as fudgers, delayers or disingenuous. Their prevarications based on personal ambitions serve only to undermine our trust in them and therefore in democracy as a whole.

Cicero had to do exactly the same in order to progress or even survive. Cicero's actions and words may not have been assessed immediately – his speeches could take years to be disseminated – but they have, on the other hand, been studied for over 2,000 years. It is still not really certain what he was doing when he did not stand against the *Lex Gabinia*. Cicero has been criticized in the past by Mommsen who said 'When he exhibited the appearance of action, the questions which his action applied to had as a rule just reached their conclusion.' In other words, Cicero swam with the current to the very last moment and when he felt the swell of a stronger one, he moved. Such fine political timing is a remarkable and dangerous skill – it avoids early commitment without betraying a position, but it can lead others to suspicion of motive. This strategy, if it was indeed a strategy, does show itself more than once in Cicero's career – waiting for just the right moment to ride the right wave to ensure one is on the winning side. Does this suggest a man of no conscience, or a man with a careful attitude towards survival? A man whose morals were easily moved, or a man of such stringent and dedicated morals that, to survive and apply these beliefs, he had to swim with changes in the political currents? That Cicero was changing as a personality can be sensed from these extracts from a letter to Atticus –

Cicero to Atticus in Athens
Rome, 66

You keep on making me expect you again and again. Only the other day, when I thought you were on the point of arriving, I was suddenly put off by you till Quintilis (July). Now, however, I do think that you should come at the time you mention if you possibly can. You will thereby be in time for my brother Quintus' election, will pay me a long-deferred visit, and will settle any dispute with Acutilius.

At first glance this does sound rather high handed – definitely from a Cicero now used to issuing orders in Rome on all sorts of levels and almost at the top of the greasy pole of political promotion. Whether Atticus noticed any tonal change we do not know, but it is almost a demand that he attends his friend in Rome and an instruction to settle an outstanding personal matter – perhaps so that it causes no embarrassment to Cicero? It should be expected that Cicero was changing, his success at all levels both in the law and on the stage of the forum and of course, his political standing now so close to being a candidate for the consulship, may have turned his head away from service to the state and instead to service to himself as this next extract suggests –

Here at Rome I have conducted the case of Gaius Macer with a popular approval; surpassing belief and unparalleled. Though I had been inclined to take a lenient view of his case, yet I gained much more substantial advantage from the popular approval on his condemnation than I should have got from his gratitude if he had been acquitted.

So much for justice and so much for the client. Clearly here is Cicero himself assessing the social and political profit and capital he has made from another legal case. His self-assessment of 'unapparelled' applause for his performance merely adds to the indications that here is a man, mid-career, losing sight of his original ambitions, ethics and morals. Lastly we see more of the man intent on adorning his new palaces with the imagery he feels he requires to mimic the men of power and worth in Rome –

I would have you, as you say, adorn the place with the other objects also, and the more the better. The statues which you sent me before I have not seen. They are in my villa at Formiae, whither I am at this moment thinking of going. I shall get them all transferred to my Tusculan villa. If I find myself with more than I want there I shall begin adorning Caieta. Please reserve your books, and don't despair of my being able to make them mine. If I succeed in that, I am superior to Crassus in wealth and look down on everybody's manors and pastures.

One of the required skills of any historian of substance is to weigh evidence free of personal inclination or opinion. This I would suggest is impossible. It is no more possible for a person to read a letter without forming a subconscious bias than for a lawyer to care whether a person is innocent or guilty. With this in mind as a caveat what are we to make of this last extract? In essence we see a man intent on social pre-eminence – not content with being part of the body of the Senate, a tremendous achievement in its own right, Cicero wants to eclipse the richest man in Rome. We have lost the aspirational young lawyer and orator, the man his father set on the path to success as a professional in his own right, instead we have gained a man requiring his friend Atticus to hoover up all he can by way of statues and imagery and now the most sought-after item of all – books – in order to reflect his own glory onto the homes and fields of the people who lay beneath him. What a transformation.

Whatever the truth of his personality at this stage of his life, Cicero was now also seen as Pompey's man, and this catapulted his electoral success up to a new level. In most of the almost endless elections for office, coming in second was the very best a new man could hope for and yet Cicero was elected in 67 to the office of praetor for the following year on a scale that usually indicated bribery – we know Cicero never bribed, but we do not know how much money flowed from Pompey's wallet in thanks for his new friend's support. Just as likely is that Cicero had, by a mixture of silence and then unequivocal support, been assumed to be a supporter of Gabinius' proposal from the very start – we must never underestimate the power of silence, as it is sometimes the loudest scream of all. Cicero took the risk of defying the large senatorial block against Pompey and in so doing alienated many prior supporters. The die was not yet cast, but in so doing he had revealed an aspect of his personality hitherto hidden, or indeed recently developed, that of political manoeuvrability. No longer seen as a neutral, Cicero's name was added to the hitlist of those bruised and neglected by the power and arrogance of Pompey – and it was already a long list.

Notes

1. Tyrell, R.Y. & Purser, L.C. *The Correspondence of M. Tullius Cicero.* Dublin University Press, 1901.
2. Hartmann, B., *The Scribes of Rome.* Cambridge University Press, 2020.

Part IV

The Battle for Democracy

Chapter 9

Was Democracy in the Roman Republic Doomed to Fail?

At the point where Cicero supported the *Lex Gabinia*, democracy in Republican Rome was already in crisis. The willing support that makes democracy work, the consensus required to maintain the delicate levels of respect for the law, the Senate and the constitution were not only challenged but badly bruised and Cicero, by his decision, played his part. That Pompey could manipulate circumstances regarding the pirate threat to his advantage and control powerful individuals with an eye to being given such extraordinary powers indicates that, in his mind at least, democracy was a failed methodology. The vision of Rome that he had clearly harked back to Sulla's absolute power, the military majesty of Marius and the kings of ancient times.

Just what the Roman Republican state was coming to terms with in the decade of the 60s echoes down the ages to our own times. Two hundred years ago Benjamin Franklin alerted those around him to the fragility of maintaining a democracy when he said his preferred option for government was 'a Republic – if you can keep it'. Western liberal democracy is not even 300 years old and the radical ideas of John Locke, even though they date to the early enlightenment regarding the partnership between individuals and the state, are still being tested. The truth is that we do not know if democracy has a shelf life and is just an option as one of the repeating social mechanisms for governance in human communities – alternating between dictatorships, communism, juntas, federations, monarchies and oligarchies.

The End of History?

In his penetrating 1992 book *The End of History and the Last Man,* Francis Fukuyama embarked upon an analysis of the future of democracy.[1] Already, prior to the Trumpian challenge in the USA, with the presidencies of Recep Erdogan in Turkey or Viktor Orban in Hungary there was evidence that liberal societies in the western world were facing another historical turning point. Just as the ancient societies of Greece and Rome had experienced, the rise of economic oligarchies who select a charismatic and ruthless commander to lead the state in a mock democratic dictatorship represent a real and present danger to democracies everywhere. But for Fukuyama, western liberal democracy has already won the battle and these are but minor setbacks and we have reached the end point of human ideological development with liberal democracy victorious. His thesis rests on a number of foundations.

In keeping with the Marxist view that history is linear, moving from one socio-economic epoch to another, capitalist economics and economies are inevitable. Technology drives private enterprise and capitalism supports, extends and maintains the pace of technological change – they work hand in hand – and this applied to the Roman Republic. The only way the empire could grow as it did, was for new talented engineers, surveyors and architects to be sponsored and for technology to prosper. Roman concrete constructed entire cities and the world that was made Roman did indeed exploit the masses, engage with capital investment and allow individuals to profit from the losses of others. Kings and generals may have lost their battles, soldiers may have died in their thousands, but the merchant and business classes of conquered provinces flourished under their new capitalist rulers.

The unequal distribution of wealth was central to the Roman Republic. Let us not forget that for the remains of every aqueduct that we admire, for every Colosseum we photograph on holiday, or every temple that takes our breath away, there were architects, engineers, designers and builders all now nameless and lost to history who were funded by huge state capital injections or private finance and whose names were celebrated. Their celebrity status made them thirsty for more and all the trappings of successful status that came with it. We obsess about the key names in Roman history, but they only existed on the backs of thousands of nameless entrepreneurial and technological success stories. The builder of the first Roman arch can be compared to Steve Jobs and the iPhone.

So too, with the technological explosions of the past 100 years Fukuyama believes that the failure of communism (the Marxist solution to these inequalities via controlled state economy and direct centralized control by government) proves that only democratic institutions, which allow for profit and free-market forces, can survive. Individuals who are successful drive economies forward, reaping huge profits at all levels, and it is liberal democracy that allows this to happen in the best way. Fukuyama takes this hypothesis a stage further and believes that the American form of democracy is the best representation of this in history.

Apart from democracy being the best environment for technology and profit to develop, the Fukuyama thesis also predicates itself on the Hegelian model of the need for social recognition as an inherent driver for democracy and its triumph over other ideological forms of government. For Hegel, societies eventually develop the best model that creates opportunity for social status and satisfies the human need for recognition. This idea, acknowledged by Fukuyama, can be traced back to Plato and his conceptualization of *thymos* or 'spiritedness' where recognition of the worth of an individual supersedes their desire for wealth. Thus, although Cicero desired wealth, it was recognition, or his *thymos*, that was more important to him and it was a democratic environment again that was the best place for this to flourish. When workers go on strike, are they demanding higher wages or really wanting better recognition regarding where they fit in the state? The rise of the expanding middle class can only fully develop in a capitalist liberal democracy. Dictatorships, Communism, Juntas, and Fascism all fail to allow for recognition of individual talent or acknowledgement of individual achievement – it is the anonymous collective that counts. But, Fukuyama believes, ultimately liberal democracy will win through, and Turkey, Hungary, Thailand and every other non-liberal democratic state will eventually come to see this. Even China and North Korea, despite their current obvious existential threats to democracy, have to spend a great deal of effort acknowledging the advantages of democracy and pay lip service to its existence even within their own state. One only has to see the Chinese Communist Party conference hall with its packed 'representatives' to sense the concern that democracy is a shadow within the state to be strangled, but not enough for it to die.

The Fukuyama thesis also highlights the growth of other factors that encourage the growth and stability of Western liberalism such as the presence of Christianity as a mainstream religion. With its emphasis on the equality and freedom of the individual, it is clear to see how democracy can thrive in Christian led states where 'commandments' create a sense of order and devotion to the community or state. These very influential mores in the sociological sense are taught from birth and, like the augurs of Republican Rome, provide a cement between the state and the well-being of the community. When religion breaks down, so polarization divides society into those who believe in the religion they grew up with and the democracy that allowed it to flourish, and those for whom religion does not exist and their loyalty to the state and therefore to the maintenance of the whole community becomes fractured down to their own interest group.

That Fukuyama sees the European Union as the ultimate expression of the successful universality of western liberal expression and governance may surprise those of us in the United Kingdom who have recently rejected his entire thesis. For Fukuyama, one day all continents will duplicate the EU model, supersede national boundaries and erupting myopic nationalism and go on to replicate what he feels is now the end of history as far as democratic evolution is concerned. The current early twenty-first century eruptions of nationalism in the face of federation – in the United Kingdom and Poland for example – are short term outbursts of *labes* (lava) on the sides of already dead volcanoes.

If these ideas are true, then was the Roman Republic doomed to fail? If democracy in the age of Cicero was providing for all the needs that Fukuyama states are necessary, what went wrong? Democracy in the Republic was allowing for technological change and development, it was allowing profits to be made to encourage further growth and it was also very adept at highlighting the individual Hegelian need for recognition. The Republic was also supported by not just one, but a series of gods for whom the state was a mother figure to be protected, and the whole of Roman society was uniformly committed to worshipping this religion. In other words, all the necessary components of the Fukuyama vision of the enduring success of democracy were in place and yet, in the space of Cicero's lifetime, democracy in Republican Rome was to transition, to use a contemporary phrase, from a high point of Republican success through to decay and, quickly and painfully, collapse.

The rubber band

So many books and PhD theses have been written over hundreds of years theorizing the reasons for the collapse of the Roman Republic, so many in fact that it would be impossible to summarize them all in a book primarily about the life and times of one man. Instead, it is possible to assess and test just one with the objective, if nothing else, of adding to the debate if not solving it.

We live in a new age often referred to as 'woke' – a time of acute awareness and focus on inequality in areas of race, sex, and social and political freedoms. First coined around 1940, 'woke' was a word associated with alerting people to racial injustice in certain American states and grew in intensity as a meme becoming an internet driven world phenomenon. Since that time, BLM has, as a construct, been corrupted and can often been seen to be used as a pejorative attack on insincerity, but reactions generally to this one, very powerful, word can be summarized in three ways. The first are those people who are indeed sincere about identifying woke causes of injustice, some dedicating their lives to ending discrimination. The second group are those repelled, mostly politically, about anything associated with being woke and, for example in America, the Republican right wing has set itself a task of eliminating woke from the dictionary. The third response is indifference – those people for whom yet more legislation, more political time and money to try to deal with more cases of discrimination is just too much. It is this last group that is of interest.

The rubber band theory suggests that democracy expands to hold as many people within its reach as possible. After all, support for democracy has to come willingly from the people because, as John Locke explained, in return for their support, democracy allows them a voice. If democracy excludes then it also by definition precludes or prevents access to involvement and a voice, thus democracies often search for more and better ways to be inclusive and to garner greater support, not less, for the maintenance of, in this case, the Republic. To do this, the rubber band theory claims, the democratic construct creates new opportunities for democracy to be seen to be completely transparent, above corruption and run by the people. The imaginary rubber band of political rules, routines and authorities that hold the people together stretches to accommodate greater demands for freedom and, over time, greater freedoms. This is a process that requires delicate management. In Rome, the fathers of the state wrestled with these problems on two levels – as the Republic grew so then did the demands for greater involvement, expanding access to positions within the state, extending the right to vote and allowing greater numbers of people Roman citizenship and these demands were perhaps at their most acute during Cicero's lifetime. The Senate produced defenders of the *mos maiorum* – the vital principles that had never changed – Cato was one such disciple and these personalities of the extreme right in politics can be both a benefit and a curse. A benefit as they remind society of what was and still is, a curse because their inflexibility towards change creates an intolerable strain for democracy. But the Senate also had to juggle a structure that had been devised to present the people with, as far as they could make it, perfect democracy – and it is these two competing demands that stretched the rubber band not so that it broke, but to the point where the essential tension needed to keep everything in place failed and it lost its shape completely.

Take the endless annual round of elections. At all levels in the Republican state, it was constant change. Devised for the best of reasons, to enable access from below to new men and to present the people with a vision of accessibility to power, this actually meant that every year good men, perhaps the best men, were lost to history. While having two consuls and changing them every year meant that there was a free flow of new faces annually, this also meant election fatigue – not just for the Senate, but for the voting electorate. It was an almost constant feature of Roman city life to be listening to aspirational speeches, thinking about one personality or another and accepting bribes. Familiarity breeds contempt and in trying to create more access, the rubber band requiring the people to respect the need for effort in electing every year began to fail.

The administrative effort to control elections not just in Rome, but across the state was immense and time consuming. Wonderful work for the *scribae*, but colossal record keeping and communications.

One can imagine that the electorate just wanted a break, no sooner had they voted than they needed to do it again – every year of their lives. For democracy to work successfully, the people must value what it does. Do we really think that Brexit would have passed in the United Kingdom if the younger voters had bothered to turn up at the ballot box? Too many 18–24-year-olds were indifferent to democracy and history changed.

Of course, the Roman State tried to collect the best into the Senate, but how many new men were lost on that journey. For the electors, however, the endless pressures to think, to decide, even to turn up were counterproductive – and did they lose sight of the value of their democracy? Far better maybe to have someone do all the thinking for you – perhaps a Pompey offering you a break from never ending elections was preferable to aspirational and ambitious young men intent on maintaining the status quo. In the USA today such a debate is running – within the rubber band of American democracy, enormous pressures have built on the matter of the dilution of support for democracy and how to reverse this – do you give even more and acknowledge the woke causes, expand access, encourage even more diversity in the hope of adding supporters of the democratic state, or do you retrench, pull the band back into shape, pass power back to one person, reduce government and decrease democracy, ignore woke causes. Matters have reached a stage that means that when Donald Trump dies, the right wing in the USA will find another Trump – the battle for democracy is not just centred on him, but the ideas that he has unleashed. In the same way, Pompey unleashed the concept of one-man rule, one man to solve the problems, one man to do all the thinking – and Cicero supported him.

The rubber band holding the Roman Republic together was also stretched by the clash of the old meeting the new. With greater sovereignty over new dominions came greater diversity. By 31, the city of Rome had been getting used to accepting in slaves, merchants and travellers from known parts of the empire, from southern France (Narbonensis), Sicily (Sicilia), northern Africa (Numidia), Southern Turkey (Cilicia) and Macedonia. But times were changing rapidly and new faces with new languages began arriving in droves from Egypt, Central Turkey (Phrygia), the Dalmatian cost (Dalmatia), Spain, Belgium, Austria, Germany, Syria and Egypt. Physically Rome as a city could not hold the numbers that were arriving, public services struggled, the noise and smell increased, as did the arrival of disease; crime and a longing for the old days also increased. Bear in mind that there was no police force to quell public disturbances or control riots – the army was not allowed to cross the city boundary or *pomerium*. Hence a struggle for the retention of old identity together with an equal desire for new identity amongst the new inhabitants ensued, and the rubber band of democracy was stretched even further – and in both directions at once.

In the same way the political and social debate in the USA also centres around the two states. No longer a simple geographical division between north and south, but a far more fractured picture emerges between the right – a return to what it means to be American, unity and conserving the past and the left where diversity and access is everything, where democracy is required to stretch and accommodate new immigrants, new languages, new people. The two Americas we see today are a mirror image of the debates and struggles fought out during the lifetime of Cicero. Again, the simplistic elector sees sense in the simple answer, where someone else does the thinking and dictatorship offers great relief.

The Fukuyama thesis has been attacked from all sides. Benjamin Barber wrote in the 1990s that *The End of History* is flawed because it fails to take account of the counter power of radical Islam and Islamic fundamentalism where ethnic and religious loyalties will always resist liberal western democracy. Equally Jacques Derrida saw Fukuyama's work through the prism of American cultural anxiety about its future and went much further

For it must be cried out, at a time when some have the audacity to evangelise in the name of the ideal of a liberal democracy that has finally realised itself as the ideal of human history: never have violence, inequality, exclusion, famine and thus economic oppression affected as many human beings in the history of the earth and humanity.

As the western world comes to terms with the spreading impact of a major international war in Europe with the parallel evils of the weaponizing of energy and attempts to recover from a world pandemic, these evils that Derrida saw across the world in the 1990s are as evident now as they ever were, and we must wonder what erosive capability they will have on support for liberal democracy.

But there is and was one other threat to democracy that plays its part in the attack on the system and alerts us as to how it can fail.

Note

1. Fukuyama, F., *The End of History and the Last Man*, Avon Books (1993).

Chapter 10

The Erosion of Morality

There are decades in which nothing happens and weeks in which decades happen.
Vladimir Ilyich Lenin

The debate over the causes of the fall of democracy in the Roman Republic has rumbled throughout history: we might be edging closer to a consensus, but historians are reluctant to fix an answer – what would be the point of studying A level History at school and beyond if a definitive answer existed? For Cicero the answer was fairly obvious, as his many letters on the subject testify. Of course, historians traditionally agreed that the rubber band was stretched too far. The Senate became increasingly exposed as weak given that its power rested on convention rather than law – a similar model to the modern-day United Kingdom. Economic problems grew in intensity; conscription into the larger more modern army and bankruptcy caused deprivations on a large scale; the influx of new wealth was distributed unfairly and disproportionately into the hands of the already wealthy; imperial government was strained and unable to control provincial administration effectively; new and ambitious men saw an enlarged standing army of legions as a weapon to intimidate both neighbours and their own institutions. But very evident alongside these pivotal problems was what Cicero identified as a sudden and serious collapse in the all-important moral compass of the Roman people. Cicero commented on these observations throughout his life and most especially towards the end of it in the 50s and 40s.

Roman success and life were centred on service and conservatism and the past, as we saw in the early education of Marcus Tullius Cicero, was revered and something to be learnt, remembered and the heritage protected. The work of their ancestors was celebrated and enshrined in those statues, temples, inscriptions and in the law and it was rare for anyone to criticize either the past or the institutions of the state. This left the actions of men for the failings and problems of the late Republican state. It was men and their inability to measure up to those that had gone before that were the problem. Whether this is actually true or not can be debated, but nevertheless the growing instability, civil and political strife and resultant events were centred around a series of political celebrities and became a matter of personality clashes. We might infer from this that there was no problem with democracy per se and that it should and would have survived, but for the actions of a few very powerful men. However, Cicero tells us a number of things. His letters not only tell us a great deal about the collapsing morality and standards of Roman public life, but they also show us that he was tainted by the same virus. As we saw earlier, his thirst for power and influence knew no bounds, to eclipse Crassus was his dream and his head had even been turned away from truth versus lies in order to measure the likely amount of praise he would personally receive on the result. If we were in any doubt about his emotional appearance and the character of the great man as he now was, we only have to look to two passing phrases in letters to Atticus for some revealing evidence –

Cicero to Atticus in Athens
Rome, December 68

We may be quite satisfied, I think, with my brother's feelings towards Pomponia. He is with her at present in his villa at Arpinum.

The date of my father's death was the 28th November.

This is about all my news, If you light upon any articles of vertu suitable for a gymnasium (an arrangement of plantations and buildings) *which would look well in the place you know of, please don't let them slip.*

In common parlance we might paraphrase – do not worry, I think my brother likes your sister, my dad died, but far more importantly, how are you doing with getting hold of some more statues for my many houses? Clearly Cicero had little depth of feeling for the death of his father whose legacy or influence on him is never referred to in his correspondence – his father is a footnote in his life.

Cicero to Atticus in Athens
Rome, 65

*I have to inform you that on the day of the election of L. Iulius Caesar and M. Marcius Figulus to the consulship, I had an addition to my family in the shape of a baby boy (*Marcus*). Terentia doing well.*

At this present time I am considering whether to undertake....

While this was ancient Rome and the attitude of men of power was something we still do not fully understand, the arrival of a baby boy is equated with the election of two men to the consulship. There is little need to dwell any more, although it is rather nice that Terentia is mentioned in passing.

There is a sense that, by 66 and in office as praetor, we have Cicero the hardening politician rather than the gifted and brilliant legal orator. His speeches and decisions were now less concerned with what was right and instead with what was useful to his ambitions. Trying to sell himself as both a man of the people, a *popularis*, but at the same time reassuring the political elite, the *optimates*, that his conservatism was his dominant philosophy. He was tested numerous times in very public trials, but his eloquence and skill were such that he just about managed to play the neutral man enough for both sides either to give him the benefit of the doubt as to where his true feelings lay – or to despise him as a clever, evasive operator. There was, however, one major exception. Having already tied his colours to Pompey and his lieutenant Gabinius, and clearly jealous of the power and wealth of Crassus, he was forced to stand in the light on one big issue – that of the bequest of the whole of Egypt to Rome. Egypt had been a client state, though not a full part of the Roman Republic for many years, but by the mid-60s, there was a strong clique in the Senate, one of many, that viewed Egypt with greed for its great wealth and they raised questions over the will of an earlier King of the ruling Ptolemaic family that had left the entire Kingdom to Rome and nothing had been done about this. It was at this moment that Cicero chose to launch his campaign for the consulship by setting out to persuade the Senate, in what was one of his first overt political speeches, not to support the agitating interests of Crassus with his accompanying huge levels of greed. This act can be interpreted as the instincts of a political statesman seeing the complete annexation of Egypt as being problematic for the Republic at this time, or someone protecting the interests of both Pompey and himself. It is possible that Cicero felt that of the two key men in Rome at this time, he could more easily contain and control Pompey than he could Crassus for the furtherance of his political career.

Cicero wrote much on what he saw as the decline in the *mos maiorum* – the rules and morals by which the Republic had always stood and been governed and yet there is evidence to suggest that he too was affected by the very same attractions of personal power and wealth that he saw as evils eroding the national spirit and strength of the state. For us, his unique eloquence and the survival of so many of his writings give a deep appreciation of what he saw and felt to be the root causes of this general decline, but our observations must come with a certain caution for a man who sought exactly the same trappings of wealth and power of those he observed.

Cicero was not alone in highlighting the erosion of tradition and *virtus* – the qualities needed for men to be able to reach and achieve the highest levels of excellence. In Cato the Elder we have a second century view of this process already under way and in 184, he vehemently attacked the decadence, luxury and extravagance that he saw as an illness slowly destroying the strict codes of morality and toughness needed to maintain the Roman Republic on its journey to world domination. Cato the Elder's famed levels of austerity and moral rectitude were bequeathed to his great grandson, known to history as Cato the Younger and whose life, amplifying his great grandfathers' views, coincided with Cicero's. Even earlier commentaries from the Greek historian Polybius made reference to the damaging effects of Roman victories over the Greeks and the luxury generated by the influx of stolen goods and wealth to Rome.

Constantly creating enemies to vanquish kept the state on its toes and maintained a focus on the need to be watchful and able to fight. Wars also gave opportunity for advancement, but they had to be good wars. Uncontested wars, where Roman military prowess simply overpowered all enemies, were viewed by the Roman historian Sallust as another cause of moral degeneration – starting in his view with the defeat of Carthage in 146. Was the momentum for the growth of empire and keeping the propaganda machines running about the constant threat of enemies on the borders merely a political tool for social control? Like a modern-day China or North Korea, enemies are constantly at the gates – real or imagined – to justify maintaining a stance of military might and central authority. In his Jugurthine War, Sallust tells us:

> But the pattern of routine partisanship and factionalism, and as a result, of all other vicious practices, had arisen in Rome a few years earlier. It was the result of peace and an abundance of those things that mortals consider important.
>
> Among the citizens, there was no struggle for glory or domination. Fear of a foreign enemy preserved good political practices. But when that fear was no longer on their minds, self-indulgence and arrogance, attitudes that prosperity loves, took over.
>
> A few men controlled military and domestic affairs; the same men held the treasury, the provinces, political offices, honours and Triumphs. The spoils of war were ravaged by the generals and their friends.

We should note that Cicero did not subscribe to this theory of the *metus hostilis*, and did not think that the threat of war was necessary for men to retain their *virtus*. For Cicero, it was not the system that was failing, but the people that the system was producing to lead it. This has echoes again in our contemporary political world where the cries of 'where are the British parliamentary leaders of the past' and 'where are the US Presidential candidates of the qualities of previous generations' are so often heard? The Republic had evolved over hundreds of years, developing an exact balance between the rights of Roman citizens and the need to invest power, through the Senate, to those whose *virtus* and *dignitas* demonstrated that they had the right qualities to use it well. But Cicero also failed to see two other new inadequacies in the Republic quickly enough to eliminate them when he became consul in 63 – the inability to control civil violence and the usurpation of military power invested through the *imperium*. Both of these were new phenomena, but critically wounding to the Republic as the state entered the decade of the 50s. It was not that men with accumulated *virtus* and immense economic and political power had not seen the opportunity for destroying the state in the past, but it was new that such wealth and power was on such a scale. Indeed, it takes only the blink of the imagination to see that these very characteristics describe the presidency and future political ambitions of Donald Trump in the United States of America. However, Cicero did agree with and see the two evils identified by Polybius, before the event, and Sallust after namely the game changers that were personal wealth and personal love for power.

Luxuria and *Avaritia*

It remains a matter for debate as to whether Cicero, the greatest orator of his time, lauded throughout the ages, if not the whole of ancient history, can be accused of a level of hypocrisy. As Plutarch admitted, Cicero was 'so unreservedly fond of his own glory' but added that he 'was quite free from envy of other people'. However, Plutarch was not writing with the benefit of the volumes of personal correspondence that we are so fortunate to be able to study at leisure and it is clear that Cicero, as we have already seen, was indeed often preoccupied with his own status and comparing himself to his contemporaries in Rome. Poor Atticus sometimes seems to be running around doing nothing but ministering to the new shopping lists received constantly from Rome.

Cicero to Atticus at Athens
Tusculum, 67

As for my statues…pray put them on board, as you say in your letter, at your very earliest convenience, and anything else you light upon that may seem to you appropriate to the place you know of.

Regardless of his own temptations for luxury and grandeur, Cicero's voluminous writings created both on his way up the *cursus honorum* and much later heading rapidly down to the bottom rung, we are never short of references to the new excesses and indulgences he saw around him. In matters of food and new foods, dress and drink and addictions to pleasure seeking without limits, it was Baiae on the northern arc of the Bay of Naples and to the south of Rome that eclipsed Capri, Pompeii and Herculaneum as the playgrounds of the rich. Famed for its hot volcanic springs, wealthy Romans had been visiting Baiae since the sixth century, but this was nothing compared to the explosion of new villas and complex gardens that took off in the middle of the first century – coterminous with the influx of fantastic wealth from overseas conquests. Some of the most famous residents of Baiae, indulging to lesser or greater degrees in the vice and notoriety, were Sulla, Pompey, Caesar and later the emperors Tiberius and Nero. Interesting to note that Cicero too had a villa here. All now lost to the sea, the archaeological remains of some of the underwater mosaics and buildings are stunning.

Cicero refers to his time at his villa here at Puteoli, most notably describing how he would often walk from his villa overlooking the bay, inland to the great lake known as Avernus which still sits about two miles north from where Cicero would have strolled between sun drenched columns of marble, sat dictating on richly decorated mosaics (now under water) and received friends and contacts away from the noise and frenetic chatter in Rome. It was here that all the books Atticus would have purchased for him were located – in Cicero's Academy – a reference to his replication of the Greek Academy founded by Plato.

In past times the lake was thought to be the entrance to Hades and the underworld. Cicero would have walked near lakeside temples, through early morning mists and past vineyards farmed on the rich volcanic soils. But close by, down in the towns beneath the great houses Cicero would sense the decay of the Republic beneath him. *Luxuria* was one of the new enemies of *virtus* with its emphasis on good living, avoidance of work and resistance to hardship – the antithesis of the centrality of *virtus* in maintaining the Republic. Baiae became a centre for *luxuria*, but it was not alone amongst the new vices created by the success of the Republic. Alongside it came *avaritia* – the thirst for wealth, a fixation with greed and the assassin of asceticism. Roman heroes of the past shared in their willingness to abhor material possessions and, as ascetics, resisted the lures of personal gratification and Cicero looked back with respect to the fathers of the Roman heritage that he had been taught to revere as a child. Too many new men with new fortunes degraded the Senate as it also meant too many poorly educated men with no knowledge of the past and certainly no reverence for it. This was a cause he took up as early as the trial of Verres, where all of the vices that he saw spreading through the state had been exhibited in one man, but he was to continue to highlight this degradation, as he saw it, for the rest of his career.

Sociologically, where interdisciplinary osmosis assists in our understanding of what was happening in Rome at this time, the leading figures in the Republic, and their wives who were equally growing in stature, we can see the impact of affluence on equality – that is, money was creating greater competition between families. Whereas in days of hard toil and a homogenous outlook on *virtus*, ostentatious displays would have been frowned upon and out of keeping with the times, they were now an essential part of social climbing and status. Just as we see powerful people cultivating more powerful contacts and social competition between families over who has the better car, so Republican wives were desperate to display their new found wealth either in personal possessions or physical displays of status in their homes. Nothing has changed between Roman society then and our own today in this respect.

It might be a dinner party to you and me, but to a Roman husband and wife desperate to climb the social ladders, the selection of guests was designed to pool together your main competitors to measure yourself against and, if possible, knock them out with one blow of a feast, or an orgy, to remember. The desire to win was not new, but the tools of victory had changed and it was no longer as much a matter of heritage or intelligence as it was a measure of wealth. It is a curious human trait that wealth mistakenly confers a perception of ability and superiority on those that have it – so it would be with numerous new men, Pompey especially, and we would be wise not to treat all the famous names with the same degrees of ability.

The cult of Leadership

One of the more puzzling aspects of history is the way in which an individual can so dazzle a nation that he or she is able to achieve what many would believe to be impossible. The secret ingredient is called charisma and the charismatic person exudes a presence and an ability that we have all witnessed, but when that is combined with arrogance, an entitlement that the law does not apply to them, and political ambition, then democracy can face a problem.

Western liberal democracy has been under attack for two or more decades and in the same way so was Republican Rome before Cicero was born. We witness, as did he, a resurgence of right-wing nationalist sentiment predicated on strong one-man or one-woman rule. The key players in the first century were men like Crassus, Pompey, Caesar and Octavian, while the modern-day equivalents are Trump, Putin, Xi Ping and Erdogan. There is a commonality of characteristics – private wealth, ruthless political ambition, a nostalgic longing for a nationalist past that never existed, a contempt for the law and, most importantly, charisma. We can see such traits in figures like Adolf Hitler and Benito Mussolini in the early twentieth century, but not all strong figures exhibit all five for, although it was true that Margaret Thatcher and Ronald Reagan shared a narrow view of national history, ruthless ambition and charisma, neither were attached to the institutions of the state.

Those figures that set out to destroy democracy do so with an intent to use it as a self-inflicting weapon, working within the state apparatus so as to be seen to be legitimate, but in reality, they use the power given to them to destroy democratic mechanisms. Donald Trump was given command of the armed and intelligence forces of the American state through a democratic process and, once he had lost the election and saw his chances of retaining power slipping from his hands, he attempted to use those same powers to strangle democratic process. The unacceptable delays in getting troops and armed Police to the Capitol riots on 6 January 2020 were manufactured by a President wanting to give time for his MAGA supporters to hang the Vice President – he could then unleash the forces of 'law and order' on the very same people, no doubt under martial law, under the pretence of stopping a revolution. In other words, these people were going to be arrested one way or the other, they just did not realize it. Hidden within Trump's system was a virus that he had injected and that killed loyalty to the state and common sense. Like COVID, people did not all catch the virus to the same degree, but certainly within the Navy (the most conservative of the three services), the FBI, the state Police forces, the National Guard and the civil service many individuals went down with this illness where facts meant nothing and lies became the truth and many are still suffering the after effects of what we might term 'long Trumpism'. Should democracy in the United States of America ultimately fall, part of the reason will be the presence of a new virus within the apparatus of state that feeds on discontent and destroys from within. Without the existence of similar viral illness within the democratic state, Hitler, Mussolini, Saddam Hussain, Mugabe, Putin, or Erdogan would possibly never have come to power – they needed assistance from within – amongst the civil service, the Armed forces, the Police, and parliament itself.

Creating a cult following is part of the skill set of the tyrannical leader, playing on fears, promises of future power and glory, spreading disinformation and an ability to focus on already festering points of anger, for example migration, the cult is gradually formed of individuals who can see a purpose for themselves rather than the state and they begin to make decisions that compromise their own values and those that they have pledged loyalty towards. All dictators share not only the presence of charismatic personality, the magnetism that overpowers rational thought, but also the ability to personify themselves as a cult figurehead where loyalty to the leader has to supersede loyalty to the state.

De Officiis (On Duties)

In the same way, leading Roman figures were populating myths about the future and Cicero witnessed these within the context of the decline of civic virtue and morality. Like America today, it was difficult to know where the truth was in a time where lies had such strong and attractive currency. The main philosophical works of Cicero, some of which rank as the most influential ever composed, did not start to take shape until after 54 – in other words after the tumultuous years about to unfold at this point in our narrative. But it would not be for a further ten years, the final eighteen months of his life, 45–43, that he wrote his last, perhaps most poignant, and arguably important work called *De Officiis*.

Despite the structure of this book adhering to a largely chronological treatment of Cicero's life and times, it may help our understanding of what Cicero experienced over the coming twenty years by moving to the end, just for a moment, to empathise with his final conclusions, having experienced twenty thunderous and seismic years of strife, war, murder and attacks upon the Roman Republic.

By 45, Cicero's son Marcus was around 20 years old – we read of his arrival earlier in a letter to Atticus in 65. Studying in Athens at the time, just like his father before him, Marcus received into his hands what has been called Cicero's major ethical writing and his final philosophical work. We can see this work as an epistle, the good news so to speak of the clear-sighted vision with which Cicero could now see the events of the past twenty years with all the strengths and frailties of men and democracy. We do not know exactly when Marcus took delivery, but it may well have been after his father's execution, and we can read the exact words that his father spoke to him. Key elements, amongst many, were:

> *Although philosophy offers many problems, both important and useful, that have been fully and carefully discussed by philosophers, those teachings which have been handed down on the subject of moral duties seem to have the widest practical application. For no phase of life, whether public or private, whether in business or in the home, whether one is working on what concerns oneself alone or dealing with another, can be without its moral duty; on the discharge*

of such duties depends all that is morally right, and on their neglect all that is morally wrong in life.

Book 1 [4]

At first reading this paragraph makes perfect sense. Natural law and natural instinct should dictate that our sense of morality should sit beside us in all that we do in our lives and *On Duties* dwells a great deal on the origins of moral decisions and how they can be balanced with expediency – specifically with decisions that benefit the state, provided that they conform to the law and justice. He himself was to sacrifice his ideals when faced with a necessary decision that benefitted the state – for example in supporting the *Lex Gabinia*, but this was nothing compared to what Cicero saw during the period from 64 to 44. The history of the Republic became littered with numerous examples of men breaking the accepted moral codes for their own gain rather than for the state and, in so doing, also committing the gravest of sins in their pretence of acting to save the Republic:

While wrong may be done, then in either of two ways, that is by force or by fraud, both are bestial: fraud seems to belong to the cunning fox, force to the Lion; both are wholly unworthy of man, but fraud is the more contemptible. But of all forms of injustice, none is more flagrant than that of the hypocrite who, at the very moment when he is most false, makes it his business to appear virtuous.

Book 1 [41]

In his reference to the Lion, Cicero is almost certainly conscious of the actions of Pompey, who was a Lion in a cage full of foxes named Crassus, Caesar, Octavian, Gabinius and others too many to name. But Cicero had not finished the education of his son there. He had all the lessons from the Catiline Conspiracy, the efforts to mobilize men to recapture the moral ground that had been lost to profligacy and greed and how he himself had been prepared to give his life for the Republic he loved and believed in. In a long, detailed treatise, Cicero allowed his philosophic findings after a lifetime of study to be punctuated by anger at the foxes and lions and how they tore at the lifeblood of the state:

But when with a rational spirit you have surveyed the whole field, there is no social relation among them more close, none more dear than that which links each one of us with our country. Parents are dear, dear are children, relatives, friends; one native land embraces all our loves; and who that is true would

hesitate to give his life for her, if by his death he could render her a service?
So much more execrable are these monsters who have torn their fatherland
to pieces with every form of outrage and who are and have been engaged in
encompassing her utter destruction.

Book 1 [57]

We can only wonder the lengths to which Cicero tried to weave his beliefs
on natural law, the importance of loyalty to the state and rising above worldly
possessions. *On Duties* is written with Stoicism at its core. Although not a
Stoic himself, Cicero seems to have felt that Stoics were the best qualified
to highlight the duties of men to one another and to the state and thus he
wove their teachings into his final words of advice for his son to lead a good
life. Although shortly after the completion of this work Cicero was murdered,
he first had to set out in 64 on his election for consulship. What could have
gone so wrong in the succeeding twenty years to see both the Republic fall,
democracy collapse and Cicero's execution – and was it all preventable?

Chapter 11

Troubled Times – Mithridates

Anyone who has been stabbed in the back knows how difficult it is to know who held the blade.

Philip Bujak

By the time that Cicero had completed his year in office as praetor in 66, he had already been seen to stand firm as an open supporter of Pompey. With the *Lex Gabinius*, Cicero had been forced to make that decision he spoke about in *On Duties* between the honourable and the expedient. However, Pompey was not satisfied and a second moment of truth arrived when the ongoing matter of the continuous rebellions by Mithridates VI, the talented and ruthless ruler of Pontus, the region of the south coast of the Black Sea and northern Turkey.

Born around 135, Mithridates was a heroic figure in the history of his nation. His father had been poisoned at a banquet while he and his younger brother were still infants and his mother reigned as regent – ultimately preferring his younger brother as successor. Mithridates ran from the plots to kill him orchestrated by his own mother, but returned a man of considerable stature and physical strength, combining extraordinary energy and determination with a talent for politics – no doubt honed as a young man trying to survive assassination and schooled by loyal lieutenants during his adolescent years. He became a real challenge for the Roman Republic as he strove to unite the principalities under his leadership in an area where Rome was seeking to expand. During the 90s, Mithridates inflicted a series of heavy losses on both local kingdoms and on an army of two legions sent to defeat him in 89. The following year, he witnessed the ravages of mercenaries assisting the rival Bithynians moving through Pontus and objected to Rome, but when no response was forthcoming, Mithridates orchestrated a mass genocide in Roman population centres across the region to be rid of the Romans once and for all. In what became known as the Asiatic Vespers, between 80–150,000 Roman men, women, and children were slaughtered over the same few days in Ephesus, Pergamon, Caunus, Nysa and many other towns and cities – although impossible to date this event with certainty, Ernst Badian places it in the first half of 88 when Cicero was around 18 years of age. It is equally impossible to verify the numbers claimed to have been killed, which were likely highly exaggerated, but widescale murder there was with even slaves who helped kill their Roman owners and families being spared and a succession of three Mithridatic Wars began. In the first it was Sulla who forced Mithridates out of Greece, to which his reign had spread, and Marius concluded the peace talks with Mithridates when Sulla returned to overwhelm Rome.

Two more wars broke out, with the third having been under way since 73 and lasting into the mid 60s while Cicero was electioneering and serving as praetor. Well known in this period was the prominent general Lucius Licinius Lucullus. Lucullus was from a very patriotic and noble family and had fought in many campaigns. He had risen to the rank of consul in 74 and would have been both well known to Cicero as well as admired and was so famous in his time that he later made it into Plutarch's *Parallel Lives*. Known to be a brilliant general, he was also generous, intellectual and a traditionalist – he stripped those he vanquished in battle bringing home vast fortunes, but building libraries and gardens for contemplation and living a lavish lifestyle, but equally was a symbol of the former regime in that he stuck rigidly to the *cursus honorum* with its mix of military, political and social duties at the right times in life. This was in stark contrast to Pompey, who disregarded such rules – usually with his own army at his back.

Dispatched in 73 to finally crush Mithridates, Lucullus created an army and naval command to successfully manoeuvre the huge 300,000 strong army of Mithridates towards Cyzcus, a town on the coastal plain of north-west Turkey. Here Mithridates was to suffer unmitigated defeat. Setting out to lay siege to Roman Cyzcus, he discovered that Lucullus and his much smaller but well-trained army was behind him. Lucullus was careful not to be drawn into battle, but instead laid a counter siege around Mithridates and waited for the massive army to starve to death. In the space of a few weeks, disease and famine struck and Mithridates was forced to break the siege and escape with only a fraction of his army. The conflict carried on for another three years with Lucullus further annexing more territory to the empire and drawing the attention of the frustrated and ambitious Pompey. Perhaps it was the length of time that the legions had been away from home, or it could have been because the legions felt they had not been awarded enough plunder from their conquests, but disquiet and then open insubordination spread through the army of Lucullus. Armed conflicts took time: time to muster; time to prepare; time to march; even more time to locate the enemy and bring him to battle, and the Third Mithridatic War was dragging on. There had already been signs of danger for Lucullus when the Fimbrian Legions, who had previously murdered one commander and deserted another, mutinied. Lucullus probably did himself few favours by treating them lightly, as opposed to the brutal punishment of decimation, because the unrest remained and was stoked by the primary reason for the troubles – the agitation of one of the Claudian brothers, in fact the most reckless of the family, Publius Clodius Pulcher. The aim of the provocation was to see Lucullus removed from command and replaced by, of all people, Pompey. Thus in 66, while praetor and in that office largely through the obvious support of Pompey, Cicero was part of the deliberations in the Senate about whether or not to remove Lucullus.

Anyone who has been stabbed in the back knows how difficult it is to know who held the blade and, for Lucullus, this must have been a crushing few weeks being forced to defend Roman positions from a resurgent, and still

Silver Greek Tetradrachm of Mithridates VI of Parthia with a contrasting heroic or 'Alexandrian' representation.

alive, Mithridates while at the same time knowing his future was being plotted thousands of miles away in Rome. Within his own army there was widespread discontent and he was forced to take extreme measures to protect himself and retain control. Ordinarily a commander with the reputation of Lucullus could expect the full support and loyalty of his senatorial colleagues, but these were not ordinary times. Rome had entered a new phase of distorted democracy where events like the Mithridatic War provided catalysts for pressure groups to make ground – a political and economic opportunity that provided a chance to make money and bring down another member of the old guard. Against what seemed a background of military failure and unrest in the army, the tribune for 66 Gaius Manilius proposed a law, *pro lege Manilia*, that the commander in the east, Lucullus, be recalled to Rome and removed from office. It further proposed that Pompey the Great be given command of all the forces and the conduct of the eastern campaign – by a stroke of luck or careful preparation, Pompey was already in the east somewhat easily dealing with the pirate 'threat'.

This time the Senate did not split asunder, although there was opposition. Many senators and former consuls supported the act, as did Cicero who was now fully aware of the centrality of his place on the stage within the political drama – this was a moment where he had to make a decision and sensed the changing tides. The most notable opponents of Manilius' proposal were Cicero's old legal adversary Quintus Hortensius and Quintus Lutatius Catulus and they were not alone in seeing Pompey as continuing to perform as he had always done – breaking conventions, ignoring traditions and bullying his way to victory, fuelled by his popular standing with the people and his association with the heroics of Sulla. Pompey posed a constant threat that his popularity and majestic presence was probably enough for him to usurp democracy and impose his own dictatorship should he so desire. Fortunately for the tottering Republic, this was not Pompey's aim nor was he politically agile enough to place the more powerful chess pieces in the right places to enable this to happen – that was to be Caesar's role before too long.

Becoming Pompey's man – De Imperio Cn. Pompei 66

Though not often seen as one of his greatest works, Cicero's speech in favour of the *Lex Manilia* is of real significance on a number of levels. It was his first political speech to the *populus Romanus*, the people of Rome – hitherto Cicero had constrained himself to legal speeches or orations to senators. He judged this moment as his best opportunity to date of unveiling his mastery of speech – the law was going to be passed anyway, as Mithridates was now a real threat to the outer regions of the south-eastern empire and the tragedy of the Vespers had to be avenged. Naturally, Cicero was also putting down his marker for the consulship for which he was planning to run within the next year or two, and what better way of ensuring one's own popularity than being associated with and seen as a successful supporter of Pompey.

The downside was, of course, that any neutrality that he had claimed prior to this oration would now evaporate and he would be tied to Pompey for good or bad. The reactionary right wing conservative block in the Senate, the *optimates*, now led by Cato the Younger, were against any further moves by Pompey to ignore convention or gather greater power to his person but, as mentioned earlier, Cicero may have sensed or thought all along that Pompey, the *adulescens carnifex* (youthful butcher) was a man whose vainglory and hot-headedness he could control and influence while he strove to further his own career and at the same time preserve the Republic. In both his speech and in private conversation Cicero would need to assure the doubters on all sides of his ability to control Pompey. Alongside Cato was Gaius Calpurnius Piso, harsh critic of Pompey, talented orator himself and former consul the year before in 67. Piso was already a supporter of Cicero, indeed they worked with each other in later years trying to defend one another from rabid attacks from the supporters of tyranny, and it may be that the support of Piso helped Cicero persuade the *optimates* that all could be achieved in the interests of the state if they could hold their noses, use expediency and allow Pompey the command. The other strong intellectuals and political giants in the Senate such as Caesar and Crassus were too independent and clever ever to be manipulated. Narcissism, a newly resurrected phrase we often hear in relation to some modern-day leaders, can be a weakness if one fails to recognize the same traits in one's followers. So it was that, against the background of the threat from Mithridates, the prominence of Pompey and the opportunity for glory, Cicero arrived onto the rostra to make his speech sometime during his praetorship in 66.

There was no pressing requirement for Cicero even to make a speech, it was entirely his choice to ask to take part in the debate – and it was clear that the electoral tribes were unanimous in their support. Tactically, Cicero could have kept quiet and not risked exposing his views at this point in time, but all the portents seemed lined up in his favour to reveal himself to the waiting audience and it is in this speech that we see more of the man himself, knowing as he did that every word would be cheered. We can also see just how superb Cicero was in the practice of emotional manipulation, how he was able to be responsive to individual situations and audiences and his power of persuasive speech. But we can also see a man of 40, intellectually strong, a talented orator, holding the senior office of a praetor and well-travelled and studied – not a man to be taken for granted, but still naïve perhaps in the ways of the Senate. Cicero began:

Quamquam mihi semper frequens conspectus vester multo iucundissimus, hic autm locus ad agendum amplissimus, ad deccendum ornatissimus est visus, Quirites, tamen hoc aditu laudis, qui semper optimo cuique maxime patuit, non mea me voluntas adhuc, sed vitae meae rationes ab ineunte aetate suscepte prohiberunt. Nam cum antea per aetatem nondum huius auctoritatem loci attingere auderem statueremque nihil huc nisi perfectum ingenio, elaboratum industria adferri oportere, omne meum tempus amicorum temporibus transmittendum putavi.

Although it has at all times given me a special pleasure to behold your crowded assembly, and this place in particular has seemed to me to afford the amplest scope for action, the fairest stage for eloquence, nonetheless, fellow citizens, this approach to fame, which the best have ever found most widely open, has hitherto barred me, not certainly by any wish of mine, but by that scheme of life which, from my earliest years, I had laid down for myself. For previously, seeing that I was debarred by my youth from aspiring to this proud position and was resolved to bring here nothing but the mature outcome of my talent, the finished product of my industry, I considered that my every hour should be devoted to my friends in their hours of peril.

Before he gets into the issue of Pompey and his command, Cicero therefore lays out a number of subtexts for the audience to register. The use of three striking superlatives of *multo iucundissimus* (a very special pleasure), *amplissimus* (the most abundant) and *ornatissimus* (highly decorated) is a deliberate effort to butter up the vast crowd assembled around the rostra, praising them for their superior amphitheatre where the most serious of matters have always been placed before them. But with such compliments, bordering on fawning, comes the question, well, why have you taken so long to speak here? Cicero then lays out a second subtext, namely that he never considered himself worthy until he had put in the years of study, *industria*, that elevated his ability to the levels he felt were necessary to speak to the Roman crowd – suggesting as it does that all others who had spoken to them in the past were far less than the perfect orator that he now considered himself to be – and that they deserved. As if they were not flattered enough by the opening paragraph, the crowd was then also told that he, Cicero, had been prevented, *prohiberunt*, from coming to them earlier by this self-imposed target of brilliance but the subtext was there – that he was also not a member of the nobility, he was like them and had had

to build a case for himself to be accepted as one of the *optimates* and the Senate
– and here was the proof, he was now a *praetor*.

We do not know if the reaction around the layered stone seating was
widespread applause, stunned silence at the quality of his words, or rolling eyes
– perhaps this last image is best reserved for the senatorial members seated on
the rostra. Having lauded both himself and those listening, Cicero, like a bee
buzzing around his audience, laid out a further subtext that the skills of the
orator were, at least, the equal of those of the commander. He who commands
troops is not as powerful as he who commands words and the mental image
of complementary 'generals' begins to take shape – one in a metal breastplate
– the other in a toga. But he went much further:

*testorque omnis deos, et aos maxime qui huie loco temploque president, qui
omnium mentis eorum qui ad rem publicam adeunt maxime perspiciunt, me
hoc neque rogatu facere cuiusquam, neque quo C. Pompei gratium mihi per
hanc causam conciliari putem, neque quo mihi ex cuiusquam amplitudine aut
preasidia periculis aut adiumenta honoribus quaeram;*

*And I call all the gods to witness – most especially the guardians of this
hallowed spot who clearly see into the hearts of all who enter upon public life
– that I am acting thus neither in deference to any man's request nor with any
idea of winning for myself by my support of this cause the favour of Gnaeus
Pompeius, nor the hope of gaining for myself from any man's high position
either protection from dangers or aids to advancement.*

Elaborating how he risked friendships with others and that he was only
putting Rome first and above his own popularity and indeed safety has been
examined very closely in the outstanding work edited by Ingo Gildenhard &
Louise Hodgson et al where they play with the Cicero text and eliminate the
negatives so it might read:

*I am acting thus (neither) in deference to (any) a **man's request** (nor) **and
with** (any) the **idea of winning for myself by my support of this cause the
favour of Gnaeus Pompeius**, (nor) **in the hope of gaining for myself from** (any
man's) someone's **high position** (either) **protection from dangers** (or) and **aids
to advancement**.*

It is possible therefore to read how Cicero, in making such an effort to deny
that he was acting in any self-interest actually admits that this is in fact the

case. As Gildenhard and Hodgson interestingly pose the question: does he (Cicero) in fact protest too much?

In terms of protesting too much, Cicero delivered a speech of fulsome praise regarding the qualities of Pompey, indeed it was the eastern provinces who viewed Pompey as a god – he was not of course in the Roman sense, but Cicero used this veneration felt by the peoples of the east to further amplify the qualities that would make Pompey a success. Added to these were his experience, his success in defeating the pirates so quickly, his assumption of Triumphs (illegally) before the due age were indicators that he was not a normal being and that the state was lucky to have such a shining star to command their forces. Pompey's prestige throughout the Roman world was equivalent to many additional legions and there was something of the divine providence about him being alive and amongst them at this time – as if sent by the Gods if the mere mortals can but see that the good fortune they have been dealt and the good luck that Pompey has always enjoyed had a divine root. Pompey had

> more often clashed with his country's enemies than any other man has quarrelled with his own, fought more wars than others have read of, discharged more public offices than other men have coveted; in his youth, he had learned the lessons of warfare not from the instructions of others but under his own command, not be revered in war but by victories, not through campaigns but through Triumphs.

Cicero was also able to drag Sulla back into the lives of Roman citizens of all classes. It was barely fifteen years since the last of the proscriptions, mothers were still in mourning, families still healing, and memories of the bloodthirsty violence were still fresh. Sulla had left a number of things undone. His 'police' action in securing Rome from what he saw as imminent collapse from *populares* revolution had led to many things, but there were still loose ends, one of which was the holdouts still fighting his cause. In Spain, Sertorius remained in charge of a small Marian army and Cicero was quick to point out that Mithridates had extended a mission to Sertorius to join with him and fight Rome. That this did not happen, Cicero emphasised was a matter of luck for Rome, but left the notion of needing to finally end and crush enemies front and centre of his selection of Pompey to do this. Cicero needed to choose his words carefully, as in a court where every pause, nuance and word matters. There were many in Rome who owed their positions and fortunes to Sulla, and equally there were those for whom Sulla was the devil incarnate.

There is, however, yet another backcloth against which we should see Cicero and his support for this anti Republican measure. Rome was a city of immensely powerful commercial interests. Mithridates had not only disrupted trade, as he prevented further exploitation of a huge area of southern Asia, but he was also cutting off a valuable supply of taxes and resources which Rome sorely needed. Twenty years earlier Cicero had watched as the Republic battled with inflation as the Senate found itself dangerously short of money to fund wars and pay bills and wages to the legions. The result in the 80s, as current research is showing, had been to debase the coinage. In their work during 2021, Kevin Butcher and Matthew Ponting of the Universities of Warwick and Liverpool respectively studied the reduction of silver content in the denarius and found that the 95 per cent silver purity of coins in 91 had dropped as far as 86 per cent by 87, being replaced by bronze, and had it not been for the financial reforms of Gratidianus, Cicero's cousin (very soon to die a terrible death in the coming proscriptions of Sulla at the bloody hands of Catiline) then rampant inflation was on the near horizon. By the 60s, the Republic's appetite for income was far greater and was funded by successful wars, pillaging of resources and taxation of newly conquered peoples. Cicero had referred to the financial problems of the state in *De Officiis* and, as he stood on the rostra in support of Pompey, would have been acutely aware of the need to eliminate Mithridates in order to open up vast new areas for exploitation, not just for private commercial gain, but for the state to pay its accumulating debts. Cicero rammed the point home – he reminded the audience that it was partly due to the 1st Mithridatic War in the 80s that Rome suffered near economic collapse, but this war was much bigger and threatened even greater problems if they did not select a General certain to defeat the 'puffed up' (*inflatum*) Mithridates.

Finally, Cicero spread his words to encompass a number of other key figures listening to his words. He ignored Manilius, whose proposal this was, completely. This may have been because Manilius was already marked as a troublemaker as tribune, it could also have been that the proposal was not actually his idea. Whatever the reason, Cicero steered well clear of saying anything about the potentially dangerous Manilius. He was kind to Lucullus, still bruised from his recall, in so far as he recounted all his many victories both at sea and on land against Mithridates, but he had not finished the job and it was only due to the fact that Pompey and his huge presence as a general was nearby that the Roman armed forces had not already collapsed altogether. Cicero was able to deal with the opposition of Hortensius in his speech quite straightforwardly – you opposed his command against the pirates and look what happened. I think the people of Rome know better than you who should be in command. Cicero also took aim at Catiline, ever noisy, ever opinionated, ever angry and always looking for a door to kick open for his own advancement. Blended into his magnificently persuasive speech were barbs at Catiline and his behaviour in the past – he pointed out that Catiline had been very supportive of Pompey in the past so why not now – was it jealousy? Catiline was also looking down the gun barrel of complaints about his governorship in Africa and Cicero pointed out to the crowd that Rome was very unpopular abroad at the moment due to the behaviour of many of its provincial governors – a definite swipe at Catiline, and Cicero finished off mocking Catiline for his 'novel' past with a reputation for murder, adultery and bloodied hands – was he really the right voice to listen to?

The Wall Street of central Rome was the *Via Sacra* and Cicero would have been well aware as he strode down this famous roadway with its massive stone slabs and its bustling shops, warehouses, merchants and traders that there was an expectation of someone needing to do something to ease their real economic fears – he took it upon himself to be that man. The *Via Sacra* was also part of the route taken by those rare individuals accorded a military Triumph by the Senate and no doubt Cicero had his own notions of triumph as he ascended the steps to the top of the rostra. From the high semi-rounded platform, looking both north a short distance to the *comitium* and south over the forum packed with people, he gave his speech, recognizing that Rome was now a military – financial complex, and began to change history.

Cicero could not lose in the short term, his own political star continued to rise, the people of Rome felt they had a new and powerfully eloquent patron and interest groups in the Senate had to accept that Cicero was the real deal. But we can also see more evidence of the 'expediency' that Cicero referred to when he wrote to his son Marcus. That he was able to support giving so much power to one man in the interests of the state, Cicero shows us that he was not above intrigue or moving to cash in on events if they gave his own career political momentum – very close in other words to the 'monsters' he so hated, but who used the same tactics. He was also not above manipulation whether this be emotional, psychological or political. The fact that he later had his speech published is not only testament to his ego at the top of his career, but also quite confusing for those of us down the centuries wondering why a man so committed to democracy and the Republic could advocate the giving of almost total power to one man and thereby set the tone for the later advancement of even more unscrupulous and ambitions men – Catiline, Crassus, Caesar and Octavian.

Becoming Consul 65–63

With his praetorship complete, his aura glowing throughout Rome, and family settled, Cicero spent the next two years focussed on being elected consul. His brother Quintus, not cut from the same cloth, but nevertheless a keen supporter, wrote a short treatise or handbook for his brother called *Commentariolum Petitionis*, or what we might call a short guide to being prepared to do what it takes. To what extent Cicero took the advice in it or just paid it lip service we do not know, but it did lay out some of the practicalities of being elected – the need to lie for example and promise what you may not be able to give – all good stuff that we might assume many modern-day politicians carry a copy of in their pockets.

A letter to Atticus in the summer of 65 indicate the upbeat and excited temperament of Cicero as he planned his next moves:

Cicero to Atticus
Rome, July 65

The position as regards my candidature, in which I know you are deeply interested, is as follows, so far as can be seen up to date: Only Publius Galba is canvassing, and he is getting for answer a plain, unvarnished, good old Roman 'No'. It's generally felt that this premature canvass of his has rather helped my prospects, for people are commonly refusing him on the ground that they are obligated to me. So I hope to draw some advantage when the word goes round that a great many friends of mine are coming to light.

It is a commonplace practice that people wanting to win an election prepare the ground with bribes – this is as true today as it ever was. This may not mean a financial payment because our warped sense of morality would see this as illegal, but surely it is equally illegal to offer medals and honours or jobs and promotions that deprive others of the same benefits? Offer a man the Freedom of the City of London in return for support in one's pursuit of becoming Lord Mayor and that is not considered a crime, but put £10 in his pocket and it is. Abuse of office and power is as old as democracy itself and let us not be so naïve as to assume that Cicero was different from any other, but with the exception that he did not have the money of a Crassus or Pompey.

The letter of July 65 was a very long one and Atticus was appraised of all manner of gossip and concerns, including Cicero's concern for Pompey. Although hopefully preoccupied with tracking down and destroying the armies of Mithridates, Pompey's arms were long and his pockets deep enough to pay well for spies and information. Cicero was concerned that he might even put forward his own candidate and, by way of trying to seal off this potential threat, he added in his letter:

For my part I shall spare no pains in faithfully fulfilling the whole duty of a candidate. I shall run down to join Piso's staff in September, in the dead period after the courts have closed, returning in January. When I have made out the attitude of the nobles I will write to you. I hope the rest is plain sailing, at any rate as far as these local competitors are concerned. You must answer for the other phalanx, since you are not so far away, I mean our friend Pompey's. Tell him I shall not be offended if he does not turn up for my election!

As Gaius Piso had been consul in 67, he was clearly an important ally and Cicero needed to ensure that he was and could travel to assist him in a nominal role, perhaps as *legatus* in a legion as Piso was now Governor of Gaul on both sides of the Alps. As for the reference to Atticus sorting out Pompey, this was a big ask from Cicero. Atticus had substantial political connections and could be and was a good behind the scenes operator for Cicero, he was also living in the right area now to get access to Pompey in modern day Turkey, on Corcyra (Corfu), but the distances were still great and whether Atticus really did feel he could influence Pompey we do not know. It was a tongue in cheek, but serious request.

A second letter followed shortly after, the one we have read informing Atticus of the arrival of baby Tullia, but it continued:

I need you home pretty soon. There is a decidedly strong belief abroad that your noble friends are going to oppose my election. Clearly you will be invaluable to me in gaining them over. So mind you are in Rome by the beginning of January as you arranged.

At this distance we have no reference point as to what Cicero had felt in the air or why he sensed that the nobility were against him, but clearly it rattled his composure enough for him to write, in pointed style, to his friend almost demanding he be there when he said he would (a reference to Cicero's oft-stated low opinion of Atticus' punctuality).

According to Anthony Everitt, 'Of Cicero's six rivals, four were hopeless electoral prospects, respectable but dull – and in one case probably dull witted.' Clearly Everitt did not have the advantage of seeing, as we did in the USA in 2016, that being a hopeless electoral prospect means nothing when it comes to the electorate. In 2016 I had the fortune of being in Boston at the very time that voting opened in the US presidential election of that year of Trump v Clinton. Surely Trump was a hopeless prospect – and to a large extent he was, with the key exception that he therefore shared a sense of the hopelessness of millions of Americans who themselves had no hope. He was the hope of the hopeless and this is another lesson the modern world should remember – if history has a value at all then here is a prime example. As I was driven around various sites of significance, I was struck by the sea of Trump posters on lawns – far from being a joke, as they had been in earlier months, they were now the dominant one in every garden. Sharing the over-fertilised east coast grass with the bronzed and golden leaves of the late fall in Massachusetts, was the face of Donald Trump. The man who said the system was corrupt was believed, the idea took root and grew – and is still growing. The man who had no hope of being elected because he was 'dull witted' was starting to keep Bostonian democrats awake at night and he went further – while Clinton celebrated with celebrities, Trump favoured the forgotten and spent time in blue collar, rust dominated states that supposedly did not matter. So how did Cicero approach his campaign for election?

In the first place he carried on with his legal work alongside patronizing the key friendships he would need. His was to be a delicate balancing act trying, on the one hand to continue to reassure the powerful *optimates* in the Senate that he was as much a conservative as they hoped for and had no intention of becoming so close to Pompey that his independence would be compromised. On the other hand he needed the support of the *popularis* – he was not rich enough to bribe them, nor was he either a celebrity or a great charismatic figure – his strengths were his intellect and his words. All in all, a tough challenge even given the apparently hopeless opposition.

In the second place he wisely took note of the changing atmosphere in Rome. Like the change of a Queen to a King, much stayed the same, but everything was different. Emerging onto the political stage from the wings was Caius Antonius – a corrupt and disgraced member of the nobility who had been expelled from the Senate, but was now largely forgiven and with powerful friends. Alongside him came new and more aggressive and ambitious players such as the young and calculating Julius Caesar and the unscrupulous Lucius Sergius Catiline. It was quite possible that Caesar was working with, if not controlling, the older but more impetuous Catiline.

If Cicero was to become consul in 63, then he would need to find a strategy to deal with the different styles of politics now present in Rome, and he chose a course of elevating his position and the discourse above the obvious factions and ambitions. In his youth Cicero read and studied Plato a great deal and naturally was influenced by Plato's *Republic*, perhaps one of the defining texts of the ancient world and where the concepts of the just state led by just men took root in Cicero's guiding principles. As he approached the defining promotion of his career, there is no doubt that he aimed to be the synthesis of the just consul, acting in a just way to help preserve the perfect –

or almost perfect – democratic state. Another of the central themes in Plato's *Republic* was the notion of the philosopher-king. This, according to Plato, was the perfect leader, moulded not through war, but by intellect and knowledge and again it is certain that Cicero saw himself as the embodiment of this refreshing style of leadership for Rome – perhaps the first of a new generation of philosopher-consuls. Cicero was acutely aware that he was still a new man and the last election of a *novus homo* to the consulship was in 95.

In reality, Cicero had already prepared the Roman crowds in the forum and the majestic senatorial body for the concept of the philosopher-consul as the positive democratic mirror image of the negative philosopher-king. If we refer back to his speech in support of Pompey's command in the east, the *De Imperio* in support of the *Lex Manilia*, we can see how much time Cicero had put into describing the attributes of the perfect general – the *felicitas, auctoritas, virtus* and *militaris*. According to Cicero, not only did Pompey have all of these talents in abundance, he had invented a new class of super-being, one who transcended normal generalship, but with a key difference: on his return he could be trusted not to become a new Sulla. The super-being was able to subdue his abilities in the service of the state. In this way Cicero was continuing the theme and painting his own super-being qualities as a civil match for Pompey, and Rome could trust in his abilities to control his own superpowers. Today as we breathe in the history of the partially destroyed stone columns, walk the stone slabs of 2,000 years of history and do our best to imagine the noise and tumult of this place in Republican days, we can almost see how Cicero would have walked through the throng of the forum on most days cultivating this image of the man the people could trust.

Responding to his friend's demands, Atticus returned to Rome where he stayed for the next three years. With his sister married to Quintus, the family ties were there for him to feel the need to be closer, for a while at least, but he would certainly have been watching his positioning carefully so as not to be seen to be too close to any one candidate. We can imagine the scenes when Atticus joined the Cicero family, re-joined his sister plus met the new baby in Rome or at one of Cicero's fabulous estates that he had helped to decorate. It must have been a happy and memorable reunion with many late nights of intense discussion and strategy. Unlike Cicero, Atticus had strong and reliable connections with numerous noble families and he would not have been short of many invitations to visit across Rome. His presence not only helped to allay any lingering fears about the reliability of Cicero – his support for Pompey's commands against the pirates and his eastern command had left a bad taste with many senators – but Atticus was also able to lean on his close friendships with Hortensius and Manlius Torquatus who had been consul in 65 – and at least buy their silence in the election.

His white gown – *In Toga Candida*

There was one deviation away from the 'philosopher-king' strategy and that was the way in which Cicero dealt with Catiline and Antonius. Perhaps it was a side of his character that was always there lurking, but was controlled by his stronger emotions, or maybe it was a result of reflecting on his brother's advice on how to approach the pragmatic issues surrounding the election – the *Commentariolum Petitionis* (Handbook on Electioneering). Quintus had written:

> *Make sure you have the backing of your family and friends*
> *Surround yourself with the right people*
> *Call in all favours*
> *Build a wide base of support*
> *Promise everything to everybody*

And most cutting of all

> *As regards the Roman masses, be sure to put on a good show. Dignified, yes, but full of the colour and spectacle that appeals so much to the crowds. It also would not hurt to remind them of what scoundrels your opponents are and to smear these men at every opportunity with the crimes, sexual scandals, and corruption they have brought on themselves.*

One could be forgiven for thinking that Donald Trump was a scholar of classical texts when, in his electoral campaign of 2015 he followed the advice from Quintus almost to the letter in his attacks on Barack Obama and Hilary Clinton. Never before in the history of the United States had such a clearly populist candidate for the presidency set out on a campaign of such lies and contempt for the truth. Two thousand years ago, Cicero did not go that far, but he did decide to attack his two key opponents and ridicule their credentials for the highest office – and, being Cicero, he did it well.

During all the speeches, meetings, house calls and walks through the forum in the election campaign of 64, it was clear that Catiline in particular was overtly and obviously using bribery to grow his support. Electoral bribery was illegal, but accepted as long as it was not thrown in the faces of society. Towards the end of the campaign and only a few days before the elections, a motion was put forward in the Senate to impose stricter penalties and punishments for proven electoral corruption, but all this did was heighten the temperature of debate and friction amongst the candidates. The motion was vetoed, as was his right, by the tribune of the people for that year Quintus Mucius Orestinus. This was not perhaps a surprise given the amount of money the people stood to lose, but Orestinus faced an avalanche of criticism about his abuse of the power of his veto and it was as a part of that debate in the Senate that Cicero made his stand. We do not have the entire speech, but only fragments related after the event by a later historian Quintus Asconius Pedianus (3–88 CE), but we have enough of a guide to see the depth of Cicero's invective: wearing his chalk white toga he reminded everyone in graphic detail of the past charges against Catiline for extortion while a Governor in Africa, recounted how he had been involved in vicious murders, plundered allies, lied, violated laws, committed adultery 'Oh wretched man'… 'by what insanity he has been induced to despise me, I have no idea'…. Cicero went on to ask Catiline on what basis he felt he could even think of standing for the consulship, the senators had stripped him of honours and decency and nearly handed him back to the Africans in chains, the equestrian order of knights had been put to death in great numbers for their opposition to Sulla to whom he had been devoted and people had long memories and still groaned when they recalled the slaughter that he, Catiline, had led. Without doubt, by the end of the speech Catiline knew his chances of winning the election had been ruined by Cicero. Both Catiline and Antonius stood and defended themselves shouting back in a tense Senate that Cicero had no right to be there, that he was a squatter from the lower orders sitting amongst the greatness of Rome, that he had no breeding, no noble blood – in other words all the characteristics that Catiline so despised in others. We can imagine a scene where, after all was ended on that day, Catiline and his supporters stormed out of the senate house enraged by what Cicero had done to their pride, as much as their electoral chances.

In the end, by constant networking to overcome the lack of a noble heritage, negotiating and entertaining hard along with Atticus, ensuring the support of the entrepreneurial classes and being the only sensible option to defeat the menacing presence of Catiline, Cicero won the election by a handsome margin with the 'sad rogue' Gaius Antonius coming second to be appointed as his co consul. At this moment in late 64 Cicero had a great deal of support both inside and outside the city. As Quintus had reiterated, Cicero was backed by

all the publicani, nearly the whole of the equestrian order, many municipal towns specially devoted to you, many persons who have been defended by you, men of every order, many collegia, and, besides these, a large number of the rising generation who have become attached to you in their enthusiasm for rhetoric, and, finally, your friends who visit you daily in large numbers and with such constant regularity.

However, still with their seats in the Senate were the bitterly disappointed and humiliated Catiline – hero of up-and-coming noble troublemakers – the complicated and intractable Cato; a raft of venerated conservative nobles looking to be reassured of Cicero's loyalty, and the Crassus/Caesar partnership, forever plotting.

Chapter 12

Consul at Last

The crowd is the gathering place of the weakest; true creation is a solitary act.
Charles Bukowski

The state of the Senate in 63

It was not of Cicero's making or choice that his consular year was so full of incident and turmoil – perhaps a pivotal year in the fading life of the Republic. In any other year, history could have looked back on Cicero's time as consul with admiration and a passing interest in how he performed. But destiny was not on Cicero's side. The election campaign had been dirty and vicious, wounds were open and tumult had been brewing for a number of years. This was the legacy that Cicero inherited after the celebrations of his success, no doubt orchestrated by the now very influential Terentia.

Naturally and unfortunately, we have no correspondence with Atticus to rely on as both men were in Rome. This means that historians have only the records left by Cicero himself, especially his targeted and occasionally biased speeches, and Sallust, who would have observed many of the events first hand and wrote about them later. What we can establish is that Cicero was arriving at the position he always craved at the exact time when many of the issues facing Rome were becoming acute. It was always going to be a tough consular year of office and if the augurs had been asked for an opinion, the birds would no doubt have been dropping from the skies across Rome.

Rarely mentioned in all the hundreds of historical texts, books and research papers is that Cicero himself added to the issues facing the Republic – because of who he was and his style of leadership. His upbringing, past experience and emotional perception of what Rome had been and should be were completely out of step with the new era. Not only this, Cicero, in his desire to be seen as the philosopher-king of Plato's imagination, was regarded by some as not only arrogant, but harbouring a desire to become a dictator himself.

In attempting to be a steward of all that was good, Cicero was manifestly psychologically wedded to Plato's transcendent figure, preferring to rise above the political chatter and float on a higher philosophic plane than everyone else. While there may have been a hope and desperation that this might work amongst the elder statesmen of the Senate, Cicero was missing the point – what worked for Athenians hundreds of years previously was not going to work now. To return to our earlier discussions of Cicero's love for acting and the stage, he was misjudging his audience if he thought that they would appreciate his version of the philosopher-king. So much of success and failure in life is timing and the arrival of the philosopher-king was an actually an encouragement to those with destruction on their minds. Cicero may have recalled another of Plato's teachings and that was that men should stick to their class – the imagery of the 'myth of the metals' and how allowing the citizen from the lower classes made of bronze to mix with those of silver and gold in the upper classes creates an alloy – a weakness that those in power wished to avoid at all costs. If he did, he did not show it. Cicero was still seen as the *novus homo* and Catiline wasted no time in pointing out that Cicero was debasing the strength of the Senate by virtue of his birth.

To make matters worse, tactically Cicero was not above humiliating his opponents as was seen with Catiline, his ability to use words as his weapon with which to embarrass and demean his opponents would have created not only a hatred of his abilities, but also a jealous reaction in a society where true honour was won through military glory, strength and force and not just by words. Cicero had no great military victories behind him, indeed he had only the lightest touch of being in a uniform serving the state in war. Far better to have beaten Catiline with rods from the *fasces* than humiliate what was left of his honour with sarcasm as he had done in the previous year with *In Toga Candida*. Within the Senate therefore were those who from day one of Cicero's consulship had but one objective – to cause Cicero difficulty and to pierce the shield of his eloquence and bring him down. Men like Catiline had already displayed their hatred for the Senate of corrupt nepotism and, as he saw them, weak old men of the Senate. In Catiline's eyes and the minds of those supporting him, Cicero was protecting this weakness and was typical of the problem of puffed-up arrogance, vindictiveness borne of old age and financial power which Catiline no longer had in his own right – he had to take it in the shadows on the night.

Add to this mix the Machiavellian ambitions of men such as Crassus and Caesar to pit Catiline and Cicero against each other while they awaited their moment on the side-lines, each with their own retinue of loyal followers, and there was an awful chemistry in the Senate at the start of 63.

Finally, as if the gods of Rome were playing a mischievous game with their human chess board, what a time for a man like Cato the Younger to arrive on the political stage in what was his first year in the Senate – and what a year it was to be. Brittle to the point of fanaticism, eloquent in his own way, admired and uncompromising, Cato would have been a challenge even in the calmest of waters, let alone this seething white water that the Republican raft was trying to navigate.

The problems begin

Cicero donned his bright white consular toga at the beginning of 63, took his seat in the consular chairs alongside Antonius, and trouble began almost immediately with land reform. The economic position of the mainland was not good. That Pompey would win and once more open up huge trading routes with Asia was not in doubt – what was in doubt is when this would happen. In the meantime, unemployment had been rising, city life for the poor was precarious and mob violence and criminality on the streets were increasing as a result. The countryside was faring no better and many farmers were struggling to make a living as were the new farmers given land by Sulla – his retired legionaries still with their rusting armour (*lorica segmenta*) and trusted short swords *(gladii)* on the walls. The rich too, with the exception of men like Crassus, were noticing the higher costs of building villas in Baiae, purchasing art works (far better just to steal them), entertaining and the cost of bribes had gone through the roof. In the face of these problems, the leaders of the *populares* turned to Crassus and Caesar to lead their case for redistribution of lands.

The reallocation of land either already owned by the state or to be purchased and then given was a perennial issue and no worse combination of state personalities with *populares* support could have joined together to present Cicero with his first headache – neither Crassus nor Caesar were supporters of Cicero and both were nobles with malevolent long term intent. The idea was laudable, as land reform and distribution was needed, but it was the manner in which they suggested it that concerned Cicero and he decided to oppose the proposed laws and successfully did so in the Senate and assemblies. Cicero argued that reform was needed, but not in the way it was being proposed, which was open to corruption and although he was not an arch conservative, this decision merely confirmed that he was wedded to the *optimates* in the eyes of any reformers. As for Crassus and Caesar, the result was not all bad – they didn't need the land anyway, they had now manufactured an image of Cicero as not being the hero of the people that he had professed to be and they could claim the moral high ground as caring about reform.

Having begun by opposing Caesar and Crassus and with the knowledge that he was Pompey's man still in the air, the die was cast for a bumpy term of office, but first Cicero did make one politically admirable decision. In order to ensure that he was left alone to stand in the light and did not have to navigate conversations with Antonius, Cicero offered him his pro-consular province of Macedonia in return for his support and non-intervention. Giving up such a rich prize would normally be surprising but not in Cicero's case, for him the prize of being seen as '*princeps civitas*', or 'leader of the community' was even more cherished than all the wealth that northern Greece could offer. He still strode the city and the Senate as a great man no doubt surrounded by loyal followers, groupies and hypnotized youths, but much more was to come.

Caesar as Chief Pontiff and the 'trial' of Rabirius

'*Fate has terrible power. You cannot escape it by wealth or war. No fort will keep it out; no ships outrun it.*' One can only wonder whether Cicero, with his scholarly knowledge of Greek philosophy and literature, ever mused on this saying from Sophocles as he wondered why his life and purpose was to defend Rome from Julius Caesar? By 63 it would have been abundantly clear to Cicero that Caesar was the main threat to everything. Why his time as consul should have arrived at the same time as Caesar strove for power may have played on his mind – it was his fate and Sophocles was right – there was no stopping it.

In his strategy, Caesar clearly saw Cicero as a fundamental target for his plans. To ridicule Cicero would be to embarrass the Senate and to embarrass the Senate would be to show the Roman people that the time for change had come. Cicero was at this juncture something of a bastion against change and radicalism – if Caesar could not actually humiliate the talented Cicero, then the next best thing would be to exploit his arrogance and draw him into the open with a series of pulls on the donkey's tail that would show his true position and poke the ribs of the senators who supported him. The support for land reform had been one attempt, but at least two more torments awaited.

So it was that without any warning a tribune, Titus Labienus launched an unexpected accusation of treason against an elderly, unsuspecting and politically impotent senator, Caius Rabirius. The sentence for a guilty verdict was execution and overnight poor Rabirius and his entire family saw the world change before their eyes. They were no doubt even more shocked given that the accusation involved an event thirty-six years previously. In short, in 100 the young Rabirius, a committed and perhaps hot-tempered supporter of Marius, found himself on the very high roof of the senate house throwing huge red rounded tiles (*imbrices*) and the flat roofing tiles (*tegulae*) down onto the heads of the tribune Saturnius and his followers who had barricaded themselves into the square-shaped Curia Hostilia after a pitched battle in the forum. The Senate had passed their rarely used, but ultimate sanction the *senatus consultum ultimum* – this instructed the consuls to ignore the law and do whatever is necessary to protect the state – it is the act of last resort and it was Marius' supporters, including Rabirius, that took matters into their own hands and killed the three-time tribune Lucius Appuleius Saturnius and all his followers – effectively stoning them to death and cutting the throats of those still alive.

We might wonder why Labienus had taken quite so long to bring this to court – perhaps he had a burning desire for justice that he just could not contain any longer, or maybe he was angry at the cost of repairing the senate roof. The confusion, however, clears when we discover that he was a close confidante of Caesar and later was to become one of his most trusted generals. So, what was the point of this clear plot? According to Everitt there were a number of possible explanations – was it just to keep the Senate on its back foot, part of an ongoing campaign of challenges from the *populares*; it could also have been a matter that had been kept up Caesar's sleeve just waiting for the right moment to challenge the Senate and the *optimates*, should they look like regaining stability under Cicero; or perhaps it was to protect Catiline should he again lose the election for consul and overstep the mark? All have an element of truth in them, but there is yet another more sinister explanation. Was it that Caesar knew full well that Catiline was plotting a coup and he wanted to test the resolve of the consul and Senate to ensure that they would follow through with an execution if pushed into using the *senatus consultum ultimatum*. It would follow that Cicero would be exposed to great criticism if he did act. For Caesar then, poor Rabirius was simply an expendable test case.

To ensure the result, Caesar and a cousin of his were selected as the judges – already further evidence of his control over the entire episode – and an execution post was erected in the Field of Mars in advance of what was expected to be an open and shut case. In the public trial no doubt in front of the rostra, Hortensius spoke to the mass assembled crowd and under the eyes of Caesar in the judge's chair, for the likely shell-shocked Rabirius, pointing out that not one tile could have been tied to Rabirius and a slave had already been identified many years before as the actual culprit. Nevertheless, Cicero was also drawn out of cover. Knowing this was just a show trial, he wasted no time gathering evidence or preparing a lengthy defence oration, he just cut to the chase and pronounced to the people of Rome;

We must be on our guard against our own passions [his own anger that this was happening], *against men of violence* [Pulcher], *against the enemy within* [Caesar and Crassus], *against domestic plots* [Catiline]. *But against these evils your forefathers left you a great protection* [the consultum ultimatum]. *Cherish this pronouncement.*

But with these judges the verdict was certain and it was only after he had failed to appeal to their better natures, if they had any, that a praetor named Quintus Caecilius Metellus Celer reverted to one of Rome's numerous historically dormant, but still effective, constitutional choke points and ran to the top of the Janiculan Hill and took down the flag raised in the fort there which indicated an assembly was being held. In this act Celer was able to halt proceedings, as historically it suggested Rome was under attack, which it was politically, and the trial had to be halted and the assembly dispersed. Would Caesar have been determined to execute Rabirius, had Celer been briefed to do this all along, was the whole charade just to prove a point we shall never know, but Cicero had now openly declared that he knew who the enemies of Rome were, and there were a number of them in various causes, and he was wedded to the notion of using the final act if he had to.

Taking a breath, but not for long, Caesar had also plotted a campaign to become Chief Pontiff. We might recall that this role came with a home in the forum next to the Temple of Vesta and enormous prestige, being the senior religious figure of the state and the man in whom the power to make all decisions on feast and business days rested. Usually such a role was reserved for former consuls, which Caesar was not, or elder statesmen in which category he clearly had some years to complete. Nevertheless, Caesar triumphed. Using enormous sums which he had borrowed, probably mostly from Crassus, to pay the *populares*, the common people of Rome, Caesar really did prove that bribery was alive and well in the city and that any laws recently passed to curtail it were not effective. Cicero could do little but watch this unfold before him. The net result was that Caesar was now in a prestigious position rivalling that of consul and he had reminded the Senate that real power, when mobilized, lay in the hands of the people, not in their blood lines.

Naturally, Catiline watched as Caesar achieved what he had so far failed to do. Almost the same age as Cicero, although his family had lost their old money fortune, he was still of noble birth and, since his humiliation the previous year, had become nominal leader of a new movement of young men who were breaking free of the traditional family stranglehold on behaviour and obligation. Young men with money, some with far more than others, but all with connections made it easy for Catiline to enlarge his following – and equally difficult to hide it. Catiline had been discouraged from aiming at the consulship in the past because of his reputation and criminal trials and he had lost to Cicero and Antonius at the second attempt the previous year. Undaunted, he was determined to use his new found popularity with the disaffected to try for a third time. No doubt his impulsive nature was encouraged by Caesar and it was not long before Cicero became aware that Catiline was, yet again, preparing for the elections that summer for the consulship in 62.

At home, in the long summer evenings, having arrived back after walking through the forum with his usual groupies in tow, Cicero must have been very grateful for the calming and wise counsel of Atticus, quietly but attentively watching events from the shadows, and the support of his brother.

Fulvia

It is to the historian Gaius Sullustius Crispus (Sallust) and Cicero that we must turn for the events as they now unfolded, as there are no other contemporary sources that we are aware of. Deploring and mourning the decline of the Republic, Sallust set out to amplify what had gone wrong and why there was so much civil strife in Rome surrounding Cicero – culminating in all out rebellion, with Cicero as the target of disaffection.

Before the seismic events of 63, Sallust wrote of an earlier conspiracy led by Catiline in 65. Historians continue to debate the veracity and likelihood of this and it keeps the 'what was Catiline all about really' pot boiling. It is a confusing question to understand Catiline and to see a man doing all he could to become consul through the electoral channels, while at the same time plotting to bring the entire edifice down.

Whatever the truth of this so called First Catilinarian Conspiracy, events moved forward and it was becoming increasingly obvious to Cicero that something was wrong. Crucially he was aided in his strategic assessments by information flowing from Terentia. Although the role of women in the Republic remains relatively undiscovered territory, recent research shows that the wives of the most prominent men in Rome played their own equally vital roles in political and social events. One of the earliest and still most attractive lives to be fully explored and understood is that of Fulvia. Together, Terentia, herself a mystery to be uncovered, and Fulvia were part of the highest social circles in Rome by virtue of their husbands, but also their own connections. While Terentia was all that Roman society expected – matronly, loyal, respectful of the Gods, and her place serving men – she was also a woman who could hold her own, advise her husband, and most importantly gather intelligence from all the other wives with whom she associated. Gossip in Rome was the TikTok of the time and their husbands' loose tongues the Instagram. Terentia was now in a vital role as she helped her husband navigate his position as the highest authority in Rome and Fulvia had already learnt the skills so important to a Roman woman – how to overhear gossip.

There was also a wedding to celebrate in 63, that of Cicero's dear and only daughter Tullia to Gaius Calpurnius Piso Frugi. Tullia was a mere 16, but of typical age and her new husband not much older. No doubt the great consul ensured that the celebrations were something special and, like any proud mother, Terentia and perhaps Fulvia together with many of their female circle played their part.

Literature has been generally critical of Fulvia. Often portrayed as a calculating, ruthless and power hungry woman of flexible sexual morals, many of the myths and facts surrounding her life come from her marriages to three great men of Roman Republican history – Publius Clodius Pulcher (one of the period's most colourful and fascinating political personalities), Caius Scribonius Curio (later to be one of Caesar's lieutenants) and lastly Marcus Antonius know to history as Mark Antony (supporter of Caesar and later ruler of Egypt with Cleopatra). Although numerous references to Fulvia appear throughout many books and papers on the history of the last Republican period, no one has been able to form quite such an image as we now have thanks to the work of Allison Weir who says of Fulvia:

> *The recurring references to Fulvia as domineering, cruel and jealous in the ancient sources should thus be understood in the context of her portrayal in the propaganda of her enemies.... Whatever her role was in the events...[it] is clear is that she was a remarkable woman who played no small part in the history of her time.*[1]

Plutarch is helpful in that, in his *Life of Antony*, he tells us quite a lot about Fulvia. A member of the Fulvi, one of the most distinguished and wealthiest families in Rome, she owned an impressive home in Rome and, along with numerous other influential families including that of Cicero, she also had an impressive home on the hills of Tusculum – no doubt Cicero was well aware of where she lived and possibly, they knew each other well. Various of Fulvia's ancestors had been consuls and senators and her mother was Sempronia and as such, Fulvia may have been the last in her family line and an heiress of great worth and value in her own right. In 63 Fulvia would have been in her very early 20s and, although we know little of her at that time, it is likely, given her achievements in later life, that she was a vivacious, much sought after and intelligent young woman, well connected to almost every noble family, independently minded and surveying the city life of Rome for excitement, opportunity and fun.

Given that she married her first husband (as far as we know) in 62, it is likely that Fulvia was already closely involved with the political life and social network of Publius Clodius Pulcher – himself a member of the very influential Claudian *gens*, one of Rome's most noble patrician families. Nobility, however, was no guarantee of financial strength, and Clodius has a reputation in history for his scandalous lifestyle, feuding with Cicero, who routinely exposed him as 'rapacious and spendthrift'. The Roman historian Marcus Terentius Varro also recorded how Clodius' brother Appius once spoke about the poverty the family had experienced after their father's premature death ten years earlier while proconsul in 72. It is worthy of note at this point that Clodius was related to Licinius Lucullus, consul in 74 and recently recalled general replaced by Pompey, who was married his sister Clodia. However, Lucullus blamed the troublesome Clodius for the revolt of his troops in his eastern command so their relationship was less than cordial – especially as, when the marriage had hardly begun, Lucullus found Clodia guilty of adultery and divorced her. It must have seemed to the wealthy and noble Lucullus that the whole Claudian family were rotten to the core and he instead went to the other extreme, asking the pious and virtuous Cato for the hand in marriage of his sister Servilia in order to try to protect what was left of his *dignitas* and *auctoritas* – such were the risks of marriage for dynastic survival as opposed to love.

For the opportunistic Clodius, Fulvia looked like a godsend with her intelligence, inheritance and connections, while for Fulvia, Clodius looked an interesting prospect for a husband with his noble connections, family history and raffish lifestyle. A marriage of convenience for both indeed. In 1965 in another study of Fulvia, Charles Babcock wrote:

> *Not only through the institution of political or dynastic marriage, so vital to the balance of affairs in the last century of the Republic, but also in the exercise of personal talents and influence were women able to attain power in a state wherein their official potential was limited strictly to certain religious positions. Few women even in this period of marital manoeuvring could claim so remarkable a progression of husbands as Fulvia.*

Whether she was already a close confident of Terentia is unknown, but it was likely that they met and socialized in the Roman equivalent of 'Loose Women' and daily exchanged city gossip – who was seeing who, the latest fashions coming in from the empire, planning the next dinner party and guest list, who was dying and who needed to die, problems with servants and slaves and of course, what their husbands or boyfriends were like to live with. To us a normal life and, as we sit in our kitchens and coffee shops, so they did too on dusty warm evenings or hot sweltering sunny days of Roman summers. We must try to remember that, within the written black and white typeface of books on their lives, they were real people, laughing and crying at the fortunes and misfortunes of life and, but for the accidents of time and space, we could have known them. In one of their many meetings it was to Terentia that Fulvia relayed the first serious warnings regarding Catiline.

According to what we know, Clodius had a loose tongue, which became especially loosened with wine. It was as a result of one of his throwaway remarks that Fulvia learned of an apparent plot and began what was to become her hobby – political intrigue.

Note

1. Weir, Allison, *A Study of Fulvia*, (2007) Queens University.

Chapter 13

Cicero's Finest Hour?

If you tell the truth, it becomes part of your past. If you lie, it becomes part of your future.

Anonymous

Historians throughout the ages have been sensitive to the fact that we only have Cicero and Sallust to view the events that unfolded from the summer of 63 through to January 62. While Sallust was present, he was not a participant, but an observer and his account in his *Catiline's Conspiracy* is that of a man attempting to produce a historical record without all the facts. Cicero on the other hand produced his speeches, which had many of the facts, but were not meant to be a historical record. Thus, like thousands of students before us, we too have to don our glasses of circumspection as we try to piece together the evidence – as far as we can and from what we have. Particularly relevant for Cicero is that we must always keep at the forefront of our mind that he was first and foremost a lawyer. Whatever this may mean to some people, he was not a deliberate liar, but he was prepared to bend the truth. His abilities were beyond comparison and he was, as May described him 'the most attractive character whom antiquity produced. However the bottom line is that his objective was always to win the argument whether that be as a letter writer dictating to his *scribae*, an author writing a book to his son, a lawyer persuading a jury, a politician speaking to the people of Rome or a philosopher recording his thoughts – one thing he was not, therefore, is a historian seeking to portray the truth – whatever that may mean to us.

By the summer of 63, Cicero was having to prepare to oversee the next consular election for the coming year. The known candidates were again L. Sergius Catiline, Ser. Sulpicius Rufus, D. Junius Silanus and L. Licinius Murena – Murena had fought as an officer under the command of Lucullus against Mithridates. At some point Fulvia, at that stage a mistress of Quintus Curius, passed on information to Terentia that a secret meeting had been held at which it had been decided to assassinate Cicero and other leaders of the Senate – probably in July, the day before the elections for consul would be held. This was the next stage of Catiline's anger, frustration and desire for revenge against Cicero, but it was also part of an escalating strategy to topple the Republic.

Despite there being no evidence other than a changing atmosphere in the city, Cicero convened the Senate. The Senate seating plan was not semi-circular as in Cesare Maccari's 1888 painting, the most famous image we have of Catiline, but archaeology tells us that it was originally oblong. Cicero adored this place with the history of events woven into the stone floors and wooden banks of seats on each side. This was his place, his theatre, he knew how to carry his voice around the walls, and he knew its particular smell – a mixture of damp must, spent candles and stale air. Cicero confronted Catiline with the rumour – Catiline in a display of cockish bravado responded that the idea was false, but so what if the people saw him as a better head on the body of Rome – was that so bad? By invoking the notion that he was a popular choice of the people, Catiline warned the Senate that he could at any time exploit this popularity to bring the whole edifice down. Catiline was smuggling an image into their minds of chaos and bloodshed should he, the self-anointed leader of the reformist senators, not be given his rightful role and his and their dissatisfaction with their governance not be recognized. But no action was taken other than the postponement of the consular election, and Cicero's decision to begin wearing a breastplate under his toga – enough that all could see as he continued to walk through the forum accompanied by a bodyguard. Why Cicero treated Catiline so carefully is a matter for conjecture. His tactic may have been the result of a lack of evidence – he was Rome's greatest legal advocate after all – but it may also have been an appeal to Catiline to ponder, to recognize that he was exposed and to pull back from his thoughts. Cicero was a kind man; his writings betray an emotional bottomless pit and possibly he saw a little of himself in the frustrations that Catiline displayed. It may also have been the concern of what might explode if he did arrest Catiline.

At the same time as Cicero was trying the stabilize Rome, a number of other developments took place around him. The summer months also required that other constitutional orders took place, and one of them saw Cato the Younger continue his rise to the top of the leadership of the *optimates* in the Senate. Not really political parties as we would understand them, but rather groups of individuals with matching interests, the *optimates* saw the idiosyncratic Cato as someone capable and brave enough to speak out on their position against the gathering forces of change. Cato was in many ways the anti-hero – he did not have open invitations to his home, he was not flamboyant nor interested in cultivating his client base, he had only one famous ancestor, but most of all he was an arch traditionalist – his morality and virtue were above reproach almost to the point of unbending stubbornness. He could be frustrating and

The Temple of Saturn at the foot of the Capitoline Hill at the western end of the Forum. The Republican treasury was stored here, the Aerarium as well as the accounts of the public finances were also stored here.

inflexible, if not a figure of fun in his plain attire, he also put the letter of the law above pragmatic solutions, which could alienate both friends as well as enemies. During those summer months Cato took his seat in the Senate as tribune elect for 62 and gave his first speech.

Pompey had been making great strides in vanquishing Mithridates and at some point, he would return. For all we know, Pompey in some ways may never have left, as his agents were everywhere, as was his money and a regular flow of communications to Pompey from Rome would leave every week. A proposal that, on his return, Pompey should be allowed to wear a laurel wreath, the ultimate symbol of success, at all public events was put forward by two tribunes – and with the vocal support of Caesar again playing his part as rabble rouser extraordinaire. Cato is the only senator recorded as standing against this, although one might be certain that Lucullus would have also been on Cato's side; he failed, but established his opposition to Pompey and the aggrandisement that he represented.

October 63

Naturally the consular elections could not be delayed for long and when they came it spelt yet another humiliation for Catiline as he was unsuccessful for the third time and Murena and Silanus were voted as the two consuls for 62. No doubt Catiline fumed, plotted and discussed the next step and around mid-October, perhaps the 20th, Cicero received a late-night delegation, headed by Crassus and two other leading senators. Earlier that evening, Crassus explained, he had read an unsigned letter stating that Catiline was about to unleash a city-wide massacre and warning Crassus to leave. Crassus further explained he was doing this for Rome and to remove himself from suspicion, as he had been a friend of Catiline. Cicero acted straight away and called the Senate together the next morning. Rome was buzzing with rumours and the atmosphere was becoming more tense. The letters were read out loud and Cicero was also able to announce that he had received reports of armed groups of men gathering in Etruria (modern day Tuscany, Lazio and Umbria) 150 miles to the north of Rome. Within these armed groups were no doubt many of the disenchanted retired legionaries of Sulla's old disbanded army and we know that one of the leading figures in support of Catiline was Caius Manlius, a former centurion under Sulla.

In the next few days, Catiline kept his nerve. Nothing concrete establishing his connection with these rumours had surfaced, no one had called for his arrest and the levies being gathered to put down the expected rising in the north were nothing to do with him and he, the smuggler of radical ideas, carried on being present in the city. He even had the nerve to offer himself to be placed under house arrest – in Cicero's home. Cicero declined, but one of the noblemen that offered his services as part of his bodyguard was the ever-opportunistic Publius Clodius Pulcher – history does not record how Cicero felt about being 'protected' by men such as this.

6 November 63

The next act in this unfolding drama was that, on the night of 6 November, Catiline was able to walk in the shadows of Rome's side streets, evading recognition to join with other so-called 'conspirators', so-called because there is another interpretation which we will come to shortly. The meeting was meant to be secret, but yet again Fulvia proved a pivotal part of Cicero's intelligence network and she was able to inform him of the meeting. Pausing, no doubt to take in wise counsel from Atticus and Terentia amongst others, Cicero prepared the ground and there was a one-day delay while Catiline and his supporters waited for a response to the news that his meeting had been discovered.

The First Oration, 8 November 63, in senatu habita (delivered in the Senate)

The senators, having received their instructions to attend, and dressed in their gleaming white togas, again walked amongst the jostling and noisy crowds across the forum and along the *via sacra*, but this time, as they gathered in small groups, they ascended up high marble steps to be seen by all below, as Cicero had called the meeting to be held in the Temple of Jupiter Stator. This was both a symbolic choice and a practical one. Practical because it was easier to defend than the senate house, should armed rebellion break out during the meeting, but also the high and imposing temple, with the immense Palatine Hill rising up behind it, had been part of the life and skyline for over 200 years. In the legends so important to the Roman people, the temple was over the spot where Romulus and his soldiers had stood and fought 700 years before, defending the future of Rome against the Sabines – 'stator' indicating stationary or preserver of order – in other words, Catiline was going to be challenged in a very holy place, revered by Romans of countless generations, dedicated to the preservation of Rome – the symbolism was immensely empowering for Cicero and all those present listening, as was the seriousness of the occasion as the room was surrounded by armed guards.

Walking across the marble floor of the Temple and addressing Catiline face to face with an electricity generated by his years of interrogating witnesses, Cicero opened the first of four speeches against Catiline – known collectively as *In Catilinam* or the *Catilinarians* – with his First Oration:

> *I am able to report how* [on 6 November] *you came into Scythmakers' Street (I will be perfectly specific) and entered the house of Marcus Laeca; and many of your accomplices in this lunatic, criminal enterprise joined you there. Do you dare deny it ...? You parcelled out the regions of Italy. You decided where you wanted each of your agents to go. You divided up the city for the benefit of the incendiaries* [to set light to the city]. *You confirmed that you yourself would be leaving and added that the only thing that held you back for a little was the fact that I was still alive.*

Cicero continued his damning report to the effect that two assassins had been dispatched to kill him in the morning, but he had been forewarned, again no doubt by Fulvia, and they had been refused permission to enter to wish him a special good morning. Not only that, but of equal concern, was the news that simultaneous uprisings were planned across Italy. The senators listened intently, looking at Cicero and Catiline in turn wondering if what they were hearing could possibly be true, and if it was, where did it leave them? According to Cicero and later Sallust, Catiline had sent arms and equipment to Manlius in the north and his assembling army of veterans was to march south towards Rome to support the takeover of the city and the Senate at a given signal – this would be followed by the installation of Catiline as the sole consul and a reign of terror along Sullan lines would begin and a mass slaughter take place. According to Sallust, Catiline sat and then stood alone as he listened to a more personal attack including some of the phrases that have echoed down the ages, through university texts, in political speeches around the globe and in text books:

> *In the name of heaven, (Quo usque tandem abutere, Catilina, patientia nostra) how long Catiline will you go on abusing our patience? Do you really suppose that your lunatic activities are going to escape our retaliation for evermore? Are there to be no limits to this audacious, uncontrollable swaggering? Look at the garrison of the Roman nation which guards the Palatine by night, look at the patrols ranging the city, the whole population gripped by terror, the entire body of loyal citizens massing at one single spot! Look at this meeting of our Senate behind strongly fortified defences, see the expressions and countenances of every one of these men who are here! Have none of these sights made the smallest impact on your heart? You must be well aware that plot has been detected. Now that every single person in this place knows about your conspiracy, you cannot fail to recognise that it is doomed. Do you suppose there is a single individual here who has not got the very fullest information about what you were doing last night and the night before, where you went, the men you summoned, the plans you concocted?*

Despite trying to gather the Senate together and thereby nullify hidden supporters of Catiline sitting around him with statements such as '*see the expressions and countenances of every one of these men*', Cicero knew full well that he was talking to a fractured Senate and towards the end of the speech, he was forced out into the open when he admitted:

> *And yet there are some men here in this Senate who either genuinely fail to see, or make a pretence of not seeing, the disasters by which we are menaced.*

At the end of the speech Cicero looked to the high ceilings and walls of the great temple of Jupiter and his echoing voice appealed to the god as the 'Stayer' of the city to keep Catiline away from *the dwellings and walls of Rome, away from the lives and properties of all its citizens'.* There is just a sense there that he wanted to ensure that he had the total support of the Senate – in referencing the fact that their property was at risk he reminded them that they stood to lose everything if Catiline was successful. Does this give us a clue as to the vulnerability he felt, that an appeal to their baser instincts was needed to ensure that they were on side. If it does, then we can also sense just how fragile the Senate was as a bastion against the fall of democracy, that it was only the fear of losing their money, homes and status that would force them to protect it. Catiline rose and delivered his own verdict, insinuating that Cicero had no place amongst the nobility of the Senate and suggesting he was out of place, an immigrant who should go back to where he belonged. All pretty vicious stuff.

In order to achieve a clean victory, Cicero attempted to persuade Catiline that there was no way back and that he should voluntarily do the honourable thing and go into exile – this would have saved Cicero the problem of dealing with a still very much alive and revolutionary Catiline and taken one of the heads off this writhing viper. Exile was the neat and tidy end that Cicero hoped for, but Catiline had no intention of doing any such thing. Perhaps encouraged that Cicero had not gone further and arrested him, Catiline again furiously criticised him as 'an immigrant', an imposter amongst the nobility, a failed leader and everything he despised and when senators began shouting him down, he stormed away issuing threats as he left. He swept away that night, with some 300 of his compatriots – others remained in Rome to cause trouble – and rode to the camp at Faesulae to join his gathering army of revolt.

The Second Oration, 9 November 63, habita ad populum (delivered before the people)

The next day Cicero called the people of Rome together and mounted the rostra yet again as consul, the wise man, the literate man, the man they had elected the previous year, surrounded by his lictors and attended by a fanfare of trumpets and colour, to deliver the second oration. Here he had to craft a completely different speech from the one the day before. Perhaps surprisingly, he would need to use all his powers of persuasion, language and emotional appeal to gain the support and approval of the people of Rome, what Mary Beard describes as 'the haves and have nots' – the wide spectrum of people that made up city life. They pushed and squeezed their way into the forum and down the surrounding streets, between carts and alongside horses, tripping over gutters and steps, standing on walls and holding onto marble pillars or climbing high on the plinths of statues to hear what their consul had to say. From literate merchants to illiterate beggars, from calm clean professionals to thugs and graffiti writers, from servants to bakers, the clean and the unclean, laundry workers and weavers, bankers and café owners, retired legionaries and doctors, our friends the scribes and government clerks, all crowded beside each other to hear what had happened the day before and how their consul had acted.

If we are to believe the versions of the speeches that we have inherited through the various copies – no originals survive – then Cicero unleashed a stream of invective against Catiline, painting him not just as the enemy of the people, but the synthesis of evil, a man with no honour and a history of vice and bad deeds, a murderer and now a would-be dictator and assassin, the destroyer of democracy.

> *For every type of criminality and wickedness that you can think of, he has been behind them all. In the whole of Italy there is not one single poisoner, gladiator, robber, assassin, parricide, will-forger, cheat, glutton, wastrel, adulterer, prostitute, corrupter of youth, or youth who has been corrupted, indeed any nasty individual of any kind whatever, who would not be obliged to admit he has been Catilina's intimate.*

We have no record of how the crowd reacted, but we do know that the Senate was concerned enough to pass the *senatus consultum ultimum* and declare Catiline and Manlius enemies of the Republic (*hostes rei publicae*). It was now down to Cicero to use whatever means he felt necessary to control the situation, which clearly was not something just affecting the city of Rome. This was the pivotal moment for the future of democracy in Rome. This was the QAnon moment where it was possible that the people, or those led by the equivalent of the American QAnon supporters of Catiline (read Trump), could march on the Senate. 6 January 2020 in the USA was a mirror image back to a point in 63 where executive authority could be used either to protect democracy or destroy it – Donald Trump was only a few hours short of being able to declare martial law, having used his supporters as the battering ram into the Senate House in Washington and Cicero was in the same position. Trump would have arrested his own people, Cicero arrested Catiline. Had Cicero in fact been using Catiline as an excuse for his own purposes then power was there in his hands – something that Donald Trump very nearly had. Cicero had the power, via the Senate, if he so wished to introduce martial law and become dictator of Rome – twenty years ahead of Julius Caesar – but he chose to save democracy, however, we can wonder if the thought did cross his mind to save democracy through dictatorship as Caesar was to claim. Instead, Cicero very quickly ordered retired generals loyal to the Republic, current office holders of praetor and quaestor ranks and his not so convincingly loyal co consul Antonius to disperse to the provinces to raise troops and put down any risings while he, Cicero, had others implicated in the plot placed under house arrest and kept watch over Rome and this is how the next two weeks unfolded, with uncertainty, expectation and unease.

The life and work of Cicero is without doubt one of the wonders of ancient history and he ranks amongst humanity's greatest individuals. This alone justifies his place in the history of the world, in books and university research papers, but is there something else that nags away at us? Why does Cicero fascinate every generation and why does he fascinate me? Personally speaking, there is a feeling that under his umbrella of oratorical and literary magnificence, there is something not quite right. Cicero pressed home over and over again in his second oration that it was he that had risen to the challenge of conspiracy against the state and it was because of his steadfast defence of democracy that Catiline had, in a way, gone into exile – well he had at least left Rome. He is of course correct, but was the challenge as dreadful as he imagined? Further, the accusations that Catiline and his supporters were debauched criminals intent on destruction and perversity, monsters determined to bring down the Republic and create a world of pain, were extreme. It is because of the lack of documentary evidence, other than Cicero's own speeches – no doubt touched up numerous times in the three subsequent years before they were published – and Sallust's book twenty years later, Mary Beard asks us to ponder and reflect that we should try to read between the lines of the speeches to 'prise apart' the text looking for other possible interpretations of what was actually happening. In his determination to paint Catiline and his supporters as negatively as possible, Cicero, in his first two orations, perhaps inadvertently reveals a great deal more about himself and the state of Roman Italy in 63.

Five examples, before the main events unfold in December 63, will suffice.

Firstly, in the initial two orations Cicero, understandably, is focussed on Catiline, his faults, dreadful past and failing friends. But it could be claimed that Catiline was in fact no different from many other 'failing' nobles at this moment in the history of the Republic. So much new money was flowing into Rome from the conquered provinces, yet it was being concentrated in fewer and fewer hands. As we have seen, Cicero did not hold back from flaunting his newfound wealth, his many homes, statues and libraries, and in so doing he magnified the manifest corruption in the eyes of Catiline and his friends and

Lucius Antonius, brother of Mark Antony – from a noble family but the subject of much scorn by Cicero in the Philippics.

allies. If one failed to gain election to office, and there were only so many, then one stood no chance of sharing the spoils. As Cicero said

> *The second group (of the five Cicero identified as supporters of Catiline) consists of those who are overwhelmed by debt but still expect to enjoy absolute power. They want to gain control of the government and think that revolution can bring them the offices of which they have no hope in times of peace. This is my best advice to them – as it is, needless to say, to all others – give up any hope of attaining their goal. First of all, I personally am on the alert, I am right at hand, I am guarding the Republic.*

But what if you did not have the necessary funds to bribe your way to office? What if you had been unlucky in business, perhaps squeezed out by Crassus and his money-making machine. What if your debts were brought on by the corrupt nature of the state or the incompetence of a parent? Cicero makes no allowance that some of this 'motley assortment of trouble-makers' may in fact be good people ruined by a corrupt state which he is now defending. As for his defiant statement that they would never get past him, Cicero does perhaps ignore the fact that Rome is a democracy, that there is a senate also prepared to defend it. In modern parlance, it's not all about him.

Secondly, all well and good to slate Catiline's character for his excesses, debauched lifestyle and murderous past, but that hardly made him an exception. One could argue that these were all the essential elements of a strong CV in ancient Rome. There were many sitting in the Senate who must have seen their own past reflected in Cicero's words and Catiline's eyes and there is a certain amount of hypocrisy here, that suddenly all scandalous behaviour is wrong. The fathers of the state were happy enough to ignore his behaviour until he became a problem to them. What was the impact of the arrival of the pious Cato – had his presence heightened an awareness that they had been bad men for too long? In any event, society enjoys stories of sleaze, the abrogations of youth and there may be an element that Catiline was in fact 'cool' amongst certain elements of society – so much so that Cicero had to work his lexicon hard to capture enough of the indiscretions of Catiline to push his reputation beyond acceptability.

Thirdly, why was it necessary to arm and alarm the whole country if Catiline was not a national hero? Cicero made much of the fact that Catiline was only leaning on a small group of city based, poor quality, disaffected, evil men. Surely Cicero's actions speak louder than his words here and the reality was that disaffection with the government had been growing for years and Catiline was just the latest and most vocal expression of it. The background to these events was that rural poverty compared with the excesses of city *luxuria* was no longer tolerable and even Cicero could see that many of Rome's elders had lost their dedication to the traditions of the Republic. Perhaps Cicero was punishing Catiline to show the Senate a mirror of their own weaknesses in no longer being totemic indicators of the Roman *virtus* – he had once written to Atticus that they (the senators) showed more concern for their fishponds than for the Republic. If the contagion of *avaritia* had spread across the whole country then no wonder Cicero was concerned about a national uprising and this makes Catiline no longer a city based, small time conspirator, but the leader of a national movement, a hero of the underclass, the dispossessed and those who had lost everything trying to get elected in a system totally corrupted by money rather than being judged on their merits.

When it comes to the word *coniuratio* or conspiracy, we enter the realm of the keystone of Cicero's oratorical strategy. The key question is: was it a conspiracy, or the start of the national uprising? For Cicero, it was vital that the people of Rome did not sense anything greater than a conspiracy of evil, greedy men and so his orations had to ram home the clandestine nature of events even though it was quite possibly something far larger than that. Sallust for example, uses the term *coniuratio* twenty-nine times in his account and Catiline's supporters are referred to as conspirators. In his study of the terminology used in relation to the events of 63, Claude Kananack points out that both Cicero and Sallust are constantly at pains to point out the clandestine nature of events, things happened in the dark, at night, on street corners, meetings were in the shadows, late at night, in hidden places. Cicero sees his role to *aperire* (to uncover or make apparent) and to identify what happened at secret meetings *priore nocte* (the night before) or to point out *de hac nocturna excursione Catilinae* (Catiline's night journey). Naturally the leaders of the rebellion, if that's what it was, had to meet secretly and night was better than day, but Cicero had a definite motive in mind, like the very best lawyer of the land would do, in that he wished to convey the hidden and secretive, underhanded and small-scale nature of these madmen rather than this be part of the planning of an open revolt across the nation.

If Catiline was so bad a figure, so out of control and so insane, then why did so many people sympathize with him or go further and follow him? Quintus Lutatius Catulus, a respected senator and one of the leaders of the *optimates* along with the much younger Cato, had been consul in 78, an opponent of Pompey's extraordinary commands and a follower of Sulla, in other words sympathetic to everything that Catiline believed in. Most relevant, however, is that he had also recently been defeated by the young ambitious Caesar – in normal times Catulus would have been expected to receive the post of Pontifex Maximus – but these were not normal times and, like Catiline, he had felt rejection. When Cicero had foolishly called for support in the Senate for the exile of Catiline, none was forthcoming – or if there were voices, they were whispers. Cicero then suggested they exile Catulus – he had no obvious connection with Catiline's activities, but he was clearly in sympathy with the young man – the outcry was loud and angry, thus by implication Cicero had his man. When Catiline therefore wrote in haste to Catulus, it was to a respected figure, one that empathized and understood his anger, but was not prepared to rebel:

Lucius Catiline to Quintus Catulus – cited in Sallust in his *Bellum Catilinae*

Your eminent integrity, known to me by experience, gives me a pleasing confidence in the midst of great perils, to my present recommendation. I have determined therefore, to make no formal defence with regard to my new course of conduct [leaving to go to war]; *yet I was resolved, though conscious of no guilt, to offer you some explanation, which, on my word of honour, you may receive as true. Provoked by injuries and indignities, since, being robbed of the fruit of my labour and exertion* [failing to win the election to consul twice], *I did not obtain the post of honour due to me, I have undertaken, according to my custom, the public cause of the distressed* [all of those insulted by the current state of affairs]. *Not but that I could have paid, out of my own property, the debts contracted on my own security; while the generosity of Orestilla* [his wife], *out of her own fortune and her daughters', would discharge those incurred on the security of others. But because I saw unworthy men ennobled with honours, and myself proscribed on groundless suspicion, I have, for this very reason, adopted a course, amply justifiable in my present circumstances,* [I'm not running because I cannot pay my debts incurred by two failed election campaigns but for other reasons] *for preserving what honour is left to me. When I was proceeding to write more, intelligence was brought that violence is preparing against me. I now commend and entrust Orestilla to your protection; entreating you, by your love for your own children, to defend her from injury. Farewell.*

Sallust certainly felt that this moving and emotional letter was genuine, and there is little reason to doubt its veracity, so we have a small window through which we can sense the thoughts and feelings of Catiline rushing to write before taking to his horse and escaping Rome on the night of 8 November. If one were trying to defend him, say with a lawyer as good as Cicero, then one could suggest this was a proud man, too proud to argue any more, given the insults thrown his way by certain orators. Also, that he was a caring man thinking of his wife's safety and a man wanting to explain himself to someone he respected. A good defence counsel might also argue that the real reason he was in this mess was nothing to do with madness, licentiousness or murderous intent, but because those with bigger purses were able to bribe the electors in two elections more than he was and, as a result, he was now in financial ruin – but that even now he could still settle his debts in contrast to what was being said about him. Lastly, a lawyer as talented as Cicero might have pointed out that he was taking a stand on the succession of poorly qualified, weak and corrupt politicians that now characterised the leadership of Rome – protected by Cicero.

The final point worth making is that Cicero also tried to demean the character and numbers of important figures who were supporting Catiline. In reality, these were leading figures in the Roman political system, many former senators and magistrates, bonded together by a mixture of anger and disappointment at how their careers had turned out, jealousy of those whose fortunes were thrown in their faces and genuine hatred of a system that was so corrupt. Although the men left behind in Rome may have made a mess of their roles in the 'conspiracy' or 'rebellion' this did not mean that they were the *'vile characters of every kind'* that Cicero called them or *'nactus es ex perditis atque ab omni non modo fortuna, verum etiam spe derelictis conflatum improbum manum'* – *'You have a band of evil men, swept together from the refuse of society and from those who have been abandoned by all fortune and hope'* (1.25). Apart from the brave and experienced centurion Manlius in the north, there was Publius Cornelius Lentulus Sura 'an imposing and popular orator', Gaius Cornelius Cethegus 'a man of formidable [and murderous, according to Cicero] energy' and Publius Cornelius Lentulus Sura, praetor in 75, Governor of Sicily in 74 and consul in 71. It was to Lentulus that Catiline devolved the plans for the burning of Rome to create chaos as the rebel army came down from the north.

For the next few weeks Cicero monitored events in Rome, had Lentulus watched closely, received reports from the provinces and planned the next stage of dealing with the declared public enemy and rebel Catiline. He also had to find the time to prepare a defence for Lucius Licinius Murena. As consul, Cicero had superintended the election back in the summer of 63, after the pause caused by Catiline, and Murena was one of the two men elected ahead of Catiline and Servius Sulpicius Rufus – it was Sulpicius that brought a claim of bribery against Murena. It was probably very true that Murena had bribed the population, everyone did, it was more a question of how obvious it was. Murena was well connected – he was something of a war hero having commanded a legion under Lucullus in the Third Mithridatic War as *legatus*, or legionary commander, and he was popular with his men and the Senate – in addition Lucullus, still with his immense military reputation and *auctoritas* intact, spoke in defence of Murena. Still, this was a chance for Cato, prosecuting for Sulpicius, and Cicero (plus Crassus and Hortensius) defending for Murena to lock horns for the first time. Cato had sworn to prosecute all bribery and corruption so he was going to be busy. In *Pro Murena*, Cicero, despite being exhausted, yet again produced another winning attack focussing on Cato's Stoicism being too insensitive to the reality of the situation that faced Rome, thus undermining his credibility. Murena was needed as a general and, despite Sulpicius being a friend of Cicero, Murena was unanimously acquitted and became consul in 62.

The Third Oration, 3 December 63 habita ad populum (delivered before the people)

The Catiline issue was brought to a head suddenly and terminally. At some point in mid to late November a delegation from the Allobroges, a Gallic tribe unhappy about their treatment, arrived in Rome, travelling the length of the country and down the Appian Way. On their arrival Lentulus made contact with them and spoke to them in terms of joining the revolt on Catiline's side – history has missed the possibility that they had already been intercepted on their journey south, which would almost certainly have taken them through Etruria. Unsure of how to respond, the delegation spoke to Fabius Sanga (whose ancestor had conquered their tribe in 121) and he in turn took them straight to Cicero. Entrapment is not something that is normally associated with Cicero, but this is exactly what was designed and we can safely assume that his plan was worked through as the best option in his discussions with his closest confidantes – Atticus included. The Allobroges asked for written confirmation from Catiline and the other leaders in Rome of the plan so that they could take these to their own leaders, however, they were intercepted by an ambush planned by Cicero as they left Rome on the Milvian Bridge over the Tiber.

Cicero finally had all the proof he needed and he once again convened the Senate early in the morning of 3 December – this time at the Temple of Concord at the foot of the Capitoline Hill at the northwestern end of the forum. With its huge columns towering down over the forum, casting a shadow each day for the previous 200 years, this was another of the holiest of places for Cicero to enter, this time to spend most of the day hearing reports and giving evidence in front of the white-toga-clad senators each with their purple stripes of office. Four were asked to take down verbatim notes along with various of the most trusted *scribae*. Reports were received that the house of Caius Cornelius Cethegus had been searched and was found stacked with weapons, Lentulus himself was put under questioning in front of the Senate and resigned in a show of frustration as praetor, taking off his toga of office, but admitting nothing. The letters were still sealed and the wax seals of the implicated men were shown to the Senate before they were opened and their contents read out. For Lentulus and for them all it was humbling and humiliating that they had been caught out in this way and it must have been plain to all what Cicero had in fact done, but the proof was louder than the circumstance. It was a long day and no doubt attention often turned to the faces of Crassus and Caesar – both of whom have been credited with being the real masterminds behind the whole plot. There was no evidence against them, they had been careful to withdraw from any link with Catiline, but, although it is hearsay given the lack of any evidence of association, both stood to gain from any successful toppling of the government. It was more than likely that they saw Catiline as a test, a Trojan horse to see how Cicero and the Senate would react, so that they could learn from the events about how to approach something similar themselves at a later date.

Although not put in chains, the leading rebels were taken away and placed under arrest at the homes of the remaining praetors and in the late afternoon, after a tiring and emotionally draining day, Cicero emerged onto the steps and surveyed the scene. There stretching away in front of him through the length of the forum, between the basilicas on either side and surrounded by the statues and pageantry of history he made a speech to another packed crowd.

The whole story was told in exciting terms – after all, this matter had been gripping the population for days if not weeks. Like a political melodrama today, the people spoke of nothing else other than all the different ways this might end – but few had in mind the way it would. Making the most of the drama, Cicero put on a fine show using the strengths of his ability to paint an image of how he, primarily, had uncovered the plot, saved Rome from flames, protected property and all of this had been achieved with the blessing of the Gods who shone down on him:

> *Romans: your country, and the lives of every one of you, your property, your fortunes, your wives and children, this centre of your illustrious government, this most fortunate and beautiful of cities – today has been made manifest to you that the outstanding love which the immortal gods bear you, as well as my own labours and endeavours at the risk of my life, have rescued all these blessings from fire and the sword, from the very jaws of death, and have given them back to you safe and sound.*

> *Power is when we have every justification to kill, and we don't.*
> Oskar Schindler

A cynic might say that, to place property and fortunes ahead of the salvation of government, in the order of things saved from fire and brimstone, rather betrays what mattered most to the Romans. She or he might also say that Cicero protests his singular role in saving the state too much. It is a matter of context. Cicero was a man relieved that this episode was almost over, but he was also a man revelling in being centre stage at one of the pivotal moments in the history of the Republic. Cicero knew that his words would no doubt echo through eternity, which they have, and so it is understandable that his part in the Catiline affair, I resist the word conspiracy, should be framed so carefully in his preparations. If there was a blatant conspiracy then it could be said it was Cicero in his deliberate entrapment, with all the secrecy and shadowy planning that this entailed, who was the guilty party. Therein lies a significant truth. That for liberal democracy to survive in the way that Fukuyama envisions, those given power are most at risk of misusing it. Clearly Cicero had won, if he saw this as a personal test of his superior being then he was vindicated, but true power means not killing someone when you have the right, the means and the reason to do it.

There was a day long delay between the end of the third oration and the start of the final and fourth one, delivered on 5 December. In these twenty-four hours we have no record of the events regarding Cicero's day, but we can surmise that it was spent partly recovering from the strains of the previous one, holding the Senate together, trying the evidence if not so much the accused, constraining Caesar, Cato, Lucullus and the myriad of other powerful personalities and writing a speech – or at least preparing some draft notes. In addition, Cicero would have taken the counsel of his closest advocates such as Atticus and indeed his wife Terentia – to what extent the latter we can only guess. No doubt a steady stream of senators made their way to his house mulling over the options as they walked through the forum, there may have been those dangerously close to the plot wishing to shore up their image by supporting Cicero with plaudits, others to plead for clemency for friends now under threat of execution. There was much to consider.

This had been and still was a time of crisis. A firm hand needed to be shown and indeed, given what Cicero had said about the plotters and the aims of the plot, there seemed little doubt that execution was necessary. If Cicero had embellished, magnified, twisted and finally entrapped the evidence then he had the two things every prosecution lawyer wants – a cast iron case, regardless of where the information came from and centre stage to perform. But Cicero was now in the awkward position, for the first time in his life, of also being judge. Not only was he consul, but he was absolute master over life and death – powers given to him by the Senate back in October. He could there and then have issued orders to round up the plotters from the various homes in which they were kept and had them quietly executed. He could not let them go, and to imprison them for life was a fudge that would not work. Consequently, having discussed long and hard that day, Cicero reached out once more for the endorsement of the Senate.

The Fourth Oration, 5 December 63 *habita in senatu (delivered in the Senate)*

After hearing the evidence, Cicero asked those senators present, some had not been willing to attend, to declare their opinion in favour or not of execution. But the Senate was badly divided and fractured and Cicero had no idea how this meeting might unfold, but he began by calling for the statement of the most senior present at the time, D. Junius Silanus, consul elect for 62, who asked for the severest penalty. Ambiguous, but a positive enough start and the senators endorsed execution. All went this way until it was the turn of Julius Caesar who was speaking early, despite his comparative youth, as he was praetor elect for the coming year. The mood began to change. Caesar spent time eloquently describing how he looked back to the forefathers of the republic for guidance, how they often showed clemency to their enemies and how important it was not to act in passion or emotion, but in calm reflection. He began:

> *All human beings who debate on matters of uncertainty, conscript fathers, ought to be free from hatred, enmity, anger, and pity. The mind cannot easily see the truth when those emotions get in the way, and no one has ever been simultaneously governed by the demands of his desire and by practical considerations.*

As Caesar continued, the mood changed and he concluded that it was his view that time was needed to make the correct decision and so the accused should have all their estates and fortunes confiscated, if they had them, and be held in custody for longer, but this time dispersed across towns in Italy that would hold them until Catiline had been defeated and then they could be brought back to Rome for a trial or referendum by the Assembly of the people. Caesar praised Cicero *'a most distinguished man'* and suggested that Silanus had voted through fear – a comment that no doubt ruffled feathers – but none of them had to worry as they were in the safe hands of Cicero. So it was that, according to Sallust writing twenty years later and consulting both the hurried notes being taken by the *scribae* and Cicero's own records, murmurs of agreement with Caesar began to rumble around the room and those initially in favour of execution stood to announce that they had changed their minds. Cicero, despite attempting to remain neutral could feel events slipping from his grasp and he chose this moment to try to recover the Senate's support with his speech, the fourth oration.

Senators, I see your heads and eyes all turned in my direction. I see you not only feel anxiety concerning the perils which menace yourselves and our country, but also, even if those be averted, that you are worried about the personal risks to myself.

The opening line of Cicero's fourth speech delivered this time in the senate house itself belied the speeches still to come. Cicero's speech this time was one of engagement with Caesar's arguments, but also on the legal aspects of the extent to which the *senatus consultum ultimatum* allowed for execution without trial. Opinion was divided in the same way that the whole Senate was riven by factions and Cicero was thinking about his own immediate future in respect of any action he would have to authorise and what posterity would make of his decision – the best insurance being the support of the Senate. One might imagine that the last thing on the minds of many of the senators present was what might happen to Cicero – much as he would have liked to think that. Some would have been happy to see him in prison with the plotters, others looked to him to carry the responsibility for making the decision on their behalf. Many were now confused about what to do. No different from any other group of politicians, the key concern was how to escape this moment unscathed and still in control and many were undecided about how to act.

Historians have debated Caesar's motivation ever since, but regardless of whether it was to protect his friends or establish a precedent for the future that might involve his being accused of treason, it was very likely that he was also playing for the support of the people, who did not like executions without trials. He may also have been the devil's advocate continuing his strategy of causing Cicero the maximum distress he could to disrupt the *optimates* even further and continue to inflate the air of fallible and indecisive government that would suit his personal designs well. There was plenty of talk about this Caesar, what his real plan was and there were those that went further hoping that the mud flying around regarding the plotters could somehow stick to Caesar's toga too. Both the former consul Catulus, still steaming in fury from being robbed in the election for the Pontifex Maximus and Piso tried to get Cicero to fabricate evidence in his speech to drag Caesar into the quagmire, but Cicero refused. Cicero saw Caesar as 'a man in progress', by this he meant that he admired much about Caesar and recognized that he could be of great service to the Republic once he, Cicero, had been able to mould and shape him – much like he thought he could Pompey. Sadly, he was to be proven profoundly wrong on both counts.

Cicero continued to try to press home the eloquent arguments and there are many references in his oration to his being but a vessel, and an expendable one at that, of the Senates' will. He is willing to lose his life in the defence of Rome and even at the very end places the care of his son into the hands of the Senate should he meet his own end. As a final push in his masterly style, Cicero reinforced the senator's imagination on the scene outside, lest they be in any doubt of what the people were thinking:

> *Everyone, of every order, class and age, is assembled here today at this one spot. The forum is crowded with people, the temples round about are packed tight, all the approaches to this shrine and this place are crammed. Since the very beginnings of the city there was never before a crisis in which all Romans have been so thoroughly of one accord.*

> *Heaven alone could measure the size of the multitude, and its enthusiasm, and its determination, and the courage with which it is united in defence of the security and greatness of Rome!*

We might interpret these words as saying, 'The people have the enthusiasm, determination and courage to see these men executed – do you? What have I got to do to restore to you the traditional values of the *mos maiorum*? This sorry episode is but the latest example of more to come – this is the vanguard of an onslaught on the values we are elected to preserve and you have allowed to decay, we must stand and been seen to stand. Bring back heroes – look I am prepared to be one of them and stand up for you!' This fourth speech was therefore an exhortation to recover political probity, traditional strengths and standards. Cicero was not using this moment to become a dictator himself, he was after all the philosopher-king, a man gifted to explain why, secure acceptance, and carry out implementation. If there was a moment in Cicero's life where the battle was joined between his beliefs and concerns for the Republic and the enemies of democracy then this was it. Another less scrupulous man, a Julius Caesar, could easily have taken this moment to seize power, but there was no MAGA movement outside in the forum because Cicero was trying to save an ideal, not create a new one.

Sallust tells us that Cicero's speech failed to rally the Senate and at this critical moment Cato rose to speak. There are questions regarding why Cato managed to jump the queue, it was not his turn, but Cicero nodded and Cato was invited to speak and this is a prime example of the right man at exactly the right time in history. The atmosphere was tense, confused bordering on unruly, Cicero's speech had been too long, too pleading and it had missed the target. Cato had no concerns about eloquence or offending his audience. He was not

The marble head of a Roman senator from around 50 BCE displaying all the authenticity of nobility, age and power of Roman imagery from this period.

Looking northwest over the Forum Romanum as it stands today and towards the Senate House. The scene of momentous occasions in Republican, and later Imperial, Rome.

The most famous marble bust of Marcus Tullius Cicero in the Musei Capitolini in Rome.

Women born into noble or aristocratic families were educated to equip them for marriage to a man destined for greatness and Terentia would have been able to work alongside Cicero throughout his political and social careers. (*Louvre Museum, Paris/ Wikimedia*)

Marble bust always associated with Crassus, richest man in Rome and determined to have his *Imperium* and Triumph alongside Pompey and Caesar.

The troublesome Parthian Empire and scene of the great military disaster at Carrhae. Note how close to the eastern flank of Roman rule the Parthian threat was, something which enabled Cicero to terrorize the Roman crowd with economic destruction in his *Lex Manilia* oration of 66.

A legionary helmet dating to the Republican period. Made of iron, this was a symbol of Roman power recognized throughout the ancient world. This example can be found in the National Archaeological Museum, Madrid.

The steps of temples in the forum were common sites to give orations about important events, block legislation, stir up riots, or begin a revolution. This is one reason why being educated in the skills of rhetoric was so vital to any aspiring Questor, Aedile, Tribune, Praetor or Consul.

The ruins of the Roman Temple at Baiae painted in water wash by J. W. Abbot in 1790. The temple looked over the thriving metropolis of Republican luxury living, which can now be seen via scuba diving all around the modern day bay.

The Appian Way south of Rome. This Republican 'motorway' was often travelled by Cicero and his large retinue and was the route for Pompey and his fleeing army southwards to Brundisium. Wayside taverns and waterpoints extended the length of the route, as did stabling and new horses for military couriers. Towards Rome itself began the roadside tombs built outside the Pomerium.

Lest we become lulled into thinking the Roman world was as grey as their statues appear today, we must remind ourselves that every day, Pompeii opens new windows into a world of colour, energy, fashion – a world where Cicero revelled in the displays of wealth so important to Rome.

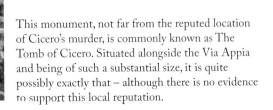

This monument, not far from the reputed location of Cicero's murder, is commonly known as The Tomb of Cicero. Situated alongside the Via Appia and being of such a substantial size, it is quite possibly exactly that – although there is no evidence to support this local reputation.

Gnaeus Pompeius Magnus, three time Consul of Rome, five time husband and father, celebrator of three Triumphs, hero of the Roman people, victorious general, conqueror of numerous territories and administrative genius, but unimaginative, flawed in political decision making, vain, and problematic for Cicero.

Cicero's letters provide the modern world with a panacea of correspondence between the most prominent personalities of the Roman Republic. Those that he received deserve as much acclaim as those he wrote. Statesman, orator, lawyer, father, husband, brother, and friend – Cicero shines a light on how he felt, what he saw, how he saw others and what he experienced in his life at one of the most important periods in human history.

Fulvia, as the wife of Mark Anthony – and thus reaching her final destination as a powerful, manipulative political operator in a man's world, was the first woman to be represented on Roman coinage. Her coinage was struck in the Royal Mints such as at Lugdunum (Lyon in France) during the brief period of power that she enjoyed. Coins provide the only likeness we have of Fulvia – unlike this one shown here, some less flattering proofs no doubt meant that the artist had to go into hiding.

The scribes that went everywhere with Cicero would have taken their inks, tablets, parchment, stylus and sealing wax equipment and seals with them in trunks or leather satchels ready to start work at any time of day or night.

Gaius Octavius – later Caesar Augustus – in a rare early and pre-propagandist representation depicting him as a younger man and as Cicero may have recognized him. This can be found in the Museum of Art & History in Geneva, Switzerland.

in the mood or by nature someone well disposed towards Caesar or indecision on matters of law or justice.

In his excellent biography *Cato the Younger*, Fred Drogula embarks on a journey through Cato's short but exemplary speech that was to seal the fate of the accused men. Cato had little more than contempt for Caesar, but this was not his main driver for this speech, it was justice he sought as he always did. If, by some chance, Caesar could be implicated well then that would be down to the gods, but Cato pressed home his argument:

> *When I consider the facts and the danger we are in, conscript fathers, I'm of a very different mind from when I think of the proposals some have made* [But] *I call on you, you who have always valued your homes, villas, statues and paintings more than the Republic. If you want to keep those possessions, whatever they are that you embrace, if you want to find leisure for your pleasures, then wake up at last and take control of the state. We are not talking about taxes and the complaints of our allies* [clearly a reference to why the Allobroges were in Rome in the first place]; *your freedom and our life are at risk.*

Cato continued to condemn the senators present, in a way that Cicero could never do, for their weakness, decadent lifestyle and corruption, but he appealed to their honour towards the fading values of the Republic, the *virtus* that they had once had and the vision of the contracting veins of the *mos maiorum*. Cato even referred to the historical milestone of the case of the general A. Manlius Torquatus, who ordered his own son to be executed because he had attacked the enemy without waiting for orders. How far had the strength and dedication of the senators of Rome deteriorated from that time? Similarly, to Caesar Cato argued that the past was speaking to them – his style was fearless, moralizing and reactionary compared to Caesar's ice-cold delivery. Cato was passionate, loud and the senators were roused, they stood and applauded in a faux display of newfound courage – they 'called each other timid' and many shouted for execution.

Sensing the moment was ripe, Cicero acted quickly. A register of verdicts was taken from all the senators present and the sentence of execution confirmed. There are numerous versions of what happened next, but it is wise to leave the main description we have to Sallust:

> *After the Senate supported Cato's recommendation...the consul thought it best to take precautions for the coming night and to prevent any new developments during that time. He asked three men to make the necessary preparations for*

the execution. Guards were deployed and he himself led Lentulus to prison. [Lentulus and the others would have been first collected from the houses where they had been guests under house arrest]. *For the rest, praetors were responsible. In the prison, when you have gone up a little to the left, there is a place called the Tullianum which is a depression of about twelve feet into the ground. Walls protect it on all sides and above there is a dome made with stone arches, but squalor, murk, and stench make it hideous and terrible to behold. After Lentulus was sent down into this place, the executioners strangled him with a rope as ordered* [he was hung]. *Thus, that man, an aristocrat from the glorious family of the Cornelii, a man who had held consular power at Rome, found an end that suited his character and his actions. Cethegus, Statilius, Gabinius and Caeparius were executed in the same way.*

From later accounts it seems that the men were collected from local houses, where they were under house arrest, soon after the Senate was dismissed. The dispersing crowds in the forum saw the men being taken to an old cistern, used as a small prison cell, assuming they were going to be detained there overnight. The public were kept well away as they watched each man being lowered down, unaware that each was being strangled before the next was lowered down. When the five were dead, Cicero turned to what was left of the dispersing crowd and famously shouted 'They have lived!' Shock and silence turned into a sort of hysterical party – except for the friends and family of the executed men, who faded into the shadows. Cicero had been verbally anointed 'Father of the Country' by the Senate and Cato shouted the same across the forum as Cicero, surrounded by armed guards, made his way back to his home through the flaming torches held and alight on posts in the now dark forum.

We can only guess at Cicero's feelings as he arrived home. It may have been a mixture of great relief, certainly great exhaustion, and no doubt great elation. He was at this moment, in these few hours and in the days ahead before his consulship ended, the greatest Roman, the man who had saved the Republic, and no doubt Atticus, Terentia, Quintus and his children were waiting for his arrival. Maybe Tiro was there too, or perhaps he had walked in his retinue having been taking notes all day beside him. As the still bodies of the five executed men began to cool and former consuls of Rome were quietly removed back up through the round hole at the top of the old cistern Cicero tells us in his later writings that this was the highest moment of his life and he saw himself as that saviour he had always read about. He believed in and inhaled his own aura and reflected on his remarkable journey to this moment and enjoyed his finest hour.

There is one thought that is worth exploring as a postscript. The denial of a trial for Lentulus and his fellow accused men has been the centre of historical attention for centuries. The debate has largely centred around the legalities of whether what Cicero did, and the Senate endorsed, was legal. This is a justifiable area of continuing debate, however, there may be other dimensions to this issue briefly worth exploring. A trial would have created huge problems for Cicero and the Senate – not only would the publicity be enormous and the whole peninsula interested in receiving daily bulletins from Rome, but what might such a trial expose? Cicero had managed, through his four orations, to be the main purveyor of information – the characters of the men, the plots and plans, the danger to Rome and the entire Republic and the evil of Catiline – the majority of this information was provided to the people by Cicero. A trial would give the accused men an opportunity for their own platform to speak, to be cross examined – to name names. Who knows how far the plot really extended? How many of the senators in the final analysis knew of the plot and had done nothing, and how many had actively aided the planning? This is the last thing that Cicero would have wanted, but also the very last thing many senators wanted either. The accused men were never given their time in open court to state their case, when they were questioned it was by a bombardment of already proven facts to illuminate their guilt. There is something of the July Plot of 1944 in the events of December 63. General Fromm made himself judge and jury over Von Stauffenberg and his close retinue of plotters – also called conspirators by the Nazi state – they were taken to the courtyard outside and executed immediately after sentence was pronounced. The speed and the ignominy of their deaths was remarkable under the circumstances. Who knows what Lentulus may have said to posterity not only about others in the plot under torture or open cross examination, about his true aims and reasons for involvement and, just as we continue to learn about Von Stauffenberg's plot to kill Hitler and peel away the layers of contemporary propaganda designed to smother any sense of justification, so we should do the same with the Catiline Conspiracy.

Part V

Plots, Power and Pompey

Chapter 14

Plots and Power 62–58

Fate whispers to the warrior, you cannot withstand the storm ...
The warrior whispers back, I am the storm.

Anonymous

When the news of the executions in Rome in December 63 was given to Catiline in his headquarters tent, a shock wave ran through the camp. Reports of some 20,000 men having gathered under Catiline may have been exaggerated, but whatever the number, it drained away far quicker than it had gathered and the grand plan, the national uprising, the crusade was over. Each day, during a cold December, in the snow-covered hills of northern Tuscany more men deserted. Imagine the scene: Catiline and his officers and friends gathered around a table warmed by a brazier of burning logs, the light reflecting in the silver of the Eagle of one of the legions of Marius looking down over their gloomy faces. What to do – there were few options. Eventually it was decided to continue the battle from Transalpine Gaul, but news also soon arrived that their withdrawal, or escape northwards, was blocked by three legions under the command of Quintus Caecilius Metellus Celer – Metellus Celer had been a *praetor* under Cicero and had been sent north quickly to take command. Cicero needed someone dependable and, as far as he could judge, loyal to push down on Catiline from the north. In early January 62 Metellus Celer moved his legions southwards to Pistoria (modern day Pistoia in Tuscany) where Catiline was camped, while Gaius Antonius Hybrida, whose period as consul had been extended to cover this mission, advanced from the south with a larger force against his friend.

According to Sallust, although he was not present himself, Catiline made a speech to his troops and followers just before they marched to face certain death. It may have been taken down *verbatim* and in which case we are lucky that it survived but, even if it was passed on through a few hands by oral memory, it suggests that we should at least give Catiline credit for being a brave man even if Cicero did not or could not risk doing so. Catiline began by being honest with his men:

I know for a fact, soldiers, that words cannot create manly virtue and that a general's speech does not make an indolent army energetic or a frightened army brave. Whatever daring has been put in each man's heart by nature and training, that's what he will show in war.

Catiline then described how they were in this position because Lentulus had failed in Rome and no more troops could be expected. This had delayed his departure with them for Gaul and now they were trapped.

Wherever you choose to go, you must open a path with your sword.

Then a clue into the mindset of a man so vilified by Cicero as to make him seem like an insane madman, a creature from hell to be exterminated and reviled, but causes reflection on how the propaganda of Cicero has dominated 2,000 years of history:

And you must keep this in mind as well: the need that presses on us is not the same that weighs on them. We are fighting for our homeland, for freedom, for our lives; theirs is an inane struggle for the power of a few.

Towards the end of his words, the last he knew he would be making by way of an exhortation:

Do not lose your life without taking vengeance. Do not be captured and slaughtered like cattle; rather, fight like men, and leave for your enemy a victory filled with blood and grief!

Taken as a whole and even with the knowledge that this speech may have been adjusted before it reached the pen of Sallust, this is not the speech of a madman or a money grabbing, licentious lunatic as Cicero would have us believe. Cicero had always spoken of Catiline in ways that meant there was never going to be a chance of a reproachment or healing – was Catiline therefore a sacrificial lamb for Cicero's personal political objectives? This is a speech of a rational, courageous man, knowing he was about to die a grisly death, pushed into a corner for his beliefs that the Republican system was already broken, that the immense power of a few meant that democracy was already dead – it did not need Pompey or Caesar to prove this – and Cicero was the main defender of corruption and greed, not Catiline. The time for a revision of Catiline's reputation in history is long overdue. This is not to suggest that he was faultless, but then neither was he the man Cicero painted with his legal mindset – to win the case at all costs, to lie if necessary and with impunity as all prosecutors can do. For Catiline, Cicero was just another fox guarding the henhouse of the Senate and he died trying to change this.

Like all battles in this period, it was a bloody affair. Catiline, with a force of about 3,000 men, decided to fight the larger force and marched to take up positions in front of Antonius – with the emotional pressure of fighting someone he had lived and laughed with, Antonius developed or feigned a sudden attack of gout and transferred command to a man who had no such qualms, his legate Marcus Petreius. The clash between the hardened and veteran legionaries of Catiline and the men under Petreius was face to face, short and brutal, but superior numbers told and the Praetorian cohort under Petreius cut their way in to the centre of Catiline's line through to the standard by which Catiline was later found dead along with his loyal men. A heroic and courageous end on a bitterly cold, snow-covered Tuscan hillside for someone so vilified by Cicero's speeches, but so admired by his men. There is a paradox there still to be resolved but that cannot be done here, the battle of Pistoria was soon over, the Catiline rebellion was at an end, but the ripple effect of what had taken place over the previous two months was to echo for years to come.

Fighting for his place in the sun

With the execution of the plotters, Cicero was left with the firm conviction that he had saved Rome, but was aware of the fact that many others did not feel the same way. Breathing in the acclamations of his fellow senators with their plaudits and praise, he must now have felt that at last he was one of them, a noble in all but name and deserving of his rightful place amongst them. Accordingly, we read that he began work on his departure speech for December and, to reinforce his place as saviour of the nation; however, Cicero felt the wind of change hit him like a hurricane. Immediately he realized that his actions had, and would continue to, divide opinion. Plutarch later wrote:

> One could not attend the Senate or a public meeting nor a session of the law courts without having to listen to endless repetitions of the story of Catilina and Lentulus.

This self-belief and sense of pre-eminence was nothing new, instead both were reaching much higher levels. Developing a kind of voluntary blindness, Cicero received an early wakeup call and an indication of the fragility of his own position. On 10 December a new tribune took up his office and immediately began criticising Cicero and agitating for his general, Pompey, to be appointed to deal with Catiline. This was Caecilius Metellus Nepos, Pompey's brother-in-law commanding the forces in the north. Thoughts of yet another extraordinary command for Pompey filled the air and Cicero realised that, in reality, he was even more exposed after the Catiline affair than he had been before it. Cicero had to work hard to contain this new virus injected by Pompey from far away, which demonstrated just how effective his intelligence network was. Pompey knew everything that was going on and was able to develop his own counter measures from afar.

Pro Sulla 62

One other matter that directly concerned Cicero and is most worthy of note in 62 was the matter of the trial of Publius Cornelius Sulla. The series of destabilizing and embarrassing events in the decade of the 60s indicated, as much as anything else, that democracy was in peril. Despite being nephew of the great dictator, Publius had not relied solely on his family reputation and connections – there were as many enemies as there were friends. Success in making his way through the *cursus honorum* saw Publius Sulla rewarded with the offices of both *quaestor* and *praetor* and he arrived in the year 66 ready to stand for election as one of the consuls of 65 along with his colleague Publius Autronius. The result went their way, but celebrations were not to last long as they were to be impeached on charges of bribery by their opponents Lucius Manlius Torquatus and Lucius Aurelius Cotta. Such accusations were pernicious at best, given that the law that provided for harsher punishments, the *lex Acilia Calpurnia*, had only been passed the previous year – naturally with substantial support from Cato – making this in effect a test case and, as such, the Senate no doubt saw it as important to set the first and strongest example. To their disgust both Sulla and Autronius were found guilty, losing not only their elections to consul, but also being expelled from the Senate in disgrace leaving Cotta and Torquatus a clear run in a second election and they were duly chosen.

It was Sallust that linked the abortive efforts by Catiline to stand against Cotta and Torquatus with what became known as a first Catiline conspiracy. The friendship between Catiline, Sulla and Autronius must have been very close already as they sought to support each other in terms of the consular elections, but also in their cause in fighting against what they saw as a failing state being led by failed leaders. In reality, there has never been any evidence to prove that this 'first' conspiracy ever took place, despite there being a great deal of gossip and rumour. The plot was supposed to require the murder of the two consuls on the day they took office, 1 January 65, and to then rise up with armed supporters to seize the government of the state. This may sound much like the second and actual Catiline Conspiracy – so much so that there is debate over whether the accusation of a preliminary plot was just used as further damning evidence against Catiline. Whether or not there was a plot, 1 January 65 came and went without incident.

For Sulla though, the damage was done and was dramatic. As one might imagine, his whole life was ruined both personally, professionally and financially. Like Catiline, he too bore a serious grudge against a system that seemed designed to prevent younger and more able men from succeeding, but after Catiline's death in early 62, the spotlight fell solely on Sulla, and the stored vengeance against him or his family name resurfaced. He was able to persuade both Cicero and Hortensius to defend him and the resultant trial became another platform for Cicero to exhibit and deliver what is sometimes referred to as one of the best speeches of his life. As in the first impeachment, the so-called evidence against Publius Sulla was largely circumstantial and hardly strong, but nevertheless Cicero still threw the entire weight of his reputation and skills into the fight on Sulla's behalf, clearly in the belief that he was indeed innocent and not complicit in the Catiline Conspiracy.

Over the past 100 years, historians have vacillated between praise for Cicero's delivery technique and eloquence and absolute condemnation, seeing him as devoid of morality in how he handled himself. Interpretations therefore vary, but *Pro Sulla* remains, by any measure, one of Cicero's strongest defences of any client. Described as a 'paradigm of Ciceronian persuasive technique' the main thrust of the defence is that if Cicero believed in Sulla's innocence, then so should everyone else and that seems to have worked, as Sulla was indeed found innocent of the charges against him as being complicit in the conspiracy to bring down the state.

Rome's greatest orator refused permission to make an oration

If the trial and acquittal of P. Sulla was another success for Cicero, the next manifestation of Pompey's influence brought him back, yet again, into the realms of concern for his own position. In December 63, Nepos, clearly under instructions from Pompey, vetoed Cicero's valedictory oration to the people, which traditionally took place in front of a huge assembly of the population in the assembly ground of the forum and on the last day of the year. It was traditional for consuls leaving office to give an account of their year in the role and Cicero must have been in a buoyant mood having prepared an oration largely about himself and how, yet again, he had saved Rome and, in his own estimation, just like the very best of generals who had won a great victory.

But with everything set to begin, Nepos stood up and with another tribune sat on a bench in front of the podium and vetoed, as was his right as tribune for the coming year of 62, Cicero's right to speak. Further he informed 'the father of his country' that he could only make the traditional oath of leaving the position of consul and then must step down. What might the atmosphere have been like at that moment – shock from Cicero for sure – this was an unexpected embarrassment, but also a very sinister development. Gasps from the crowd, astonishment from some senators, glee and satisfaction from others, this was a small but pivotal moment. Cicero, like a man shouting at a judge as he was taken down from the witness box, called out a new oath:

I swear to you that I have saved my country and maintained her supremacy.

The growing clash between Cato and Caesar

If Cicero had thought that harmony between the orders in the Senate would last as a result of his philosopher-kingship, he had badly misjudged the political situation. He may have been an excellent lawyer, but he still had much to learn about politics and politicians, who were even more unscrupulous than lawyers. Events may have turned out more positively for Cicero had he actually accepted the usual proconsular appointment to a province where he could have calmed his nerves, taken a break from the intensity of trying to be the central figure in Roman life and not always been there to remind everyone of what he had done, but he had given Macedonia to Antonius to keep him out of the way in 63 and it has been said that not going was the biggest mistake of Cicero's life.

It was evident that Pompey was now working to expand his influence prior to his return to Rome and Cicero could sense that he was already being squeezed out into the shade as the man of yesterday, with Pompey being the man of today. The next destabilizing issue to arise was the proposal by the tribunes Nepos and Caesar, working together, that Pompey be allowed to stand for the consular election for 61. This brought direct and swift opposition from many in the Senate as it again opened up yet another direct challenge to the democratic process for Pompey, who had already ignored so many of the accepted protocols in his career. The clash between Cato and Caesar now reached new levels. In his assessment of both individuals, Sallust tells us:

And so I turn to them. They were nearly equal in birth, age and eloquence; their greatness of soul was similar, likewise their glory; but in other respects, they were different. Caesar was considered great for his benevolence and generosity; Cato for integrity of life. The former was made famous by his compassion and mercy; intolerance added to the latter's stature. They both attained glory: Caesar by giving, helping, forgiving; Cato by not bribing. In one there was refuge for the wretched, the other death for the wicked. Caesar's easy disposition was praised, Cato's steadfastness. Finally, Caesar's heartfelt purpose was to work hard, to be vigilant, to neglect his own interests while being devoted to his friends', and to deny nothing that was proper to give; for himself he longed for a great command, an army, a new war in which his excellence could shine. But Cato's drive was for self-restraint, propriety, moral absolutism. He did not compete with the wealthy in wealth or with the partisans in partisanship; he competed with the fervent in virtue, with the restrained in moderation, with the blameless in abstinence; he preferred to be good than to seem good; and so, the less he sought renown, the more it followed him.

Naturally we cannot accept these characterizations at face value. Sallust was a supporter of Caesar and indeed profited at a high level from his patronage – he was the commander of a legion under Caesar and supported him in the coming civil wars – thus he sought to paint only the positives in his histories which he wrote in his retirement. We are fortunate to have them as contemporary sources, but his work must be treated with the usual cautionary intake of breath and pauses. Sallust's characterisations of both Caesar and Cato are superficial, but are what most people would have recognized at the time. There is little forensic analysis in his work and his writing style has been described as having an antipathy to Cicero – Sallust gets to the point in his condensed and often severe way as opposed to the opulence of Cicero's writing, but in that way leaves a great deal unsaid.

Sallust saw the collapse of the Republic in real time and it was no doubt extremely hard to capture the substantive causes with all that surrounded him – he had little benefit of hindsight or evidence other than the judgements he himself made. A good example is that Sallust saw the moral decline of the Republic as the main cause and was unable to see the far wider and deeper manifestations of decay. Nevertheless, we do have an eyewitness to the friction between Cato and Caesar and their vastly different stance on the same issues as in the case of the Nepos proposal. Cato saw another Catiline in Caesar as Drogula states:

Like Catiline, Caesar was in a difficult situation: if he did not reach the consulship and receive a further lucrative command, his debts would crush his family [those incurred from Crassus for the bribery and feasting of the people need for his election as Pontifex Maximus] *sending it into permanent obscurity.*

The two men were on a collision course, with Cato on a mission to restore values to the Republic and fight corruption and Caesar, who had already proven his willingness to corrupt anything in his election as Pontifex Maximus. Cato had already locked horns with Caesar over Catiline and when he became tribune officially in December 63, he proposed a new *popularis* measure to give cheaper corn to the people of Rome – this was a clear attempt to pull the rug from under Caesar and secure the Senate's standing in Rome itself. This bill, the *lex frumentaria* was enacted quickly and before Caesar took his own office on 1 January 62. At some additional 30 million sesterces a year, this measure was very costly to the state treasury, but it was hoped it could be paid for once trade with the east opened up again thanks to Pompey, and it was worth it to undercut Caesar's progress as hero of the people. There is one other point to note – the fact that this was needed at all adds to the picture of a nation and city in dire economic straits just as Catiline and others had claimed – the rich were getting richer and the poor were starving.

In the Senate, Cato spoke vehemently, even irrationally, against the proposal to allow Pompey to stand as consul whilst still in the east. Nepos did no better but the Senate, uneasy about either direction, eventually sided with Cato. Nepos then went into the forum and the streets agitating for the Assembly of the People (the Plebian assembly) to come together to support this act and the Assembly did indeed meet in the forum in the shadow of the great temple of Castor and Pollux at the southeastern end of the forum – only a short number of yards from the new Pontifex Maximus' home, the *domus publica*. As Cato arrived, he saw a crowd sitting on benches on the top steps of the temple and at the centre were both Caesar and Nepos and he had been warned that many senior senators had changed their minds (no doubt encouraged by Caesar and Nepos regarding how grateful Pompey would be to them). As was his abrupt way, Cato strode up the steps directly towards them accompanied by a fellow courageous tribune Q. Minucius Thermus, togas flowing and faces fixed on them both and pushed their way onto the bench where they were sitting and forced his way in between them so they could not communicate. As a tribune he was quite within his rights to be there and was not afraid to show the whole of Rome how he felt, despite the armed men and atmosphere that changed into a mix of cheers for his courage and anger that he had turned up at all. Plutarch relates how:

> *When the people were about to vote on the law, in favour of Metellus* [Nepos]
> *there were armed strangers and gladiators and servants drawn up in the*
> *forum, and that part of the people which longed for Pompey in their hope of a*

change was present in large numbers, and there was strong support also from Caesar, who was at that time praetor [and Pontifex].

A climactic moment then followed, and as the clerk stood to read the bill, Cato shouted his veto – again which was his right as tribune, just as Nepos had stopped Cicero from speaking a few weeks earlier. When Nepos grabbed the document and continued, Cato stood and grabbed it back and a fight ensued on the steps of the temple – a riot followed in the forum with the armed Gladiators part of the melee. The fighting continued, but Cato won the day as the Assembly was unable to sit, but this was an indication of just how volatile relations were in the Republic and how hard it would be for those in the moderate camp to hold both sides together. The elastic band of democracy, mentioned in an earlier chapter, was being stretched to breaking point just as Pompey arrived back in Rome.

Chapter 15

The Return of Pompey

The man of knowledge must be able to love his enemies, but also to hate his friends.

Frederick Nietzsche

The aftermath of the executions

If Pompey could have been in two places at once, then he would have been. The war against Mithridates was nearing its end and events in Rome were creating the opportunity he craved – to return, to save and stabilize Rome and, like Cicero also hoped for himself, to be seen as the saviour of the state. The main difference between these two men being that Pompey wanted to be asked to do it whereas Cicero had created a certain current for himself.

For Cicero, the post-consular year of 62 had been troubling. He had returned to his legal work, but was also balancing this with trying to retain the status, which he believed he had, of the senior statesman of Rome. But he now had far more enemies than before – the execution of the so-called conspirators had exposed his vulnerability and unpopularity with some elements of the Senate and, in his endeavours to hold the statesmanlike line he recognized that opposition was growing. A letter to him from Q. Metellus Celer, brother of Caecilius Metellus Nepos who had such clashes with Cato, was blunt and to the point:

Metellus Celer to Cicero
Cisalpine Gaul, 12 January 62

Greetings. I hope you are well!

In view of our reciprocal statements and the restoration of our friendly relations I had not expected that I should ever be held up by you to offensive ridicule in my absence, or that my brother Metellus would be attacked at your instance in person or estate because of a phrase. If his own honourable character did not suffice for his protection, the dignity of our family and my zeal on behalf of you and your friends and the commonwealth should have been support enough. Now it seems that he has been beset, and I deserted, by those whom it least behoved.

So wear the black of mourning – I in command of a province and an army conducting a war! ... I did not think to find your own disposition so changeable towards me and mine.

The context of the letter was that in the hostility Metellus Nepos had shown towards Cicero since becoming tribune of the plebs in December 63, not only had Nepos requested that Cicero be indicted on a charge of murder (this failed) for the execution of the conspirators, Metellus Nepos, as we have seen, also stopped Cicero from speaking in his final address and then tried in January 62 to force through a bill allowing Pompey, to whom he was related, to stand for consul while away from Rome. Cicero for his part had spoken harshly against Nepos which resulted in this letter of criticism from Metellus Celer which would have been written in his camp in Gaul and carried by riders down the main roads to Rome over a journey of about four days.

We have an indication of just how quickly communications could work across the empire – if money and status was available – in that Cicero responded in typically verbose style with a very long explanation of why Celer had misinterpreted what had happened. Cicero pointed out in rather patronizing tones that his brotherly love was understandable, but he should realize that he was only in Gaul as commander as he had appointed him and because he himself had declined to accept one of the two pro-consular options on offer (Macedonia and Cisalpine Gaul) and that the two of them had both acted as saviours of the nation – Cicero had saved Rome and Celer had saved Etruria and the provinces. What this had to do with anything is unclear. Was the point that Cicero had been generous to Celer therefore he should back off from daring to criticize him? Furthermore, Cicero said he had nothing but affection for the family. The following excerpts show how well Cicero dealt with this criticism and what set him so far apart from most with his eloquence, logic and how language was his weapon of choice:

Cicero to Metellus Celer
Rome, Mid January 62

I suspect you have heard a report to the effect that, while arguing in the Senate that there were very many who regretted my saving of the commonwealth, I remarked that relatives of yours, to whom they could not say no, had prevailed upon you to suppress what you had decided you ought to say in the Senate in commendation of myself. In making this observation, I added that you and I had made a division of duty in the preservation of the commonwealth: my part was to guard Rome from domestic plots and the enemy within the gates, yours to protect Italy from armed forces and underground conspiracy. This partnership of ours in so vital and splendid a task had been impaired by relatives of yours, who feared you might make me some gesture of mutual goodwill in response to the ungrudging warmth of my tributes to yourself.

As if that was not enough of a warm rebuke, it was merely the start:

If I were to say that I forwent a province for your sake, you would think me less than sincere. It suited my purpose to do so, and I draw more pleasure and profit every day from my decision. What I do say is, that having announced the relinquishment of my province at a public meeting, I lost no time in planning how to transfer it to you.

In respect to how Metellus had prevented Cicero from giving his final oration as consul, Cicero could not but search for the moral high ground and continuing justification for what he had done:

When I learned that he was planning and preparing his entire programme as tribune with a view to my destruction, I addressed myself to your lady wife Claudia and your sister Mucia [Mucia was at this time still married to Pompey hence the closeness of Metellus and his efforts on his brother in law's behalf – this marriage was about to end, as was the relationship that Metellus had with Pompey] *(her friendly disposition towards me as a friend of Cn.Pompeius had been plain to me in many connections) and asked them to persuade him to give up his injurious design. And yet, on the last day of the year, as I am sure you have heard, he put upon me, consul and saviour of the commonwealth, an insult which has never been put on any holder of any magistracy, no matter how disloyal: he deprived me of the power to address an assembly before retiring from office. This affront, however, redounded greatly to my honour. In face of his refusal to let me do more than take the oath, I swore in loud tones the truest and finest oath that ever was, and the people likewise in loud tones swore that I had sworn the truth.*

We can only surmise how Celer reacted to this epistle from Cicero. Reading more like a legal brief and with overtones of fawning and sycophantic phraseology, Cicero displayed both his magisterial position along with magisterial vocabulary and reasoning. It is hard not to be impressed, but also hard not to feel a sense of self justification or approval far in excess of what was needed. Cicero would go on defending his actions and needing, if not demanding, acclamation in the years ahead for the events surrounding the Catiline executions in Rome; this was to be the cross that he had to bear and that he had manufactured for himself.

As for Pompey, Cicero needed and wanted his admiration. The need may have its roots in a maldeveloped sense of self-esteem whereas the want was essential to any political future when Pompey returned. If we need further evidence of the former, that is that Cicero may have exhibited a less than authentic character in order to present to his peers what he thought they wanted to see, then we can look in detail at a very carefully worded letter to Pompey in April 62. The glowing report submitted by Pompey to the Senate on his successes in Asia had one obvious omission – Pompey failed, no doubt deliberately, to make mention of, let alone commend Cicero for his actions in respect to 'saving' Rome from Catiline and his plans. For someone with a maldeveloped sense of self-esteem this would represent something of a crisis. The drive for abandoning our true nature in order to derive approval from others is a soul defeating exercise because whatever approval we get, it is never enough. In so much of Cicero's more personal correspondence, as in many of his speeches, there are clues that suggest he was indeed a very needy man in constant search of acclaim.

Marcus Tullius Cicero, son of Marcus, to Gnaeus Pompeius Magnus,
son of Gnaeus, Imperator, greetings.
Rome, April 62

I hope all is well with you and the army, as it is with me.

Like the rest of us I was immeasurably delighted with your dispatch, in which you hold out the bright prospect of a peaceful future; such a prospect as I have ever been promising to all and sundry in reliance on your single self. I must tell you, however, that it came as a severe blow to your old enemies, nowadays your friends; their high hopes dashed, they despond.

Your personal letter to me evinces but little of your friendly sentiments towards me, but you may be sure that it gave me pleasure all the same. My chief joy is apt to lie in the consciousness of my services to others. If these fail of a like response, I am perfectly content that the balance of good offices should rest on my side. I have no doubt that if my own hearty goodwill towards you does not suffice to win your attachment, the public interest will join us in confederacy.

[I have been telling everyone how great you are and that you will sort out the problems in the east all on your own. Your success has really put a spanner in the works for Caesar and Crassus – they hoped that you would be stuck in the east forever. However, I wish you could be more friendly towards me but your hints are enough for me to know you like me. Anyway, I don't mind being the more friendly one – after all – we both work for the good of the state so we have that in common – don't we?]

Not to leave you in ignorance of the particular in which your letter has disappointed me, let me speak plainly, as becomes my character and our friendly relations. My achievements have been such that I expected to find a word of congratulation upon them in your letter, both for friendship's sake and that of the commonwealth. I imagine you omitted anything of the sort for fear of giving any offence in any quarter. But I must tell you that what I have done for the safety of the country stands approved in the judgement and testimony of the whole world. When you return, you will find that I have acted with a measure of policy and a lack of self-regard which will make you well content to have me as your political ally and private friend – a not much lesser Laelius to a far greater Africanus.

[In case you are asking yourself why I am disappointed, well you know me, I am a lawyer and always get to the point quickly (!) and clearly so you need to know I am very annoyed and upset that you have not praised my efforts especially as we are such close friends. I expect it was because you are frightened of what Caesar might say if he knew! But, just in case you were in any doubt, the whole world agreed with what I did and when you get home you will realize what an asset I will be as your friend and to guide you in politics – just like Laelius did for Africanus – although you stand much higher than him in history of course].

This letter helps to clarify the relationship between Cicero and Pompey at this time. Cicero was at great pains to justify his actions, point out to Pompey that everyone agreed with his decisions and that he would be wise to strengthen their friendship on his return. The longing for acceptance and endorsement is obvious and this in turn reflects how vulnerable Cicero felt if Pompey were to continue to ease him out of the way – as clearly Nepos had tried to do on numerous occasions acting on Pompey's instructions.

The Good Goddess scandal and Pretty Boy

One of the most notorious events of 62 occurred towards the end of the year and concerned the young, rebellious and, as we know, largely poor, Publius

Clodius Pulcher – the new man in Fulvia's life. Clodius cared little for the proper formalities and protocols of living amongst the noble families in the city, nor did he have much control over his often-reckless temperament. Sallust was explicit in his condemnation of the younger set at that time:

Men prostituted themselves like women, and women sold their chastity at every corner. To please their palates, they ransacked land and sea. They were to bed before they needed to sleep, and instead of waiting until they felt hungry, thirsty, cold or tired, they forestalled their bodies' needs by self-indulgence.

Roman literature is enriched by our ability to read about the debauched activities of these young people as an antidote to politics which surrounds the history of the period and equally suffocated their lives. Expectation and honour were everything, and sometimes that strain showed itself. Clodius was well known in this circle, but others had their moments. Marcus Antonius (son of the great orator of the same name, stepson of Lentullus and future general under Caesar) accrued huge debts as a young man and in later years was the subject of one of Cicero's speeches where Cicero said of him:

You [Marcus Antonius] *assumed a man's toga and turned it into a prostitute's frock. At first you were a common rent boy; you charged a fixed fee, and a steep one at that. Curio soon turned up, though, and took you off the game. You were as firmly wedded to Curio as if he had given you a woman's dress.*

The poet Catullus wrote of his lost love Clodia, elder of Clodius' three sisters recording her loose morals and sexual misconduct recounting in a poem how she would hang around the crossroads at night ready to toss off the generous sons of Rome. So Clodius was far from alone in his circles, but he was somewhat unique in that he was also politically ambitious.

The festival of the Good Goddess was held every year at the start of December. A very secret ceremony held in the house of a very senior official, chosen by discussion, formed part of the celebrations and was attended by the Vestal Virgins. In 63, Terentia and Cicero had hosted the ceremony, but this year it fell to Caesar and was held in the official house of the Pontifex just to the side of the forum. Clodius had fallen in love with Caesar's wife Pompeia and, for whatever impetuous reason thought he could dress as a woman, enter Caesar's house and not get caught. He was wrong. Cicero wrote to Atticus with glee, especially as Clodius had needed the help of a servant girl to escape, but the scandal rocked Rome. Religion was not something to be mocked, it was a core belief in all that mattered and Clodius was in real trouble. Cicero, surprisingly, was ambivalent towards this activity. Despite his war of words on declining moral standards and the decay of *virtus* in the modern age of the Republic, he was also understanding of, if not even affectionate towards, younger men – seeing them perhaps as his protégés rather than in any homosexual way and for which there is little evidence save a love poem to Tiro, which could be interpreted in a number of ways other than a homosexual act. The most notorious of those young men he patronized would be Octavianus, later to become Emperor Augustus.

In the case of the Good Goddess and the invasion of Caesar's home, however, matters were very different. Caesar divorced his wife very quickly, admitting that she may have been innocent, but that was not enough for him, the atmosphere it created around him was what mattered. What mattered most to Cicero was the relationship with his wife. He spent so much time talking to Fulvia, gleaning information and reconnaissance, that Roman tongues wagged and he needed to make sure that Terentia understood that his relationship with Fulvia was merely political and not in any way emotional – and as far as we know that was the case. The Senate were perplexed about what to do – a trial would inflame the *populares* in Rome and of course stir up further enmity against them, fuelling further protests about them being out of date and corrupt, but they could not ignore what Clodius had done. The compromise was a decree from the Senate to the popular assembly that a tribunal be set up to try the case. This all fell apart when, on the day of the assembly meeting, Cicero tells us that *'there was a flocking together of our goateed young bloods'* and a riot was on the cards so that it was not until the following year that the matter was once more debated.

In the meantime, and to keep up appearances and his high station in Rome, Cicero had invested 3,500,000 sesterces of borrowed money on the purchase of a wonderful property on the Palatine Hill. Antonius had begun, at last, to deliver Cicero's cut of the profits and plunder of Macedonia into his hands and he was able to pay back Crassus for the money he had loaned to him to buy Crassus' own house.

As for the rather ridiculous episode of Roman cross-dressing, what does this matter to this assessment of the life of Cicero and the lessons we might learn from the decay and collapse of democracy? It matters because when the state establishment feels intimidated by its own children and fails to act as any parent would, then a breakdown of control is not far away. Although there are no actual children in this episode, we can take 'children' also to mean those brought up by any democratic state. Whether part of a family or the inhabitants of a state, children fail to show any understanding of how the world in which they live has been created, the lives of millions sacrificed to defend it or the responsibilities of maintaining it.

Not even 100 years before, such openly disruptive behaviour and intimidation of the people and the Senate would never have happened and the same is true today. The punishment would have been swift and brutal. The elastic band of liberal tolerance is always being tested, new horizons opened up, new words entering the vocabulary and this was yet another such test for the Republic just as Extinction Rebellion and many other social protest groups are for modern liberal democracy. We share a certain sympathy with Extinction Rebellion just as the senators did, we share an awareness of impotence when it comes to the unorthodox methods being used to demonstrate unhappiness with the state and we also share anger that we seem to be out of step with the youth of our respective worlds. However, we can also see how modern protest fails to appreciate what it is they threaten, how fragile freedom is and how weak government can be in response. In the precise case of Cicero, that misplaced arrogance is not something restricted to young people. When the case resumed in July 61 the whole matter was resolved by Crassus and his money, bribing more jurors to lose their reputations than those that wished to retain them and Clodius Pulcher was acquitted, but not before Cicero had ruined his relationship with him and made another enemy by giving Clodius the nickname 'pretty boy' as *pulcher* was the Latin for beautiful or attractive and was the *cognomen* much used by the Clodian family and indeed where we today derive the word pulchritude.

Apparently, it was Terentia that wanted Clodius found guilty and his main defence of not being in Rome on the day of the ceremony was upended by Cicero, the consul, the unbribable man, the saviour of his country and intimidated by Terentia, stating that he lied – and that he had seen him in Rome on the day of the event. This angered Clodius of course and Cicero told Atticus:

> *Our little beauty* [Clodius] *gets on his feet and accuses me of having been at Baiae – not true, but anyhow.... 'Well', I reply, 'is that like saying I intruded on the Mysteries?'* [the Good Goddess ceremony]. *'How long' cried he, 'are we going to put up with this king?' 'You talk about kings', I answered, 'when rex didn't have a word to say about you?'* [That Clodius could be so openly accusative of Cicero behaving like a king does suggest that many felt that he was viewed by many as behaving like one. The accusative *rex* was a reference to Clodius' brother-in-law Q. Marcius Rex who was consul in 68 and left him nothing in his will – this was a really barbed comment from Cicero and would have cut deeply.] *'So, you've bought a house' said he. I re-joined, 'One might think that I had bought a jury'......The roars of applause were too much for him and he collapsed into silence.*

Cicero further ridiculing and humiliating Clodius so sarcastically in public has distinct echoes of how he treated Catiline. With his man on the ropes, fumbling for words to punch back, Cicero piles in the invective with sword cuts so sharp and so witty that he not only humbles, but demeans and embarrasses his opponent. Any respect for his prosecution is destroyed by the hatred of the humiliation that Cicero was able to pile on to a beaten man. Cicero, using his tremendous intelligence, overstepped the mark repeatedly and hubris took over. The essential lawyer came to the surface, as if he was unable to contain his undoubted skill for debasing his perceived opponents, so much so that he often overestimated his own ability to contain and crush others – he made enemies not so much politically but, more dangerously, personally. This need to prove oneself, to achieve victory at all costs suggests an occasional loss of contact with reality, perhaps brought on by stress or anxiety as the ability to berate a challenger dominated the common decency of humility. Cicero so often claimed that he was humble, but he simply was not. The cross-dressing affair should not have had any lasting impact on Cicero, but his mishandling of Clodius in fact resulted in massive collateral damage. Clodius never forgave Cicero for calling him 'pretty-boy' to his face or for his witty insults – neither did he forget, and he would have his revenge.

The arrival of Pompey

Somewhere between the end of December 62 and January 61, Pompey at last landed at the busy and vital Roman port of Brundisium. Situated on the back of the heel of Italy and today modern-day Brindisi, a vast amount of trade and shipping of all sorts came and went from this vital port. Brundisium was hectic and packed with the usual flotsam of any port in the world, in addition there was a cultural mix probably unequalled anywhere in the world at that time derived from the vast number of trading ships coming and going from all parts of the known world.

Imagine the scene then when the ship and accompanying vessels carrying Pompey, who had been away for nearly six years expanding the empire, was spotted on the horizon. The great man had been expected for weeks and, as the news went out from Brundisium by word of mouth, so messengers were despatched directly to Rome. The Stanford University ORBIS calculator suggests that the fastest route by horse relay would take just over two days to arrive at the Senate and no doubt Rome became alive with rumours of what might develop next.

For Cicero, the return of Pompey had been on his mind for years. Pompey was a shadow image for him to try to emulate, the brightest star for Cicero to equal in magnificence and a reputation he had tried to equal. Clearly his superior in intellect, but his subordinate in glorious ventures, Cicero always knew that one day he would have to prove himself the master of Pompey if he was to remain at the forefront of Republican political life, or else retreat into the dusty shadows of the back row of the Senate.

Thousands of Pompey's men arrived by ship into Brundisium each day, disembarking onto home soil after so many years to greetings, cheers, congratulations, each loaded down with their armour, chain mail, weapons and shields, some kneeling and giving thanks to the gods for bringing them home safely, others no doubt with memories of those they had buried across Asia. This army had done great things. Writing much later, the Greek historian Appian, who in fact worked in Rome for much of his life as an advocate just like Cicero had done, wrote numerous books, many of which have not survived. One that did, however, was his *The Foreign Wars* and part of this series of detailed accounts contains Appian's 3rd Mithridatic War.

History may have largely forgotten the nameless legionary soldiers who actually built the empire through blood, sweat and toil, but their sandals marched thousands of miles under Pompey and added riches beyond belief to the Republic. They also profited quite well themselves as vanquished kings one after the other gave tributes to Pompey, his legates, tribunes, centurions and legionaries – it was the promise of rich rewards from plunder rather than the salary that motivated an army. Appian recounts how Pompey and his men marched through modern day Georgia, through Turkey, across Syria and as far south as Egypt. Eventually Mithridates was cornered. After nearly fifty years of fighting the Romans, he was not going to be captured and paraded as a trophy through Rome as part of Pompey's Triumph and decided to commit suicide. His two daughters, Mithridates and Nyssa, pleaded with him to let them die first and took poison which quickly did its work. For Mithridates the King and their father, things did not go as planned. Watching his daughters die he too took poison, but after a lifetime of preparing to resist poisons, his body would not die, Appian continued:

> *Seeing a certain Bituitus there, an officer of the Gauls, he said I have profited much from your right arm against my enemies, I shall profit from it most of all if you will kill me, and save me from the danger of being led in a Roman Triumph.*

Seeing the body of his adversary for the past six years, Pompey commanded that he be buried as a king and even paid for the ceremony himself.

On a later part of the campaign, while Cicero was consul in 63, Pompey headed south and conquered large parts of modern-day Israel. Josephus, a Roman-Jewish writer of the first century CE who accompanied Titus, son of the Emperor Vespasian, on the second siege of Jerusalem in 70 CE looks back to the first siege 100 years before in his histories:

And when he [Pompey] *was come to the city* [Jerusalem], *he looked about where he might attack: for he saw the walls so firm, that it would be hard to overcome them: and that the valley before the walls was terrible; and that the temple, which was within that valley, was itself encompassed with a very strong wall.*

Pompey successfully laid siege to Jerusalem and bombarded the walls with his catapults – some of these boulders are being discovered by archaeological excavations today. Pompey then had walked in the holiest of holies in the Jewish temple and saw many of the great Jewish treasures – the Jews were lucky on that occasion, as Pompey had no desire to inflame further insurrections, but this was not the case when Titus walked in the same place and took everything from the Jews, in stark contrast to making friends out of the conquered, as Pompey had tried to do.

Alongside annexing territories directly to Rome and setting up direct control, Pompey also created client states wherever he could rely on a local ruler – this was the case in Galilee and Judea, laying the foundations for the Biblical predictions of the coming of Jesus. In Israel alone, Pompey was able to secure many tons of silver and gold which was all sent under guard to the treasury in Rome.

While it is undeniable that Pompey was a talented and charismatic commander, these attributes alone would not account for the military success that he achieved. There had been many notable charismatic generals before him and there was an even better one waiting in the Senate for his own opportunity. What gave Pompey a distinct edge over his predecessors was that he led a completely reformed military machine. The Marian reforms restructured the army from mainly militia-based formations into standing units of professional soldiers and created new numbered legions that did not disperse at the end of every campaign. Of course, there were sizable financial costs to the state, but the benefits far outweighed the extra tax revenue that was needed. The esprit de corps was central in these new legions, binding men together to fight for each other as well as their commanders, additionally the accumulated experience of campaign life and battle was preserved and passed on to new recruits. Central to the whole structure were the professional centurions. Veterans of numerous campaigns and with honour crests and badges to prove it, these men ran the battle and the daily life of the legion and supported the constant flow of new officers serving their time from Rome. The *legati* were chosen by governors to serve in legions and gain the military experience so essential to political promotion – but it was the centurions who made the real difference. Thus, Pompey was able to conduct his campaign against Mithridates with probably the finest, best equipped, and best trained Roman army that ever took the field.

Contemporary sources suggest that Pompey took his time returning to Rome. Plutarch says that Pompey travelled *'as if he were coming back from a foreign holiday'* – the most famous man in the Roman world accompanied by just a few friends. But before he left for Rome, Pompey made a decision to disband his army and so, over many days, he gave many orations, recounted many tales and said goodbye to men who had fought and bled for him. These legionaries, like Sulla's army thirty years previously, took their weapons and their fealty for their overlord with them. A legionary's bond with their commander could be fickle, but it could also be the total opposite, and Pompey would be able to rely on the feudal loyalty of his veterans for the rest of his life.

Disbandment was a huge relief to the Senate. Again, they would have received news of this development via regular couriers riding up and down the main route to the port, which was the *Via Appia,* there was to be no march on Rome, no great dictator taking over the state and instead Pompey became celebrated as perhaps the greatest hero of the Republic – his past misdemeanours and flouting of constitutional rules conveniently forgotten by most – but not by Cato.

Cicero watched and weighed up Pompey in the coming months of 61 – as did everybody else. Pompey made it plain that he had two main objectives from the Senate. Firstly, he wanted his wide-ranging settlements and agreements made in his conquered territories to be ratified – he had made many promises, connections and agreements which needed to be signed off. Secondly, he was determined that the veterans be given land for their service and retirement. Pompey had laid plans in advance, and his nominee Pupius Piso was now consul for 61, which gave Pompey a distinct advantage. So where did Cicero figure in Pompey's plans now that he was back in person? We have a first indication in that Piso relegated Cicero to second place in senatorial debates which was a slap in the face for the saviour of Rome – although Cicero tried to pretend to Atticus that he really was not bothered at all when he wrote to his friend who had now said his goodbyes after three tumultuous years advising Cicero and was now back in Epirus living a quieter life:

Cicero to Atticus
Rome, January 25 61

Since you left me there are things that well deserve a letter of mine, but I must not expose such to the risk of getting lost or opened or intercepted. First then you may care to know that I have not been given first voice in the Senate, the pacifier of the Allobroges [Gaius Piso a kinsman of the consul] *being put in front of me – at which the house murmured, but I myself was not sorry. I am therefore relieved of any obligation to be civil to a cross-grained individual, and left free to maintain my political standing in opposition to his wishes. Moreover, the second place carries almost as much prestige as the first, while one's inclinations are not too much fettered by one's sense of the consular favour. Catulus comes third, Hortensius, if you are still interested, fourth. The consul himself is of petty and perverse mentality, given to the sort of peevish sneer that raises a laugh even in the absence of any wit.*

Later in the same letter Cicero moved on to relations with Pompey and revealed his true feelings for the man to whom he had written less than a year before professing his support, affection and friendship:

As to that friend of yours (you know whom I mean? The person of whom you write to me that he began to praise when he no longer dared to criticise), he professes the highest regard for me and makes a parade of warm affection, praising on the surface, while below it (but not so far below that it's difficult to see) he's jealous. Awkward, tortuous, politically paltry, shabby, timid, disingenuous – but I shall go more into detail on another occasion.

Hardly what one might expect in terms of objectivity and a good insight into the very personal relationships between the senators of the late Republican period. So much political power rested on personal status and survival that policies and strategy were of far less significance. There were no political parties as such where one might feel safety in numbers, instead popularity and plotting ran parallel to each other and those less able were wise to stay out of the limelight as some modern-day politicians would do well to recognise. Within two weeks, Cicero was again writing to Atticus at some length, but this time with a completely different tone and containing some wonderful imagery for us to peer back 2,000 years into the life of Rome:

Cicero to Atticus
Rome, 13 February 61

An irresponsible tribune, Fulfius, egged on by consul Piso, called Pompey out to address the Assembly. This took place in the Flaminian Circus, on market day just where the holiday crowd was gathered.

Imagine for a moment the adulation for Pompey as he walked in the market, being so close to the great man himself, as if we were in touching distance of a mix of Barack Obama and Elton John, Pompey in his bright white toga with golden cords and his adoring followers always close by. These lines show just how approachable and close everything was in Rome, there was no motorcade, FBI security, barricades, or bullet proof glass, and speaking to the 'dregs' as Cicero sometimes referred to the bottom of society was, in its way, as important as speaking to the most noble of senators.

Subsequently consul Messalla [co consul with Piso] *asked Pompey in the Senate for his views* [on the bill to try Clodius in the Good Goddess affair] *about the sacrilege and the promulgated bill. He then addressed the Senate, commending in general terms all decrees of that body, and remarked to me as he sat down beside me that he hoped he had now replied sufficiently to questioning on these matters. When Crassus saw that Pompey had netted some credit from the general impression that he approved of my consulship, he got to his feet and held forth on the subject in most encomiastic terms, going so far as to say that it was to me he owed his status as a senator and a citizen, his freedom, his very life. Whenever he saw his wife or his house or the city of his birth, he saw a gift of mine.... This day's work has brought me very close to Crassus, not but what I was glad enough to take whatever tribute Pompey more or less obliquely vouchsafed.*

Still searching for Pompey's true feelings and for his endorsement, Cicero writes like a desperate man trying to persuade Atticus that all is now well and that to his great relief Pompey has, more or less, obliquely approved what Cicero had done in the Catiline affair. Pompey was not an eloquent speaker and certainly did not enjoy soap boxing in the forum and found speaking to the Senate little better. That Pompey was in support of Cicero's measures may not have actually been true at all, but we often hear what we want to hear rather than what has been said. Equally, the praise heaped upon Cicero came as a welcome surprise to his vanity and anxiety – even though he knew full well he was kidding himself if he thought Crassus was genuine about anything.

Elation took over and in a significant feat of self-congratulation Cicero told Atticus that:

> *I brought the house down. And why not, on such a theme – the dignity of our order, concord between Senate and equites, unison of Italy, remnants of the conspiracy in their death-throes, reduced price of grain, internal peace? You should know by now how I can boom away on such topics. I think you must have caught the reverberations in Epirus.*

And so with these relaxing thoughts in his mind, Cicero was able to take a deep breath, sigh and believe that all was well and finally, in the concluding sentence of a very long letter largely about himself, his problems and his ambitions, he wondered how Atticus was getting along. Around this time in the middle of 61, Cicero's brother Quintus was appointed to a provincial governorship in Asia. It was most likely that Cicero had a hand in arranging the necessary support for his brother and his credit was strong enough to pat the right backs and praise the right egos. Quintus had served as Plebian aedile in 65 and praetor in 62. As an administrator, Quintus is regarded as ruthless and efficient – a rather old school governor who ordered punishments that were overzealous and cruel. His emotional state was notorious for being in such contrast to his brother – hot tempered, tactless and outspoken, but his heart was in the right place and he was, as most younger brothers can testify, always in the shadow of his elder brother and the frustrations of never being regarded as good enough spilled over into his daily life – taken out on others.

But all would never be well and, as if to illustrate just how reliable Crassus was in regards to probity, good governance and the stability of the Republic, within a matter of weeks, over the summer in fact, the trial of Clodius took place and, as we know, the matter was ended by manipulation of the jury and widescale bribery by Crassus, and Clodius escaped any sort of punishment. Cicero should not have been surprised, but still he obliterated any regard he had for Crassus in a letter to Atticus in the July of 61:

> *As soon as the jury took their seats, honest men feared the worst. A more raffish assemblage never sat down in a low-grade music hall – fly blown senators, beggar Knights, and Paymaster tribunes who might better have been called 'Paytakers'. Even so, there were a few honest men whom the accused had not been able to drive off at the challenge. There they sat, gloomy and shamefaced in this incongruous company, sadly uncomfortable at their exposure to such a miasma of disreputability.*

> *You know Baldhead, my encomiast, of whose complimentary speech I wrote*
> *to you. Inside a couple of days, with a single slave (an ex-gladiator at that) for*
> *go between, he settled the whole business – called them [the jurors] to his house,*
> *made promises, backed bills, or paid cash down. On top of that (it's really too*
> *abominable) some jurors actually received a bonus in the form of assignations*
> *with certain ladies or introductions to youths of noble family.*

It was on 30 September 61 – Pompey's birthday – that the much-anticipated Triumph for Pompeius began, and what a show he put on for the people of Rome. Around the central part of the city and along the Via Sacra wooden stands and seating was erected and also in the Forum itself, which is where the parades would finish. The temples were opened and decorated, great houses invited guests to watch from their gardens and terraces, the poorer citizens planned feasts as best they could and it was a national holiday – festivity was everywhere. The planning must have taken weeks and involved many parts of the government and meetings with Pompey himself. On the day itself, the massive procession lined up along the route outside the city and began its march, crossing the boundary of the city, the *pomoerium* and now, flanked by tens of thousands of cheering and waving men, women and children, Pompey began his grand march into Rome as Plutarch accounts:

> *He was awarded a Triumph exceeding in brilliance any that had gone*
> *before...it occupied two successive days, and many nations were represented*
> *in the procession.*
>
> *Among these peoples no less than 1,000 strongholds had been captured,*
> *according to the inscriptions, and cities not much under 900 in number, besides*
> *800 piratical ships, while 39 cities had been founded...but that which most*
> *enhanced his glory and had never been the lot of any Roman before, was that*
> *he celebrated a third Triumph over the third continent...his first over Libya,*
> *his second over Europe and his last over Asia.*

No doubt many of Pompey's legionaries would have made their way to Rome and formed up outside the city as part of the parade, his officers and his precious centurions with their polished steel helmets, shields and blood red cloaks, in their thousands they marched through Rome to the cheers and adoration of the people. The noise of trumpets and music must have been deafening. On day two, prisoners of war were brought through the streets, harangued by the crowds and in chains, they saw the true brutality but also the power of Rome in all its blatant ceremonial and barbaric contrasts. Mithridates should have been there but he was dead, his place was taken by five of his children accompanied by the King of Armenia's wife and son and also the King of the Jews.

All the personalities of this story so far were present: Cicero, Cato, Lucullus, Metellus Celer, Metellus Nepos, Hortensius, Curius, Fulvia, Terentia, Clodius and hundreds of members of the Senate, the noble families and the youthful renegades, all were gathered in their hundreds in the forum to greet the, if not their own, hero. Caesar, however, was not there: as if by fate, he was already away leading his own praetorian command in Spain and demonstrating his own prowess as a general. As the noise intensified, here was the epitome of Rome, harmony amongst the orders, unity and glory and, in front of them along the Via Sacra as its cobbled street snaked towards them with the immense crowds on either side, the gleaming temples, flowers and rose petals strewn across the streets and then, at last, a huge portrait of Pompey appeared, to gasps from the watching crowds. Made entirely of pearls it heralded Pompey himself in a chariot covered in precious stones, on his head the wreath of bay leaves for the hero and a purple toga with golden stars. Imagine if you will his face, painted with red lead to represent Jupiter, king of the gods, but beside him someone whispering in his ear 'Remember that you are human' – it must have been hard to believe that he was.

Chapter 16

Finding his Way in the Wilderness

After climbing a great hill, one only finds that there are many more hills to climb.

Nelson Mandela

I t is always much easier to climb up a ladder than to climb down. This was true for Cicero as he entered his post consular period – there were no more rungs on the *cursus honorum* to climb and he could not stand forever at the top. But coming down the ladder was something he did not want to do so we see the years from 62–58 as transitional ones for Cicero, coming to terms with having reached his personal and career ambitions and working out ways to remain relevant. But of course, the world changes around us, and the backdrop of how we achieved our success in life is not necessarily the same one that we have to survive later on; this was acutely the case for Cicero in his immediate post consular period. Context in history is everything. In the years up to and including 63, Caesar was young and still finding his own momentum, he was also poor and in huge debt, ergo he was not yet a threat. Pompey was away in Asia and would be for almost six whole years, although he was in constant receipt of intelligence, he too was not a threat – he may have sent his acolytes, like Metellus Nepos, to unsettle the Senate, but they were not Pompey. Crassus was devoted to intrigue and money rather than a leadership, and Cicero himself was at the height of his rhetorical powers. However, the old contextual situation changed; Cato became a new power in the Senate for the *optimates* and some of the *nobiles*, Caesar returned a hero from Hispania (Spain), Pompey was back in person, while Crassus remained devoted to conspiracy and his money. The post 63 ladder could only hold so many people at the top at one time and it was inevitable that clashes would come.

Perhaps unsurprisingly, it was Cato who had the most trouble accepting Pompey as a demigod amongst mortals. Despite Cato's resentment towards Pompey's love of power and all the peacock display that went with it, it was hard not be too mightily impressed by what Pompey had achieved. In raw financial terms alone, he had taken the annual tax revenues of the state from 200 million sestertii each year to 340 million and vast amounts of already minted coined money arrived in long guarded wagon trains to be stored and counted in the Treasury. Captured weapons were too many to count, as were the polished gold and silver trophies looted from over a dozen new territories annexed to the empire – John Leach in his book *Pompey the Great* estimates the value of all the booty handed over by Pompey to the Senate as 480 million sesterces. All in all, Pompey had not only solved the current financial crisis affecting Rome and her territories, but he had set her on a new path to expansion unrivalled in the history of the world to that time.

When Pompey reached the end of his processional route at the foot of the Capitoline Hill, he spoke plainly, as was his way, to the assembled crowds of all classes and dedicated 8 million sestertii to the Goddess Minerva. After those gasps at his personal generosity and wealth, he further promised to build a new theatre on the Field of Mars – just to the west of the forum in what were then large flat fields with a large tracked circus marked out for games and racing. In hindsight, although he did not know it, those very moments were the zenith of Pompey's life. To huge applause, cheers, throwing of flowers and acclamations the Triumph ended, the crowds dispersed, and his troubles began.

For Pompey the timing of his two requests from the Senate was all important. He needed to know where support would come from and where the opposition would be. Like the good commander he was, he spent time gathering intelligence and doing his reconnaissance before making his move. When December arrived so too did two more problems, which rather put the timing of his move onto the hard shoulder. The first was that Cato was still incensed by the ability of Crassus to corrupt the legal system and he had proposed a new bill to ramp up and extend the punishment levels for bribery into the equestrian classes – the *Lex Cornelia* had really only provided for punishing nobles for bribery in election and legal matters, but even then, it was rarely used. Although typically morally strong, this proposal caused uproar – tens of thousands of knights and property owners expected bribes at some point in their administration of the law and the state relied on their goodwill for the administration of law in the provinces. Cato successfully undid all the good work that Cicero had done in creating harmony of the orders. As was often the case, Cato had the ability to self-identify with being the champion of the *mos maiorum*, which in turn created an inflexible, alienating presence in the Senate devoid of, or not caring to, build unity, but accuse and point to the morality of his causes. The Senate was often rocked by Cato's demands and, much as they saw him as a bastion against tyranny, lamented his lack of willingness to compromise. The Senate could hardly argue in favour of bribery and so, reluctantly pushed into a corner, approved the bill – though the popular Assembly did not so it never became law.

The graffiti was on the wall

The objective that Cicero was striving for was to retain unity amongst all the classes in Roman society against a backdrop of continual expansion and change. Cato was an immovable object that reminded everyone of what was being lost and stood as an anchor against the decaying standards of political power. But democracy continued to fight back, demand more, expect more and therein we can see Hegelian theory emerging with Pompey, Crassus, Cicero and others exhibiting both their wealth, but especially their *thymos*. As was explored in Chapter 4/Part One, social recognition begins to supersede devotion to a state of equality – something that goes hand in hand with democracy. The growth of empire, an explosion in revenue, wide ranging military superiority all worked against the notion of society working together and encouraged competition between individuals and Cicero was as guilty of this as much as any other. Partly, Cicero was protecting a Republic already riddled with inequality but as that became more obvious, less hidden in the shadows, not so easily brushed under the carpet, then he fought back hence his regard for, but irritation with Cato.

That the Republic was therefore already in real trouble as early as 61 and 60 is not in doubt. Numerous long-term factors had created a state that was already unstable even before the impact of massive administrative and financial growth. The contextual change which saw the presence of a small group of men in Rome at the same time was also crucial – their paths to glory and *auctoritas* had taken different routes, but they had all now arrived at the same crossroads at the same time.

Short term squabbles for power and constant realignments made the situation even more difficult to contain and the longed-for stability seemed impossible. In other words, the elastic band needed to accommodate these new pressures within a democracy was being stretched beyond its limits. But worst of all, reactions to what was developing merely added to the challenges and it was fate that brought numerous important senators to the end of their careers at the very moment that the Republic needed them.

Cato was one of the few committed to saving the spiritual core of the Republic, closely followed by less zealous supporters like Cicero. Both saw the *mos maiorum* as under attack and both saw the decay in standards within public office as potentially terminal, but they came at the problems from a different lineage. Cicero may have saved the Republic (he also may contrive to manipulate events for his own political ends) but no matter how many houses he purchased, he was never going to be accepted as a member of the *nobiles*. Cicero clearly was aware of his 'deficiency', but saw his immense intellect and skills as an orator as equally vital to the salvation of democracy and leadership of the *optimates*. On the other hand, Cato had revered ancestors – his great grandfather, although also a *novus homo*, had been consul, and equally importantly, he had many noble connections and close family friends. His young, conservative blood ran in his veins and it was a natural drift towards Cato and away from Cicero that was to characterize the strategy of the *optimates (*wealthiest classes) and *nobiles* (aristocratic) sections of the Senate – with all that entailed.

The continual political struggles in the Senate were exhausting and it was just not tenable for some important figures to carry on and so it seemed sensible to delegate the struggle to a younger man. The variable of the right people at the right time often appears in history. We can refer to it as fate, lack of succession planning or just bad luck, but whatever name we give to the vital element of chance in history the impact is significant. The Catiline rebellion was not the end of the challenge to democracy, it was just the start – it had been a trial run and now Clodius and his cross-dressing escapades were another – they both led to a shock for the elderly senators and a reactive tightening of restrictions at a time when flexibility and understanding may have been a wiser course. That would have meant strong leadership and there was a shortage of those who wanted to act in the interests of the state and possibly suffer the consequences and those magnetic and charismatic leaders that did exist were rightly viewed with suspicion. Then fate took a turn. Within months, Lucullus retired from politics – he was suffering from indifference to events and retired to a life of luxury and indolence as a mixture of a bitter and fatalistic man. The loss of his *gravitas* and *auctoritas* in the Senate was compounded by the retirement of Hortensius – another substantial figure of reason and standing. To this were added the deaths of Metellus Pius in 63 [a hugely experienced Sullan general, leader of the *optimates* and the distinguished Pontifex Maximus replaced by Caesar], Q. Lutatius Catulus in 62 [another respected leader of the *optimates*, former consul and accuser of Caesar in the Catiline affair], D. Junius Silanus after 62 [consul in 62, supporter of Cicero in the Catiline affair] and Cato's uncle Mamercus Aemilius Lepidus Livianus, who had been consul in 77 and was also a famous military commander and member of the aristocratic *nobiles* party in the Senate.

Recognition that Cato was now a leading force in the Senate came with a proposal of marriage. In a cynical political move, Pompey divorced his then wife Mucia – this caused not a little unrest with her two powerful brothers Metellus Nepos and Metellus Celer. Pompey, in what can be seen as a naïve decision, asked to marry Cato's niece and for another niece to marry Pompey's son. Naturally, Cato saw through this plan to influence him by this alliance and rejected the proposal, leaving Pompey having to plan an alternative route for his sweeping plans. This meant that he drifted in the direction of massaging the ego of Cicero and so all was set for the next stage of developments, meanwhile Cicero found himself wandering in spirit and missing Atticus:

Cicero to Atticus
Rome, 20 January 60

I must tell you that what I most badly need at the present time is a confidante – *someone with whom I could share all that gives me anxiety, a wise, affectionate* *friend to whom I could talk without pretence or evasion or concealment. My* *brother, the soul of our candour and affection, is away* * is not a person at all* [the MSS has the consul Metellus Celer noted for the name but it may have been copied in error], *only 'sea-shore and air' and 'mere solitude'. And* *you, whose talk and advice have so often lightened my worry and vexation of* *spirit, the partner of my public life and intimate of all my private concerns, the* *sharer of my talk and plans, where are you? I am so utterly forsaken that my* *only moments of relaxation are those I spend with my wife, my little daughter* [Tullia] *and my darling Marcus. My brilliant, worldly friendships may* *make a fine show in public, but in the home they are barren things. My house* *is crammed of a morning, I go down to the Forum surrounded by droves of* *friends, but in all the multitude I cannot find one with whom I can pass an* *unguarded joke or fetch a private sigh. This is why I am waiting and longing* *for you, why I now fairly summon you home.*

Domestic problems were a new concern for Cicero, not so much his relationship with Terentia but the temper of his brother Quintus, both as Governor of a province in his own right and as a husband. Problems between Quintus and his wife Pomponia, we recall the sister of Atticus, were becoming more obvious and these tested Cicero and were matters also best discussed with his closest friend.

Caesar's sense of political timing

It was the wont of the immortal gods sometimes to grant prosperity and long *impunity to men whose crimes they were minded to punish in order that a* *complete reverse of fortune might make them suffer more bitterly.*

Caius Julius Caesar

When we assess the character of Caesar we start at a huge disadvantage. Does anyone really ever understand the mind of a genius? Caesar is regarded well in those parts of history that assume, incorrectly, that his well-known clemency was based of some sort of strongly held humanist conviction not to punish his enemies. He constantly, sometimes the same person repeatedly, pardoned his enemies, but not because of some high-minded innocence or sense of honourable decency, but because seeing his ultimate success would punish them more. The quotation above captures his thinking on this point. He was the immortal god that granted impunity – but only so his enemies could see the play full length – not just the opening scenes. When we understand this, we understand a little more of the mind of Caesar and how he was able to control all in his path. Cicero, sadly, was way out of his depth with the man he thought was similar to Pompey – they shared nothing in common.

Atticus replied with concerns over how hard Cicero was trying to reconcile with Pompey – he feared a reaction from Caesar, whose spies were everywhere – often in the same room. However, what Atticus could not know was that this was all part of a grand new plan for Cicero to reposition himself, as he climbed down the ladder, to work within his new contextual situation redefining himself as the friend to all, the trusted counsellor of the great, and controller extraordinaire:

Cicero to Atticus
Rome, June 60

In a mild sort of way you take me to task for my friendly relations with Pompey. I should not wish you to think I had drawn close to him for my own protection.... You may be interested to learn he eulogises my achievements, which many persons had prompted him to attack, in far more glowing terms than his own, acknowledging himself as a good servant of the state but me as its saviour.... Supposing I manage to make a better citizen even of Caesar, who is riding on the crest of a wave just now, am I harming the state so very much?

Thus, as Cicero developed a new role, he saw himself as a moderator and go between, representing the Senate to the *equites*, who were still angered and distanced, but also between the strong personalities and their own orbits and objectives. We should note here just a word of caution. Pompey is rarely regarded in history as a man of acute political sense, but this may be doing him an injustice. He was no longer the arrogant bully of his early 30s, the consul at 35 (in 70) or ignorer of convention. He had matured and fashioned his skills and it could just be that the flattery Cicero had remarked upon when he wrote to Atticus, was him being manipulated by Pompey and not the other way around. If Pompey knew anything about winning wars, it was to identify where the enemy was weak and Cicero certainly had a weakness for flattery and it seems that Pompey was laying it on with a trowel.

So, with his father of the nation epithet, Cicero manoeuvred himself into the good books of all and this is possibly why he mentions Caesar at the end of this letter in the summer of 60. Caesar had just returned a hero from his Governorship of Spain where he had been on campaign for the past year as *propraetor* and was now putting a major effort into his campaign for the consulship for the coming year of 59. However, he had not just wandered back to Rome. Caesar's keen sense of timing and a smell for opportunity meant that he in fact almost ran headlong from Spain. Caesar had a great love for Spain and visited it four times during his life. He had been there as questor in 68, where Suetonius remarked in his *Divine Julius* that Caesar was near Cadiz (*Gades*) when he came across a statue of Alexander in the Temple of Hercules and remarked how he had yet done nothing with his life, although he was the same age as Alexander when the latter had already conquered the world. But for now, he had used surprise and speed to successfully defeat various tribes in the Herminian mountains and waged war wherever he felt like – in line with the authority given by the Senate.

Caesar was acclaimed *Imperator* by his legions, but needed to get back to Rome quickly because there was a deadline if he was to celebrate his Triumph earned in Spain and submit his application, or *professio* to stand for the consular elections in Rome. Thanks to Cato's legislation in 62, which barred Pompey from submitting his name in absentia, Caesar had a dilemma: he could not plan and hold a Triumph in time to then make his *professio* before the due date and he could not make his *professio* without crossing the pomerium and forfeiting his Triumph. In making a request to the Senate for a one-off exemption, Caesar was being reasonable, but Cato erupted and managed to block this request. The expectation was that no commander would give up his Triumph and that he would wait until the following year to try for election, but that is exactly what Caesar did and he forfeited the proudest moment of his career to date in order to enter Rome and submit his *professio*. If senators, Cato especially, needed any evidence of Caesar's true aims, then this was it.

Meanwhile, the consul for 60 was Q. Metellus Celer – he of the frosty exchange of letters with Cicero and returned hero of the defeat of Catiline three years before and, if we recall, half-brother to Mucia, whom Pompey had just divorced. Thus, this was not a good time for Pompey to ask his lieutenant and tribune L. Flavius to introduce the agrarian bill that Pompey had planned in order to fulfil the promise he had made for the distribution of land to his veterans. Yet another tense and destabilizing, not to mention ridiculous, series of events followed whereby Cato and Celer joined to persuade the Senate to object to the measure, not because it could not be afforded or because the land was not available, but through fear of Pompey further increasing his power. Pompey had his own man in Afranius as co-consul, but he does not seem to have been a match for Celer and Cato. History can reflect on whether this was wise or not, but Pompey ignored Afranius and turned instead to Flavius and, using his considerable tribunician powers, had the consul Celer taken to jail. In a show of constitutional solidarity, senators attended Celer through the bars until Flavius then sat on a bench in front of them but, with public opinion turning against him, Pompey called off his hounds and the consul was released. For Pompey this was an unexpected reverse, he had been used to being able to bully the Senate with his popular appeal and aura, but now the gulf that Cicero had hoped he could bridge between Pompey and the Senate was wider than ever. Celer proved himself more than able to withstand a little political turbulence.

Neither was this the end of matters and the year 60 continued as one long political stalemate between Pompey and the Senate. Cato intended to really balance the scales with Pompey by blocking and delaying the latter's settlements in the East. Normal practice in the years before had been that any commander could make decisions, through his *imperium* granted by the Senate, while on campaign, but on his return and with the laying down of his armies and that same *imperium*, a *lex* or law of the people or an act by the Senate was required to formally ratify such measures. Prudent generals sometimes invited a group of senators out to the frontiers for preliminary agreement, facilitating a much smoother passage in Rome. Pompey did none of this – he expected ratification of the dozens of agreements he had made and boundaries he had created, not to mention cities he had founded, and Cato was having none of it. Cato even lured Lucullus away from his 'fish ponds' and dinner parties to ask that every detail of Pompey's decisions be investigated – presumably he enjoyed his opportunity for payback against the man who had relieved him of his command.

With Crassus also feeling a chill wind of resistance from the Senate over a major problem with tax farming concessions that needed a revision having bid too high a price for them in the first place, Cato had undone much of what Cicero had built by way of a spirit of co-operation. Like the modern-day Conservative party in the United Kingdom where 'unity' is too strong a word to associate with 'party', the fault lines in the late Republican Senate ran deep and were pulling away from each other. On Cato, Cicero had this to say about a man whose desire to maintain the traditions of the Republic was so strong that he would rather see it fall than compromise:

Cicero to Atticus
Rome, June 60

I love our Cato as much as you do, or even more, but nevertheless that man,
possessing the finest soul and the greatest honesty, sometimes does real harm to
the state. For he pronounces his judgements as if he was in the Republic of Plato
rather than in the dregs of Romulus.

Caesar, now with his huge debts incurred for the election as Pontifex Maximus
paid off and a successful campaign in Spain behind him, did not need to
expend a fortune in bribes to be elected consul for 59. As part of his strategic
repositioning, Caesar worked his relationships with everyone that could possibly
be of use to him. These now included the repeatedly rebuffed and frustrated
Pompey and Crassus, the man in power but with none. Caesar also saw a pliable,
still ambitious and needy Cicero if he handled him correctly. Cicero did not have
the financial power or influence to affect power struggles in the normal way, but
his eloquence and status as the more pragmatic conscience and mouthpiece of
the Senate, compared to Cato, made him someone to be carefully managed.

It was Cato that bore an implacable mistrust of Caesar and despite Caesar's
acute sense of timing and feeling that this must be his moment before the
sunlight faded on his career, Cato persisted with trying to put Caesar off
from running for consul. Cato managed to get the Senate to confirm that the
consuls of 59 would receive, as their provincial commands, the *sylvae callesque*,
or the paths and woodlands of Italy. There was no glory or profit in those,
but Caesar saw their bluff and evidently did not rise to the bait. Trouble was
brewing to the north in Gaul and that is where Caesar was aiming to make his
bid to equal or outdo Pompey.

But Cato must have felt that additional political insurance was needed in
the case of Caesar to the point where he even sanctioned the use of bribes to
make sure that his future son-in-law, M. Calpurnius Bibulus, was elected co-
consul for 59. From a historical point of view, poor Bibulus is often seen as a
footnote to Caesar's dominance in the coming consular year, something of a
point of ridicule and insignificance, but this is not a fair or accurate assessment
of him either as a man or as a politician, he just happened to be part of that
contextual accident of fate that we referred to earlier. Without Caesar arriving
back in Rome at this point in time, without Cato deciding it was vital to have a
strong co-consular presence to reign in Caesar's ambitions and without having
been Caesar's mirror image in terms of the *cursus honorum*, then Bibulus may
well have gone down in the annals of the Republic as a strong consul and
a good man for the Republic – but no man would survive easily if Caesar,
reasonable, bridge building, forgiving Caesar, had decided your fate.

Chapter 17

The First Triumvirate

An unfaithful friend causes more pain than a hundred enemies.
Anonymous

Even before the new consular year of Caesar and Bibulus had begun, Cicero was questioning what his role was and where he should place himself in the maelstrom of the Senate. The reference to the festival of the *Compitalia* (the Festival of the Crossroads) was perhaps a missed opportunity to see a useful metaphor for his own political position:

Cicero to Atticus
Rome, December 60

Either I put up a stout resistance to the agrarian law [now being put forward again by Caesar as consul to support Pompey's veterans] *which means something of a struggle but an honourable one, or I lie low, which is nearly tantamount to retiring to Antium or Solinium, or I actually lend it my assistance, as they say Caesar confidently expects me to do. I have had a visit from Cornelius* [Lucius Cornelius Balbus of Gades, Cadiz, who had come to Rome at some point in 71 under Pompey but was now an advisor to Caesar, no doubt as a result of Caesar's time in Spain], *Balbus I mean, Caesar's intimate. He assured me that Caesar will follow Pompey's and my advice in all things and will try to bring Pompey and Crassus together.... But let's keep all this for our strolls together at the Compitalia. Remember the day before. I shall have the bath heated. Terentia invites Pomponia as well, and we shall have your mother over too. Please bring me Theophrastus 'On Ambition' from Quintus' library.*

While Cicero mulled over his options, events moved on, and lengthy private discussions took place between Crassus, Caesar and Pompey on forming a three-way alliance to pressure the Senate, control the government agenda, and achieve their most desired goals. All three shared having been frustrated or even embarrassed by the tactics of Cato with his willingness to stand out from the senatorial crowd, risk everything and compromise on nothing, and it was Cato that was the main obstacle to their future aspirations. It seemed logical then that, despite their differences, all three came to recognize that they could gain what they wanted individually if they worked collectively and pooled the political acumen of Caesar, the money of Crassus and the network and influence amongst the *popularis* of Pompey. As we can see from Cicero's December 60 letter, Caesar was also reaching out to him for support, which suggests that the formation of the triumvirate was not the initial purpose – instead he may have been seeking to create a block of the most influential men in the Senate and saw Cicero as pivotal to his cause. When Cicero wobbled and then actively showed reluctance to be drawn, the grouping hardened into a triumvirate, and Cicero had cast his cards outside of the three most powerful men in the Republic.

Caesar began as consul by softening his tone, seeking to work with the Senate, and his first act in the role was to order all the business of the Senate to be published in and around the forum so that the public knew what was being discussed and, as importantly, who was saying what. This was a huge and new task for the *scribae* and likely saw a considerable expansion of the number of administrators required to service the needs of the Senate. But Caesar was not just acting to increase the transparency of the senatorial proceedings, he also saw this as a way of undermining Cato – his stubbornness and often unreasonable behaviour was not now just hidden to 600 senators – all could be revealed to the people.

Inevitably, next came the *lex agraria*, the long overdue land bill which would allow private and public land to be freed up for sale to army veterans (both Pompey's and Caesar's) and the poor. Cato's resistance and that of the *optimates* was well known and so Caesar tried an alternative route rather than the probable and inexorable journey into a direct clash between the two sides. Sensibly, Caesar instead 'studied their past objections carefully and crafted his bill to make it as palatable to the aristocracy as possible.' Caesar planned ahead like any good commander, seeking intelligence on what the likely objections would be and building the solutions into his bill – not only did this show an unexpected deference to the Senate but, in asking for views and amendments, it became very difficult for Cato to obstruct or object. Difficult situations, however, did not intimidate Cato and he continued to find ways to object and obfuscate. In many ways Cato was role reversing with *popularis* tribunes – very often it was they who acted with their power of veto to obstruct the business of the Senate, but now Cato was the obstructionist, determined not to let Pompey and Caesar have their way for fear of the popularity, and power, such a far-reaching act would bring them as individuals.

In hindsight, Cato was perhaps picking the wrong fight at the wrong time and on the wrong ground – Caesar was the master of timing and strategy and he did not mind losing the occasional battle as long as he won the war. Cato ran the risk of being seen as damaging the good governance of the Republic – made worse by his resorting to the filibuster, talking for hours on why and why not Caesar's bill should be resisted and managing this for a whole month in January 59, preventing any vote from being taken. Inevitably, Caesar lost patience and ordered Cato's arrest. Instead of rebellious complaint, Cato's reaction disarmed Caesar: he had lured the would-be dictator into his trap to expose Caesar's true personality as a natural tyrant and bully. Without hesitation Cato said he was glad to go to prison and, as he left, other senators stood and followed him out from the Curia and down the steps into the forum. According to Dio, when Caesar tried to prevent one of these senators from leaving, the unknown man said that he would rather be in prison with Cato than in the Curia with Caesar.

Although not a politically fatal moment for Caesar, it was nevertheless an embarrassing stumble and he was forced to move quickly to calm the situation by swiftly releasing Cato from arrest and tempers cooled. Cato knew he had won this battle and the Senate witnessed both a clear demonstration of what Caesar was capable of and the notion of Caesar the tyrant was born. Equally, Cato's willingness to risk all positioned him even more front and centre as the leader of the *optimates*.

The issue of land reform, however, was as live as ever. Plutarch relates how Caesar was not built to capitulate and he agreed with Pompey to invite as much of Pompey's retired army to Rome as he could to then hold a legal assembly of the people, a *comitia*, and with the support of a tribune, Publius Vatinius, get the measure passed. Step forward into history the much-maligned consul Bibulus whose time had come. Thousands of rugged, whiskered and battle scarred faces began arriving in Rome over the next few days, clearly old soldiers with some still wearing parts of their old uniforms, but all, of course, without weapons – these were Pompey's veterans and on a set day they surrounded the *comitium* cheering their old commander Pompey when he turned up – the theatrical aspects as well as the levels of intimidation must have been quite something to observe and the forum, so often a place of epic events, watched yet another pivotal moment in the history of the Republic.

Despite bad omens seen by Bibulus, Caesar would have his way and ignoring the portents, the measure was read out by Caesar on the steps of the Temple of Castor again with veterans all around, but the rancour between the various groups, with some it has to be said, encouraged by Cato, meant that there was so much fighting and scuffling that no vote could be taken and Bibulus confined himself to his home, issuing unfavourable pronouncements almost daily to obstruct the vote. On the final occasion of the assembly meeting, courageously Bibulus arrived and Caesar 'pleaded' with him to support the veterans probably in a mock show of deference, knowing how it would paint his co-consul as an enemy of the people if he refused and the atmosphere changed as Caesar knew it would. When Bibulus tried to announce his veto, he was chased down the steps cowering and covering his head shouting 'You will not have this law this year, not even should you all want it', and as he fled into the forum, he was variously pelted with faeces or had an entire bucket thrown over him and the *fasces* of his lictors were grabbed and broken – an appalling result for a man of such standing right in the forum where all could see democracy and the Republic on the edge of destruction. The bill was carried and again through the Senate who accepted *force majeure* and even Cato was forced to agree under great duress. Lands across Italy were now released for sale to the poor and to veterans with their hard-earned savings of gold and silver. In Campania alone, enough land was released for 20,000 extra citizens. The land reform issue had been an emotionally tumultuous test for Caesar and his opponents and the result was a tectonic shift in the disposition of authority in the Senate.

During 59 Crassus benefitted from the remission of the tax farming concessions, Pompey's eastern settlement was agreed and Caesar was granted the proconsular provinces of Cisalpine Gaul and Illyricum for five years with a force of three legions. There was opposition, but it struggled against the popularist strength of the appeal of Caesar together with his manipulation and bare-faced rejection of the normal democratic rules. Cato had always maintained that Caesar was a tyrant in waiting and events supported his fears – Caesar restricted the meetings of the Senate by only calling them when he needed to and he continued to ignore Bibulus. For those who had stood against Caesar, they were marked men. When Cato opposed the settlement of Campania by standing on the Rostra and shouting his speech to the crowd, he was forcibly dragged away on Caesar's orders while the still respected Lucullus, despite his great *auctoritas*, was cowed back into obscurity by legal threats. Aware of his political impotence and redundancy, Lucullus was in despair and retreated into his own world of decadent living, no doubt appalled and homeless in the new atmosphere that Caesar had unleashed in the Senate.

Bibulus confined himself to writing long letters of objection to Caesar's laws calling them illegal, and his wit and cutting sarcasm was even remarked upon by Cicero so that, like a satirical magazine, people eagerly looked forward to every new edition. Other opponents of Caesar fared little better and even the powerful *optimate* Metellus Celer could do no more – he died suddenly in April of 59, some say poisoned by his wife Clodia, we might recall the sister of Clodius Pulcher – callousness clearly ran in the family, but we should note that her brother, Pretty Boy, was also very much in the orbit of Caesar's influence and Caesar would have been pleased to see the demise of Celer – however it came. Despite threats of violence or death by poison, Cato persisted in his resistance. Like a modern-day Liz Cheney in her opposition to Donald Trump and her determination to prevent his anarchic and destructive presence in American democracy, Cato went on the offensive. As part of an active resistance to Caesar, Cato became a central part of a successful propaganda campaign that started to turn against the Triumvirate. As the year of 59 came to an end, senators deliberately failed to turn up in large numbers when Caesar declared there would be a meeting in the curia – their absence preventing the normal democratic processes and serving as an insult to Caesar's authority and an embarrassment to his standing in the Senate. Like many others, Cicero chose discretion as the better part of valour and withdrew to his estates, thereby boycotting being seen as part of this sham democracy. Caesar reacted badly to these insults, but continued to slowly strangle democracy rather than kill it decisively as Cicero sensed:

Cicero to Atticus
Rome, July 59

For we have experienced the rage and immoderate behaviour of these men, who – being furious with Cato – have destroyed everything. But they seem to be using so gentle a poison that we seem to be able to die without suffering. Yet now I fear they will blaze in fury at the hissing of the mob, at the remarks of the respectable, and at the tumult throughout Italy.

The trials of Antonius and Flaccus 59

One other development that was to dramatically affect Cicero the following year, came in March 59 after he offered to defend his former co-consul Antonius from charges of corruption and mismanagement. Described as 'a thoroughly disreputable character' by Anthony Kamm, as well as 'the alleged murderer of his own son and a violator of a Vestal Virgin', we last saw G. Antonius Hybrida in Macedonia as Governor there, sending back Cicero's cut of his proconsular earnings so he could buy his house from Crassus – hopefully the gout he had suddenly suffered in the battle against Catiline had healed. It seems that Antonius had not only mishandled his treatment of the population (in this he seems to have been merely following the established traditions), but also lost two small scale military engagements – more alarmingly for the Senate together with the significant amounts of plunder. Antonius was recalled by Caesar and prosecuted. Emerging from his smoke screen of silence, Cicero acted for Antonius, not out of friendship or some perverted sense of loyalty, but to give himself an opportunity to return to the stage and deliver a carefully worded condemnation of Caesar and the Triumvirate. Cicero must have weighed up whether this was a wise move but, given what we know of his egotistical character, it is most likely that he could not help but feel that the Senate wanted to hear from him. Sadly, Cicero again miscalculated if he thought his status and rhetoric would impress Cato and the Senate or cause Caesar distress. Depressingly for Antonius, Cicero lost the case and Antonius went into exile until 47, but this was not to be the only result of the trial, as Caesar would demonstrate a few months later.

A second case in 59 was that of L. Valerius Flaccus, whom Cicero also agreed to defend against charges of maladministration. Facing some considerable damaging direct evidence and many witnesses, Cicero planned his defence with his usual forensic zeal in three stages and his defence speech *Pro Flacco*, which is regarded by many as one of his greatest, alongside *In Verrem* in 70 and *In Catilinam* in 63. The first of his arguments went to the pressing situation in Rome at that moment recounting the sparkling and dedicated military career of Flaccus to offset the debaucheries of his youth highlighted by the prosecution – as Cicero had done many times in an effort to blacken the past reputation of the man even before the evidence was given. Secondly Cicero attacked the credibility of the witnesses. In doing so he spoke in stereotypical terms of the national characteristics of the witnesses and especially the Jews whom he painted as worthless liars embroiled in a conspiracy to bring down the Republic. The third strand was to deal with the evidence stacked against his client – which Cicero dealt with largely by referring back to his second strand.

In an article from The Historical Society of Israel published in 1942, the approach taken by Cicero was adduced to 'correspond with the rules established by Roman rhetoricians for the discrediting of witnesses'. Thus, it is even more important that we do not judge the polemics used by Cicero from the standpoint of the twenty-first century as his speeches were a) for the standard prosecution approach of winning a case rather than ascertaining the truth b) in line with a strategy used by all Roman advocates in regards to destroying the character of witnesses prior to them giving their evidence and c) therefore not necessarily indicative of Cicero's own views regarding the Jews. Flaccus was accused of stealing gold, not just any gold, however, but gold collected throughout Asia for the Temple in Jerusalem, but the case was far more important than that, for lurking in the background was Cicero's nemesis,

Clodius Pulcher. How could this be? Put simply, there were thousands of Jews living in Rome who flocked to the trial of Flaccus in support of their fellow Jewish witnesses because their own rights had been undercut by the Senate. Concerned at the rise in revolutionary attitudes amongst the various *collegia* or corporations, the legal status of the Jewish community had also been questioned and whether they could be regarded as a threat to the state. Clodius had been courting the *populares* for months in his desire to build a power base amongst the dispossessed and threatened and he had associated himself with the Jewish claims for protection from the power of the state. Backed as he was by Caesar, Crassus and Pompey, it was easy for Clodius to see this trial as another way of dealing a body blow to the authority of the Senate – he was after all working to bring it down from within. So for Cicero, the trial of Flaccus was not just about defending a friend, but also symbolically defending the state, and in so doing he had to attack the character of the Jewish population.

Cicero began with mock apprehension – the prosecution had selected the Steps of Aurelius as the venue for the trial (so named after Lucius Aurelius Cotta, consul in 119), so Cicero alleged, in order for a large Jewish mob to attend and intimidate – adding to his claim that the Jews were indeed a threat to the state. We may recall that in 63, Pompey had been resident in Jerusalem and visited the Temple and left it, and its treasures untouched. The prosecution contrasted this with Flaccus, who had been high handed and disrespectful to their religion as Governor. But Cicero was able to state clearly that Flaccus had his agents and prefects in the provinces collect the gold legitimately, account for it in his books and place it in the *aerarium* – in other words all completely above board and not for his own benefit, but for the state, in fact the evidence the prosecution produced poured credit on his client, not criticism.

The trial of Flaccus is important for reasons other than the beauty of Cicero's defence. The evidence in Cicero's speech clarifies for historians that there was an already flourishing Jewish community in Rome by 60, one with enough influence for Clodius to see them as an important group within the city. Equally, it is an opportunity to see how far Cicero was prepared to go to secure convictions. Naturally, accusations of antisemitism have been a feature of the assessment of Cicero's approach, but crude national caricatures hardly constitute deep held racial prejudice. Another aspect that makes this trial of greater interest is its timing. It was over three years since Flaccus was in post and it could be argued that the charges were brought now not just to discredit Flaccus, but also Cicero for his actions as consul in 63. Flaccus had been a strong supporter of Cicero in the Catiline affair and the dark powers at work behind the scenes may have been seeking to tarnish them both as corrupt individuals supporting each other in the maintenance of an equally corrupt regime. In the end, Cicero was successful in his defence, but again it came with a cost to his armour of invincibility and was another test set before him, almost certainly by Clodius.

In response to Cicero's speech in the trial of Antonius, Caesar decided it was time to let Clodius loose. Most likely Caesar had hoped that Cicero would have seen the futility of obstruction – let alone thinking of some heroic return to centre stage in Rome. Given what he knew of Cicero, it was unlikely that Caesar could secure his silence, but the next best thing would have been Cicero's benign acceptance of the new realities and possibly even his support – but Cicero's speech ended these calculations and our young renegade Clodius managed to get the support he needed from Caesar, as Pontifex Maximus, to be adopted into a plebeian family and thus be eligible to become elected as a tribune of the plebs – with all the considerable power that entailed. This is exactly what happened in the delayed elections held on 17 October and after 10 December 59, when his tribunate became active, Clodius was, at long last, able to conduct his own political agenda of popular measures, but more personally, his new position allowed him authority to exact his revenge on Cicero for the Good Goddess affair.

Lessons for our own age

...the enablers......

So, what of Cicero against this backdrop of a semi coup against the Republic and why was Caesar able to achieve so much relatively easily? Let us look at the latter first of all. Caesar could not have achieved the success he did so relatively easily without an element of connivance amongst certain senatorial groups and individuals. At a time when the concept of personal sacrifice to preserve the democratic state had long since withered away, some no doubt saw an opportunity in active non-participation – showing Caesar their support by doing nothing. These people exist in every country and every democratic state – they are the 'enablers'. For any tyrannical ruler to come to power there must be enablers, officials or advisors, the hidden powers who revel in seeing old scores settled, an opportunity for advancement or just the joy of seeing others fail before their eyes. Hitler depended on them, Mussolini was one of them, Stalin had them everywhere, and every other dictator who sought to bring down democracy has needed them. In every cabinet, senate, congress, parliament or assembly these are the people who walk in the shadows, able to make a difference, able to prevent collapse but they do nothing as their own weapon of either survival or success.

...the appeal of popularism...

Across Europe we are witnessing the rise of the popularist right. Popularism appeals to ordinary people who feel they have been and are being ignored by the establishment and, with economic pressures as acute as they are now, popularist parties are in the ascendant. Caesar stuck to his agrarian reform agenda not because he cared so much about the poor, but because it was popular with the ordinary people – he made the establishment look unreasonable, out of touch, selfish and greedy. He was also a charismatic leader and across the world there are a number of these such as Bolsonaro in Brazil, Modi in India, Erdogan in Turkey and, closer to home, Meloni in Italy. We may recall in an earlier chapter that the combination of unpopular establishment parties and the existence of a charismatic leader can spell real problems for democracy with large voting turnouts for popularist parties, for example 65 per cent in Hungary, 54 per cent in Greece, 51 per cent in Poland, 50 per cent in Italy and 49 per cent in the Czech Republic.

...the normalization of extremist rhetoric and actions...

Just as in the Roman Republican Senate, when established democratic representatives fail to respond to ever more extreme actions and use of offensive terms, then they have already lost control. Donald Trump has played a key role on the world stage, aided by social media, which has changed the face of world communications, in bringing down the thresholds of what is acceptable. Such a threat was predicted in the book *The Sovereign Individual* in the 1990s and we as a world are still coming to terms with the reach and power of the internet. The QAnon theories and the MAGA – Make America Great Again – movements harnessed the power of the internet to take ideas, no matter how extreme, into the homes of the individual – there was no Roman equivalent except gossip, but we can assume that this acted in the same way. It is no longer taboo to be discriminatory, to lie to the people, to ridicule and vilify your opponents and, just as Caesar did, unless there is an even stronger reaction against this strategy, then democracy just looks weak and ineffective and this aids and enhances the appeal of popularist leaders who espouse dictatorial powers to get things done. As we read and discover the history of the Roman Republic, we can reflect on how history does repeat itself and look for the lessons in our own time. One lesson is that democracy has always needed defenders, they must be as strong as the tyrants, use the same weapons as they do to defeat them and react quickly to any erosion. Like any playground bully, the charismatic leader is only as strong as the person that allows them to bully them.

But what of the former question, what of Cicero? After failing in the trial of Antonius and playing his part in the boycotting of the Senate, Cicero left Rome and dictated to his scribe Tiro at length, writing to Atticus from a number of his country homes and estates:

> But why all these questions, when I want to put all such matters aside and concentrate my whole time and energy on study? Yes, that is what I intend. I wish I had done so from the first. Now, having discovered by experience the emptiness of all the things that I prized most highly, I mean to concern myself with all the muses.

From Antium (Anzio) he wrote:

> One can hardly believe that there could be a place so near Rome where many of the inhabitants have never seen Vatinius, where no member of the board of twenty has a single well-wisher besides myself, where nobody disturbs me and everybody likes me. Yes, this is surely the place to practise politics. In Rome that is impossible, and what is more I am sick of it.

From Formiae, 26 April 59:

> How you whet my appetite about your talk with Bibulus, your discussion with Ox-Eyes.

From this we can see that Atticus was either in Rome or corresponding both with the pro consul, up to his eyes in his fight with Caesar, and Clodia who had 'large brilliant eyes' but Atticus was not willing or able to commit the contents of those conversations to paper. Further in the same letter:

> You are always urging me to composition, but it's out of the question. It's not a country house I have here, but a public exchange, so many of the good folk of Formiae come in…. But my closest neighbour is one C. Arrius, or rather room-mate, for that is what he has now become. He actually says he won't go to Rome because he wants to philosophise with me here all day long…where is a man to turn?

A few days after this letter Cicero dispatched another and after some cutting jibes at Pompey and how he was in the dark about 'What our friend Gnaeus is up to now I simply do not know.' Cicero went on to say:

For I think I have done quite enough to satisfy Dicaearchus; now I turn to the other school, which not only permits me to rest from my labours but scolds me for labouring in the first place. So, Titus mine, let me throw myself into my studies, those wonderful studies which I ought never to have left and to which I must now at last return.

After a line or two about his brother Quintus wanting him to edit and publish a history book he had written -

We shall see you in Arpinum and welcome you in country style since you have scorned our seaside hospitality.

Cicero played with the possibility of travelling to Egypt on a mission from Rome – there was a hint in the air that Caesar may offer this opportunity. King Ptolemy XII had been ruler for some years, but his was an uneasy relationship with Rome and Crassus had tried and failed to formally annex Egypt to the empire in 65. Ptolemy had reached out to Pompey during the Mithridatic war and sent large amounts of money to help in the great general's war in Judea. Finally, in an attempt to secure his future, Ptolemy came to Rome in 60 to meet with the Triumvirate for official recognition – paying 6,000 talents in gold and silver (the entire revenue of Egypt for one year) to Caesar and Pompey. So, there were many wide opportunities for trade and political advancement as well as missions for men of status – such as Cicero:

Yes, I am eager and have been for long enough to visit Alexandria and the rest of Egypt and at the same time to get away from this part of the world where people are tired of me and to come back when they have begun to miss me a little.... What will our optimates say, if there are any left? [Should Cicero leave for Egypt] *Perhaps that I have been somehow bribed to change my views. 'Polydamas will cry me shame first – I mean our friend Cato who is worth a hundred thousand in my eyes'* [From a Greek proverb 'One to me is worth tens of thousands' which has its roots with the philosopher Heraclitus.] *And what will history say of me a thousand years hence? I am far more in awe of that than the tittle-tattle of my contemporaries. But I think I had better wait and see. If the offer is made, that will give me some sort of latitude, and then will be the time to deliberate. Also, dash it all, there is some glory in not accepting.*

So, what do we and history more widely have to say of Cicero not one but 2,000 years hence? In terms of whether or not he should have taken Caesar's offer and gone to Egypt, subsequent events will show that he certainly should have jumped at the chance regardless of what Cato might say in the Senate. There had already been more than one occasion when Cicero should have kept his counsel to himself or gone abroad – the classic example being not taking up his proconsular role in Macedonia after the Catiline affair. Egypt would have been good for his mental health, given him a chance to again feel that he was doing something worthwhile for the Republic, replenish his bank account and most important of all, got him away from the firing line that Clodius had in store for him. The sense that he wanted to be missed in Rome and hunt out more glory by refusing Caesar, however, indicates that, despite his protestations to Atticus that he was finished with politics, he was just fooling himself. When Jo-Marie Claason wrote in her 1992 article on Cicero's banishment, 'The events leading to Cicero's banishment read like a catalogue of the forces of retribution mustering against a man intent on self-destruction', she was revealing the concept of professional suicide. This can be driven into a person for a number of reasons – perhaps the exhaustion of clinical depression and anxiety means that death or exile is a pleasant release, or it could be part of a self-destructive trait whereby the individual would rather burn in their own fire than be seen to capitulate. A third explanation for professional suicide is that it is part of a plan to return one day even stronger than before and when the circumstances are more appealing. Cicero had opportunities to avoid what was coming but he decided to stay and was eventually forced into exile. We can only ponder why he did not leave Rome and take up these offers to avoid ruin, however, it is somewhat easier to interpret the probable reasons when we look at his speeches after his return seventeen months later.

Chapter 18

The Return of Pretty Boy

A nation can survive its fools, and even the ambitious. But it cannot survive treason from within. An enemy at the gates is less formidable, for he is known and carries his banner openly. But the traitor moves amongst those within the gates freely, his sly whispers rustling through the alleys, heard in the very halls of government itself.

Marcus Tullius Cicero

It is remarkable just how much correspondence there was in April – possibly there was a lot to catch up on after the turmoil in Rome, as we have no letters between Atticus and Cicero for January, February or March 59. After all these musing letters regarding a peaceful transition, almost retirement into writing, travelling around his various homes with Terentia, Cicero wrote of a strange occurrence on 19 April. Apparently, Cicero and his, no doubt considerable train of wagons and attendants, was travelling north out of Antium and had just joined the very busy Roman *autobahn* the Appian Way at the popular stopping point of Tres Tabernae or Three Taverns. The Queen of Roads, as the Appian Way was called, still stands strong in places, a testament to the surveyors and engineers of over 2,000 years ago. Much of the archaeology of Tres Tabernae is still evident, as are major parts of the Appian Way and the tombs and mausoleums that lined it (burials were not allowed inside the city) so it is not a great feat of the imagination to see Cicero getting out of his sedan chair and stretching his legs while Terentia did the same as they looked in either direction as the sun set. The direct equivalent of South Mimms on the M25 north of London, Tres Tabernae offered a pit stop to change and feed horses, no doubt kill off those at the end of their mileage, watch fellow travellers arrive and head south towards Naples or north to Rome, soldiers delivering important messages to and from Rome and everywhere people resting and eating. According to his letter:

I had just come out of the Antium district and joined the Appian Way at Tres Tabernae, on Ceres Day actually, when my young friend Curio runs into me on his way from Rome. At that very point along comes a boy [slave] from you with letters. Curio asked me whether I had heard the news. I said no. 'Publius [Clodius] says he is standing for tribune.' 'No, really?' 'Yes and as Caesar's deadly enemy, and means to undo everything they've done.' 'What about Caesar?' 'Says he had nothing to do with proposing Publius' adoption.' I bade the fellow an affectionate good-bye in a hurry to get to the letters.

Atticus had certainly spoken to Clodia about Cicero and no doubt hoped that she could calm her brother's anger – or at least let it blow itself out so that it did not reach his friend – but Cicero really was in a quandary about how to start to protect himself. His long and industrious campaign to seduce Pompey into friendship had, so far, resulted in very little in tangible terms but Cicero contented himself that he had Pompey's assurance that he would keep Clodius in check and told Atticus that he would make Pompey regret it if he let him down:

If, however, the bargain as respects myself is not observed, I am in excelsis – just wait for our friend from Jerusalem [code for Pompey] who manufactures plebeians so easily, learns what a fine return he has made for my toadying speeches!.... It is plain enough to me now to what quarter the wind of unpopularity is veering and where it will set. You can say I have learned nothing from experience and nothing from Theophrastus [Greek philosopher who took all knowledge as his province rather than land] if you don't soon see people regretting the old days when I was in the saddle.

There was little chance of Cicero hearing the trumpets recalling him to save Rome again. Like Boris Johnson in his first wilderness after his fall as Prime Minister in 2022 and his quotation of Cincinnatus, Cicero also hoped he would be recalled as consul. But times had changed, the Senate had changed, and even Cato had changed – although he was still standing firm and fighting hard. The Triumvirate further secured their partnership when Pompey married Caesar's beautiful daughter Julia signalling that this arrangement was to be permanent and highlighting the necessity of marriage as a political tool. Not only this but Caesar, the most eligible bachelor in the whole of Rome, married the daughter of a loyal supporter Lucius Calpurnius Piso Caesoninus – and shortly after proposed him for consul for the following year of 58 along with the loyal supporter of Pompey Aulus Gabinius, the man who had proposed the *lex Gabinia* to give Pompey his eastern command back in 67 and whom Cicero had so vocally supported. Naturally both were elected and secured the next year for Caesar while he began his work in Gaul and of course both Pompey and Crassus remained behind as well so the Triumvirate looked secure, despite a resurgence of resistance in the autumn against Caesar's illegal legislation led by Cato's brother-in-law Ahenobarbus, a new praetor.

As time passed in the summer, Cicero felt increasingly uneasy and isolated, resentful at a perceived lack of support amongst the *boni* or good men and by the first two weeks of July he was back in Rome, sensing danger, noting the instability as these extracts illuminate:

Cicero to Atticus
Rome, 7 – 14 July 59

The truth is that the present regime is the most infamous, disgraceful, and universally odious to all sorts and classes and ages of men that ever was, more so upon my word than I could have wished, let alone expected. These 'popular' politicians have taught even quiet folk to hiss.

Caesar wants to have me on his staff [in Gaul]. *That would be a more acceptable evasion of the danger* [than Egypt], *which however I do not decline. It comes to this, I would rather fight. But my mind is not made up. Again I say, 'If only you were here!' However, if the need arises I shall send for you.*

What else now, let me see. This, I think. I am certain that Rome is finished. Why go on mincing words?

The threats and abuses promised by Clodius did not abate and in a series of letters in late July and throughout August we can see that Cicero was increasingly uncertain of which way to go or what level of support he had amongst his supposed allies – Pompey and his promises, Cato and the *optimates* and the other *boni* who had professed their support for him and these extracts from letters to Atticus speak volumes:

Clodius is still threatening trouble. Pompey says there is no danger, he swears it. He even adds that Clodius will attack me over his dead body. Negotiations proceed. As soon as there is anything definite, I shall write to you.

Clodius is hostile. Pompey continues to assure me that he will do nothing against me. It would be dangerous for me to believe that, and I am getting ready to defend myself. I hope to have strong support from all classes. I miss you, and the facts of the case call for your return to meet the crisis.

Oh how I wish you were here in Rome! No doubt you would have stayed if we had expected all this to happen. Then it would be easy to keep Pretty-Boy in hand, or at least we should be able to find out what he is up to. Now the picture is as follows: he rushes wildly up and down, without any definite programme, threatening numbers of folk with this, that, and the other. Apparently he will take whatever line chance puts his way. When he notices how the present regime is detested he makes as though to attack its authors; then again, when he remembers their power and ruthlessness and the armies behind them, he turns upon the boni. Myself he threatens sometimes with violence, sometimes with the law courts. Pompey has spoken to him. Strongly, as he himself informed me (I have no other witness), telling him that he, Pompey, would be branded as a traitor and a villain if I were brought into jeopardy by one whose weapons he had furnished in allowing his transfer to the plebs.

It was Atticus who often advised Cicero to make his peace with Clodius before the elections for tribune would be held, but something seems to have prevented him from doing so. We can only surmise that this was possibly ego and that the bright light of having been a consul still affected his political vision or perhaps he wanted matters to deteriorate to a fragile point where he could look to be the salvation of all and mount the stage once more as the philosopher-king but if he did, then he was badly mistaken.

Clodius had little regard for talent or intelligence let alone respect for any part of Cicero – both men shared a common failing and that was a careless use of their tongues with Cicero's being as much to blame for this collapse between them as anything. Cicero seems to have felt, on the surface anyway, that even if Clodius was elected as tribune he had more than enough protection both from his own status as a hero of Rome, plus the promises of Pompey and finally the *boni* who continued to profess their support.

In response to Cicero's speech earlier in the year, Caesar had hoped that he could draw Cicero into his own tent either in Gaul or by sending him away to Egypt. However, with the arrival of December 59, we find Cicero still in Rome, no doubt with a very concerned and emotionally strained Terentia by his side, and to his great relief his closest friend Atticus too. On 10 December, as Caesar prepared to leave for Gaul and with Cicero not either ready to travel with him or be packed off to the hot climate of Egypt, the new tribunes took office. It soon became very clear that Clodius had plans and ambitions that went much further than anyone expected. Caesar carried on completing his command and putting all in place for the long wars ahead until March and watched as resistance stiffened against him and as Clodius revealed his intentions.

Caesar was now immune from prosecution as he had been granted his imperium as commander in Gaul, but even this was threatened now as Cato and another new tribune Memmius tried to prosecute Vatinius for his actions in proposing a five-year command for Caesar, when the normal proconsular length was a two-year maximum. Caesar had seen this coming of course and Vatinius had been offered a post of legate in his command which also secured his position as an official away from Rome, and they were camped outside of the Pomerium which gave them further protection from prosecution. He could hear the noise on the streets of Rome, but he could not be touched.

The storm breaks

In February of the new consular year of 58, Clodius released paid gangs onto the streets of Rome to create an atmosphere of instability. Similar to the MAGA instability unleashed by Donald Trump, the gangs put together by Clodius were the equivalent of the Oath Keepers in the USA in 2020 and their masters had the same objectives – the acceptance of the notion of a standing army of armed civilians waiting to pounce on any political leader or group targeted as an enemy of the right wing. This was a new tactic and to further solidify his power base with the people, in February 58, Clodius promulgated a *lex Clodia de capite civis Romani* – this affirmed a citizen's right of appeal and outlawed anyone who had executed a Roman citizen without trial. This was to be the law that St Paul would cite in his defence some 80 years later. No names were mentioned but it was clearly aimed at only one man. Shackleton Bailey believes that Cicero now 'lost his head'. Instead of using the tools fate had given him and perhaps challenging the law in court and proving that he had acted with the consent of the Senate and they were therefore all guilty, he in fact opted for wearing the clothes of mourning – just as Celer had done those few years before and, representing one who is under attack, Cicero allowed his hair and beard to grow and wore torn clothing smeared with ashes and dirt. This was known as *mutatio vestis* – literally the mutilation of clothing. To us, this may seem like an extreme display, but the notion of wearing particular types of dress as a way of publicly displaying deference or emotion is not unusual – black arm bands, top hats and tails or sombre black clothing are still recognized as displays of those in mourning. The key difference in this case is that *mutatio vestis* was designed to indicate that their life was under threat, typically taking place in public places to appeal directly to people by supplication and hoping for support by others doing the same thing.

This very visual representation of ritual sorrow was studied by Aerynn Dighton in a 2017 article for the Classical Association of Canada.[1] In her research, Dighton highlights the difference between the very personal and individual display that Cicero undertook and that encouraged by senatorial decree. Plutarch tells us that the Senate met in the Temple of Concord in support of Cicero and passed a decree signifying that the attack on Cicero was also an attack on the *res publica*. The proposal was adopted, having been put forward by another tribune named L. Ninnius. We do not know how many of the senators decided to change their clothing but, after return from exile, Cicero reminded the Senate that the vote had been carried in a 'full house' and that 'all of you changed your dress'. Cicero further elaborated, rubbing salt into the wounds of those that had prevaricated, 'all good men had already done so'. We can imagine then that a large number of the 600 or so senators filed out of the Curia, under attack verbally and physically, and walked to their homes to change into their own morning clothes and then returned to gather in the forum as an expression of 'the grief of the country' and that great misfortune or *calamitas* was threatening the state. As Dighton commented:

> *The Senate could appeal emotionally to the people without ever saying a word by wearing mourning clothes and making themselves a spectacle of humility and wretchedness. The power of civic leaders...is partly dependent upon how citizens respond to their public behaviour and visual self-representation. Mutatio vestis, as used by the Senate in the late Republic, seems to have been a symbolic acknowledgement that the masses had power over them just as a jury controlled the fate of a defendant. This was a powerful form not just of protest against the tribunes, (in this case Clodius) but of recognizing the people as a force capable of influencing the course of politics in the republic.*

Cicero had been demonstrating that he was under attack for a few days before the Senate met and his dishevelled state of unshaved beard and uncombed hair was a more extreme form of expression known as *squalor* – a word we associate today with slums, filth and poverty. By walking around the forum and talking to the populace about what was happening, Cicero was not asking for a pardon, but making a political protest – he was in fact objecting to his treatment rather than just retreating from the onslaught of invective against him. This was a world where communication had to be visual and tangible, where there was no social media platform to engage in personal slanging matches at a distance (perhaps on either side of the world and never actually meeting one's adversary face to face). The creation of the cowardly and vile online troll shows how much personal courage we have lost and the power of social media has become another inherent weakness in the elastic band of modern democracy. The whole sorry episode continued and the forum, once Cicero's stage of bright enlightenment for the Roman public and the scene of so many great orations, was now a place where he was chased through the streets and pelted with stones and mud by the street thugs paid by Clodius. The senators too were dispersed and attacked.

Cicero appealed to the two consuls that Caesar had put in place – but further lukewarm support belied the fact that, in truth, Gabinius vehemently protested against the passing of the *mutatio vestis* and remained in his consular *toga praetexta* as the crowds of senators returned in their changed clothes, at the same time he actively began to support Clodius – no doubt having received a prod from Caesar, who was about to depart for the north, but not until he had separated Pompey from Cicero's influence. The two consuls further passed their own edicts forcing the senators to change back into their regular togas. Cicero decried this action as 'consular tyranny' that 'prohibited the Senate from obeying its own decrees'. Later in exile he was to write:

Caeci, caeci inquam fuimus in vestitu mutando, in populo rogando.

Blind, blind were we, I say, in changing our clothes, in begging the people.

Perhaps now Cicero could see why Caesar had offered two very good opportunities for him to leave Rome. Caesar had no interest in providing retirement gifts for Cicero, instead his tactical objective in the preceding months had been to remove Cicero from Pompey's company and, if at all possible, use him as a very public ally in his long game to seize power. Caesar had correctly assessed Pompey as a politician with the ability to wobble at the key moments and Cicero could have been able to work his skilful magic over him while Caesar was away. Having failed to attract Cicero, he was handed over to Clodius like a friend who had outlived his usefulness and Clodius eagerly accepted. But in this, what about Cato and the *optimates*?

Even for Fred Drogula, Cato's failure to support Cicero is hard to explain. It was possible, but unlikely, that Cato had been bought off with an offer of a special command in Cyprus. More convincing is that Cato had never seen Cicero as part of any grouping and as likely to give a speech against himself as anybody else – intellectual overconfidence, hubris, a sharp tongue, sarcasm all of these were the tools Cicero could access to destroy his enemies and they were not endearing political characteristics. By maintaining his air of independence and aloofness as the philosopher-king, Cicero actually had also left himself friendless – only Atticus retained a strong loyalty towards him and thankfully that was not put to the test in the Senate. Finally, the key question was what could Cato actually do? The consuls were kept men, Clodius was a very powerful and aggressive loose cannon protected by the triumvirs, which meant that trying to save Cicero was possibly not the best reason for opening up what could become a civil war. If war was to come then planning was needed and, in the meantime, Cicero would just have to be sacrificed.

The end came for Cicero when in March 58 a delegation of senators went to Pompey to ask him to intervene, but he declined – hiding behind a thin shield of protocols requiring the consuls to ask him to act as he was only a private citizen and would also need martial law declared. Years later, Cicero wrote that he too knelt at Pompey's feet only realizing when Pompey did not even ask him to stand to speak, that he had completely misjudged his years of careful courtship and that Pompey was unable – or unwilling – to stand independently to protect anyone. According to Cicero, Pompey said he could do nothing against Caesar's wishes – the implications being two-fold; Pompey was in fact powerless as long as Caesar was part of the Triumvirate and secondly, Caesar had made it clear to him that he wanted Cicero gone from Rome. We should ponder the sense of utter betrayal that Cicero must have felt as he left Pompey's country estate at Alba. He had never completely trusted Pompey, even though he very much wanted to, but he had done much to support him in his career, spoken for him in the debates on his eastern commands and praised him to the heavens as some sort of super-being. Cicero had always harboured a hope, if not a belief, that at the end of the day he could influence and control Pompey and that they had a mutual interest in working together. These hopes and dreams were now dashed upon the rocks of terrible misjudgement and anyone who has ever prided themselves on their good sense of judgement will know how painful and debilitating it is when one realizes that they have got everything completely wrong – especially so if the person they trusted was a former friend.

In utter dejection, feeling betrayed and in depression, Cicero asked for the counsel of fellow *boni*. It seems that both Hortensius and others encouraged Cicero to leave and go into exile, for how long no one knew, but he should go. Later, Cicero wrote that they did this out of pure jealousy, possibly true but equally likely that they too were scared. Their options were limited as Caesar had an already loyal army quite nearby and, if Pompey was the only possible counterweight, then he needed to be separated from the clutches of the Triumvirate, meaning that now was not the time to act. The consuls, who had the authority to disperse Clodius and his gangs, were not going to act against the interests of Caesar either. So, on the night of either 18 or 19 March 58, Cicero fled Rome and the bill to accuse him was passed in the assembly, not the Senate, the following day – no doubt with considerable bribery and obstruction of anyone who would vote to the contrary.

Note

1. Dighton, A., 'Mutatio Vestis: Clothing & Political Protest in the late Roman Republic'. Classical Association of Canada, 2017 in *Phoenix Journal*.

Chapter 19

Into Exile

I know how men in exile feed on dreams.

Aeschylus 525–456

T he days following his escape from Rome were spent at full speed heading for the south. Cicero was not in any immediate danger, but Clodius had stipulated that, as the traditional punishment, Cicero should be denied food and water and that he should live at least 400 miles from the city boundary. This was exile Roman style and often a convenient way for significant figures to avoid capital execution.

So, as a motivated and excited Caesar ordered his new voracious and talented army to begin their march northwards to Gaul, a despondent and shattered Cicero began his journey south travelling back down the Queen of Roads. Only weeks before, Cicero had been riding the other way so full of hope and optimism as he returned to Rome. Thankfully there were enough allies en route who were willing to ignore the threats from Clodius. We have no idea who or how many people decided to go into exile with him, but we do know from the mass of correspondence that was now to flow to Atticus, that Terentia stayed behind and we can assume Tiro and possibly other scribes and trusted slaves went with him. In a later letter, Cicero reports that Terentia was both unwell and emotionally exhausted from the events in Rome in recent years and months, but she had young Marcus, now aged around seven, to consider. The apple of her father's eye, we might recall, had been married five years previously so we can be fairly certain that although fully aware of the tragedy that had overtaken her father, she was at least safe and in contact with her mother – it may in fact be that Terentia and Marcus fled to Tullia for protection. This would be especially relevant because once Clodius had discovered that Cicero was gone, he was to name Cicero personally in further legislation and then order that Cicero's beautiful house on the Palatine, so expensively purchased and furnished, be burnt to the ground. Pretty-Boy really did have a deep hatred for Cicero and knew that the *domus* of Cicero was the most potent symbol of the man and his story – destroy that and you destroy Cicero – and no doubt the house was also looted by the local populace prior to its being torched. There is a reference that Cicero took a small statue of Minerva from his home on the night he left and placed it secretly at the foot of the hill asking the goddess to look after Rome while he was away. If true, then we can imagine a small square hole in a main wall of the house, shaped like a mini temple and painted with bright colours. This was the *lararium*, which housed miniature clay and bronze figures representing various gods and goddesses to which offerings and prayers could be made at any time. Possibly lit by a small oil lamp, it is from here that Cicero would have taken the small Minerva – goddess of the home – and then placed her discreetly with his prayers before leaving.

Cicero to Atticus
c. 24 March (?) 58, location unknown

I hope I may see the day when I shall thank you for making me go on living. So far I am heartily sorry you did. But I beg you to come to me as soon as possible at Vibo, where I am going. I have changed direction for many reasons. But if you come there, I shall be able to make a plan for my whole journey and exile. If you do not do that, I shall be surprised: but I am confident you will.

We know that Cicero varied his route numerous times on the journey south as he initially headed for Sicily and then Malta. However, the governor of Sicily, a former friend of Cicero's, refused him entry and again he had to adjust his plans seeking help wherever he could find it. The former Greek settlement of Vibo lay on the northern coast of the toe of Italy. Cicero may have chosen Vibo as it was a small and discreet Roman town but one with a fishing fleet that could provide him with a quick deep sea sailing vessel when he was ready to depart. It may also be that he had arranged some last minute meetings before his departure and needed a safe and obscure venue to say a final goodbye. His reference to thoughts of suicide indicates just how emotionally depressed and hopeless he felt – the awareness of his own miscalculations weighed heavily on a man so used to victory and controlling all around him. How the mighty can fall and the higher the position the further the drop, but in Cicero's case the words of Jim Butcher seem appropriate: 'Some fall from grace – others are pushed.'

Possibly due to the changes of direction, Atticus did not join Cicero at Vibo and nor did Cicero arrive there either, instead he was next writing at much greater length to Terentia from Brundisium and almost a month later and these excerpts display not only thoughts of suicide, but great sadness that their life had come to this:

Brundisium, Cicero to his family
29 April 58

From Tullius to his dear Terentia and Tullia and Marcus greetings

I send you letters less often than I have the opportunity, because, wretched as every hour is for me, when I write to you at home or read your letters I am so overcome with tears that I cannot bear it. If only I had been less anxious to save my life!

I want to see you, dear heart, as soon as I can, and to die in your arms, since neither the gods whom you have worshipped so piously nor the men to whose service I have always devoted myself have made us any recompense.

I have stayed in Brundisium for thirteen days with M. Laenius Flaccus, a very worthy gentleman. He has disregarded the danger to his own property and status in his concern for my safety, and refused to be deterred by the penalties of a wicked law from carrying out the established duties of hospitality and friendship. I pray that one day I may be able to show him my gratitude.

Be sure of one thing: if I have you, I shall not feel that I am utterly lost. But what is to become of my Tulliola? You at home must take care of that – I have nothing to suggest. But assuredly, however matters turn out, the poor little girl's marriage and good name must be a primary consideration.

You urge me to hold my head high and hope for restoration. I wish the facts may give ground for reasonable hope. Meanwhile, as matters wretchedly stand, when am I going to get your next letter? Who will bring it to me? I should have waited for it at Brundisium if the sailors had let me, but they did not want to lose the fair weather.

Take care of your health as best you can, and believe that your unhappiness grieves me more than my own. My dear Terentia, loyalest and best of wives, my darling little daughter, and Marcus, our one remaining hope – goodbye.

Having sent this letter, Cicero set sail for the coast of Greece at the end of April – a journey of three days in good weather – with the intention of moving through Macedonia and then on to Cyzicus where Atticus, it was always Atticus, offered Cicero the use of his estate in Epirus but, according to Shackleton Bailey, there were already enemies and supporters of Catiline in exile in that area so that destination was ruled out. With his small retinue, Cicero changed direction and headed east through Macedonia bound for Thessalonica and reaching the regional capital of Salonika on 23 May and he went no further eastwards. The quickest route would have been along the *Via Egnatia*, the military road through Macedonia and on to Thessalonica and it is likely that Cicero travelled those many miles along this road.

Having walked and ridden on the dusty and hot roads, across streams and rivers, foraging for food and always on the lookout for bandits for three weeks, Cicero located a place to recover his abilities to see events in context. The Roman town of Salonika had a Roman garrison and Plancius is noted with giving him lodgings and it was not only a beautiful city with a great deal of Greek history, but also a thriving trading port – today it's a property developer's nightmare with layers of Byzantine, Roman and Greek remains and it is famous for being one of St Paul's headquarters on his missionary journeys 100 years after Cicero lived there, in around 50 CE. Cicero may have written in the depths of despair, and no doubt he was suffering from a partial nervous breakdown, but he would have been heartened by the local diets of apricots and mulberries, the Greek fountains in the old town, religious shrines to Philip and Alexander of Macedon who both stayed there on their travels, Roman arches and temples near the harbour and, to cap it all, a forum with shops and a square paved in white marble for him to wander through as the most illustrious Roman visitor in its history.

Relations with Quintus in 59–58

After a few weeks trying to settle into a new way of life, Cicero wrote to his brother Quintus. In all we have twenty-seven letters from Marcus to Quintus and they all date to the period between 60 and 54 when Quintus was, for the most part, serving overseas. Quintus has just completed his third year as one of the governors in Asia and he had acquired quite a reputation for brutality and was now looking forward hopefully to an appointment on Caesar's staff – something Cicero felt may now have been jeopardised by his fall from grace and exile. Early in the previous year Cicero had written at least twice to his brother trying to convey to him the need for a measured approach to his power in Asia. In early 59 Cicero had addressed a commentary to his brother entitled 'Advice to a Governor' – perhaps intended for publication, but no doubt a response to Quintus and his 'How to win an election' written for Cicero five years earlier in 64. It would seem his words had little impact. Quintus was reputed to have written rather foolhardy and indiscreet official letters which had been leaked into Roman society – governmental leaks have always been with us – for example in writing to a knight named Catienus, Quintus had boasted about having his father smoked to death to the cheers of a local crowd, others detailed orders to burn people alive or to send them to him and he would ensure it was done. Finally, Quintus had a new reputation for punishing parricide by *poena cullei*, or sewing the offender into a sack with wild animals such as dogs, snakes, or cockerels and then throwing them into water. Quintus had ordered this twice already and was keen for a third instance in the case of a man named Zeuxis. We can view 'Quintus the Quintessential Roman' as one of those mind-boggling characters that we have to become used to in our understanding of what it was to be Roman – that unnerving and disturbing combination of intellectual prowess and yet bewildering and disturbing cruelty contained within the same character. Later in 59, Cicero had also taken his brother to task for the manumission, freeing, of his slave Statius. Manumission was always within the power of the owner, but in this case Statius, as private secretary and *scriba* to Quintus, had acquired a reputation for rudeness and arrogance beyond his station in life and Cicero was enraged:

> *I have many things on my mind, arising from the grave political crisis and these dangers that menace me personally. They are legion, but nothing distresses me more than Statius' manumission.*
>
> *And yet I don't know what to do, and after all the talk is more than the thing itself. Moreover, I can't even be angry with those I really love. I am only pained, deeply pained.*
>
> *You must understand (for it is equally my duty to avoid ill-advised statement and crafty reticence) that Statius has given the gossip of those who want to run you down all the material they have. Previously it could be gathered that certain persons were annoyed by your severity; but now that he has been manumitted, the malcontents have something to talk about.*

Relations with Quintus then could be strained as with any brotherly love, but matters were not helped either by Cicero spending a large sum sent to him by Quintus, now wealthy from his extended period as Governor, to be looked after and then not paying it back. Circumstances do change in people's lives, but Quintus never forgot this action by his elder brother.

Excerpts of other letters serve to give a sense of how Cicero was feeling at this time – a mixture of deep self-pity, regret and love for his brother in his fashion – by which I mean he professed love in flowing prose, but there is a sense of knowing how to describe love rather than how to give it. It is hard to place much of Cicero's more emotional letters into context – for example how far do we read into his words the attitudes we hold today compared to those of 2,000 years in the past? Yet it is not only time that divides us, but also feelings – the feelings of a Roman man, borne into an ambitious equestrian family, trained in the affairs deemed vital to political success with the rigid disciplines expected of the *mos maiorum* – compared to our own very liberal age with our comparatively poor levels of education. To edge ever closer to Cicero the man, we have to take his life and writing in the round – seeing him as the product of his time, but also his own character, proven already to be ambitious, a driven man, capable of warping the truth, perhaps selfish and without doubt egotistical. We may be inspired by much of what Cicero writes in public, but how do we view his most personal correspondence? To Quintus he wrote explaining why they had not yet met on his way into exile:

Cicero to his brother
Thessalonica, 13 June 58

From Marcus to his brother Quintus greetings.

My brother, my brother, my brother! Were you really afraid that I was angry with you for some reason and on that account sent boys to you without a letter, or even that I did not want to see you? I angry with you? How could I be? As though it was you who struck me down, your enemies, your unpopularity, and not I who have lamentably caused your downfall! That much lauded consulship of mine has robbed me of you, and my children, and my country and my possessions; I only hope it has robbed you of nothing but myself. Sure it is that you have never given me cause for anything but pride and pleasure, whereas I have brought you sorrow for calamity, fear of your own, loss, grief, loneliness.

If I had died, the fact itself would stand as ample proof of my brotherly love for you. Instead through my fault you have to do without me and stand in need of others while I am alive, and my voice, which has often defended strangers, is silent when my own flesh and blood is in danger. [Quintus had many good reasons for concern that his own conduct as governor might be the subject of the courts.]

You can imagine how I weep as I write these lines., as I am sure you do as you read them. Can I help thinking of you sometimes, or ever think of you without tears? When I miss you, I do not miss you as a brother only, but as a delightful brother almost of my own age, a son in obedience, a father in wisdom. What pleasure did I ever take apart from you or you apart from me? And then at the same time I miss my daughter, the most loving, modest, and clever daughter a man ever had, the image of my face and speech and mind. Likewise my charming, darling little boy, who I, cruel brute that I am, put away from my arms. All too wise for his years, the poor child already understood what was going on. Likewise your son, your image, whom my boy loved like an elder brother. As for my loyalest of wives, poor, unhappy soul, I did not let her come with me so that there should be someone to protect the remnants of our common disaster, our children.

Regarding Terentia 58

As someone who was himself taken away from his own children when they were of a similar age, I can immediately identify with the pain and grief that Cicero felt. His all-consuming career now seemingly in tatters and with his challenge to stay at the top ruined he now had time to reflect on the emotional cost of his ambition to all those around him, and it was a painful realization to see the damage done to those that loved him – perhaps more than he had loved them. Much as this would be understandable and, in part, an identification of a man coming to terms with the reality of existence as opposed to the pretence of politics, there is still concern that much of what Cicero wrote was how he wanted people to see him, not how he actually felt. Take the final sentence from the above passage. It is entirely plausible and laudable that Terentia should be left behind to tend the children and clearly that is how he wanted to Quintus to view his decision not to have brought her with him into exile. But, if we look back at a previous letter written to Terentia only six weeks earlier we read:

> *Ah, what a desperate, pitiful case is mine! What now? Shall I ask you to come – a sick woman, physically and spiritually exhausted? Shall I not ask then? Am I to live without you? Perhaps I should put it like this: if there is any hope of my return, you must build it up, and help in the campaign. On the other hand if all is over, as I fear, then come to me any way you can.*

Here we have a completely alternative reason why Terentia was not brought out with him – she was being asked to stay behind and work on his behalf for his return. Only if that turned out to be a fruitless task was she to come to him. If one were to be very critical then a case could be made for seeing Cicero even twist his words so carefully as to make it seem that he was in anguish about whether she should come or not. The phrase *'shall I ask you to come – a sick woman, physically exhausted?'* is heavy with faux concern – so presumably Terentia was not so exhausted or sick to work herself to death in agitating for her husband's return? He went further: *'If there is any hope of my return, you must build it up, and help in the campaign'*. In other words, if you detect that there is a groundswell of people wanting me back (he hoped) you must throw everything into this movement – whether you are sick or exhausted. Cicero could easily have brought his entire family to him, spent time regrouping, loving and recovering but no, he wanted to use Terentia as a Trojan Horse to work on his behalf for his return, presumably as a hero if she could manage it, meanwhile he would sit and write and feel sorry for himself.

While this does not paint a particularly pleasant picture of the character of a man idealized throughout history as a most noble Roman of virtue, a saviour of the state and greatest intellect of the ancient world, politicians of any age are very rarely noble and in the Roman period even less so. We must accept that, in order to survive, let alone be as triumphant as Cicero was, that he shared in the abilities required for political success – cunning, scheming and conspiracy. Perhaps sadly, Cicero did not openly write about these more dubious aspects of his character, but they were undoubtedly present and it is important that, in trying to get a true sense of the man himself, we accept that they were a key part of his character. As we have seen numerous times already, it was important to Cicero that he left to posterity the most positive view of his life and achievements as possible but in exile Cicero lets his guard down through a mixture of anger, resentment and desperation. The cut throat nature of his experience in Rome and especially the Senate was such that ruthlessness superseded any thoughts of Greek theories on democracy, emotion or love. Knowledgeable though Cicero was about the philosophy of the Greek poets, this was not used as a way of leading his life or relationships but just an ideal – an ideal totally out of keeping with the realities and necessities of gaining and maintaining power and that Terentia was used a tool to these ends exposes a more authentic view of Cicero than all the philosophic writings could ever do.

For the historian, the period that Cicero spent in exile offers the best and most informed opportunity to build a stronger psychological understanding of him as a personality. Nearly thirty letters have survived from that period, almost all to Atticus, allowing the reader into the very personal world of a man with time to reflect on the world and himself. There are no speeches prepared for delivery to an uncertain public in the forum, no orations minutely conceived to sway 600 disparate senators, and no prosecution embellishments or downright lies to achieve a conviction. But there are letters, poems and speeches about how he coped with what he allowed to be a miserable seventeen months. They reveal far more about Cicero the man than any of the contrived theatrical performances he gave either in court, in the Senate or on his stage in the forum. The central focus throughout is on himself, his mistakes, moaning and self-pity and minutely assessing every small detail of events in Rome looking for clues to his future, his return, his salvation. So much revolves around *meus* and *noster* – as Jo-Marie Claassen said 'the banished man is wrapped in a cocoon of misery'.[1]

When he eventually returned from exile, Cicero reconstructed his experience to create an entirely new image of himself. There was bitter recrimination against those that had allowed his banishment to happen and a reinforcement of the concept of betrayal, the illegality and injustice that had been meted out to him – and all of this was wrapped up in the new image of a brave and intrepid hero now returned to become the saviour of the nation yet again. Cicero would underpin his epic journey as though part of some Greek tragedy where he emerges, thanks to his own courage and the mercy of the gods to vanquish the threats to Rome, a real masterclass in the reinvented self. Historians and history have reacted variously to the literary output from the period of Cicero's banishment and that generated by him after his return. This period allows us to ponder over how Cicero's philosophic foundations changed and to see him in many ways unmasked as he wrote without the knowledge that every word would be pored over by historians for hundreds of years to come, be interpreted and reinterpreted depending on the contextual debates of the time and not at all flattering judgements made about his true character and personality. The period of Cicero's exile offers us a challenge – rather like assessing an actor both on the stage and in the dressing room – trying to work out which is the real person. Was the real Cicero the man on the stage speaking his mind, freed from restraint, able to explode forth his innermost feelings, or was that all contrived as only a talented actor can do. Alternatively, are we closer to the real Cicero in his letters and writings, his books and orations – or were these written for appeal, impact and a legacy? Oliver Goldsmith could have been referring to Cicero when he said *'On the stage he was natural, simple, affecting, 'twas only when he was off, he was acting.'*

Ironically, although Cicero could easily have cut himself off from politics in the city, he remained as close as possible to events. Cicero could have been at the start of a Lucullus moment and moved on to that new phase of Epicurean luxury life that he, apparently, so yearned for when he was writing to Atticus only the year before. Instead, we discover Cicero working his *scribae* hard, writing with tremendous length and intensity, purging his anger while at the same time no doubt starting to recover his zeal to return to Rome and beginning to feel the urge to plot his return in glory as the politician in him regained control in the streets and sounds of Salonika. Not in the mood for philosophic pondering or poetic wandering, this is a fallow period for literary pursuits other than correspondence littered with regrets for what he had lost and the false friends he had trusted. In the same letter of June 13 to Quintus:

Now if you can do what I, whom you always thought a strong man, am unable to do, then stand up and brace yourself for the struggle you may have to sustain. I should hope (if any hope of mine counts for anything) that your integrity, the affection in which you are held in the community, and in some degree also the pity felt for myself will bring you protection. If, however, it turns out that your hands are free of that danger, you will doubtless do what you think can be done, if anything, about me. I get many letters from many people on the subject and they make themselves out to be hopeful, but for my own part I can't see any grounds for hope, when my enemies are in power and my friends have either deserted or actually betrayed me. Perhaps the idea of me coming home frightens them as involving blame for their own villainy. But please see how things stand in Rome and make them clear to me.

And towards the end of his long letter

How much faith you should put in Hortensius I don't know. He behaved to me most villainously and treacherously, while pretending the warmest affection and sedulously keeping up our daily intercourse.

In June 58 Cicero received word that could have been quite heartening – with Caesar gone to the north the inevitable clash between Clodius and Pompey broke out and on 1 June, while Clodius was out of the city, a motion was put before the Senate for Cicero's recall. Although blocked by another tribune, Atticus was at least able to send on some positive news that he was far from forgotten, but Cicero remained depressed as though Salonika and the people there held nothing of any regard for him. Cicero write to Atticus on 17 July 58:

You are at pains to argue what might be hoped for, particularly through the Senate, and yet you write that the clause in the bill which forbids any reference to the subject in the Senate is being posted up. So silence naturally reigns. And in these circumstances you take me to task for tormenting myself, when I am tried beyond any mortal that ever was, as you well know.

I am still stuck here, with no one to talk to and nothing to think about. I may have suggested to you, as you say, that you should join me; but I give that up, and realize that you are helping me where you are, whereas you could do nothing even verbally to lighten my load here. I can't write any more, nor have I anything to write about. I am rather waiting for news from your side.

With Clodius in office until the end of his year on 10 December and with Caesar's consular block of Piso and Gabinius, Cicero could hardly expect anything to change during 58, but the summer elections in Rome heralded positive possibilities for the following year. Not only were a number of the new tribunes well disposed towards the Republic, but also one of the consuls-elect was Lentulus Spinther – a close ally of Pompey and supported by Caesar, but also a friend to Cicero. Sadly, the co consul would be Metellus Nepos – he of the continuing onslaughts against Cicero after the execution of the plotters, the attempt to recall Pompey from the war in the east to deal with Catiline's army, siding with Caesar in the brutal physical encounter with Cato on the steps of the Temple of Castor and Pollux and cousin to Clodius.

Towards the end of the year, Cicero decided on a move to a new location – closer to Rome and therefore earlier arrival of news and correspondence. In November, Plancius, Cicero's host and protector while in Salonica, returned to Rome and Cicero followed him back probably once again on the *Via Egnatia* through Macedonia and on to Dyrrachium – today the city of Durres on the coastline of Albania. This was in itself a slight tonic for the disconsolate and dejected Cicero, he knew the town well and referred to himself as a patron of the town in his letter to Terentia on 30 November 58. Originally a very ancient Greek trading sea port called Epidamnos, Roman Dyrrachium was already hundreds of years old in its relationship with Rome and was a busy nexus for travellers to and from Thessalonica, Macedonia and Thrace. Almost exactly ten years later in 48, Dyrrachium was to be the site of a major battle between Pompey and Caesar during the Civil War – but that was on the far horizon as Cicero settled into lodgings in the town and waited for news, writing as follows to Terentia in these extracts of 30 November 58:

> *I have been given three letters by Aristocritis, and almost blotted them out with tears. I am overwhelmed with grief, dearest Terentia; and my own distresses do not torture me more than yours and my family's. But my wretchedness is greater than yours (and yours is bitter enough) because while we both share in the disaster, the blame for it is mine and mine only.*
>
> *The hope of restoration held out to me is very slender. Many are hostile, almost all are jealous. To drive me out took some doing, but to keep me out is easy. However, as long as my family continues to hope, I shall do my part, for I would not wish to seem responsible for every fiasco.*
>
> *Our last hope now lies in the new tribunes – and in the first few days: for if novelty is lost, we are finished. I have therefore sent Aristocritis to you straight away* [poor Aristocritis, no sooner had he arrived with letters than he is dispatched back again the way he had come] *so that you can write me an immediate account of the initial stages and a conspectus of the whole business.... I am staying at Dyrrachium at the present time expressly so that I can get the quickest possible news of what goes on.*

What actually went on was that Cicero was still writing letters from exile in the February of the new year of 57 responding to dreadful events that he was informed had occurred the previous month.

Where was Cato?

In Rome the new consuls and tribunes had taken up their posts and Cicero still waited upon events – powerless to affect much change directly. But Clodius was not going to exit stage left – his time as tribune had been frenetic and fractious, single handedly he had tried to intimidate democracy into submission. His gangs roamed the streets at will and democratic process had withered. But where was Cato? Back in February and March of 58, just as Cicero was in anguish about what to do and whether to go into exile or stay and fight, Cato had accepted a magistrate's position in Cyprus. The annexation of Cyprus was another of tribune Publius Clodius Pulcher's decisions in his year of office. It was originally conferred upon Gabinius for his pro consular year, but after he rejected the offer in favour of Syria, Clodius put forward a bill nominating Cato for this honour. Historians cannot agree why Cato left Rome at this juncture. Given his determination and propensity for resistance against tyranny, why did he accept the offer from the lawless and reckless Clodius who was terrorizing Rome with the connivance of the Triumvirate? It could have been that Cato was encouraged to go – Caesar desired all opposition removed while he was away in Gaul so why not accept the reality and take the offer. Additionally, a period in Cyprus would allow him to recharge his own coffers and prepare for his own run at the consulship – he was well advanced on the *cursus honorum* and he had the support of the *optimates* in the Senate. Thirdly, he would be returning soon after Caesar and thus ready for the next coming stages of the fight for the survival of the Republic. Perhaps it was a mixture of the three, but in any event, Plutarch tells us that Cato was given minimal staff for his role with only two clerks – one a known thief and the other a paid henchman of Clodius so we can perhaps forget any notion that Clodius had tried to reach out and form any sort of friendship with Cato – like Cicero, Clodius wanted him gone.

During his journey to Cyprus, Cato stopped at Rhodes for a few weeks where he paused to see how King Ptolemy might react to losing the island which had belonged to Egypt until Clodius unilaterally annexed it. Ptolemy however had bigger problems on his mind. He had again been ejected from his own country by an uprising and was heading to Rome hoping for a return on his investment and to receive further resources to help him back to the throne again – he would be waiting for three long years. On Cato's arrival and presentation of the Senate's decision, the local King committed suicide rather than suffer the indignity of capture and death – perhaps an event that struck Cato deeply, as this would ultimately be the way he met his own end – from which point onwards Cato governed Cyprus in his own inimitable style. At the end of his special commission (he was not after all a pro consul) Cato was supposed to return with a detailed copy of his account books – something he was acutely aware of, both as a sponsor of the new laws on bribery in 59 and the *lex Julia de repetundis*. It was crystal clear – he should return with one copy, to be stored in the Temple of Saturn where all public accounts were stored, and a second identical set of accounts should be left in the province to avoid embezzlement. In Cato's case, one set was mysteriously lost at sea and the other accidentally burnt in his tent before he left – a terrible combination of bad luck. Much as we like to believe that Cato was a Stoic hero, above the crimes and fraud perpetuated by almost every Roman of note we have to be open to the notion that, just like Cicero, Cato had to abide by the needs of men aiming for the top. This in turn meant a modest amount of embezzlement, bribery and corruption – how else could men of moderate means compete at the top levels? Cato received high praise for his honesty perhaps because his profiteering was not as extreme as others – but he was nevertheless just as culpable.

Cicero is recalled to Rome

Meanwhile Rome continued to lurch through further pain as two new faces arrived on the political scene in the spring of the new consular year of 57. Almost the first item of business put to the Senate in the new year was a proposal by consul Lentulus to recall Cicero to Rome and the measure passed, not with a majority, but a worthy number – hardly the clamour that Cicero hoped for. However, when the measure was taken for ratification out to the Assembly, Clodius unleashed his roughs into the forum to shout and disrupt events to prevent the measure being heard, fighting broke out, blood and screams filled the air and bodies lay in the streets – including a wounded Quintus, who was in Rome supporting the return of his brother. This was serious stuff as tribunes were also attacked and their sacrosanct position should have warranted a very serious response, but events moved too fast for the Senate and two new tribunes Titus Annius Milo and Publius Sestius, a noted supporter of Cicero, recruited their own groups and regular fights broke out in various parts of the city between these sects. It was not to be until the Imperial period, when emperors stationed the Praetorian bodyguard in the city barracks that Rome eventually had its own armed police force of sorts.

Over the spring and summer there were numerous discussions and persuasions. Atticus was there now acting as agent and public relations manager for his friend Cicero and made a good case for needing Rome's greatest orator and lawyer back in the forum to articulate the need of the Republic for calm and decency. Gradually Caesar's premonition came true and even the vacillating Pompey was persuaded to support the movement for Cicero's return – for many months Clodius had been too intimidating for Pompey to do much in the full knowledge that Clodius had Caesar's support – for the time being. Eventually Caesar, receiving almost daily briefings by despatch riders from Rome, was persuaded that the time was right, but this needed to be handled with care. Clodius, for all his scandalous behaviour, lies and violence was popular with the people. Like a MAGA supporter in the USA of 2022, he had a strong base that believed what he said and admired him for direct action and getting things done. The popular view may not have been agitating for the return of long lingering speeches with a vocabulary few could understand. Equally, as Cicero was well aware, he had his enemies and his jealousies – there would be some in the Senate not at all happy that he should return once more to lecture them at length – but lest we forget, none of this could have happened without the absent Caesar's blessing.

Lentulus, very sensibly, proceeded in stages and in May 57 the Senate agreed to thank all those who had acted to help and assist Cicero during his banishment from Rome. The Military Assembly was convened to consider his recall – this was a clever way of convening the popular vote without relying just on the Roman mob and Clodius – and representatives from across Italy were invited to attend in August at The Field of Mars. The Senate met in July and the consuls were asked to prepare legislation for the recall of Cicero – at last. The motion was almost unanimous with no tribune voting against it and the only men of note opposed being Clodius and his brother Appius. The Military Assembly convened and included many veterans ordered by Pompey to vote in favour and finally, guarded by Milo and his own hired gladiators, the bill was passed triumphantly.

We have no letters of this period from Cicero – sadly they were either lost accidentally or perhaps destroyed by Atticus as they showed either the true levels of despair of the hero or the disagreements between them. There is little doubt that anyone could understand should Atticus lose his patience with Cicero's never-ending demands on him or his often sarcastic and sharp criticisms. Cicero was indeed fortunate to have his Atticus. We do know, however, how Cicero felt soon after his return. On 4 August Cicero had left Dyrachium earlier than he should, confident that he was going to receive a positive outcome and landed back in Brundisium the next day on the *Nones* (5) of August. The day itself could not have been more auspicious and indeed it could not have been luck that Cicero landed not only on the day of the festival of the founding of the city, but also Tullia's birthday, as she was there to greet him. While we naturally focus on just the letters to and from Cicero to Atticus and a small circle of contacts, it is important for a fuller picture to remember that thousands of other letters planning events, organizing people, making things happen are all lost.

The apple of her father's eye was there waiting to hug and hold her father on this warm August day as he stepped ashore, perhaps a lot thinner, probably a lot more lined in the face and almost certainly very emotional. But Tullia's husband Caius Calpurnius Piso Frugi, who had done so much in his own way to work for the return of his father-in-law, was not there. He had recently died, leaving Tullia a widow from what was, by all accounts we have, a happy marriage to a good man. Having rested for six days being treated no doubt as a true celebrity in Brundisium, Cicero received word from Rome that the law had been carried by the democratically convened and run Assembly of Centuries and he set off the following day. As he wrote to Atticus a few days later after arriving in Rome:

> *On 11 August, while at Brundisum, I learned by letter from Quintus that the law had been carried in the Assembly of Centuries amid remarkable demonstrations of enthusiasm by all ranks and ages and with an extraordinary concourse of country voters. Thence I set out, after receiving the most flattering remarks of regard from the townspeople, and as I travelled along I was joined by congratulatory deputations from all quarters.*

The next ten to fourteen days were spent travelling as the returning hero – the adulation he had always hoped for lined the roads and small villages as he passed. According to ORBIS, the quickest route would have taken Cicero firstly north up the back of the heel of Italy to Barium then cutting westwards into central Italy heading for Beneventum on the Appian Way, before travelling north west to Rome where he arrived on 4 September. The entire journey was uphill as if reaching the heavens at the end – Cicero described the scene to Atticus:

> *So I arrived at the outskirts of Rome. Not a man whose name was known to my nomenclator* [literally a man who remembered names for his master], *no matter what his rank, but came out to meet me, except for enemies who could neither conceal nor deny that they were such.*

There is a distinct change in the air in this very short extract. Naturally the ego of Cicero once again is the dominant characteristic of his personality and he cannot soak up enough acclaim and applause to satiate his need for acceptance and acclamation but now, instead of speaking in shades of grey regarding his popularity, Cicero openly accepts that he has enemies, that he is hated by some and any resistance that he may have had to the notion that he could turn anyone back to his side, has evaporated. It is now a battle of skills and wills. In the same letter:

> When I reached the Porta Capena [the gate to the city from the Appian Way] I found the steps of the temples thronged by the common people, who welcomed me with vociferous applause. Like numbers and applause followed me to the Capitol. In the forum and the Capitol itself the crowd was spectacular.

On 5 September 57 Cicero made a speech to the Senate (presumably having stayed with his daughter at the home of a friend overnight as his house was now but a black ruin). This oration was structured in what was to be a pattern for all his speeches in the months to come, made up of lavish praise for Pompey and the consul Lentulus, pointed condemnation of the consuls of the previous year and of course Clodius, references to the enormous upswell of happiness amongst the people of Rome at his return and the inevitable reframing of his flight from Rome as the actions of a man prepared to sacrifice his freedom for the nation and prevent a civil war.

Now ever present with Cicero was the air of vengeance against what he termed 'false friends'. Indeed, there were numerous plotters who could be included in a list of those wishing to see Cicero brought down – he was a man that made enemies easily even if he did not realise it – but it was he that manifestly felt that he could make all men his friends through his eloquence and reason and so naturally it comes hard to realise that actually this is never possible. In the world of politics and especially at this stage in the history of the Roman Republic, identified enemies are and were to be trusted more than friends.

Note

1. Classon., Jo-Marie 'Cicero's Banishment: "Tempora et Mores"', *Acta Classica*, Vol. 35 p. 19–47.

Part VI

Readjustments

Chapter 20

Time to Reflect

Few things are brought to a successful issue by impetuous desire, but most by calm and prudent forethought.

Thucydides

Let us be clear, Cicero did not heed these words from one of the greatest of ancient Greek historians. Overflowing emotion and thoughts of his indispensable presence at this stage of the events in Rome clouded the usual careful symmetry of Cicero's thinking. Instead of a lawyer's forensic assessment of the merits and strengths of a case, Cicero engaged as if he had never left, using a rhetoric out of step with the current temperature and not having taken time to assess how positions had adjusted over the period of his absence.

What had changed was important and significant. The situation in Rome was complex. Some things were self-evident though – despite Milo and his own attempts to check chaos on the streets, Clodius was still present as were his gangs and he was still a powerful force of disruption so necessary to disrupt democracy to the point where the people cry out for a tyrant or dictator. The rift between Pompey and Clodius had created the gap Caesar had feared through which Cicero escaped back to Rome. In the shadows behind Clodius was Crassus, egging him on, paying the bills for the gangs and attempting his own form of destabilization. Caesar was in Gaul creating his own history enough to rival Pompey, and the Triumvirate was showing numerous cracks of jealousy and frustrations. Once a junior partner to Crassus and Pompey, Caesar was self-evidently now the major player. Finally, Cato was absent still in Cyprus and the *optimates* were largely inactive and rudderless.

Step forward the ebullient Cicero into what he described *'It is a sort of second life I am beginning'*, with his aspirations to take charge of the situation he was only seeing from his own position. Almost immediately Cicero was given a chance to plant his flag back at the centre of Roman politics. Grain prices had been rising and Clodius wasted no time in blaming Cicero. Ridiculous though that was, Cicero had to respond and as a large crowd gathered outside the senate house, Cicero immediately felt the adrenalin of history, back in his old hunting ground and back on the familiar stage in the forum he spoke. The general clamour was for Pompey to be asked to take over control of grain supplies. Clearly behind the scenes agitation and no doubt money had created this demand for Pompey to be drawn out of retirement and boredom. Cicero wrote or rather crowed to Atticus in a letter of or around 10 September:

> There was a general demand, not only from the populace but also the boni too, that Pompey be asked to take charge of supplies. He himself was eager for the job, and the crowd called on me by name to propose it. I did so in a full-dress speech. In the absence of all the consulars except Messalla and Afranius, because as they alleged, it was not safe for them to speak, the Senate passed a decree as proposed by me, to the effect that Pompey should be asked to undertake the matter and appropriate legislation be introduced.

In effect Cicero was returning to his old mantra of believing himself to be central to any major development in Rome and that the 'Harmony of Orders' was in turn the ideal state of affairs which only he was able to manage, create and maintain. In fact Cicero was adrift from reality, harmony was no longer the objective for many senators, instead self-enrichment and self-glorification together with a large piece of selfishness characterized the most senior levels of government and Cicero was deluded to think otherwise. Even Cato was away losing his account books prior to his imminent return. Additionally, Cicero conveniently and naively forgot Pompey's betrayal eighteen months before and again tied himself to that mast of a man proven many times to be both a military and administrative genius, but with a talent for vacillation far beyond any contemporary political figure. Pompey still could not decide what his political ideology was – he traversed the gap between *optimates* and *populares* like a free climber without ropes, never aligned to anyone and could never be relied upon to hold fast to the rock face. Pompey wanted the approval of the people and his soldiers, but he was also wary of the contempt of the nobility – he was after all a new man like Cicero and sensitive to his image. On the other hand, some traditional Roman rules still applied – *dignitas* was paramount, and marriages for alliance essential, *amicitia* and political friendships came and went as fast as the daily weather and the Senate was never as disparate as it was now, the urban mob of Rome was dangerous and clients rather than true friends meant power. What was new was that these older, traditional values were being undercut by a new force – Julius Caesar. In the same 10 September letter Cicero reflected on his property situation:

Of my general position it can so far be said that I have attained what I thought would be most difficult to recover, namely my public prestige, my standing in the Senate, and my influence amongst honest men, in larger measure than I had dreamed possible. But my private affairs are in a very poor way – you are aware how my property has been crippled and dissipated and pillaged – and I stand in need not so much of your resources, which I count as my own, as of your advice in pulling together what is left and putting it on a sound footing.

It may well be that the reference to his 'private life' was the first indication that we have that his relationship with Terentia was heading towards collapse. The strain on them both had been serious and it was no doubt difficult to simply pick up from where he had left off – this is sadly an all-too-common result of emotional separation through imprisonment. As for the property issue, again Cicero may have been better advised, if he ever listened, to have taken a softer approach to his return. He was not the conquering hero that he supposed, the reactions to him were not the same as his career up to 63 and he had many enemies – something he kept saying he knew, but failed to adjust his position regarding them. Thus, instead of a softer approach in respect to his property, and perhaps starting afresh, Cicero went to the College of Pontiffs – as Clodius had cleverly and carefully built a shrine to Liberty on the site and in so doing hoped Cicero could never regain the land – and the Senate with his case for compensation.

De Doma Sua, 27 September 57

Domo per scelus erepta, per latrocinium occpata, per religionis uim sceleratius etiam aedificata quam cuersa, career sine maxima ignminia rei publicae, meo dedecore ac dolre non possum

The house that has been snatched away by wickedness, acquired by robbery, built upon through a violent form of religion, even more criminally than it was destroyed, cannot be taken from me without the greatest ignominy to the state, and dishonour and pain to myself.

This was the final statement from Cicero arguing for the full return of his house from the hands of Clodius and those who supported him and echoes the argument that he had made throughout his speech – that Catiline was impure, his actions therefore polluted by hatred and that the actions were a disease within the state that needed to be purified.

This approach was not uncommon for Cicero. The historical evidence contained in Cicero's extant speeches and orations is clear that, as a prosecutor, it was Cicero's job to win a case almost regardless of the truth – truth was for the defence to ascertain and prove. Thus, Cicero regularly set out to demean, destroy or otherwise pollute the character of his intended victim. In respect to Verres, Catiline, and now Clodius, the strategy was to display the defendant as a plague or pestilence within the Roman state and those who acted against the best interests of the Republic were guilty in the eyes of the gods. In this particular case of course Clodius was an easy victim – not that the Collegia needed reminding – but his past resonated with crimes, intrusions on religious ceremonies which made the erection of a shrine a hypocrisy, along with incest, violence and widespread bribery. However, in *De Doma Sua* it can be argued that Cicero went to extreme lengths to gain his victory. No doubt driven by the very personal nature of his extreme hatred of Clodius and the attack on his home, Cicero certainly went the extra mile in ensuring that Clodius was an enemy for life. In his article of 2004, W. Stroh states that 'posterity has not always followed Cicero's self-assessment without hesitation' and a commonly held view remains now that Cicero was outrageous 'in spiteful polemics against his enemies and unscrupulous glorification of himself, or, at any rate, that he went a great deal further than he needed to in order to win the case'.

By going so far Cicero ratcheted up the animosity that would flow from Clodius – but he was not the only target for Cicero's charges of pestilential influences and plague within the Republic. Piso and Gabinius also received the same treatment with references to the evil Catiline as the final insults and insinuations that they deserved the same fate. Rome and its politics were to suffer much in the months ahead thanks to this speech from Cicero and as ever, words were his weapons of choice and he could cut deeply into any heart.

Four days after the speech and after much debate on how to treat Clodius with due care in their findings, on 1 October the consuls, together with city surveyors agreed on the return and rebuilding by the state of Cicero's home, valuing his house on the Palatine at 2 million sestertii – as opposed to the 3.5 million he had paid Crassus for it, and the villa at Tusculum at 500,000 with 250,000 for the Formiae site. All in all, not a good result and Cicero was immediately peeved and angered – not content that he was fortunate to get anything at all because had the Chief of the College been in Rome instead of in Gaul, he may well have received nothing. In a resentful tone, he wrote to Atticus:

The valuation is sharply criticised, not only by better-class people but by the populace as well. You may wonder why this happened. They say my modesty was the reason, in that I neither refused compensation nor pressed my claim with vigour. But it isn't that. That would have been in my favour rather than otherwise. No, my dear Titus Pomponius, those same gentry (you don't need me to tell you their names) who formerly clipped my wings don't want to see them grow back to their old size. However, I hope they are growing already.

In the confrontational tone in Cicero's letter, we can sense the increasingly bitter divide between Cicero and a significant part of the Senate. The men of the College of Pontiffs were the same men who had to sit in the Senate, but Cicero could appreciate the difficulty he placed them in. Far from being the bridge builder he imagined himself to be, the philosopher-king above the melee of petty rivalry, Cicero was allowing himself to be drawn into the mud of intrigue and segregation which now was the hallmark of government in Rome. He would have to devise a strategy to rise above all this if he was to be the philosopher-king and risk even greater resentment. Cicero's own phrase of *o tempora, o mores* – Oh the times! Oh the customs! would ring in his ears as he viewed the sorry state of the Senate and of democracy and decency.

Cicero to Atticus
Rome, October 57

.....As to my private life, my affairs are in a terrible tangle. My house is being rebuilt, as you know at what expense and trouble. My Formian villa is being reconstructed, and I cannot bear to let it go nor look at it. I have put up the Tusculum property for sale, though I can't easily do without a place near Rome.

Nor was he able to rid himself of Clodius, who had spoken out in public against any form of compensation for Cicero and criticized the weak Senate for agreeing to compensate a man whom they had previously banished. But one key aspect marked Cicero out from his predecessors who had returned bitter from banishment – he did not wreak violent vengeance. Unlike Marius or Sulla, his arrival was *in pace atque otio* – in peace and leisure or calm – for Cicero the aim of revenge was to display his statesmanlike approach to stabilizing the administration of the state and in so doing, provoke even more anger at his superior bearing – a red rag to those who still resented the *novus homo*. This was all part of what Cicero saw as his rebirth, his 'second life' energized by the acclaim he had felt on his return to the city.

Why was the house on the Palatine so important to Cicero?

In her April 2000 article 'At home with Cicero', Shelley Hales explains just why the matter of the house on the Palatine Hill was so important for Cicero. It was partly about the money, no one wants to borrow such incredible sums only to see their capital pillaged, burnt down and built on with a temple. By so doing, Clodius was trying to erase the image of the man as well as the man himself. In Rome the *domus* was indicative not just of status and an awareness of fashion and culture, but it was also a statement of success. As in the USA, ancient Roman society prized status and class above most things and the display of wealth was built around the visual impact of the home. In the United Kingdom, for the most part but not always, such displays are thought of as vulgar so the palatial residence or the humble bungalow is often hidden by high fences or hedges – it is a nation of hedging – but it is also a statement of reluctance to engage with neighbours, an unfriendly act in a nation that protests its welcoming nature. Not so in ancient Rome or modern-day USA where anything that could obstruct a 100 per cent frontal view of the home is removed. This is unabashed achievement and status in your face.

Across the Roman world, the house was inseparable from the man that lived there. In *De Officiis,* Cicero advises his son Marcus to make sure he has a well-appointed house and this meant a good position for others to see you, the number of visitors to your home and your awareness of the latest cultural fashions and styles. The aim was to be featured in the Roman equivalent of *Good Housekeeping* or *Vogue* magazines. Cicero understood that full restoration of his place in society and the Senate rested on full restitution of his properties just as Clodius Pulcher understood that the destruction of his house was central to the destruction of Cicero, his reputation and his future. As Hales reminds us, the concentration of property in such a small area was the collective identity of the top of society, but it was also part of the breeding ground for blatant competition on a social and political level. If we imagine that all Members of Parliament saw their political identity linked to the visual status of having a home within sight of the Houses of Parliament then we can start to imagine the clamour for property, the prices houses would reach and the nature of the struggle for political visibility.

Cicero was determined to excel in his property holdings in one way or another. Despite being short of funds, he borrowed again and told Quintus 'I am building in three different places' as well as 'refurbishing my other properties. I live in a more expensive style than I used. It was called for.' What was called for was perhaps a more subtle reintroduction of his presence on the political scene, but Cicero did not see matters that way. He had returned ebullient and drank the air of what he interpreted as recognition of his martyrdom as the saviour of the state and thus justified to himself why he needed to exceed what he had before as recompense for his past pain – all of which he eulogized to the Senate on countless occasions. His romanticized memory of his experience became symbolized in the rebuilding of his house on the Palatine, at the state's expense, and even the purchase of a new villa complex at Cumae in the Bay of Naples.

But Clodius just would not let go. His determination to crush Cicero and all he represented was, after the *doma sua* speech, now more poisoned than ever and, in a reference to the rebuilding work on the Palatine Hill, Cicero recorded in a letter to Atticus:

> On 3 November an armed gang drove the workmen from my site, threw down Catulus' portico which was in process of restoration by consular contract under a senatorial decree and had nearly reached the roof stage, smashed upon my brother's house by throwing stones from my site, and then set it on fire. This was by Clodius' orders, with all Rome looking on as the fire-brands were thrown, and loud protest and lamentation – I won't say from the boni, for I doubt whether they exist, but from all and sundry. Clodius was running riot even before, but after this frenzy he thinks of nothing but massacring his enemies, and goes from street to street openly offering the slaves their freedom.... On 11 November, as I was going down Holy Street, he came after me with his men. Uproar! Stones flying, cudgels and swords in evidence. And all like a bolt from the blue! I retired into Tettius Damio's forecourt, and my companions had no difficulty in keeping out the rowdies.

The reference to the *boni* is interesting. It seems that Cicero now despaired of the concept of the good men of the Republic – to him they seemed no longer to exist and that may have been so, but such a generalization may also mask the reality which was that Cicero had less and less genuine friends in response to the political strategy he was following and indeed the character and personality that he was allowing to dominate his thinking. The needy man continued to be needy, and the people he really wanted respect from were withholding it – but why? That the streets of Rome continued to be beset with violence between Clodius and his gangs set on creating instability against those of Milo and Flaccus, whom Cicero had so successfully defended in 59, could be laid at Cicero's door and the strategy of trying to further demean Clodius was only resulting in more of the same. It was a personal clash of wills that was making Rome such a difficult place in which to live and there was more to come. The day after the attack on Cicero, 4 November 57, Clodius vented his wrath directly on the home of Milo intending to kill him. A nasty fight ensued where a large number of the key henchmen of Clodius lay bleeding to death in the street so for the time being Clodius had to pull back and regroup.

Egypt…again

The end of the year saw a return to the problem of Egypt. It was nothing to do with any sort of feeling or moral support for Ptolemy that drove the interest of the Senate, it was the grain harvest that Egypt produced that was vital for the Roman people – grain from Egypt and Sicily made up the major part of supplies for the state. A competition developed between the former consul, Lentulus Splinther, now Governor of Cilicia, and Pompey – the latter seeing a chance for a new military campaign and great wealth from a grateful king. Cicero was conflicted. On the one hand he was keen to align himself with the great Pompey – of the three men in the Triumvirate, Pompey was still the only one likely to be swayed by Cicero and he knew Caesar only acted on behalf of Caesar – Crassus was never going to be loyal to anyone. On the other, Lentulus had been instrumental in his return to Rome – even though Cicero saw him as letting him down in the matter of compensation for his damaged property. Cicero resolved this dilemma by writing at great length to Lentulus protesting how hard he was working on his behalf, at the same time, he tried to work out exactly what Pompey wanted as this extract from a letter from Cicero to Lentulus dated from Rome, 15 January 56 indicates:

> I happened to be dining with Pompey that evening. It was a better moment than had ever come my way before, because we had just had our most successful day in the Senate since your departure. So, I talked to him and I could flatter myself that I led his mind away from all other notions and focussed it upon upholding your position. When I listened to him talking, I quite acquit him of all suspicion of selfish aims. But when I look at his friends of all classes, I see what is now plain to everyone, that this whole business has for a long while past been bedevilled by certain individuals, not without the connivance of the king himself and his advisors'

In other words, don't blame Pompey if he gets the job and not you. It's not his fault nor mine. Cicero was correct, there was a great deal going on behind the scenes that made securing the command to sort the grain problem from Egypt more than a little difficult. Ptolemy had spent so much on bribing eminent Romans to support his restoration that he had raised taxes so high his people threw him out. The annexation of Cyprus had further eroded his treasury and, being aware that he had once more fled to Rome, 100 senior figures had decided to travel from Alexandria to Rome to make their own protests and representations. According to Cassius Dio writing 200 years later:

> *Now he [Ptolemy] heard of it in advance, while still in Rome, and sent men out in various directions to ambush the envoys before they could arrive. Thus he caused the majority of them to perish en route, while of the survivors he had some slain in the city itself, and others he either terrified by what had happened or administering bribes persuaded them neither to consult the magistrates touching the matters for which they had been sent nor make any mention at all of those who had been killed.*

The Egyptian issue of the restoration of the King and the grain supply issue continued during January of the new consular year and became embroiled in yet another challenge from Clodius. Again, the bitter former tribune created trouble for both the Senate and Cicero with a charge this time against Milo of – wait for it – disturbing the peace! The irony and hypocrisy were breathtaking, but Cicero again saw it not so much as a duty, but an opportunity yet again to lock horns with Clodius. On 7 February and acting for the defence, Cicero called on his presumed ally Pompey to speak in defence of Milo as he wrote to Quintus:

> *Pompey spoke – or rather tried to speak, for no sooner was he on his feet than Clodius' gangs raised a clamour, and all through his speech he was interrupted by shouting, even by insults and abuse. When he wound up (and I will say he showed courage; he was not put off, but delivered all he had to say, sometimes even managing to get silence by his personal authority) – well, when he wound up, Clodius rose. Wishing to repay the compliment, our side gave him such an uproarious reception that he lost command of thoughts, tongue and countenance. That lasted till half-past one, Pompey having finished just after midday – all manner of insults, ending up with some highly scabrous verse to the address of Clodius and Clodia. Pale with fury, he started a game of question and answer: 'Who's starving the people to death?' 'Pompey', answered the gang. 'Who wants to go to Alexandria?' Answer 'Pompey.' 'Whom do you want to go?' Answer 'Crassus' (who was present as a supporter of Milo, wishing him no good). About 2.15 the Clodians started spitting at us, as though on a signal. Sharp rise in temperature! They made a push to dislodge us, our side counter-charged. Flight of gang. Clodius was hurled from the rostrum, at which point I too made off for fear of what would happen in the free-for-all. The Senate was convened in its House, and Pompey went home. I did not attend, however,*

*not wishing to keep mum about so remarkable an incident nor yet to offend
the boni by standing up for Pompey, who was under fire from Bibulus, Curio,
Favonius, and young Servilius.*

Roman politics was entering yet another new phase on a downward spiral that
few were trying to stop. Cato the Younger was still away from Rome and he
needed a replacement to try to restore the dwindling authority of the Senate.
Cicero was more of a red rag to Clodius than a block and his presence at the
forefront of trials defending members of the establishment did little to calm
the anger that Clodius was constantly stoking – if he had been wounded and
killed on the streets instead of his gladiators, then history may well have been
very different, just as if Hitler had been killed in the bomb attempt against
him right back in 1923, or if the legal process in the USA had been able to
prevent Donald Trump from running for President for a second time – at the
time of writing we await the result of that last example of whether fate helps
or hinders the survival of democracy.

Pompey drew back from the forum, he was not only shocked by his
treatment and the lack of respect for his *auctoritas*, but also fearful for his
life as he mentioned to Cicero and openly to the Senate – as Cicero wrote
to Quintus on the 8 February warning that '*he* [Pompey]*is getting ready and
bringing up men from the country. Clodius on his side is reinforcing his gangs.*'
With Pompey needing to call on his veterans to assemble in Rome ready to
defend him against threats from Clodius, with open spitting and fighting in
the forum, the Senate and anywhere that a political meeting was being held,
Clodius was achieving his, or Caesar's aims, namely spreading chaos that could
only be solved by martial law and the arrival of a strong man at the centre – in
other words the end of the democratic state.

Chapter 21

Back to the Courts 56

A lawyer will do anything to win a case, sometimes he will even tell the truth.
Patrick Murray

The matter of Pompey and a possible command in Egypt was settled in a strange way. The Sibylline Books were of great sacrosanctity within the plethora of Roman items of virtue. Supposedly purchased from a sibyl or priestess of ancient Greece by the last king of Rome, the 'books' were a collection of prophecies which were consulted at times of extreme danger in order to avert a calamity to the state. Originally kept in a sacred vault under the Temple of Jupiter on the Capitoline, they were then moved to the Temple of Jupiter on the Capitol but when that burnt down in 83 they were lost. The Senate sent envoys throughout Ilium, Samos and Sicily to find replacements and then stored them again, under the safety and supervision of chosen senators and the Pontifex Maximus in the restored temple. When consulted, the prophecies were interpreted and read out to the public leaving much room for oversimplification. However, in this case the prophecy was clear – do not remove your support for the King (Ptolemy), but equally send him no army and this was enough to satisfy Pompey that he should remain in his now fortified villa.

The trial of Milo, February 56

The situation was becoming perilous, but did not deteriorate further at this point. No doubt the population of Rome and the rest of Italy longed for a period of calm compared to the almost constant fighting in the Senate and Cicero needed funds and a reason to exist outside of politics where, at present, it seemed impossible to get a resumption of normal business. The year had already started with the disruptions of the attacks on Pompey over the Egyptian issues and the trial of Milo, instigated by Clodius and more were to come. The trial it seems fell apart, but Milo would not escape a further attempt on his freedom four years later in 52.

Pro Sestio March 56

In this case and against the backdrop of continual realignments in the Senate with Clodian inspired attacks on anyone supportive of the status quo, the tribune of 57 that had supported Cicero for his return to Rome, Publius Sestius, was also charged with bribery and breach of the peace. These charges were against a man who had shown a dignified political career, loyalty to Cicero for many years, helped put down the Catilinarian revolt in 63 and been on the streets with Milo trying to control the mobs paid by Clodius to create anarchy – this latter point no doubt being the central reason he was targeted for attack by Clodius. The importance of this trial is that Cicero used this platform to frame a speech specifically designed to lay out an alternative for the Republic – and achieve an acquittal for Sestius. With relations between Pompey and Crassus at an all-time low, both having been agitating for a command in Egypt, and with Caesar in Gaul, Cicero seems have judged that the time was right to attack the Triumvirate. We have already established that Cicero chose the path of full-on activity on his return, eschewing the strategy of a slow build up to a new position, and instead firing vitriol at every opportunity. Whether or not this was a miscalculation, the end result was that his *Pro Sestio* speech triggered a number of things – it revealed once more that his political philosophy had not changed, it pointed the finger at the enemy within rather than without and pledged a new message to the people *otium cum dignitate*. This concept had a Greek root and clearly Cicero had been musing on how the future could be changed for the better – the current mess in Republican politics could not carry on for much longer – and he laid out the concept of leisure with dignity – what we might call peace and security with minimal political involvement in the process. If respect for the hierarchical order could be reaffirmed, honour to the Senate and the establishment achieved, then social harmony would result – just as it used to be and the people could leave the government of Rome to those best placed to manage it. The speech was also a blatant recounting of his own career and suffering, like Sestius, enduring hardship in the name of the Republic, a relentless list of the gestures of welcome made towards him by the people, senators and consuls on his return – linking his own safety with that of the Republic. Yet again he ignored the private letters of utter dejection and despair written to Atticus and his brother safe in the knowledge – or so he thought – that his words to them would never be made public or form part of world study for millennia to come.

Cicero thought he had worked out what was wrong and offered his own, perhaps naïve solution, explaining that the central problem was a clash between the *populares* and the *optimates*, pointing out that the latter group are neither insane, criminal nor bankrupt – ergo Clodius was. This was a fragile political assessment ignoring the far wider problems of the state and the changes it was experiencing, failing to adjust to new pressures and attempting to adopt the established to deal with the disestablished. There were far more fundamental reasons why the Republic was suffering and *Pro Sestio*, while a brilliant piece of oratory, does not capture these at all. Sestius, Cicero's loyal ally if not friend, was unanimously acquitted, but a lot of damage had been done which was yet to reveal itself – it did after all take the best part of ten days for reports to reach Caesar in northern France.

Pro Caelio April 56

Cicero was still Rome's foremost orator and he was enjoying using the stage given to him via public trials to tangentially bruise his enemies. He took them down with a mix of supreme rhetorical skill, a swagger borne of immense ego and a confidence that he was unbeatable. He was also now using the same stage to promote a new political dimension of his character – the solution to Rome's problems. Another burdensome case that would burn many nights of midnight oil for Cicero and his *scribae* in 56 was the case of his former pupil Marcus Caelius Rufus. The charges were numerous –

Inciting civil disturbance in Naples
Assaults on Alexandrians at Puteoli
Taking gold for the attempted murder of Dio of Alexandra and the attempted poisoning of Clodia
The murder of Dio

This was a troubling and complex matter, and it gave rise to one of the most outstanding examples of Roman oratory in history and arguably the best of Cicero's speeches – he was clearly in a rich vein of creative writing.

Caelius had been educated in the house of Crassus and as such in his youth came under his sway around the same time as he was apprenticed to Cicero for his legal studies so in a way he could be seen as being conflicted as to his loyalty. In the Catiline affair, Caelius was implicated as being a supporter of the plotters and his background was certainly similar to those that followed Catiline – he was from a noble background, influenced by Crassus from the shadows, short of money with a financially conscious father, and ambitious. Nothing was proven, however, and he was admired by Cicero with elements of a homoerotic affection – being 'tall, of fair complexion and strikingly handsome'. Cicero described him as precisely the kind of orator he likes –

passionate, bent on winning, needing to be curbed rather than spurred. Perhaps we have another clue in this phrasing of the difficulties Cicero created for himself. To win in politics requires an awareness that one cannot always win – in fact losing in the right way at the right time can be an integral part of ultimate victory. However, the lawyer in Cicero, moreover the prosecutor that was Cicero's central role, meant that he was always committed to winning and being 'bent on winning' can be a real weakness.

Cicero had been pitted against the young Caelius, who had been the lead prosecutor in the trial of Antonius, and lost to him, but all was fair in love and war and in this case, Cicero was only too happy to act for him. The background is typically Republican Roman – simple on the surface, but riddled with hidden tunnels and plotting under the surface. After winning the trial against Antonius Hybrida, Caelius moved into an apartment on the Palatine Hill – near Clodius. It could have been an act of generous spirit by Clodius, but it was more likely that Caelius was already romantically involved with Clodia and the apartment was very close to where the young, recently widowed 32-year-old sister of Clodius lived and they were, or quickly became, lovers – but not for long. For an unexplained reason, Caelius broke off from both Clodius and his sister, and in February 56 Caelius charged L. Calpurnius Bestia with corruption in the elections of 57 for praetor – the previous year. Bestia's son, realizing that if Caelius were convicted of a charge, he could not proceed with his prosecution, counter charged Caelius in the violence court, which meant an almost immediate trial.

The texts of the prosecution evidence do not exist, but we can glean something of their case from who the prosecutors were and how Cicero responded to them. The team lined up against Caelius was made of three speakers – L. Sempronius Atratinus, a 17-year-old son of Bestia, L. Herrenius Balbus a close friend of Bestia and finally, yes, P. Clodius Pulcher. Lined up for the defence were Caelius himself, who intended to defend himself along with M. Licinius Crassus and Marcus Tullius Cicero – a formidable legal trio. Cicero presented Caelius as a type of clone of himself, forensic and above the charges levelled at him and he supported his approach in the usual Ciceronian style of ridiculing the witnesses against him – Clodia was especially singled out as the root of all evil, a reveller in scurrilous activity like her brother and the instigator of the charges – a jilted woman with a higher plan. In the end Caelius must have been acquitted of the charges as he remained in Rome and went on to have a fine career, becoming a tribune of the plebs in 52 and praetor in 48. Again, Cicero was victorious, but at the cost of creating more bitterness amongst the Clodii and by enshrining his reputation as having the sharpest tongue in Italy able 'to cut him up to the applause of gods and men' anyone that he chose.

Cicero next chose Publius Vatinius – the man who as tribune in 59 had proposed Caesar's five-year command and who was one of many eyes and ears for Caesar sending regular letters to keep him up to date in Gaul. Vatinius had appeared as a witness for the prosecution in the trial of Caelius and Cicero had cut him to pieces, but while doing so inferred that all of Caesar's legislation was illegal. This was a very risky business, but Cicero reassured his brother that he had everything under control and then went further and put Caesar's Land Reform Act on the business of the Senate for May. He could easily have left this matter; yes the Campania lands were huge; yes the Senate needed money and could raise funds by taking back these lands given away to poor families and some veterans, but the cost would to be to anger Caesar and undoubtedly place Cicero in uncertainty. As part of his support for Cicero's return the previous year, Pompey had asked for a guarantee from Quintus that his brother would not cause trouble and Quintus was becoming alarmed at the pace and scale of his brother's re-entry onto the stage. Quintus was in Sardinia on a commission from Pompey, but Cicero wrote and reassured him that he had everything under control – especially as the senators purred warmly at his bravery in taking on Caesar on their behalf. April was an extremely busy month and we can but wonder whether Cicero was doing too much in too many areas, he was but a man, and stress and anxiety can drive a man harder than he realizes and therein he can miscalculate.

In a letter to Lentulus Splinther two years later he wrote:

> *On 5 April the Senate accepted my motion that the question of the Campanian Land should be debated in plenary session on 15 May. Could I have found a better way to penetrate the citadel of the coalition? Could I have shown myself more oblivious of my present situation or more mindful of my past record?*

In trying to *'penetrate the citadel'* Cicero was more than just poking at the ribs of the Triumvirate, he was attempting to undercut Caesar, separate Pompey from what he saw as the clutches of Crassus and Caesar and restore himself to being the centre of political gravity. The matter had been raised the previous December by a tribune of the plebs named Lupus who wanted the ongoing distributions blocked and Caesar was no doubt pleased, thinking the matter had gone away so Cicero, by highlighting this again was clearly instigating a direct attack on Caesar himself. Not only these matters concerned Caesar, but in addition L. Domitius Ahenobarbus had announced his intention to stand for the consulship of 55 and he declared that one of his first acts would be to recall Caesar from Gaul. Cicero did not assess the cumulative effect that all these changes had on Caesar and rather casually wrote to his brother:

Cicero to his brother
en route to Anagnia, 9 April 56

From Marcus to his brother Quintus greetings.

I sent you a letter the other day telling you that our Tullia was betrothed to Crassipes on 4 April, along with the rest of the news, public and private.... On the Nones of April the Senate decreed HS 40,000,000 to Pompey as Grain Commissioner. The same day there was a warm debate on the Campanian Land – the shouting in the House was like a public meeting. The shortage of funds and the price of grain made the question more acute.

I went over to your site. Work was going ahead with a crowd of builders. I said a few animating words to Longilius the contractor, and he convinced me that he wants to give us satisfaction. Your house will be splendid. One can see more than we could judge from the plan. Mine too will be built rapidly.

I dined that evening at Crassipes' and after dinner had myself carried to Pompey's villa, not having been able to see him because I was leaving Rome next day and he had a trip to Sardinia in view. So I met him and asked him to send you back to us as soon as possible. 'Straight away' said he. He would be leaving, he said, on 11 April and taking a ship from Labro or Pisae. Now as soon as he arrives, my dear fellow, be sure to take the next boat, providing the weather is suitable.

On 9 April I dictated this letter before daylight and am writing the rest on the road, expecting to stay the night with T. Titius near Anagnia. Tomorrow I intend to stay at Laterium, and then, after five days in the Arpinum area, go on to Pompeii. I shall have a look at my Cumae place on the way back, and so to Rome.

Caesar is always watching

For the previous two years Caesar and his model legions, packed with veterans and experienced officers and generals, had been marching, fighting, building encampments, dealing with disease and exhaustion across southern and eastern Gaul. Major battles had been fought in the Vosges mountains and he had secured the eastern flank on the Germanic border, killed and captured Suebi and Nervii numbering over 280,000 and his wagon trains were becoming longer and heavier with the pillaged gold and silver that had been stolen from the tribes they encountered. Many captives had been beheaded and thousands of slaves had been sent south into Italy and the junior partner of the Triumvirate was now proven as a military commander to rival Pompey and a wealthy man to rival Crassus.

As the year of 56 unfolded, Caesar had to take a pause from the campaign in the northwest against the Venetii in what we know as the Cotentin/Brittany area to regain control over events in Rome. The news had been increasingly concerning – Clodius was still running dangerously around the city causing disturbance wherever he could (not that this was necessarily a bad thing from Caesar's perspective as it occupied the idle hands of the Senate) and now most concerning of all, Cicero on his return had also returned to his former meddling ways, even threatening his own command, his Land Act, and now the security of the Triumvirate.

We can imagine Cicero departing from Pompey that evening feeling rather pleased with himself and confident that Pompey was once more under his sway (that is of course if he ever was) and then heading southwards with a smug feeling of control as he visited his various properties and finally arrived in Pompeii. While in the north, Pompey was indeed heading for Pisae (modern Pisa) on the west coast ready to depart for Sardinia – however, rather crucially he had arranged a previous engagement with Caesar at Lucca, some twenty-one kilometres to the south – something he had not mentioned to Cicero, and once more Cicero had miscalculated his ability to read events. Caesar arrived at Lucca having already met Crassus on the east coast at Ravenna. Both meetings as far away from Rome as possible and held in secret. At Lucca, Caesar was keen to mend fences and restore the three of them to a stranglehold on Rome. Part of their agreement was that both Pompey and Crassus should both stand, and no doubt win, the consulships for 55 – for the second time as colleagues – and then both receive five-year commands as he had done. Caesar's command in Gaul was to be extended for the same amount of time – giving him a total of ten years in Gaul should he so wish it. They also discussed Cicero and we have a fairly close account of what may have been said from a letter from Cicero written two years later to Lentulus Splinther:

> *This speech of mine caused a sensation, not only where I had intended, but in quite unexpected quarters. After the Senate had passed its decree on my motion, Pompey (without giving me any indication of displeasure) left for Sardinia and Africa, and joined Caesar on the way. Caesar there complained at length about my motion – he had been stirred up against me by Crassus, whom he had previously seen at Ravenna. Pompey was generally supposed to be much upset by the affair. I heard this from various sources, but my principal informant was*

my brother. Pompey met him in Sardinia a few days after leaving Lucca. 'You're the very man I want' he told him, Most lucky our meeting just now. Unless you talk seriously to your brother Marcus, you are going to have to pay up on the guarantee you gave me on his behalf.' In short he remonstrated in strong terms, recalling the many discussions he had had with my brother himself about Caesar's legislation and the pledges my brother had given him concerning my future conduct, appealing to my brother's personal knowledge of the fact that his own support for my restoration had been given with Caesar's approval. By way of commending to me Caesar's cause and position, he made the request that if I could not or would not defend them I should at least refrain from attacking them.

In a separate letter Pompey also wrote to Cicero asking him to stay out of the land question until his return. Cicero had tried to force his way back into the centre of politics and was put firmly back in his place and remained outside of the molten core of power. In fact all he had done was to damage his own position with respect to Pompey, confirm to Caesar that he was a problem and reveal just how powerless Pompey felt in respect to Caesar – the Great Pompey having to look for approval from Caesar before he could even think of supporting Cicero.

De Provinciis Consularibus Summer 56

The exact date of this speech is uncertain, but it came when Cicero was feeling the pressure from Caesar transmitted through the person of Pompey and encouraged and advised by Atticus and Quintus to try to find a way of working with rather than against Caesar. Cicero was mainly disgusted by the majority of the Senate with their lukewarm attitude towards him with some even befriending Clodius – whom they thought could be a bastion against the Triumvirate – and he felt that he had to retain the friendship, false or otherwise, of Pompey. Having pushed him into a corner, Cicero was chosen by the Three to champion their cause by drafting and delivering a speech on the allocation of provinces for the consuls of the coming year of 55. The impact of this speech was to be pivotal. Cicero attacked his enemies Piso and Gabinius (who were in Macedonia and Syria respectively) probably unaware that Crassus and Pompey were aiming to stand as consuls and wanted these two prime provinces for themselves, and he argued that Caesar should be given an extended command in Gaul. In other words, the Triumvirate used Cicero to articulate their recent agreements at Lucca and Ravenna. Furthermore, Cicero argued that, because both Piso and Gabinius should be recalled as soon as possible, the provinces should be mandated as praetorian as well as proconsular, as the consuls of 55, who had not been elected yet, would not be able to take up their positions until over eighteen months hence and a stop gap governor was needed. The evidence does not entirely support the fact that the Senate agreed with all of these proposals. Piso did indeed return early – apparently, according to Cicero, turning white and dropping half dead at the news he was being recalled from Macedonia – and arrived back in Rome in the summer of 55 to a slanging match with Cicero, whom he identified as being behind his recall.

But the most far-reaching result was that Cicero's *palinode* or recantation which he publicly announced in supporting Caesar was not only a shock for Rome and for the Senate, but also for world history, as Caesar was to go on to mark out the known world and Europe in ways that could not have been thought possible. Cicero was well aware that his attitude and position had dramatically moved from one where the Triumvirate was evil and a target for his invective and he knew that the reaction from his contemporaries would range from shock, through disbelief and onto derision and ridicule. In response to Atticus' criticism he wrote:

Ain tu? An me existmas ab ullo malle mea legi probarique quam te? Cur igitur cuiquam misi prius? Urgebar ab eo ad quem misi et non habebam exempla duo. Quin etiam (dudum enim circumrodo qoud devorandum est) subturpicula mihi videbatur esse.

What do you mean? Do you believe that I prefer that what I write be read and approved by anyone more than by you? Why have I sent it to someone else before you, then? He put pressure on me and I did not have a second copy. And – besides – I keep nibbling around that which I must just swallow – it seemed to me a bit of a dishonourable recantation.

What Shackleton Bailey describes as a 'relapse into quiescence' and what other historians refer to as a betrayal of those he purported to lead in the Senate characterizes the debate on this speech and this moment in Cicero's life. Cicero was careful not to go too far in offending the senators to whom he spoke – he reminded them that he had led them in measures to contain and control Caesar (even though underneath he had nothing but contempt for many of them who had never in fact accepted him) and he was also careful to try to promote himself as that philosopher-king, asking the Senate to respect what Caesar had achieved for Rome, while at the same time asking Caesar to respect the decisions of the Senate. As so often the case, this is a great piece of oratory given in the midst of highly charged and difficult circumstances. Cicero had reorientated himself in 55, where would this take him?

Chapter 22

Prelude to Collapse

I do not remember the height from which I fell but the depth from which I have risen.
Marcus Tullius Cicero in 54 in reference to his new position in life

The next four years were a mix of having swallowed the bitter pill of realization that power was no longer in his hands – and trying to get it back. He had written to Lentulus, to whom Cicero felt he owed a great deal for his support and advice (sadly we have no letters from Lentulus) regarding his impotence and commented:

And yet the perverseness (not to use a stronger word) of folk is beyond belief. With good will they could have kept me in the common cause; instead their jealousy has estranged me. For I must tell you that their venomous back-biting has pretty well succeeded in turning me away from my old, long-established principles and brought me to the point, not indeed of forgetting my honour, but of paying some attention to my vital interest. The two could have run perfectly well in harness if our consulars had known the meaning of good faith and responsibility.

Cicero was referring to the majority of the so-called better men, the *boni*, as the consulars rather than any two in particular. His observations that the Senate generally was being shown to have been out manoeuvred and intimidated by either Clodius on one side or the Triumvirate on the other rang true and he felt that he had no choice but to get out of the no man's land in the middle of the two, criticised by both, and look after his own interests. Times had indeed changed.

In the USA in 2022 and moving into 2023 we have a parallel situation. Both the right and left are worried about the future of democracy and they both blame each other for the possible collapse of the Republic with the result that there is now a realistic chance of a major political shift just as there was in Republican Rome during the 50s. We can only wonder how many potential saviours of the state have taken the same course of action as Cicero did and have withdrawn from the melee so far and it may be that, as in Republican Rome, this will be seen as one of the preludes to the collapse of the United States of America.

Keeping busy

For the foreseeable future then, Cicero was busy but inconspicuous compared to the past and was a mixture of responding to calls to act in the defence of one of the Triumvirate's friends, crossing swords with Cato – who had returned from Cyprus in the summer of 56 – making more speeches on the aspiration of peace and harmony which few people were listening to, or sorting out his private affairs. He was also able to witness from the side-lines the cause of democracy being led now by Cato instead of himself.

In September 56 Cicero defended Caesar's Spanish vassal Cornelius Balbus against a charge of illegally taking on Roman citizenship. Cato was busy re-establishing his presence and new found wealth in the Senate and coming to terms with Cicero's apparent defection to the power of the triumvirs. With an eye to elections for 55, his brother-in-law Domitius Ahenobarbus received all the support Cato could muster from the *optimates* and, as we know, Caesar responded with Crassus and Pompey as his preferred candidates and they were elected, or rather they seized the consulships through violence and bribery, though not until January 55 after a ludicrous charade of months of delayed elections and in fighting.

Violence and corruption were now the order of the day and an impartial onlooker could rightly have adjudged democracy already to be in a coma if not completely dead, but government of sorts continued to function in a charade of process and protocols. Even Cato, with his *optimates* and *populares* support lost the election for the praetorship due to Pompey hearing thunder (on a sunny day in Rome) declaring the augurs seeing danger and postponing an election he was going to win.

Cato was incensed almost from the moment of his return and Cicero watched as he stood throughout 55 in the forum and the Senate against the Triumvirs and the consuls Pompey and Crassus. Most worthy of note is that Cato publicly resisted a motion put forward by a tribune named Trebonius that Crassus should be given the province of Syria in his proconsular year and Pompey receive the two Spanish provinces – both for five years! Crassus had indicated that he would go to war with Parthia with all the riches that it could bring and Cato asked why, when there was no reason for war? Cato was supported by Favonius who spent the hour he was allocated complaining that an hour was not enough so this left Cato, who had been allotted two hours, to try to carry the assembly with his outright criticism of the sad state of affairs and the illegality of the proposal. Trebonius stopped Cato speaking exactly on time, but he carried on in order to force Trebonius, and by implication the lack of democratic freedom now present in Rome, to arrest him and take him to jail – again. Violence ensued and no vote was possible as the crowd noisily demanded Cato's release. In a show of just how far matters had declined, that night Trebonius had the forum blocked all around and the senate house locked, with mobs stopping Cato and his supporters from continuing the debate in the morning. Naturally under these circumstances the bills were passed and the consuls had achieved all that they desired and the Triumvirate was all powerful using the democratic process to mask their tyranny.

For Cicero, standing back from the centre gave him time to look to his own future. He had definitely moved into a new phase of his life during his early 50s. Trying to maintain a statesmanlike presence in the Senate and forum wandering to and fro now from his newly opened house on the Palatine, he maintained the pretence of a man at the centre of things, but he was hardly the father of his country any more. As an indicator of his lessening presence, his morning visitor numbers were down compared to the past, but this was not necessarily a bad thing. He did sometimes write in this period of a certain level of self-loathing regarding how he allowed himself to become a willing partner to the Triumvirate, feeling like a slave and in disgrace, writing to Atticus in April 55:

After all, what could be more ignominious than the life we lead, I especially? For you, though you are a political animal by nature, are not subject to any particular servitude, you share the common lot. But as for me, reckoned madman if I speak on politics as I ought, a slave if I say what is expedient, and a helpless captive if I say nothing – how am I to feel?

But there were also positive, reflective moments, possibly those of the rejected looking for the reassuring, but nevertheless writing to Atticus in 54 he commented:

You'll wonder how I take all this. Pretty coolly I assure you, and I plume myself highly on doing so. My dear friend, not only have we lost the vital essence of the free state – even the outward complexion and aspect it used to wear has gone. There is no Republic any more to give me joy and solace. Can I take that calmly? Why yes, I can. You see, I have the memory of the proud show she made for the short time that I was at the helm, and the thanks I got in return. My withers are unrung by the spectacle of one man all-powerful, which chokes the persons who found it distasteful that I should have any power at all. I have many consolations. All the same, I do not move away from my position, but turn back to the life that is most congenial, to my books and studies. The labour of pleading is compensated by the pleasure that oratory gives me. My house in town and my places in the country are a source of delight. I do not remember the height from which I fell but the depth from which I have risen.

In Pisonem and De Oratore 55

Cicero spent many days, late evenings and very early mornings in the summer months withdrawn into writing possibly or very likely with the trusty and industrious Tiro by his side and created at least two works – *De Oratore* and *In Pisonem*. The former was a treatise or philosophical work not just on the attributes of the perfect orator, but also the importance of oratory and the ethical ways in which it should be used. Like the philosopher-king, the perfect orator should be skilled in history, philosophy, an expert in technique and with the ability to manipulate public opinion – just like a lawyer manipulates a jury? *De Oratore* is a magnificent work, divided into at least three books that we know of and was mainly, if not entirely, written away from Rome in his villa at Tusculum – where we might suppose he spent much valuable time with Terentia after all that they had been through.

In Pisonem was an entirely different matter. In stark contrast to the many days of philosophical reflection on oratory and rhetoric, Cicero responds, in some fury to L. Calpurnius Piso, now returned from Macedonia, at least in part due to Cicero's *De Provinciis Consularibus* speech in 56. The date of the delivery of *In Pisonem* is still unclear, but either a few days before or after the great opening ceremony for Pompey's magnificent new stone theatre, and certainly after Piso had decided to insult Cicero in the Senate with a speech of his own remarking on his early recall from the provinces. This time he would have laboured intently venting the spleen that he so often mentioned in his writing. Piso, a renowned and powerful *optimate* not to be messed with lightly, was the father-in-law of Caesar and so Cicero wrote in the knowledge that Caesar would at least be aware, but may even have liked what he read. Cicero poured forth into Piso with a mixture of comedic put downs, accusations about his family, such as his mother being a prostitute and his grandfather a pimp, and abusive language and in so doing, confirmed Piso as another real enemy on the scale of that felt by Clodius. To the Senate his words created a hum of laughter and gasps as his allusions and comic references were well known – it would seem Cicero enjoyed a carefree assault perhaps feeling that if his political career was over, he could now enjoy one in comedy.

As for the opening of the new theatre entirely funded by Pompey, this occurred at around the same time on the Field of Mars, construction having taken three years and at massive cost and was designed to display Pompey as Rome's leading citizen. Sadistic shows where criminals were thrown to wild animals were accompanied by processions, music, trumpets and the heroic gladiators – the *retarius* with his helmet, net and trident set against the *mirmillo* in his chain mail and sword. The blood ran on the floor of the new theatre to wild applause as a kind of release after the constant strain and stress of political fighting in the Senate. Naturally Cicero attended and would have sat near or even next to Pompey himself as the trumpets announced their arrival, but he was unamused or perhaps jealous:

> *What pleasure can a cultivated man get out of seeing a weak human being torn to pieces by a powerful animal or a splendid animal transfixed by a hunting spear?*

Even the many stunning black panthers captured and transported from Africa or the vicious mountain tigers brought from the Atlas Mountains did not impress him:

> *Anyhow, if these sights are worth seeing, you have seen them often; and we spectators saw nothing new. The last day was that for the elephants. The ordinary public showed considerable astonishment at them, but no enjoyment. There was even an impulse of compassion, a feeling that the monsters had something human about them.*

Pompey was one of the earliest of the imperial builders. With greater wealth came a greater desire to be immortalized in stone and Rome became a vast building site with engineers, draftsmen, architects and thousands of slaves provided with work from the deep purses of individuals – in the Hegelian sense of fulfilling destiny as society moved forward, became more ambitious and individuals sought immortality.

Towards the end of 55, earlier than expected, Crassus departed for Syria. He could wait no longer to replicate the great victories of his two fellow Triumvirs and sought his share of military glory heading for Syria and then Parthia. As he left the gates of Rome to rather less than the crowd he had hoped for, one of the tribunes hurled a curse at him for going to war with Parthia. Perhaps the curse worked for Crassus would be gone for some time, in fact, he would never return.

De Re Publica 55–51

'Your work on politics is all the rage.' This is how Caelius Rufus ended a letter written to Cicero around the last week of May 51. We may recall that Caelius was a protégée of Cicero and, Cicero hoped, he could become another regular correspondent and his eyes in Rome when he was away for any reason. If there is one work that resonates with the name of Cicero then it is his 'work on politics'. Entitled *De Re Publica* or 'On the Commonwealth' is a series of six books that Cicero composed in this period of his life when he was no longer centre stage and kept his mind active by reflecting on where he was and the state of the nation he so loved. In between prosecutions and defences, letters and meetings Cicero composed this work over a number of years. The entire work does not survive in the original and large parts are missing and so history has relied upon a mixture of copies in later works and an incomplete palimpsest – a manuscript where the page has been reused, but underneath it is still possible to read the original document – this was discovered by accident in 1819.

By this stage of his life Cicero could clearly see the real dangers to democracy in the Republic as it existed by the middle of the first century. Part of the problems being faced was the constant questioning of what was and was not established custom and the elastic band of democracy was being tested constantly in the absence of a written single constitution. Cicero sets out to codify how democracy had developed to present both a philosophical debate via the characters in this work and establish some more concrete acceptance of constitutional theory and practice. As an imitation of Plato's *Republic* the work has the structure of a Socratic dialogue where characters interrogate, through conversation, the essence of an argument.

The central character is Scipio Aemilianus who had died over twenty years before Cicero was born and the imaginary debates are held on his estate over a three day period. The controversial nature of the subject and the context in which it was composed – against a background of tyrannical threats, mob violence, corruption and instability – inevitably meant that Cicero was placing the characters of the day within the context of an allegorical discussion, therefore he had to be very careful that he did not cause offence. Cicero often sailed close to the wind in representing characters in this way avoiding direct conflict but nevertheless creating tension amongst his targets. If Caelius was stating that this work was 'all the rage', then it was probably not for reason of the constitutional theory being discussed but more likely as people enjoyed identifying the characters in the texts.

'On the Republic' – or the Commonwealth – is also famous for *Somnium Scipionis* or the Dream of Scipio which takes place in the sixth and last book where the General Scipio Aemilianus is visited by his dead grandfather Scipio Africanus who is looking down over Carthage 'from a high place full of stars' and listens to the loyal duties of a Roman soldier who will gain his reward after death – a commentary perhaps on the death of the army of Crassus in 53. The celestial references continue with Africanus explaining that fame is fleeting and that greater people than him have been forgotten by history and he should do the right thing for his soul and not strive for immortality – a clear reference to those still striving for power. The work also has the benefit of enlightening the historian to seeing the extent of the world as it was seen then – to the south is the Nile, to the west is the Great (Atlantic) Ocean and to the east the Caucasus Mountains and the Ganges river.

The prosecutions of 54

> *Confessing to avoid prosecution is a time-honoured strategy*
> *Howard Tayler*

After the domination of the Triumvirs in 55, the *optimates* had cause to be pleased with the results of the elections at the end of the year for 54. Domitius finally was allowed to stand and successfully secure the consulship and alongside him was, at last, Clodius Pulcher. With his desire to please Pompey and stay within his envelope of grandeur, Cicero was in an invidious position and did nothing that might enrage Clodius sitting in his consular chair in the Senate, but was also called on to repay his debt to Pompey and Caesar throughout the year by obtaining guilty verdicts. Another successful election for 54 was that of Cato as praetor and he lost no time in spending most of the year trying to reverse the power of the Triumvirate with a constant stream of accusations and trials, the targets of which were supporters of the Three. Gaius Cato (no relation) was prosecuted for violating election laws, but was acquitted. Cicero was pressurized by Pompey into defending Messius, who had proposed extraordinary powers for Pompey's grain Mission in 57; we think he was acquitted. Scaurus was prosecuted on a charge of *de repetundis* or extortion. Scaurus was extremely well connected and furious with Cato and acquitted by 70–8, which was a pretty damning commentary of what Cato was trying to do.

The prosecution that hit the Roman headlines, however, was that of Gabinius. Initially, due to his long running *animus* with Gabinius, Cicero refused to defend him even when pressured by Pompey and indeed Caesar to do so. There were three main charges and although Cicero owed the triumvirs a great deal in his own way, defending Gabinius was a step too far. Ultimately Gabinius was able to call on both Pompey and Caesar for letters of support in the case of extortion in Cato's court and Cicero relented and offered to defend him, but the jury still convicted him and fined him 10,000 talents – a vast sum but one that he was supposed to have received as a bribe from Ptolemy for his restitution to the Egyptian throne. Without doubt Gabinius had helped Ptolemy back into Alexandria on Pompey's instructions – Pompey with an eye on Egypt for the future. The Senate had already refused this so Gabinius was in a difficult position, which perhaps over exposed him to a guilty verdict. Gabinius was the only supporter of the triumvirs that year to be found guilty which evidences just how powerful a reach Caesar could wield. Unable to pay, Gabinius went into exile for the next five years before being recalled by Caesar. Despite his reluctance to take on cases for such obviously guilty supporters of Caesar, Cicero would have rather liked still being needed for his skills and status in the courts even though he often protested the opposite, for example to his friend Marcus Marius:

As for me, in case you picture me as a free man, if not a happy one, during this holiday, I have pretty well ruptured my lungs defending your friend Caninius Gallus.

I was weary of it [his profession] *even in the days when youth and ambition spurned me forward, and when moreover I was at liberty to refuse a case I did not care for.*

Domestic matters in 54

Alongside preparing detailed defences and long speeches, dictating letters and travelling between his homes, Cicero also found time to sort out his beloved library. Assisted by Tyrannio, it was a task to restore what had been dispersed or destroyed by Clodius' gangs when in exile, but Atticus wrote that he would help by sending clerks to support with 'gluing and other operations'. The end result must have delighted him, it was after all Cicero who said to Varro 'If you have a garden and a library you have everything you need.'

Against the backdrop of work in Rome and at home, Cicero was acutely aware of his brother Quintus. Having completed his mission for Pompey in Sardinia, Quintus was now back serving under Caesar in Gaul. Indeed, the relationship of mutual respect that Cicero enjoyed with Caesar was underpinned by the use Caesar made of the competent and valued Quintus. During service in Gaul, Caesar was to write about Quintus in his commentary

The Gallic War, detailing how 'Cicero himself, although in very poor health, would not rest even at night, until a crowd of soldiers actually went to him and by their remonstrances made him take care of himself.' There is no doubt that Quintus helped the standing of his brother in Caesar's eyes and Cicero himself grew in affection for Caesar. *'In all the world Caesar is the only man who cares for me as I would wish'*, he wrote to Quintus. Cicero may have been influenced by the 800,000 sestertii loan Caesar gave him when in straitened times. One footnote to Quintus at this time is that he was part of the expedition across the waters to a little-known island the Romans called Britannia. We do not know how long he was on the island with Caesar, but long enough for his brother to have tried to write a poem regarding his service in Britain but Cicero complained that *'writing poetry calls for a certain mental alacrity of which the times we live in quite deprive me.'*

Between April and December 54, historians and classicists have a rich vein of letters to mine for information on the state of affairs as they affected Cicero. He was very much a driven man as far as the written word is concerned and the volume of information running to and from his homes and locations displays for us just how active the courier and road systems were in ancient Rome. To give a flavour rather than a detailed account of these few months is challenging. In April 54, Cicero wrote to Caesar asking for a favour regarding the jurist G. Trebatius Testa. Twenty years younger than Cicero, and like Caelius, a young man that Cicero admired for his legal ability, he is suggested to Caesar as a legal advisor. Apparently, Caesar reached out to Cicero to recommend someone on whom to bestow his favour – bearing in mind that Caesar reached out to no one without a hidden agenda:

Cicero to Caesar
Rome, April 54

From Cicero to Caesar, Imperator, greetings.
Please observe how fully I am persuaded that you are my alter ego, not only in my own concerns but in those of my friends also. I had intended to take C. Trebatius with me wherever I might go, in order to bring him home again the richer by any and every benefit and mark of goodwill in my power to bestow.... I now want Trebatius to look to you for everything he would have hoped for from me, and I have assured him of your friendly disposition in terms really no less ample than I had previously been wont to use respecting my own.
Just as I was talking to our friend Balbus at my house on the subject of this very Trebatius, a letter comes in from you concluding as follows: 'I shall make M. Curtius' son king of Gaul. Or, if you please, make him over to Lepta, and send

me somebody else on whom to bestow my favours. Balbus and I both raised our hands to heaven. It came so pat as to seem no accident, but divine intervention.

I send you Trebatius accordingly.... I should wish you to confer upon his single person all the kindness which I could induce you to wish to confer upon my friends. As for him, I will answer that you will find him...there is no better fellow, no more honest and honourable gentleman alive. Add to which, he is a leading light in Civil Law; his memory is extraordinary, his learning profound.

In fine, I put him altogether, as the phrase goes, out of my hands into yours – the hands of a great conqueror and a great gentleman, if I may become a trifle fulsome, though that's hardly permissible with you. But you will let it pass, I see you will.

'Fulsome' indeed. No doubt Caesar was used to the verbal dexterity of Cicero in written form and immune to his praises, but equally grateful that he could recommend someone so highly. This letter is a measure of how close Cicero felt, as he had once felt with Pompey, to Caesar. Despite Caesar's immense stature, Cicero was himself a former consul and yet there is a fawning appeal to Caesar to treat him and his friends well, not an equality of standing, the one thing that Cicero had always wanted – admiration – he layers on Caesar no doubt in the hope that it will be reciprocated.

In August, Cicero is writing to Quintus, thanking him effusively for his letter from Britain. This despatch, if we assume it was from near Londinium and by the fastest route across to the west coast of France, down via the Pyrenees and thence by boat via Sardinia into the River Tiber and Rome, would make a journey of 2,200km and take just over twenty-two days to reach Cicero. Not only does he congratulate Quintus on finding a mine of literary source material, but he is also anxious, again, regarding Caesar and how he sees himself.

Cicero to his brother
Rome, Late August 54

Now I come to what ought perhaps to have been put first. How pleased I was to get your letter from Britain! I dreaded the Ocean and the island coast. Not that I make light of what is to come, but there is more to hope than fear, and my suspense is more a matter of anticipation than of anxiety. You evidently have some splendid literary material – the places, the natural phenomena and scenes, the customs, the peoples you fight, and last but not least, the Commander-in -Chief!

But see here, you seem to be keeping me in the dark. Tell me, my dear fellow, how does Caesar react to my verses? [Cicero had written a poem called 'On my vicissitudes' which was all about his exile and restoration]. *He wrote to me that he read the first Canto and has never read anything better than the earlier part, even in Greek, but finds the rest, down to a certain point, a trifle 'languid'. The truth, please! Is it the material or the style he doesn't like? No need for you to be nervous – my self esteem won't drop a hair's breadth. Just write to me.*

On through 54, Cicero writes at length to bother Atticus about his admiration for Caesar and how he suited Cicero's new political perspective. To Quintus he had earlier written:

As for your Caesar, I have been chanting his praises this while past. Believe me, he is grappled to my heart and I have no intention of disengaging.

Caesar responded by using Cicero's affection along with a loyal lieutenant Gaius Oppius, to entrust a large sum of money sent by armed wagon trains to Rome for the refurbishment of public buildings – it was the absent hero's gift to the people and the city. Cicero and Oppius oversaw the allocations and wrote to Quintus:

I can have no second thoughts where Caesar is concerned. He comes next with me after you and your children. I believe I am doing wisely (it is time for wisdom), but my affection is truly kindled.

If Cicero was continually sensitive to the strength of his relationship with Caesar it would be put to the test in the near future. As Caesar continued to succeed militarily, Cicero was in awe of the man who had the characteristics he envied – inner confidence, an aura of strength, where Cicero wrote with feathery and soft phrases – Caesar was direct, hardly ever self-praising his achievements and above all, Cicero lacked the killer instinct, he played with his prey like a cat using words to wear down the opposition but never quite dealing the death blow – Caesar while tactful and diplomatic did not hesitate when it came to ordering death. It was to be Caesar though who would have to deal with acute pain and sorrow. Before the year of 54 was over, likely in November, his beloved only child and daughter Julia died in childbirth. Born around 76, Julia, like Tullia was to Cicero, was the epicentre of Caesar's emotional being. Her mother Cornelia was Caesar's second wife – his first being divorced in the light of Claudius' affections in the Good Goddess affair. Julia was noted to be a kind woman of beauty, virtue and intelligence and became the third wife of Pompey whom, it was said, was infatuated with this woman thirty years younger than himself. In the rioting of 55 she had suffered a miscarriage after the bloodstained toga of her husband had been brought home for cleaning – he was spattered by the blood of a protester but not dead as she suspected. Recovered enough to try for a child again, Julia went into labour in August 54 just as Cicero was dictating his letter to his brother but died during the birth – the child, Caesar's grandchild, died too – we do not know if it was a boy or a girl. Seneca confirms that Caesar received the news when he was in Britain – at the fastest by military courier and horse relay, this would have taken only ten days so Caesar would have known very quickly. There are no extant letters from Cicero to Caesar of which there must have been hundreds taken by courier to the great general northwards along the great Roman roads by wagon, private messenger or military courier depending on the status of the sender, but he will have written in no doubt full Ciceronian phrasing. This terrible event for any father contrasted with Tullia who, after the early demise of the likeable Piso Frugi, was married in 54 to another young nobleman Furius Crassipes.

A grieving Pompey wanted Julia's ashes to be kept at his favourite villa in the Alban hills, but the people of Rome, who had a great regard for Julia, were equally determined that her ashes be laid in a tomb in the Field of Mars. Caesar would no doubt have been hurt and angered by the consul Domitius Ahenobarbus' deliberate obstruction – hardly able to hide his hatred for both Pompey and Caesar, but the people prevailed.

The year of 54 came to an end with the last letters we have from Cicero to Quintus. Letters to Atticus continued but again these stopped until 51 leaving with us the events of the following three years little by way of Cicero's thoughts on them. He ends in November for us at least by writing a mixed, slightly depressed tone letter to Atticus with some ironic phrasing as this extract underlines:

Hurry back to Rome, come and look at the empty husks of the real old Roman Republic we used to know. For example come and see money distributed before the elections tribe by tribe, all in one place openly, see Gabinius acquitted, get the whiff of a Dictatorship in your nostrils, enjoy the public holiday and the universal free-for-all, behold by equanimity, my amusement, my contempt... and, yes, my delectable rapprochement with Caesar. That does give me satisfaction, the one plank left from the wreck. Wouldn't you love such a man?

Chapter 23

Pivotal Moments 53–52

Wars make history seem deceptively simple. They provide clear turning points, easy distinctions: before and after, winner and loser, right and wrong. True history, the past, is not like that. It is not flat or linear. It has no outline. It is slippery, like liquid; infinite and unknowable, like space. And it is changeable: just when you think you see a pattern, perspective shifts, an alternate vision is proffered, a long-forgotten memory resurfaces.

Kate Morton

icero maintained a close correspondence with Trebatius – the young lawyer whom he had commended to Caesar and through these letters we can peek at Cicero's protecting words, guiding the young jurist to be patient in the ways of the army and to be more grateful for the opportunity he has been given:

Caesar has written to me very civilly, regretting that he has so far been too busy to get to know you very well, but assuring me that this will come......
Your letter gave me an impression of undue impatience; it also surprised me that you make so little account of the advantages of a Tribunate, especially one involving no military service.

By October 54, Cicero felt reassured:

On the strength of your letter I give thanks to my brother Quintus, and can at last commend yourself in that you now seem to have fairly made up your mind [it seems likely that Trebatius had little to do – the soldiers had no need of him and Caesar was too busy to find him a role but maybe Quintus had sought him out and made him feel more part of life with the legion]. *Your letters in the first few months disturbed me not a little, for they gave me an impression (if you will forgive me saying so) at times of irresponsibility in your craving for Rome and city ways, at times of indolence, at times of timidity in face of the labours of army life, and often too, most uncharacteristically, of something not unlike presumption.*

Cicero scolded Trebatius for thinking that all he had to do was turn up, put on a uniform and take the money and return to Rome. The remaining letters into 53 had a lighter note, congratulating Trebatius on staying safe, accruing his military experience and staying with Caesar who, true to his word, did indeed find time for Trebatius – so much so that four years later when Caesar was at war with the Republic, Trebatius stayed loyal to him.

With the war in Gaul set to continue through a very cold winter, Trebatius and Quintus were with Caesar at his winter headquarters at Samarobrovia – modern Amiens and the last letter we have from Quintus to his brother comes to us dated June 53. Written and sent from Transalpine Gaul, no doubt from a legionary camp and possibly from the tent as *legatus* or commander of the legion Caesar had promised him, it is simple, non-political and merely thanks Cicero for informing him that he had decided to give Tiro his freedom. Tiro was much more than a scribe to Cicero, Quintus described him as having *'literary accomplishments and conversation and culture'* which were all part of the character that made Tiro a confidante if not friend to his master. Doubtless, Quintus will not have forgotten the angry letter he had once received from his brother when he freed his own man Statius and, perhaps, he was making a point.

Carrhae 53

True to a unique tradition of Rome, all the nearby walls had been slathered with that unique institution of the Latin race: graffiti. Daubed in paint of every colour were slogans such as Death to the aristocrats! and The shade of Tribune Ateius calls out for blood! and May the curse of Ateius fall on Crassus and all his friends! All of this was scrawled wretchedly and spelled worse. Rome had an extremely high rate of literacy, mostly so that the citizens could practise this particular art form.

John Maddox Roberts

In another military tent of a Roman Commander this time on the far eastern flank of the empire another senior commander, indeed a general, was dictating his own flow of letters. This was Marcus Licinius Crassus and he was at the head of a massive Roman army estimated to be around 40,000 men, women and children (who often followed the camp) plus 1,000 elite cavalry, sent from Gaul by Caesar to aid Crassus in his campaign, and under the command of Crassus' second son Publius. Crassus also recruited numerous sons of the wealthy and famous families in Rome, offering them tribune positions amongst his seven legions and he was supported by experienced senior officers such as C. Cassius Longinus – future plotter against Caesar, who was the brother-in-law of Brutus.

For the whole of his life Crassus had everything except military glory in his own name. He had fought before and had some military experience, but not as a field commander with an army at his disposal. He had watched and celebrated, perhaps increasingly jealously, the young Pompey claim victory after victory for six long years in the very same areas that he had marched his seven legions through in recent months, and for three years he had heard nothing but glory coming from Caesar's campaign in Gaul.

Crassus' army could not take enough supplies with it so, like a huge swarm of locusts, they had been increasingly living off the land that they moved through heading ever eastwards across modern day Turkey and on towards the river Euphrates and the border with first Armenia and through there on to Parthia, or modern-day Iran. It was in Parthia that Crassus had long seen his destiny, his opportunity for even greater wealth and, far more importantly, prestige to match both Caesar and Pompey – and who knew, possibly even sole control over Rome itself.

As his second son, Publius had already proven himself to his father. Like Cicero and other young men from good backgrounds, he had received the best conservative and intellectual education that money could buy. He had lived in his father's shadow of success and great wealth all his life, his grandfather had been a general and received a Triumph for his actions in Spain and he was named after the same man who had also been consul in 97. Cicero had praised the oratorical abilities of Publius and by all accounts he seems to have been more accomplished than his elder brother Marcus. Finally, Publius had proven himself in the field as one of Caesar's most able junior officers with the VII Legion in Gaul between 57–56 where, despite his youth, being 25 at the time, he had commanded a cavalry detachment of significant size. On his return to Rome in 56, Publius brought with him 1,000 loyal Gallic horsemen who owed their complete allegiance to him and their presence helped his father Marcus Licinius Crassus to exhibit strength during his consulship in 55 alongside Pompey. Publius had been a *monetales* in 55 which gave him the right to mint and issue his own money, and coins exist with his own mint mark celebrating Caesar. When General Lucullus died in 56, Publius, and not his brother Marcus, was chosen to replace him in the College of Augurs – this would have been on the direct order of Caesar.

But why should we divert our attention away from Cicero and focus on this episode? Even though they would not call it such, the laws of unintended consequences and the fact that history 'is slippery like liquid' made the coming campaign one of the pivotal turning points in Roman history that would affect the Republic and every Roman for years to come.

Parthia had recently been plagued by fratricide. In 57 Farhad III had been assassinated by his two sons Orod and Mehrdad. Orod became king but was soon forced out by his more popular brother Mehrdad III. Orod, or Orodes to the Romans, went to the reprobate and target of Cicero, Gabinius, who as Governor of Syria was able to assist him – at a price. However, as we read earlier, Ptolemy was able to pay more and lured Gabinius towards Egypt with his offer of 10,000 talents in gold, the gold he was ordered to pay back to the Senate and could not, leaving Orodes to fight his own battles – which he did and he went on to kill his brother in the process of becoming King Orodes II. One of the main reasons Orodes was so successful was the presence in his forces of a young and very wealthy aristocrat, no doubt with his own eye on the throne, named Suren. Plutarch described Suren in his *Life of Crassus* as:

> no ordinary person; but in fortune, family and honour, the first after the king; and in point of courage and capacity, as well as in size and beauty, superior to the Parthians of his time.

It was Suren who had only recently revolutionized the way the Parthians fought. The cataphracts were Parthian nobles who fought as heavy cavalry on war horses and were covered in mail to smash enemy lines with their charge, but the ordinary soldiers, also on horseback, were expert horsemen able to fire accurate and armour-splitting arrows both forwards and backwards as they rode away. Suren was the one who planned for 1,000 camels to provide the backup logistics to keep the arrow supply coming. Suren's 10,000 horsemen were mobile and each firing twenty or more arrows in one minute meant that any opposition would have to face 200,000 with each onslaught – the Roman army was expert at bringing an enemy onto the battlefield and killing him or her face to face, the disparity in tactics should have been obvious. Additionally, the very small composite Parthian bow was designed to fire a projectile at close range but incredibly high speeds to pierce any shield. The term 'Parthian Shot' relates directly to firing a killing remark or phrase while departing, which no doubt many legionaries experienced in the battle.

Crassus made a series of miscalculations as he issued his orders to his massive Roman war machine. Ignoring the advice of his more experienced legionary commanders and his many tribunes (there were six to each legion) he failed to head south towards Seleuceia where Orodes was besieging his brother and catch the enemy together and off guard. Instead, he headed east, crossed the Euphrates for a few weeks and then returned and wintered in Syria giving the Parthians months to recover and prepare – Crassus sent his raiding parties in all directions, some even reached Jerusalem where the temples were attacked again.

In May 53 Crassus, the former consul and triumvir, richest man in Rome, gave orders to move and his seven legions headed over the great river again east into Mesopotamia hoping to attract cavalry support from the tribes there. Incidentally, Crassus crossed in a storm which was felt to be a bad omen, but he ignored that, just as he had done with the curse as he had left Rome. Instead of taking advice to advance more slowly through the mountains so as to disable the tactics of Suren, Crassus wanted to move quickly and followed a desert route. Plutarch recounts that his large army was tired, hungry and thirsty as they camped by the river Belik. When Crassus ordered his army to move, Suren starting attacking them like mosquitoes inside the net, at which point any Arab cavalry he may have had is said to have turned north and deserted. Out in the plains, Crassus had his legions deploy into a vast square for protection but men were falling everywhere and on all sides, the hope being that the Parthians would run out of arrows. Each of the seven legions began to slowly break formation and Crassus took the decision to send Caesar's cavalry and eight cohorts (a cohort was around 480 soldiers and centurions) led by his son to destroy the baggage trains – Crassus watched as they were suddenly surrounded and crushed by the cataphract cavalry who had been camouflaged in the rear, they threw off animal skins to reveal their bright bronze and copper armour dazzling in the sunshine. The legionaries and French cavalry would have been hot, sweating profusely, dust everywhere, difficult to breathe, unable to see what was happening as a deafening noise of horses, trumpets and drums hurtled towards them followed by showers of razor-sharp arrows above. Publius recognized very quickly that his command was going to be annihilated and is said to have been carried, wounded, to a nearby hill. Surrounded by the shields of his men as the arrows rained down on them, he is supposed to have been asked to flee and save himself. Instead, Publius told his men to save themselves and he was going to stay and die on the battlefield. Unable to fight with his sword due to an arrow that had pierced completely through, he turned his side to his shield bearer and ordered him to kill him between his armour, which he did. Amongst those who died alongside Publius were at least two of his closest friends Marcius Censorinus and Magaboccus – both of whom Plutarch describes as fine young men of noble birth with careers ahead of them. It is likely that most of his Gallic cavalry also perished with him and a few minutes later his father Crassus watched as his son's head was paraded around on the top of a Parthian spear – where taunts were thrown to his

The Parthian Shot – a final deadly arrow despite leaving the battlefield.

legionaries that the son was braver than his father. The 4,000 legionaries who had marched out with Publius were also shattered, left fighting in small groups around their centurions and unable to return to the main square.

Fighting on until dark, what was left of the exhausted Legions began to move in groups to a nearby town called Carrhae, some 30 km away, leaving around 4,000 wounded men, bleeding to death and almost all mutilated by arrow wounds, to be slaughtered and stripped of any valuables in the morning when Suren's men arrived. It is reported that most said their goodbyes and remained quiet while others cried out when they saw their comrades packing to leave during the dark of night – only to receive a cut to the throat as a quicker way out towards death. Amongst these would have been seasoned veterans of numerous campaigns, invaluable sons of noble families who had been given a tribune position, like Trebatius serving in Gaul, and a whole host of loyal centurions. A further group of cohorts trying to make their way north from the battlefield became disorientated in the dark and were quickly surrounded and also killed as Crassus' losses passed 10,000 men on the first day.

Despite pleas from Cassius Longinus to plan for an organized withdrawal, Crassus refused. It is likely that he had been emotionally and psychologically destabilized by the death of Publius. Cassius with other officers attempted to withdraw during the night as their fate the next day was certain. It was not a rout and columns moved north and fought a fighting retreat only to find that their guides had cheated them and they returned to Carrhae. A second withdrawal was attempted on the second night with columns of varying sizes either becoming trapped and killed or others, such as that with Cassius actually reaching safe ground. Crassus also followed but became trapped in nearby mountain ranges where he was to receive an offer of parley from Suren. Initially unwilling to attend, Crassus is thought to have been 'persuaded' by his troops to at least try to save them and he went with a group of officers to meet Suren. The details are obscure but a fight broke out during which all of Crassus' officers were killed and he himself was held captive – the story being that molten gold was poured down his throat to humiliate the richest man in Rome. Those men that did not make it back across the Euphrates were either slaughtered or sold into slavery – there is even a myth that some marched as far as China and established a Roman colony there. All that was left of Crassus' army were those units led by officers such as Cassius and Coponius, amounting to around 10,000, who withdrew well and they in turn stood guard on the river waiting for any survivors to straggle back.

The Impact of Carrhae

For the Senate it was a dark day followed by many more dark days when news of the disaster arrived. Despatches from Cassius would have reached Caesar at almost the same time. The ORBIS calculation tells us that it would take around thirteen days to cover the 2,700 kilometres on the fast route via, Constantinople, Dyrrhachium and Brundisium, by military relay to Rome and no doubt news was spread along the route by the military couriers as they went full speed for the Senate. The country and Senate took stock of not only the loss of Crassus, the promising young noblemen who died with the Legions and even worse, the Eagles – the sacred standards of each Legion – the same standard carried from generation to generation and detailing their heroic deeds. Some of the seven eagle standards were now in the hands of the Parthians to be spread as booty amongst their temples and it would not be until seventy years later in 20 CE that they were returned.

Families across Rome would have been affected – especially those who would have lobbied Crassus to take their sons and heirs as tribunes for the military experience and their path up the *cursus honorum*. At an average of six tribunes per legion, that would mean up to forty influential families waiting for news or nursing their deep loss never to see their sons again. Many of these would have been sons of senators, adding to the deep depression no doubt felt as they met to take in what had happened. Demands for details of how such a force could be defeated were confused, but no doubt Cassius would have sent his accounts to the Senate as he took command of what was left of the army. News also filtered through that the head of Crassus had been severed, with its coating of gold in its throat, and taken to the court of King Orodes II and was used as a prop in the performance of Euripides' play 'The Bacchae' where it was thrown around the room like a toy and a Roman prisoner, with

Coin face of Mithridates IV of Parthia – note the power and authority of the design.

a likeness to Crassus was dressed in women's clothes to represent and mock Crassus. Almost certainly Caesar would have known many of the officers in the lost legions and we should not forget the human tragedies amongst men and families that such disasters created – even after such a length of time.

For the future, the Parthians now became a threat. The loss of six legions was serious and Parthian raids on the east flank of the empire increased and remained a constant threat for years to come – the Parthians of course revelled in their new found awareness of their own military prowess defeating the strongest military power in the world at that time.

For the family of Crassus there were a number of impacts. Cornelia Metella, the young widow of the brave Publius went on to marry Pompey as his fifth and final wife – like Julia before her, she was reputed to be a beautiful, loyal and intelligent woman and of course was half his age. The use of marriage as a primary tool in cementing power and wealth into the hands of a few families has been touched on in earlier chapters and it seems likely that Pompey wasted no time in wooing and captivating Cornelia and her access to the tremendous fortune of her own estates. The eldest son, Marcus, reeling from the loss of his father and brave younger brother, inherited the fortune and married Caecilia Metella whose impressive circular towered tomb commemorates their marriage and can still be seen today at the three-mile marker on the great highway of the Via Appia.

For Cicero, the death of Publius opened up a vacancy in the College of Augurs and no doubt Caesar sought to shore up and ensure his mutually respectful relationship with Cicero by offering this position to him – for Cicero this was an unexpected honour for the now elder statesman approaching his mid-50s and had been something he had sought for some years. From Gaul it seems Caesar still controlled everything – except the daily violence on the streets which really never went away and erupted again towards the end of 53.

The most important result of the death of Crassus was not immediately felt. The Triumvirate was no more and one third of the power – perhaps the balancing power – had gone too. Plutarch wrote, with the benefit of hindsight, that war between Pompey and Caesar was now inevitable. Nothing was inevitable and neither wanted war and there was no perceptible change in their relationship. What there was, however, was increasing disorder in Rome. The immediate need in the early spring was to arrange elections for the coming year – one of the weaknesses of the Republic was the endless cycle of annual elections and if anything served to create instability or democratic weariness it was this. But due to the violence it was impossible to proceed – the harassment of Clodius accompanied any senator he did not like and any meeting could expect to be disrupted especially when his arch enemy on the streets, Milo, announced that he intended to stand for the consulship in 52. Despite his commitment to trying to maintain some semblance of order in Rome, Milo did not get the backing of Pompey who was now, given the permanent absence of Crassus, the main networker and 'kingmaker' in Rome. Pompey's support went to one of his former lieutenants P. Plautius Hypsaeus with Q. Caecilius Metellus. Pius Scipio Nascia, the most noble of the three choices by some distance, was the third runner. Pompey was a busy man, bribery took time and money to distribute, conversations were needed and all the time there was the shadow of Caesar in the background. When Pompey asked the widow of Publius to marry him, he did so in the full knowledge that she was not only the daughter-in-law of Crassus with his enormous fortune behind him, but she also just happened to be the daughter of the aforementioned Scipio Nasica. What a wicked web Pompey was trying to weave and Caesar was alert to Pompey's move to broaden his client base with highly influential figures.

No consuls had been elected by the year's end and Pompey himself was behind a veto by the tribune T. Munatius Plancus which also prevented the appointment of an interrex, or overseer of the elections in January – the only interpretation can be that Pompey was worried that Milo was so popular he would be elected and he needed more time and more bribes to activate enough support for the other two candidates.

The death of Clodius 18 January, 52

As a teacher of A level history for so many years it became impossible to remember the faces of all my students, I do recall always having the most fun when we discussed the concept of synchronicity in historical events. If Carrhae was a pivotal moment in 53 then the death of Clodius was another at the start of 52 and within six months the entire political landscape of the Republic had changed due to two completely unforeseen victims of synchronicity.

The main component of synchronicity is the element of chance. Take any range of the same events and treat them individually or allocate them a separate place in time and one can, generally, predict reasonably closely what the impact would be. But place all the events together in a congested place and time where the tremors of one are felt by the others and suddenly a completely different result occurs. Synchronicity brought Crassus to Parthia at exactly the right time for the Parthian revolutions in warfare and exactly the wrong time for the traditional tactics of the legions. Synchronicity saw Clodius killed at exactly the wrong time when there was a power vacuum in Rome and exactly the right time for those wishing to take power. Synchronicity was to see Cicero available to become a major player again instead of being in exile and so it goes on.

Never underestimate the element of chance in history – as Bismarck said, 'man cannot control the current of events, he can only float with them and steer.'

So it was, quite by chance, that on 18 January of the new year, there was a brawl on the Via Appia thirteen miles south of Rome. What Cicero was later to refer to as the 'Battle of Bovillae' occurred when Titus Annius Milo and his wife were on their way to his country home, where he was also mayor, when at around 3pm he saw Clodius coming from the opposite direction on horseback with three friends surrounded by his usual array of about thirty thugs. Thankfully Milo was also accompanied by a column of slaves and, bringing up the rear, two stars of the gladiatorial arena chosen especially as his bodyguards called Eudamas and Birria. Surprisingly the two columns passed each other without any trouble until the two ends started brawling and Clodius apparently turned back and shouted at which point Birria hurled his lance at Clodius hitting him in the shoulder. A full-scale fight ensued which left most of Clodius' men dead or wounded. Clodius, with blood streaming from what would have been a serious wound, was taken to a nearby inn on the side of the road and when Milo was informed, he decided that a wounded Clodius was going to be far more dangerous than a dead one, so he rode to the inn, sent his men storming in and finished Clodius off. His body was hauled out onto the road and left there. Shortly afterwards, a passing senator discovered Clodius and sent him home to Rome in his own litter, and the body arrived at the recently purchased house just two minutes from the forum alongside the Sacred Way.

The sounds of wailing and sobbing filled the street and a crowd gathered outside his house and his wife, Fulvia, invited people in to see his wounds – some of which were in Clodius' back. On the morning of the 19th, two tribunes and supporters of Clodius suggested that the naked body should be taken down to the forum for all to see and placed on the speaker's platform. After a rabble rousing speech to a large and militant crowd, Clodius was taken inside the Senate House where any wooden furniture that could be found was piled up and they set it alight in a hugely symbolic cremation in the very place where Clodius had fought so many battles and caused such disruption. The huge fire spread to the roof and then to the large Basilica Porcia alongside – the centre of Rome was ablaze, panic and noise gripped the forum and rumours spread across the million strong city.

What happened next is the subject still of debate as the ancient sources disagree. Amid the uproar, the Senate convened in the afternoon, probably in the Temple of Jupiter Stator as it could accommodate such a large gathering and, as we know, had done so in the past. This allowed the senators to avoid walking through the forum. Neither Pompey was present, as his imperium for his proconsular office holding in Spain meant he could not cross the *pomerium* (Pompey was running Spain via legates and representatives so he could remain in Rome) and Plancus we can assume was still orchestrating rabble in the forum – this meant that the two men responsible for preventing the elections and why there were still no consuls, were absent. Even then the Senate struggled to move forward as the legitimacy of the elections had to be preserved. M. Aemilius Lepidus was appointed for the first five-day term as interrex, but it would take many more such appointments to resolve the matter. Ultimately the burning of the senate house was met by a reaction against the supporters of Clodius, even Milo felt it safe to return within a day or two as public sentiment cooled and the majority sought security and peace not revolution – Clodius had no successor either – his was a very personal crusade and it died with him. Ultimately both the Senate and people looked to Pompey to restore order and he made sure the clamour was at fever pitch before he accepted, in the absence of any consuls being appointed, not dictatorship but sole consulship of Rome under a *senatus consultum ultimatum* with the power now to raise troops to defend Rome and re-establish order. Even Cato, though with a degree of reluctance, supported this move, stating that this was preferable to anarchy and Cicero, in his new found role as supporter of Caesar, kept his own counsel playing a small part in all this change back to a form of monarchy – hopefully only for one year. A dictator had the power to do as he wished, but Pompey still had to abide by the majority feeling of the Senate – this was Pompey's third consulship and hopefully he would appoint both a co-consul shortly and hold the elections, in peace, for the coming year of 51.

Pompey reached out to Cato, asking him to act as his personal counsellor – or more likely to see if he could be brought over to the dark side given Cato's influence over the *optimates*. But to his credit and his well-established reputation for integrity, Cato refused, saying he would happily share his views but these would be done in the Senate. Interestingly, the man that Cicero had spent most of his life feeling he could influence, did not feel the need to reach out to him instead of Cato and, in the absence of letters from this period we can only assume what he must have felt. It is also interesting that Caesar was not invited back to Rome to sit alongside Pompey. There were small voices across the city suggesting this, but clearly the Senate felt they could trust Pompey slightly more than they could Caesar and certainly Cato would not have backed such a decision.

Acting swiftly, Pompey restored order. Long overdue, soldiers now patrolled the streets, insurrectionists were caught and executed quickly and legislation was passed to reduce bribery and corruption in elections which must have been to Cicero's liking. There were also a series of the inevitable public trials including that of Milo, who was charged with murder.

Cicero's defence of Milo April 52

Not unnaturally, Milo wanted the best defence jurist that he could find, but this was not to be Cicero's finest hour. Despite preparing a detailed defence in *Pro Milone*, Cicero seems to have lost his nerve and numerous commentaries and books have referred to his feeling the intimidation of the crowd and the threatening presence of Pompey's armed troops – the rioting against Cicero's defence from the pro Claudian faction on the first day can only have served to increase the tension. Pompey certainly wanted to see Milo found guilty and it was without doubt a huge personal conflict for Cicero to know how to be seen to defend Milo as well as he knew he could and yet, at the same time, not insult his great benefactor and possible friend by achieving victory. This may account for his stumbles, stuttering voice and overall sub-Cicero performance – and yet history still records this as one of Cicero's finest speeches. How can this be?

In her scholarly analysis of *Pro Milone*, Lyn Fotheringham assesses the point of Cicero openly stating his 'fears'.[1] Were these 'fears' a cover that needed to be used by references to Pompey glaring down on his performance, the soldiers and the atmosphere? Or were they a cover for a poor performance that he was going to have to give in order that Milo be found guilty – in other words asking the crowd to read between the lines. There is also the possibility that Cicero was very cleverly planting these fears in the minds of the jury and what may happen to them if they make the wrong decision – whatever that may have been.

The forum certainly was intimidating. Milo was something of a national hero to the majority – his bravery in standing up to Clodius had saved Rome on many occasions and now he had rid them of the devil for good. But opposing were the *Clodiani*, the wife of Clodius, his family, closest friends and hundreds of agitating supporters. There was also Pompey who had decreed that violence should be met by swift punishment. Thus, the forum was densely packed as far as the eye could see – not the usual '*corona*' or crown of a few hundred less than interested onlookers that would inevitably praise Cicero – instead this was a partisan crowd and Cicero could not personally win whatever happened. According to Cicero it was '*sine aliquo timore*' – not possible not to fear what was around him. Whatever the true position, history as recorded by Dio, Plutarch and others took Cicero's words as being indicative of a faltering and frightened performance – this would be very out of character. Instead, Cicero faced the impossible task as best he could, by scattering plausible defences all around – Milo had rid Rome of a pestilential threat and Milo stood bravely accepting his fate.

In later years, and from exile in Massilia (Marseilles), having been found guilty by 38 votes to 13, Milo mused on how hopeless Cicero's defence had been – this may not refer to any physical reflection of cowardice on the part of Cicero, but more the tone and textual nature of his defence speech. It was not a typical, scathing, scything, cutting, fire and brimstone speech, Cicero did not condemn the authorities for bringing the prosecution because it was Pompey that had brought it. Maybe the philosophic Milo recognized this when he spoke. Milo was referring to a copy of the speech which had been sent to him by Cicero but, as we have witnessed previously, Cicero often re-drafted his speeches for the benefit of posterity and they were often even better than the original hence Milo's famous philosophic comment:

> *Lucky for me he didn't deliver it! I should never have sampled these remarkable red mullet.*

In being found guilty and choosing exile, Milo nearly lost everything – although Cicero, always with an eye for a bargain, did purchase some of his property, he wrote to Atticus, 'for Milo's sake'.

In the same timeframe, Cicero also took on a prosecution role – as we know not his usual choice – but when it came to supporters of Clodius he would make an allowance and he stood against the 'ape' Bursa. This was an entirely different Cicero, which may help us understand what was actually going on with Milo's defence. Here we were back to normal service as Cicero wrote shortly after to his friend Marcus Marius:

> *I am sure you are pleased about Bursa, but you need not have been so diffident in your congratulations. You say you suppose I don't rate the triumph very high, because he's such a low creature. Well, I ask you to believe that this trial gave me more satisfaction than the death of my enemy. To begin with I prefer to get my revenge in a court of law than at sword-point. Secondly, I prefer my friend [Milo] to come out of it with credit than with ruin. I was especially pleased with the display of goodwill towards me on the part of the boni in the face of astonishing pressure from a very grand and powerful personage [Pompey]. Lastly, and this may seem hard to credit, I detested this fellow more than Clodius himself.*

Caesar's legal position challenged 52

The third pivotal moment of 52 was the legislation endorsed by Pompey as sole consul. In the face of the dreadful news from Parthia, Caesar continued to provide the Roman state with reasons for pride and celebration as his Gallic Wars experienced success after success. Regular despatches brought Rome, and the country, news of more tribes beaten by Roman legions, great swathes of new territories added to the ever-expanding boundary of the empire and glory for Caesar. But the problem remained that the legality of his decisions to award, or reward the Triumvirate with five commands was still questioned. There was a growing realization that, with Crassus gone and Pompey as sole consul that Caesar may be considering a return to Rome before too much longer. Amongst sensible legislation to curb abuses at elections, Pompey also supported a purely political bill on the matter of Caesar's ability to stand for the consulship in 48, his time for next office, *in absentia*. While contentious and greeted with uproar in the Senate, the impact of this measure lay in the future. Of far more direct and immediate importance to Caesar, yet another pivotal moment in 52 was inspired by Cato, accommodated by Pompey and approved by the Senate.

Everyone knew that the provinces needed better governance. Since the time of Verres and beyond, the maladministration of provincial commands was a sad and negative reflection on the Roman claims of justice and fairness. Cato played a leading part, under the new protective wing of Pompey, in drafting a bill which stated that the senatorial decree requiring a five-year gap between holding a magistracy and a provincial command now become law. This was a dramatic piece of legislation as no longer could unscrupulous politicians borrow and spend vast fortunes in bribes knowing that in the following year, they could pay it all back – they would now have to wait five years to take up their post. But this very sensible legislation also directly affected Caesar as he was definitely seeking another consulship and another command directly and seamlessly. This would maintain his *imperium* and therefore also maintain his immunity from prosecution. The same strategy has been followed by Donald Trump in the USA in so far as if he could delay the many outstanding legal challenges to him and his family long enough to become president for a second time then he would also gain immunity from prosecution – this was naturally the driving force behind his pathological commitment to his 'Stop the Steal' agenda when he attempted to hang on to the presidency by forcing through a riot on Capitol Hill in 2020.

Creating a hiatus between commands and thereby leaving him vulnerable as a private citizen to prosecution was essential to stopping Caesar and thwarting his ambitions to take over the state. Pompey's role in supporting this law is complex and full of nuance beyond the scope of this book but of even greater significance was that a second law required that all candidates were now going to be required to deliver their *professio* in Rome in person – this may sound familiar because Cato, as a tribune, had tried to enforce this law ten years earlier for the same reasons but it had never been followed. This restatement, however, had the backing of almost all of the Senate. Playing a dangerous game, Pompey still reaffirmed that these laws did not apply to Caesar and added a codicil to the *lex* stating this, but even the legality of this could be challenged. So here we were again, a perfect example of Pompey trying to satisfy everyone and in fact alienating everyone.

Pompey may not have broken with Caesar, but he was moving closer to it. To further appease and mollify the Senate, in July 52 Pompey announced that his new father-in-law Metellus Scipio was 'elected' or more accurately 'selected' as his co-consul for the rest of the year. Being a conservative traditionally minded senator, we can again but wonder how much Cicero would have or did eulogize to Atticus about such positivism from Pompey. So by the end of a tumultuous year the stage was set for a showdown on a number of issues – would it be a drift towards conflict as many were predicting or a sudden collapse? For Cicero, however, another sudden, although not pivotal, experience awaited.

Note
1. Fotheringham, L., 'Cicero's Fear: Multiple Readings of Pro Milone 1–4'. *Materiali e discussion per l'analisi dei testi classici*. No 57, (2006) pp. 63–83

Chapter 24

Cilicia 51–50

Poor is the nation that has no heroes, but poorer still is the nation that having heroes, fails to remember and honour.

                                                                    Marcus Tullius Cicero

T he new law passed by Pompey and the Senate regarding the governance of provinces meant that there was now going to be a four year, at least, hiatus in the flow of new magistrates qualified to take up their proconsular posts. To control the empire, it was suggested to some and issued as an order to others to depart for foreign shores. Cicero was not pleased to be asked to serve abroad and, during 52, he was appointed proconsul of Cilicia – taking over from Appius Clodius who had been maintaining the low bar of mismanagement for the previous two years.

At this time Cilicia covered a large coastal strip running along the southeastern coast of modern-day Turkey towards Antioch and included the recently annexed Cyprus – thanks to Clodius and where Cato had just completed his 'special mission'. Cicero recognized that he was not militarily experienced enough to handle what might become real problems with Parthian incursions spreading northwards out of Parthia post Carrhae and he appointed four legates to join him for the one year he had agreed to and one of these was his brother Quintus. Cicero was to set off for his new role, leaving the port of Brundisium, at the end of May.

It seems from later evidence that Quintus had not enjoyed quite the success Caesar had written about in his commentaries. Quintus did not get along with some of his fellow officers and he certainly had not returned home a rich man. Added to this discontented feeling were marital problems to which Cicero attested in his correspondence with Atticus, which resumes on 5 or 6 May 51. After mentioning the 800,000 he owed to Caesar and the intermediary acting for Caesar named Oppius he writes:

I come now to the line in the margin at the end of your letter in which you remind me about your sister [Pomponia]. *This is how the matter stands. When I got to Arpinum, my brother came over and we talked first and foremost about you, at considerable length. From that I passed to what you and I had said between us at Tusculum anent your sister. I have never seen anything more gentle and pacific than my brother's attitude towards her as I found it.... I stayed at Aquinum, but we lunched at Arcanum – you know the farm. When we arrived there Quintus said in the kindest way 'Pomponia, will you ask the women in, and I'll get the boys?' Both what he said and his intention and manner were perfectly pleasant, at least it seemed so to me, Pomponia however answered, in our hearing 'I am a guest myself here.' That I imagine, was because Statius had gone ahead of us to see to our luncheon. Quintus said to me 'There! That is the sort of thing I have to put up with every day.'*

Cicero continued that he found Pomponia rude and asked that Atticus talk to her, but clearly the marriage was breaking down.

On 22 May Cicero wrote again to Atticus this time from Tarentum on the heel of Italy:

As for me, after spending three days in Pompey's company and at Pompey's house I am setting out for Brundisium on 22 May. I leave him in the most patriotic dispositions, fully prepared to be a bulwark against the dangers threatening [Caesar].

Before he left for Greece, Cicero would have received numerous letters and communiques one of which was the letter from Caelius Rufus mentioned earlier which referenced how well Cicero's *De Re Publica* was going down in Rome. In the same letter Caelius wants to know more about Pompey:

If you found Pompey, as you wanted to do, be sure to write and tell me what you thought of him, how he talked to you, and what disposition he showed. He is apt to say one thing and think another, but is usually not clever enough to keep his real aims out of view.

In the three weeks spent at Brundisium Cicero was able to write many letters that were sent in all directions and his staff of scribes would continue to work all the hours of night and day as the great man got his affairs in order. Cicero had taken Marcus with him for the experience and a tutor to keep his studies moving – provided by Atticus, a cultivated and well-read freedman named Pomponius Dionysius. Sea travel of any kind was fraught with danger and even a small squall could see a boat get into real trouble. Cicero waited for one of his legates, Pomptinus, to arrive, but he failed to turn up and the next stage of his journey is established by a letter telling us that he reached Actium on 14 June and stayed at one of Atticus' houses nearby where they were well looked after before heading off inland to Athens. It seems that Quintus and his son had completed their journey independently, but all four were reunited in Athens in late June. Cicero moaned to Atticus about how he wished he was not there, how Athens was lovely, but how much it had changed and how he was having to practise greater levels of self-control:

> *Irritability, rudeness, every sort of stupidity and bad manners and arrogance both in word and act – one sees examples every day. I won't give you details, not that I want to keep you in the dark but because they are hard to put into words.*

Packed and ready to move, the proconsul and his considerable wagon train left Athens and headed on a short trip to sea this time to the island of Delos and then from Ephesus into his new command on 31 July 51 some three months since his departure from Rome. From the start, Cicero insisted that he was going to administer the province in the way Cato and the Senate now intended. He himself over many years had prosecuted and defended many former governors on charges of maladministration – Verres being the most notable – and now was his chance to set an example. The local people were not to be put upon, there was to be no expectation of largesse or any smell of corruption. This was just as well, as his initial assessment to Atticus ran as follows:

> *I must tell you that on 31 July I made my eagerly awaited entry into this forlorn and, without exaggeration, permanently ruined province, and that I stayed three days in Laodicea, three in Apamea, and as many at Synnada. I have heard nothing but inability to pay the poll-taxes imposed, universal sales of taxes, groans and moans from the communities, appalling excesses as of some savage beast rather than a human being. In a phrase these people are absolutely tired of their lives.*

The state of his province created a number of challenges for Cicero and Quintus – his almost equal partner. The people were clearly already at the end of their ability to pay anything to anyone, so thoughts of returning home with wagon trains of gold were quickly erased for the brothers Cicero. Then there was the problem of what to do about *'the savage beast'*. This was a particularly big and savage beast. Appius Clodius Pulcher was the elder brother of Publius – the Clodius and scourge of Cicero's life – and as such a devoted enemy of Cicero. Unusually, Appius avoided meeting his successor on the change of governor – perhaps due to the animosity felt between them, or more likely, when he saw the state of the province, Cicero felt that he had caught a beast in the act of devouring a carcass. Appius was a big player in Rome. He was an expert on Roman law and antiquities, the head of one of the foremost patrician families in Rome, a major beneficiary of money from the will of general Lucullus – with whom he served in the Mithridatic War (putting the family back in money as well as status), he was prominent enough an ally to be invited by Caesar to both the conferences at Lucca and Ravenna in 56 and had been consul in 54 alongside Ahenobarbus. Claudius was also an augur and a senior member of the college, again alongside Caesar. In other words, despite what he had done to Cilicia, there was little Cicero could do to touch him. It was customary for the outgoing and incoming governors to meet, exchange greetings and information but, try as Cicero might, Appius never seemed to be in the right place as agreed. Various places were suggested by Appius' representative named Phanius, but each time either Cicero had gone on the wrong road or Appius had moved on. What seemed like a boyish game of hide and seek was actually quite serious as Cicero more acutely felt that Appius was deliberately avoiding him, whereas Appius does not seem to have cared. This was almost certainly not by accident, but by design – perhaps a signal of the hatred that Appius still felt for Cicero which would be understandable. It could also have been an indication of the attitude Appius had towards the status of Cicero. In her forensic assessment of 'Cicero's Cilician Correspondence,' Eleanor Leach comments:

> The issue had not been laid to rest four months later when Cicero himself raises the point of having heard from Lentulus' freedman Pausanias of Appius' complaints. The issue that Cicero here takes up concerns the confusion of highways near Iconium, and Cicero, on his way from Laodicea, has hastily back-tracked on hearing that Appius has gone beyond. On this occasion, Pausanius quotes Appius as having said of the gubernatorial succession:[1]

> *Appius Lentulo, Lentulas Appio processit obviam; Cicero Appio noluit*

> Appius went to meet Lentulus; Lentulus put himself in the way of Appius' journey; Cicero was unwilling to do the same for Appius.

The point being that Appius, with his superior aristocratic standing, felt that it was up to Cicero to catch him, not the other way around. Snubbing the *auctoritas* of Cicero would have hurt Cicero deeply and was exactly the treatment he wanted to avoid – acceptance was central in all that he did.

The correspondence from Cilicia

In total we have thirty-two letters to Atticus from this year of office for Cicero. Added to this treasure trove of information can be a further eight to Caelius Rufus, and another thirteen to Appius Clodius Pulcher. There are numerous other individual letters too, so we can build an accurate picture not only of events, but also of attitudes and propaganda from the province as Cicero prepared the ground for his return to Rome. Similar to the letters from exile, Cicero is conscious that what he writes may become despatches for the people to read – other than Atticus, he could trust no one not to disclose what he wrote and so his letters become a valuable part of his self-promotional campaign.

Atticus was especially keen that Cicero govern well and makes a statement about his probity through his administration of the province. Cicero wrote from Actium in June 51;

> *Every day I think of how to fulfil your often-repeated exhortations (which fell on willing ears) to get through this abnormal duty with the strictest decency and propriety, and so I impress on my companions, and so in fact I do.*

Cicero funded most of his expenses himself so as not to attract criticism from the population and to avoid indulgent living at the expense of the province. In fact, he complained that he would have to raise a loan to cover all the costs – *'I don't scratch Appius' sores, but they show and can't be hidden.'*

Cicero was careful and expedient in his dealings with Appius. He knew better than to stir up any further animus while he was in Cilicia, or his period as proconsul might be extended – the very last thing he wanted. Appius and Cicero exchanged tetchy letters throughout 51 and on into 50 and Cicero heeded, for once, the advice from Atticus not to get drawn into a slanging match.

Correspondence with Caelius was brimming with light-hearted exchanges. Caelius possibly felt that his closeness to Cicero could allow him to ask for favours and he requested that black panthers be hunted, trapped and transported to Rome for the games he was hosting in 50 following his election as aedile. Having been in a similar position himself way back in his earlier career, Cicero wanted to assist, but managed to deflect a costly and potentially awkward problem:

> *About the panthers, the usual hunters are doing their best on my instructions. But the creatures are in remarkably short supply, and those we have are said to be complaining bitterly because they are the only beings in my province who have to fear designs about their safety. Accordingly, they have decided to quit the province and go to Caria.*

In other letters to Atticus, Cicero explains how he dealt with the very sensitive issue of taxes. The population complained that they could not pay the taxes and the tax collectors complained that they could not collect the taxes with the level of commission being offered – the usual intractable problem throughout the empire. By a combination of good compromise and good lunches it seems that Cicero managed to navigate this potentially volatile matter with ease – as he was keen to explain to anyone who asked the question. Cicero was well aware that provincial figures could easily be forgotten and he needed to be talked and gossiped about to keep his name awareness alive, refreshing the memory of what Cicero could bring back to Rome in yet another time of need.

Caelius kept up his flow of gossip to Cicero who, like a magnet, had, by April and May, moved closer to home and was in Laodicea dispensing justice as a magistrate. Cicero no doubt enjoyed reading about what was happening within society at Rome and this excerpt gives a flavour of the levels of close-knit sexual liaisons in and around the forum – lest we think it was all doom, gloom and street fighting:

Caelius Rufus to Cicero
Rome, 4 April 50

From Caelius to Cicero greetings.

This letter will be rather brief – I am giving it without notice to one of the tax farmer's couriers, who is in a hurry. I gave a longer one to your freedman yesterday.

The ORBIS network model of the Roman world suggests that the distance from Rome to Laodicea where Cicero currently was located was approximately 3,000 kilometres and by the fastest route by civilian transport it would take the letter from Caelius eighteen days to get to Cicero – providing it was not lost at sea while travelling across the Mediterranean via Sicily to Crete and then on to Antioch.

'Nothing new has happened really, unless you want to be told such items as the following – which, of course, you do. Young Cornificius has got himself engaged to Orestilla's daughter. Paula Valeris, Triarius' sister, has divorced her husband for no reason the day he was due to get back from his province. She is to marry D. Brutus. There have been a good many extraordinary incidents of this sort during your absence which I have not yet reported. Servius Ocella would never have got anyone to believe he went in for adultery, if he had not been caught twice in three days. Where? Why, just the last place I should have wished – I leave something for you to find out from other informants!

An old man in a hurry, hunting for his Triumph

For whatever reasons the two legions stationed in Cilicia for Cicero to use as he saw fit were in a poor state. Numbers were down, troops were missing, morale was low. Appius had left his forces angry and grumbling about missing pay and Cicero arrived to meet his commanders at the main camp at Iconium – modern Konya in central Turkey. Post review and gaining an impression from Quintus of the state of his forces as they stood at the end of August 51, Cicero and his legions marched to Cappadocia in the south to meet King Ariobarzanes. Under Cato's leadership, the Senate ordered Cicero to ensure the safety of the young king as a way of blocking any further advance of the Parthians – Cassius Longinus had been maintaining a stout defence of the frontier areas in Syria to the north and had recently won a victory over an invading Parthian force. Cassius had been under siege in Antioch, but heartened by the approach of Cicero, he emerged and defeated the Parthian force surrounding him. Cicero wrote to him in October 51 mentioning amongst other matters:

> *I am emphatically of the opinion that you should hasten to Rome. For the situation I left behind me was one of complete calm as regards yourself* [no blame for the events at Carrhae], *and thanks to your recent victory (and a glorious one it was), I can see your arrival will be a memorable event.*

Cicero may just have had Cassius' best interests at heart, but it could also be that he wanted good men and true back in Rome to bolster the Senate against the inevitable arrival of Caesar at some point in 50 or 49.

In December 51, Cicero wrote to Atticus informing him of recent military events. Cicero had led his two legions, after shoring up King Ariobarzanes' position in relation to plots against him, on towards Tarsus which he reached on 5 October. No doubt Quintus will have been instrumental in helping to reorganize and motivate the officers and men of the legions as they marched through the dusty and hot plains and passes of southern Turkey. Tarsus was the capital of Cilicia and established by Pompey – the main Roman roads through the town today are almost as they were in 67 when Pompey walked them and in 51 as Cicero arrived. It would not be so many years before a young Saul of Tarsus, the later St Paul, would also be running down these same roads.

From Tarsus, Cicero moved to battle the tribes and bandit groups in the Amanus mountains – Cicero reported to Atticus:

> *I reached Tarsus on 5 October and pressed on to the Amanus, which separates Syria from Cilicia at the watershed, a mountain range full of enemies of Rome*

from time immemorial. Here on 13 October we made a great slaughter of the enemy, carrying and burning places of great strength. Pomptinus [one of Cicero's legates] *coming up at night and myself in the morning. I received the title of general from the army* [imperator].

Cicero goes on to say how Bibulus, proconsul now in Syria, wanted his slice of the action and attacked Amanus from the east but:

He started looking for a scrap of laurel in the wedding cake in these same mountains of Amanus. The result was that he lost his entire First Cohort, including Chief-Centurion, Asinius Dento, a distinguished man in his own class, and the other Centurions of the cohort, also a Military Tribune, Sex. Lucilius, whose father T. Gavius Caepio is a man of wealth and standing.

There followed another battle further on at the fortified town of Pindenissum. Rather than surrender to the now reinvigorated legions, a siege was laid around the town and Cicero's men took it – after a number of casualties. Cicero writes that he allowed the men to keep any booty they found and to celebrate while he sold off the captives on 19 December, which had thus far raised 120,000 sesterces. Three questions come to mind immediately. Firstly, who was buying the slaves, how were they paying for them and what does this say about Cicero claiming to be out of pocket? It is most likely that Roman coinage in that amount was not available in that area so the calculation of HS120,000 is probably in silver bars or weight equivalent – this would be transported back to Rome and minted into coin and then distributed – Cicero keeping by far the largest percentage. After this battle, Quintus was given command of the legions for their winter quarters and routines.

In 50, it is thought around March, Cicero wrote to his friend Papirius Paetus using his new military title and he was able to poke fun at himself, an admirable gift, but within his cheek there was also probably a tongue poking through. He was in an ebullient and confident mood as this extract shows:

Laodicea, March (?) 50
From Cicero, Imperator, to Paetus

Your letter made a first rate general out of me. I had no idea you were such a military expert – evidently you have thumbed the treatises of Pyrrhus and Cineas [both king and minister from Epirus who wrote on strategy and war]. *So I intend to follow your precepts, with one addition – I mean to keep a few boats handy on the coast. They say there is no better weapon against Parthian cavalry!*

For Cicero, becoming a successful commander rather suited him. He freely admitted to Atticus that his new found integrity – indicated by the people wherever he went for not stripping them of what little they had left – and his abilities as a commander had gone to his head. He was actually starting to enjoy the acclaim and must have felt some of the joy of being called *imperator* by his soldiers as a compensation for never being acclaimed as such by the Senate as he boasted to Atticus:

> *Meanwhile here is a scintillation: Ariobarzanes owes his life and throne to me. Just en passant I rescued king and kingdom, by good judgement and influence and by showing those who were plotting against him that they could not get near me, much less their money.... That is all I have to tell. I am now sending an official letter to Rome.*

When we assess how Cicero had acted as a military commander, we should remember that there was no pressing military reason for his attacks in the mountains of Amanus nor his assault on Pindenissium. The province was quiet.

There had always been a pirate threat from this northeastern corner of the Mediterranean, but Pompey had done much to eradicate this. Additionally, the Parthian threat was real but there was only scant evidence that an invasion was imminent, indeed it can be argued that Cicero was talking up this danger for his own benefit – to be seen as protecting the Empire from this threat. Furthermore, the question of why Cicero was so aggressive in his military strategy has been partially answered by Mary Beard in her 2007 work *The Roman Triumph* in that Cicero saw Cilicia in a different light once he arrived in what he had always referred to as his grim and unedifying task of acting as proconsul. In a period of fifty years, some nine Roman governors sent to Cilicia requested a Triumph and six received one, so why not Cicero? A number of factors made Cilicia a good target for the glory hunter – small and easy victories against homeless mercenaries. So it was not just good administration and fairness that could impress the Senate, but also military success and the prospect of a return to Rome in glory, as Cicero had experienced when he came back from exile. It was a Triumph that he wanted and that became the purpose of his mission. This was not frowned upon – on the contrary, the Triumph was used as a lure for generals to venture out conquering new lands with the promise of glory through the streets of Rome and a lustre to their *auctoritas*.

Packing for home 50

Cicero was as good as his word and did indeed send a number of despatches either direct to Cato or to the Senate. Like Cicero's legal orations and speeches, these reports were an opportunity not only to inform people of the facts, but also to enliven and reignite his own standing in the eyes of those in the Senate. They were a platform for Cicero to expound on not only what had had happened, but why he had acted as he did and in so doing, they were also an attempt at reinforcement of approved practice or an education as to how they should govern. Perhaps they were aimed at Cato or to the forward-looking men who saw that the Empire now had to be governed more professionally. A prime example comes in a passage from one of these reports where Cicero explains how he has dealt with the matter of King Ariobarzanes – the Senate having ordered him to protect and maintain the throne:

> *The king then asked me for some cavalry and foot regiments from my army. I was aware that under your decree I had not only a right but a duty to agree. But in view of the reports coming in daily from Syria, the public interest demanded that I should conduct the army to the borders of Cilicia as soon as possible. Moreover, now that the plot had been exposed, the king did not appear to me to need a Roman army; his own resources seemed adequate for his protection. I therefore urged him to make preservation of his own life his first lesson in the art of ruling. He should exercise his royal prerogative against the persons whom he found organising a conspiracy against him, punishing where punishment was necessary and relieving the rest of apprehension.*

There is little doubt that the relevance of this passage would not be lost on those that read or heard it in the Senate. It was a restatement and reinforcement of the action he had been forced to take in 63 and the lightness of touch with which he rams this point home is a remarkable passage of writing. His action in 63 had been easy to undertake as it was the correct action undertaken in the correct way – he had merely followed the same course of action with the young king. With reports such as this, Cicero hoped not only to be welcomed home soon from his year in office, but received back with at least an ovation, if not a Triumph. Cilicia had provided him with yet another stage on which to act and he had, so far, given a great performance. Cicero was determined to exploit this new found opportunity that had been built no doubt on the back of the experience Quintus and other officers had brought to his short campaign. Cicero wrote a letter to every member of the Senate asking for a Triumph – he probably deserved it and yet Cato stood out as one of only three dissenters who opposed this great honour. The letter still survives and these passages explain his thinking. Cato conveys his congratulations on Cicero's success, but points out that a *supplicatio* – a supplication where a number of days of prayers and feasting are announced as symbol of great thanks to an individual for his service (Cicero had received one of these after the Catiline plot was put down) – was more appropriate. His reasoning was that the results achieved in Cilicia were more to do with good administration than by the swords of the army – or perhaps Cicero felt that it was the gods that deserved the credit and not himself?

Cato to Cicero
Rome, April 50

From M Cato to M Cicero, Imperator, greetings.

Patriotism and friendship alike urge me to rejoice, as I heartily do, that your ability, integrity, and conscientiousness, already proved in great events at home when you wore the gown of peace, are no less actively at work in arms abroad. Accordingly, I did what my judgement allowed me to do: that is to say, I paid your tribute with my voice and vote for defending your province by your integrity and wisdom, for saving Ariobarzanes' throne and person, and for winning back the hearts of our subjects to a loyal support of Roman rule. As for the decree of Supplication, if you prefer us to render thanks to the Immortal Gods in respect of provision taken for the public good by your own admirable policy and administrative rectitude – why I am very glad of it. If, however, you regard a supplication as an earnest of a Triumph, and on that account prefer the praise to go to accident rather than yourself, the fact is that a Triumph does not always follow a Supplication.

On the other hand, the Senate's judgement that a province has been held and preserved by its governor's gentle and upright administration rather than by the favour of the Gods or the swords of an army is a far greater distinction than a Triumph: and that is what I proposed to the House.

Cato had decided that the greatest honour for Cicero was the public acknowledgement of the Senate rather than either a *supplicatio* or a Triumph. Cicero was furious and no doubt felt that, yet again and as he had felt so often in his life, no matter what he did he was held down, still the *novus homo*, still not part of the 'in crowd'. Cicero tried to mask his desire for these honours in his response to Cato:

> *But I have explained the reason for my inclination (I will not say my desire) in my previous letter. Perhaps you did not find it altogether convincing; it means at any rate that I do not regard the honour as something to be unduly coveted, but that, none the less, if proffered by the Senate, I feel I ought by no means to spurn it. I trust, furthermore, that in view of the labours I have undertaken for the public good, the House will deem me not unworthy of an honour, especially one so commonly bestowed.*

With Cato unimpressed with this pretence at not being bothered, Cicero later discovered that Cato had supported a long *supplicatio* for Bibulus and he wrote to Atticus:

> *Cato has been disgracefully spiteful.*

Before his term in office came to an end, there was one other awkward problem that arrived on Cicero's watch and that was the loan of money that a new face in this story had made to the town of Salamis in Cyprus. Marcus Brutus was the son of Servilia, half-sister to Cato and one time lover of Julius Caesar. He was thought of as a coming man – of aristocratic bearing, handsome, careful and strong willed, the sort of man Cicero wished to court, not annoy. Brutus was making his way up the *cursus honorum* and had won the quaestorship in 54 and was thus one of the newer members of the Senate and as such he was, in theory at least, not allowed to lend money. Having ignored this, Brutus had imposed a 4 per cent per month interest charge on his loan – 48 per cent compound – and the town of Salamis had been unable to pay. Cicero took a stand against a request from Brutus for support which did not go down at all well with Brutus, whom Cicero described as 'brusque, arrogant, ungracious'. Brutus took matters into his own hands and sent cavalry to Salamis to get his money – locking up the senate of Salamis in their own senate house until they paid – four died of starvation in the process. Cicero was grateful to have handed over his position before having to act in any further way, but no doubt Brutus got what he wanted as he managed to secure a position on the staff of the new governor of Cyprus the following year.

Events in Rome

Cicero wanted to get home, he was impatient and frustrated and with or without a Triumph there were many issues that he needed to deal with. His daughter Tullia, now divorced, had decided to marry Publius Cornelius Lentulus Dolabella, who was a little younger than her, a bit of an ambitious playboy, and not the son-in-law that Cicero had in mind. To add insult to injury, all of Cicero's efforts to mollify Appius were undone as Dolabella was making a name for himself by bringing the charges against Appius that he faced on his return from Cilicia. Appius had returned to Rome to be greeted with charges of misgovernment. Perhaps not surprisingly, given what we know about how quickly Republican networks and relationships could change almost in the blink of an eye, there was a literary reproachment by letter between Appius and Cicero with the former reaching out, carefully and without begging, for Cicero's good advice and Cicero responded to him:

> Finally...at long last, I have read letters worthy of Appius Claudius. Full of graciousness, responsibility, industry. The view of the city, perchance, has brought back your customary civility.'

As Cicero commented, 'Here I am in my province paying Appius all kinds of compliments, when out of the blue I find his prosecutor becoming my son-in-law!'

In the same letter of 3 August written from Side, creeping along the coastline of southern Turkey ever closer to home, Cicero commented to Atticus on news that Hortensius was dying: 'For my own part I am deeply distressed'. There was a pressing issue regarding his handing over control of the province. The gathering political storm in Rome had meant that no successor had yet been named and so Cicero took matters into his own hands to appoint a temporary *locum*. Cicero explained to Atticus that his current quaestor, Mescinius Rufus, was not suited to the responsibility and that his brother would probably not accept – one might think that he would have been ideal, but Cicero was worried about how this would look in Rome with accusations of nepotism no doubt coming his way. For Quintus there was a lingering sore spot in this matter, as Shackleton Bailey observed: it was one thing not to accept, but quite another not to have been offered the position in the first place. In the end a new young quaestor arrived and Cilicia was left in the hands of Coelius 'perhaps a silly boy, without sense of responsibility or self-control' but he explained that, apart from his brother, there was no one that he could appoint ahead of Coelius given his rank of quaestor, and being a nobleman, not willing to insult him or his family in Rome. For Quintus, all his efforts were in vain if he expected financial gain – only a few months later he was unable to repay a comparatively small sum back to Atticus and his brother could not or decided not to help him, despite having returned with at least the income from the slaves he had sold but more likely quite a bit more on top.

Other storm clouds were gathering on the horizon and Cicero read another letter from Caelius with concern. Written to Cicero from Rome on 8 August 50, Caelius passes on some more gossip, this time about recent election embarrassments for Domitius who was beaten for election to the College of Augurs by Mark Antony – no doubt with considerable support from the still absent Caesar – the vacancy had opened with the death of Hortensius. But the real news was that the atmosphere in Rome was changing and the signs of a major clash were everywhere.

> On high politics, I have often told you that I do not see peace lasting another year; and the nearer the inevitable struggle approaches, the plainer the danger appears. The question on which the dynasts will join issue is this: Cn. Pompeius is determined not to allow C. Caesar to be elected consul unless he surrenders his army and provinces; whereas Caesar is persuaded that he cannot survive if he leaves his army......So this is what their love-affair, their scandalous union, has come to – not covert backbiting, but outright war!

Note

1. Leach, Eleanor Winsor., 'Cicero's Cilician Correspondence: Space & *Auctoritas*'. *Arethusa*, Vol. 49. No. 3 (2016), p 503–523

Tending to Tiro 50

The sole consulship of Pompey allowed Cato and the *optimates* to feel, justifiably, that the Triumvirate may be over and that they had succeeded in drawing Pompey towards them and away from Caesar and could now work on him as their man. Pompey himself was never easy to read and he has left precious little to history by way of a means to assess his inner thinking. On the surface he seemed content with not offending anyone, but this often meant that he also pleased no one. Politics was much harder to fight than an enemy on the battlefield – at least there you knew who the real enemy was, whereas in the Senate, Pompey was out of his depth. Undoubtedly vain, Pompey felt the need to stay relevant, but was not quite convinced he knew what relevant meant in the Republic where so much could change so quickly. If he was pleased to have a chance to pull away from Caesar then he rarely displayed it except perhaps in his legislation, and it is in these bills that the root cause of the next climactic events in Rome was to be found. But before these events unfolded, Cicero was returning home to re-establish his life and deal with some domestic issues.

Cicero met back with his son Marcus, Quintus and Quintus Junior and left Cilicia late in the autumn of 50, arriving back around December for his reunion with his beloved Tullia and his new son-in-law. While he had been away, his faithful confidante and friend Tiro had been working tirelessly alongside him and had now been taken seriously ill. We cannot know what the ailment was, but it certainly incapacitated him – possibly stress, some bowel disorder, but certainly a stomach issue is mentioned in Cicero's eight or so letters to Tiro as he had to be left behind on the journey unable to travel home directly. In November 50 he had written directly to Tiro from the island of Leucas, modern day island of Lefkada off the western coast of Greece, no doubt from here he planned to head for Brundisium:

Cicero to Tiro
Leucas, 7 November 50

From Tullius to his dear Tiro best greetings, also from Marcus and my brother
Quintus and Quintus Junior.
  I read your letter with varying feelings. The first page upset me badly, the
second brought me round a little. So now, if not before, I am clear that until
your health is quite restored you should not venture upon travel either by land
or water. I shall see you soon enough if I see you thoroughly strong again.
  You say that the doctor has a good reputation, and so I hear myself; but frankly
I don't think much of his treatments. You ought not to have been given soup
with a weak stomach. However, I have written to him at some length and also
to Lyso [Cicero's host at Patrae where Tiro was staying and convalescing].

After reassuring Tiro not to worry about the cost of any treatment and that he had made arrangements for money to be made available, Cicero continued:

Your services to me are beyond count – in my home and out of it, in Rome and
abroad, in private affairs and public, in my studies and literary work. You will
cap them all if I see you your own man again, as I hope I shall.

Eventually Tiro was able to also get back to Italy across the Ionian Sea and we know that he spent time recovering from his illness at Cicero's Tusculan villa, which had been rebuilt with new gardens after Gabinius had looted and vandalized it in 58 during Cicero's banishment. The villa was one of many luxurious buildings in the Alban Hills that looked north, through the early morning mists and forests, the sixteen miles towards Rome. Lucullus had retired and died here in luxury and over 130 villa sites have been identified in the neighbourhood belonging to thirty-six owners in this period of the Republic. Seneca wrote that 'Nobody who wants to acquire a home in

Tusculum or Tibur for health reasons or as a summer residence, will calculate how much yearly payments are.' In his oration for Plancius, Cicero described the clientele of the area thus:

> *You are from the most ancient municipium of Tusculum, from which so many consular families are originating, among which even the gens Luventia – all other municipia* (together) *do not have so many* (consular families) *coming from them.*

We also know that the house, the *Tusculanum*, had a library, but whether this was restocked with books is unknown. In 1920, Mabel Root wrote about her 'pre-war' visit to the area trying to locate the site of the villa and described what she felt and saw, and this excerpt gives us an imaginary journey to a place Cicero loved and to which he must have longed to return:

> *We followed the old Via Latina; in about an hour, we reached the Alban Mountains and began to climb to a long white town half buried in trees, Frascati. There we left the car and took our devious way to Tusculum. All about were the villas of wealthy Romans, great estates, where mossy marbles and deserted fountains tell of bygone grandeur.... We came out on breezy uplands with tall pines scattered over them...over grassy slopes dotted with crimson poppies, along a lane, and then we took the Via Latina, which was excavated for some distance here, so that we walked literally in the steps of Cicero and his friends.... When we had climbed for an hour and a half, we found ourselves on a level stretch with only a mass of rock and masonry above us. Here lay Tusculum, 'The long white streets of Tusculum, The proudest town of all'.*
>
> *There are no streets here now, only occasional ruined walls and a well-preserved theatre, where we sat down to rest, and imagined Cicero and his family applauding some clever Roscius.... Archaeologists who scout this location are convinced that the Tusculanum was four miles from ancient Tusculum... that Grotta Ferrata has the most evidence to support it.*

Although the exact location continues to be debated, the fact that Sulla originally built the villa that Cicero purchased suggests, to me at least, that it was near where Mabel was standing, high on the hills in the fresh country air, with green fields and wild flowers below rather than in a hollow at the base of the hills where the Grotta Ferrata is to be found. In a letter to Atticus, Cicero talks about covered walks at Tusculum indicating the long columned walkways to stroll and discuss shielded from the sun and something similar to the Lyceum outside Athens with a garden or roses, Greek statues (from

Atticus hauled up the hills on wagons), fountains and white marble colonnades amongst the green of the trees and vines, a suitable place to send his friend to recover or die.

Alongside worrying about Tiro's health, Cicero also had concerns about Terentia's freedman and agent Philotimus. On a visit to catch up with business affairs, the man was woolly enough to arouse Cicero's suspicions that he was cheating them both. Rather than challenge Philotimus or alert Terentia, Cicero ensured that Atticus stopped sending funds his way, but his suspicions were also aroused that Terentia was not being honest with him.

Earlier in the year 50, both Quintus Junior and Marcus had been sent off with Dionysius for their studies with him – we recall Dionysius had been on loan from Atticus. Residing at the court of King Deiotarus in Galatia, who was described as a loyal friend to Cicero and Rome, the young boys would have been treated with great respect given who their fathers were and the good will that might follow. When Quintus reached the age of sixteen he became a man in Roman eyes and received his 'manly gown' which, as his father was away with the army, Cicero planned to present to him on the festival of Liber on 17 March. In reference to the two boys to Atticus, Cicero remarked on how well they worked together, but that one needed pushing, the other pulling into line:

The boys are fond of one another, and are learning and practising. But as Isocrates said about Ephorus and Theopompus, one of them needs the rein, the other the spur.

Chapter 25

Rubicon 49

It has also been suggested that constant exercise of power gave Caesar a love of it; and that, after weighing his enemies' strength against his own, he took the chance of fulfilling his youthful dreams of making a bid for the monarchy: Cicero seems to have come to a similar conclusion.

Suetonius, The Life of Caesar

Two weeks after his letter to Tiro, Cicero had safely sailed across the Ionian Sea and arrived once again into the port of Brundisium to another great welcome. As he stepped ashore, he would have been followed by his group of lictors – again with their *fasces*, the bundles of rods and the central axe – but now topped off with laurel leaves as a mark of his *imperium* which he could retain until he reached the outer limits and the *pomoerium* of Rome. He seems to have been in no hurry to arrive there, rather building up his image and enjoying the warm reception and praises as he made his way north once more.

As Cicero crossed the centre of Italy travelling ever westwards over to the west coast, on 18 December or thereabouts, he wrote to Atticus from Formiae:

The political situation alarms me deeply, and so far, I have found scarcely anybody who is not for giving Caesar what he demands rather than fighting it out. The demand is impudent no doubt, but more moderate than expected.... And why should we start standing up to him now? [Then with a quote well known from Homer's Odyssey] *Sure 'tis no worse a thing' than when we gave him his five years' extension or when we brought in the law authorising his candidature in absentia.*

For the sake of clarity, Caelius had captured the essence of the issue in his letters which was that there were both political and constitutional issues at stake for Caesar, but other factors came into play as well. On the procedural side, Caesar needed to know whether the law of 52 which Pompey had passed in his favour allowing him to stand for the consulship in absentia would be upheld. If not, then he would have to attend in person to apply his credentials, which meant giving up his command and coming to Rome as a private citizen. Secondly, he was well aware that if he did do this, Cato and others had made it plain that he would be put on trial on charges of bribery, corruption and violence during his period as joint consul with Pompey in 59 where he used brutal tactics to force through his land bills, the five-year commands and the election of his successors. Thirdly, the date of the end of his Gallic command was yet to be decided, but when it came and if it were not extended to cover the period down to the last day when he could become consul again, then he became also a private citizen and was left open to charges and his future was finished. As a private citizen, Caesar was totally exposed and vulnerable and he needed either his command or an election in his absence.

Central to these matters was the position of Pompey and, through him, Cato. While Cicero was racing to get to the point where he could get back to Rome during 50 to play a part in these events, by the time he did arrive in December too much water had flowed under the bridges of the Tiber for him to be able to make any substantial impact. But within this web of constructs in the political sphere lay deeper issues. For example, if Caesar did in fact give up his command and return to Rome how likely was it that he would be arrested and put on trial? How likely was it that he would end up in Marseilles with Milo eating fish? Caesar had a stranglehold on Rome even with Pompey as sole consul. Many people were in Caesar's debt, many admired him and the people were certainly in awe of this great commander with the public and common touch. Who would have the courage to prosecute him other than Cato? Would Cicero have taken on the task? There were numerous imponderables to which we can add that Caesar himself hardly mentioned these political issues in his later commentaries and there is a consistent level of debate amongst historians about what his own motives were. Caesar was to claim that it was his *dignitas* that was being threatened – that he deserved both a further command and the consulship and if the rules denied him this then the rules must either change or the whole edifice be brought down and changed too – Caesar was not alone in thinking this either.

Evidence of where Pompey had moved in relation to his former partner comes in a number of forms. When the Senate asked both Pompey and Caesar to contribute a legion to a force to travel to Parthia to avenge the death of Crassus, Pompey asked that Caesar send one of the legions he had lent him for the campaign in Gaul – in other words reducing Caesar's force by two legions. Additionally, Cicero met with the great man on 25 December 50 and discovered that there was no sentiment for peace, Pompey was not at all fazed by Caesar and was confident that he was in the right. To Atticus he wrote either late that night or the day after about Dionysius who had now turned out to be something of a rat and a concern for Atticus' health before moving on to his many hours with Pompey:

Your forecast that I should be seeing Pompey before I came your way has proved correct. On the 25th he overtook me near Lavernium. We went back to Formiae together and talked privately from two o'clock till evening. The answer to your question whether there is any hope of a pacification, so far as I could see from Pompey's talk, which lacked neither length nor detail, is that there isn't even the desire for one. His view is that if Caesar is made consul, even after giving up his army, it will mean the subversion of the constitution; and he further thinks that when Caesar hears that preparations against him are energetically proceeding, he will forgo the consulate this year and prefer to retain his army and province. But should Caesar take leave of his senses, Pompey is quite contemptuous of anything he can do and confident in his own and the Republic's forces. All in all, though I often thought of Mars on both sides [a reference to the uncertain nature of war] I felt relieved as I heard such a man, courageous, experienced, and powerful in prestige, discoursing statesman wise on the dangers of a false peace.

Events in Rome were already starting to divide opinions openly and the more adventurous and warlike, seeing that the middle ground was collapsing, made their own plays and gambles for power and prestige as Cicero went on the explain in the same letter:

We had in front of us a speech made by Antony on 21 December containing a denunciation of Pompey from the day he came of age, a protest on behalf of persons condemned [those whom Pompey had attacked in the courts in 52] *and threats of armed force. Talking of which Pompey remarked: 'How do you expect Caesar to behave if he gets control of the state, when this feckless nobody of a quaestor dares to say this sort of thing?' In short, far from seeking the peaceful settlement you talk of, he seemed to dread it.*

We can look to sources written long after the coming decisive moment when Caesar marched his army south from Gaul up to the river Rubicon, the nominal boundary of Italy past which no army was to travel. The trouble with consulting later sources is that they often had their own reasons for writing either in favour or in condemnation of Caesar. There is little documentary evidence that helps in our own assessment of why Caesar acted in this way. Much later, looking over the decisive battlefield of Pharsalus, Caesar is supposed to have remarked that he was made to do it, he had no option, 'They wanted it', but just how reliable is this?

Caesar's reasoning

The difference between a republic and an empire is the loyalty of one's army.
Julius Caesar

When Caesar marched his army from Ravenna to Arminium he knew exactly what he was doing because he carried with him a number of resentments and thorns that had got under his skin over a long period. In November 50 when the Senate told him to return to Gaul, which he should not have left without authority, and dismiss his army, Caesar was well aware that this was at the same time as Pompey still held his Spanish provinces and was not about to dismiss his own – held for the same period as those of Caesar. This sense of double standards rankled with him, as did Pompey's legislation back in 52 which reconfirmed that candidates for office must stand in person. The original law which was passed for Caesar's benefit had contained an exemption from Pompey and yet here he was reaffirming the original law – the law of the ten tribunes – what was he to do, which law was correct? He had written and complained to Pompey that, because he now had to attend Rome in person in the summer to submit his credentials to stand, he was being robbed of the last six months of his *imperium* which were being ripped from his hands by his enemies *'ereptoque semenstri imperio'*.

The further law prescribing the five-year interval between office in Rome and becoming a Governor – that which saw Cicero, amongst other old hands, sent abroad to hold the fort – was something else that Caesar had been ruminating on for eighteen months. He could return to Rome, if he wanted to give up his command and risk legal attacks, but he would not be able to hold a province again for another five years – and Caesar knew there was much unfinished business in Gaul from a strategic point of view if no other. The original reason for the five-year rule had been sound, to prevent corruption in the provinces by ex-consuls immediately out to exploit their provinces to recoup money expended on election. Indeed, the law was to remain in place for 200 years, which does establish the merits of the *lex*, but Caesar saw it as something devised for an attack on him personally. He was right to view the law in this way because Metellus Scipio was appointed to the governorship of Syria for 49 although he had been consul in 52 – apart from only being a three-year gap, being the father-in-law of Pompey just made things worse. Further evidence that he was being stitched up came when another province was allotted, this time Caesar's own, and Transalpine Gaul was given to Domitius Ahenobarbus even though only four years had elapsed since his consulship in 54. To any observer, these seem like the actions not of a senate, but of an anti-Caesarean faction, which is in fact what Pompey and Cato led. There was no doubt that Caesar would feel affronted, embarrassed and belittled by such actions and unfairness, and possibly that is why these decisions were taken. If Caesar's *auctoritas* really was his guiding principle then why keep throwing mud at him if you did not want him to react? Did Pompey really feel so confident that he could crush Caesar, if matters came to civil war, as he had said to Cicero?

One of many other insults was the request for Caesar to send the two legions south. They could march through Italy as they had no commander with imperium with them but, expecting them to be diverted to the east and on to Parthia, Caesar became aware that they had been diverted and 10,000 armed men were in fact sitting encamped near Rome waiting for orders – indeed some of their officers were possibly being replaced with those loyal to the Republic and men being transferred. Caesar felt outmanoeuvred and lied to by both Pompey and the Senate and this just added to his anger.

On 12 January 49, Cicero wrote to Tiro and these lines taken from the letter explain his upbeat mood in contrast to the solemnity with which he had been writing to Atticus:

> *I arrived outside Rome on 4 January. They streamed to meet me on the road – a most flattering welcome. But I found myself plunged into the flames of civil strife, or rather war. I should dearly have liked to heal the mischief, and I believe I could have healed it had not the personal desires of certain people (there are warmongers on both sides) stood in my way. To be sure, our friend Caesar has sent a threatening, harsh letter to the Senate and persists in his impudent determination to hold his army and province in defiance of the Senate, and my friend Curio is egging him on. Our friend Antony and Quintus Cassius have gone to join Caesar* [they were both tribunes so were breaking the law by leaving the city]…*preparations are going very actively forward on our side too. This is taking place by the authority and zeal of our friend Pompey, who late in the day has begun to be afraid of Caesar.*

Cicero had decided that he could not influence affairs any longer in the substantial way he had once done – or felt he had done. It was wishful thinking to feel that the Senate could resist both men now intent on war under Cicero's leadership. His words would have fallen on deaf ears even though he would like to think that he could have saved Rome – again. In case his letter fell into the wrong hands he is now careful about taking sides, attempting to play a mediating role which was to be his position for some weeks to come. On 7 January the Senate issued a final decree and two Caesarian tribunes rode hard northwards to locate Caesar and deliver the message but it was too late – 'the die was cast.'

To get his army to the Rubicon River south of the Alpine passes, Caesar had to issue orders weeks before in order that his legions could move through before the snow fell – there was therefore nothing impulsive about Caesar's actions – his plan had been in place for months during 50. On the early misty morning of either 10 or 11 January, the forward troops of Caesar's hard bitten legions crossed the Rubicon with the commander and his *imperium* intact. Their destination was a series of small towns on the northern coastal plain, such as Ancona and Arretium. To some in Rome, ready and waiting for Caesar to take this step, their spies had kept them well informed and there was no shock, just a celebration that now they had put Caesar where they wanted him – in their view in the wrong place in history, a tyrant ignoring the will of the people and Senate of Rome, a monster coming to devour democracy. For others it was outright panic on 17 January and especially for those who had stood in Caesar's way. As senator looked at senator and as families met and young men beat their breasts for war – everything divided and the worst type of war began, a civil war within a society and again, within living memory, Italy divided. Cicero left the next day on the 18th and wrote to Atticus:

I have decided on the spur of the moment to leave before daybreak so as to avoid looks and talk, especially with these laurelled lictors [his status as proconsul still entitled him to his twelve lictors in procession wherever he went and no doubt the laurels, a symbol of military courage may have looked rather conspicuous as he fled the city – if fleeing is too strong a description, then what was he doing?]. *As for what is to follow, I really don't know what I am doing or going to do, I am so confused by the rashness of this crazy proceeding of ours.*

Part VII

The Beginning of History

Chapter 26

A House Divided

In October of 50 and while there was still time to heal the divides, Cicero was in Athens and on his way homewards. Despatching a letter to Atticus, he captured the central question of the problem – who to support.

I fancy I see the greatest struggle – unless the same Providence that delivered me from the Parthian war better than I dared hope takes pity on our country – the greatest that history has ever known.

I have made friends with both contestants.... And only wish I had listened to your affectionate admonitions from the first.

We calculated that on the one hand joined with Pompey I should never be obliged to go politically astray, while on the other hand as Pompey's ally I ought not to be at loggerheads with Caesar – they were so closely linked.

Each counts me as his man, unless it be that one of them is only pretending... moreover I received letters from both at the same time as yours, conveying the impression that neither has a friend in the world he values more than myself.

'Speak Marcus Tullius!' what shall I say? 'Be so kind as to wait until I see Atticus'?

I am strongly in favour of doing something about a Triumph and so staying outside Rome with the best possible excuse. [If Cicero passed over the *pomerium* he would forsake his *imperium* and thus not be eligible for a Triumph, but the likelihood of his receiving one was low, as he well knew and this was just a forlorn hope. In any event, the Senate had bigger matters to concern them than Cicero.]

Cicero even joked that it would have been better to be in Cilicia – things were that bad. The accelerated pace of events suggests that matters got out of control and too many individuals were taking steps that exacerbated the tension and created a warlike atmosphere. Being unable to prevent social and political decay suited Caesar just as it suited Donald Trump in Washington in 2020 but with the key difference that, in Rome, there was no one left inside the senate building to bar the doors – the senators had already made up their minds to fight Caesar and had left the building empty of resistance and dispersed throughout Italy awaiting orders from Pompey. Cicero's loyalty was to the Republic and thence to Pompey and that is where he tied his colours – no doubt Caesar had been expecting Cicero to remain true to form.

With panic came an attempt by Pompey to assign districts to defend and a decision to evacuate the city to gain time to create an army. Caesar already had a well-oiled machine and it was loyal – we only know of one officer who refused to follow him named Titus Labienus who had been one of his ablest commanders.

Labienus was no ordinary defector. We might recall his spell in Rome working away for Caesar and promoting the trial of the thirty-year-old supposed assassin of Saturnius and accusing Gaius Rabirius of murder. Cicero had been the defending counsel, but it was only after Metellus Celer took down a flag that the trial was halted and Caesar called off Labienus. He was also the man who stood at Caesar's side during the campaign in Gaul as his best cavalry commander and many victories were down to his leadership and, in gratitude (*gratitudo*) Caesar appointed him Governor of Cisalpine Gaul.

But Pompey had no such military machine and needed to buy time – he was always on the back foot and this added to a sense of confusion which also meant that no one thought to empty the city treasury before they left Rome. The arrival of Labienus would have felt like a victory, however, and he was put in command of all Pompey's cavalry forces. As events unfolded, Cicero discussed the situation with Terentia and Marcus, no doubt Terentia had a good idea of which women at the top of society were staying and who was leaving with their husband so to begin with, the rebuilt house on the Palatine was set into a state of defence while she decided to stay.

In January 49, Cicero wrote a long and quite bitter letter to Atticus mostly about Caesar's dirty work and pretence:

> *Pray, what's all this? What is going on? I am in the dark. 'We hold Cingulum, we've lost Ancona, Labienus has deserted Caesar.' Is it a Roman general or Hannibal we are talking of? Deluded wretch, with never in his life a glimpse of even the shadow of the Ideal!* [the letter uses the Greek word for a moral ideal translated into Latin as *honestum*]. *And he says he is doing all this for his honour's sake! Where is honour without moral right? And is it right to have an army without public authority, to seize towns by way of opening the road to the mother city, to plan for debt-cancellations* [just as Catiline had promised to gain support] *recall of exiles, and a hundred other villainies.*
>
> *I would rather a single hour with you, warming myself in that 'bonus' sunshine of yours* [free heat and a dig at Atticus' well-known austerity and

thrift] *than all such autocracies, or rather I had sooner die a thousand deaths than entertain one such thought.*

It was not until Caesar reached Corfinium that he met real resistance in the form of Domitius Ahenobarbus and a small force which decided to make a stand – without Pompey's support or legions. Cicero was on his way to join Pompey, having made a decision in haste that he was going to join that side, and was resting the night at Cales on 18–19 February when reports arrived of Caesar's arrival at Corfinium. Writing again at long length to Atticus:

> *But lo and behold! As I write this very letter this night at my lodge at Cales, here come messengers and a letter to announce that Caesar is before Corfinium and Domitius inside the town, with a powerful army eager for battle. I don't believe that Gnaeus will crown all by leaving Domitius in the lurch.... But it will be a disgraceful thing to desert Domitius when he is begging for help.*

But that is exactly what Gnaeus Pompey did, and Domitius found himself under siege for seven days before his own men compelled him to seek terms of surrender. With him were about fifty senators and Caesar was now able to display his famous clemency by releasing them all without penalty to show that he was not Sulla, not acting to overthrow the state, just to defend his dignity and that they could rest safe under him. Some left immediately to go to Rome and wait for Caesar there – others simply did not believe him and left for Pompey's camp. Many of the soldiers immediately joined Caesar's veteran legions to cheers.

This fight at Corfinium was indicative of a major strategic mistake that had already doomed the Republican forces to failure. As soon as Caesar crossed the Rubicon, Cato urged the Senate to give Pompey command over the whole of the Republican forces so that a unified strategic plan could be controlled. However, much to the disgust of Cato and Cicero, the Senate shared out commands to a variety of senators keen to demonstrate that they were militarily able and who wanted their own slice of the glory that would come from a victory in battle against Caesar. Once these commands had been distributed it was impossible to control a unified strategy, let alone a tactical plan. Hence, Domitius ended up in the north, Cato was sent to Sicily, Lentulus was to remain in Rome and guard the treasury (in which he failed) and so on. It was at this point that Cato lost leadership of the Senate and it finally broke into factions with only some members staying loyal to Pompey.

So Domitius was acting under his own initiative when he decided to take on Caesar at Corfinium and that is why Pompey refused to help him when he had ignored his orders to head south and join him. But lest we think that Ahenobarbus was an impetuous failure, he did not personally surrender and instead ordered his doctor to give him poison – it was only a sleeping potion and he awoke to Caesar's clemency. Leaving in disgust at Pompey, Ahenobarbus continued to fight alone from Massilia in Greece before joining Pompey at his camp. He named Cicero as a coward and is the only known senator to have died at the Battle of Pharsalus in 48 still fighting for the Republic.

Pompey was collecting as many of the supportive elements of the state as he could around his headquarters in Campania – not only senators but also more junior office holders, loyal officers, thousands of troops and the administrative apparatus of the various bureaucratic offices – everything it seems except the money in the treasury. When he arrived at Capua, however, Cicero found a sense of depression and chaos. Campania was where many of the key senators of the Republic had their luxury homes and they had painful decisions to make – to stay and sublimate themselves to Caesar or pack their expensive treasures and travel with the army. Much depended on what their glorious commander would decide as his strategy. During February, Cicero pondered on what the future strategy might be. Given that Rome had been deserted and left to Caesar without so much as an arrow being fired in anger, there were some who hoped that this might encourage Caesar to stop and sue for peace – they were wrong and Caesar wasted no time pressing on after Pompey. So it was that Cicero watched as Pompey led the core of his army and tens of thousands of rich and poor alike with their carts and wagon trains, servants and slaves and mules and horses in a semi-stampede to Brundisium, making it clear that Pompey had decided he was leaving for Greece and to wage his war from there. Cicero wrote to Atticus from his villa at Fomiae:

> *However, in that letter of Pompey's, at the end in his own hand, are the words 'As for yourself, I advise you to come to Luceria. You will be as safe there as anywhere.'*
>
> *I am writing back at once and sending a trusty person, one of my staff, to tell him that I am not looking for the safest place I can find....I also urge him to hold on to the sea coast if he wants to be supplied with grain from the provinces.*

But Pompey was leaving not holding on to anything and each day transport ships left packed with men and materials for Greece. One can imagine the port of Brundisium overwhelmed by the chaos of tens of thousands of men, families, supplies, horses all seeking oats for Greece. It must have been a memorable sight.

Caesar and the main body of his forces arrived at Brundisium on 9 March determined to cut off Pompey and surround him by immediately throwing up a blockade. Caesar even tried to open negotiations, perhaps to buy time for his fortifications, but he failed and by 17 March Pompey escaped with the vast majority of those who wished to travel with him. With that, those who were still in Italy now had to look to their own fences.

Cicero, still at his villa, decided to write to Caesar offering himself as a mediator. This was the role he had coveted since his return from Cilicia, or even much earlier. He told Caesar that 'surely he would find no more suitable person than myself for that purpose' before going on to expand on his extensive CV as if applying for a job. Cicero flattered Caesar in his usual lathered way using as much soap as he could find – no doubt this may have repelled Caesar rather than attracted him. He was a practical man desirous of practical solutions, but the eloquent lawyer in Cicero was still the dominating aspect of his personality, still trying to win arguments and win over the jury which included his harshest critic, his friend Atticus, especially given that his lavishly praiseworthy letter to Caesar had been copied and released:

> You write that my letter has been broadcast. I am not sorry to hear it, indeed I have let a number of people take copies.... If I called the latter [Caesar] 'admirable' in urging him to the salvation of our country, I had no fear of appearing to flatter; in such a cause I would gladly have thrown myself at his feet.

So, which was he? Cicero the honest broker, the mediator soft soaping Caesar, or Cicero the judge of Caesar as the man with no honour and no morality? Was he the defender of democracy or the beneficiary of it? Cicero was not only often lying to Atticus, he was lying to himself. Whether he had indeed had copies made of his very personal letter to Caesar we will never know – it could have been a good propaganda ploy to paint himself in this role or indeed he could have just been trying to trump the obvious criticism from Atticus – somewhere, to someone, Cicero lies. Even accepting the boundless immorality shown by prosecution lawyers and judges, there must be a limit to the extent to which an individual can justify their words – or perhaps not – and this is why others did not trust Cicero. He was a lawyer, open to the best solution to win any case regardless of the morality which he himself accused others of lacking.

Civil War in 49

The supreme art of war is to subdue the enemy without fighting.

Sun Tzu

Cicero was distraught at Pompey's departure and is recorded as such in his words to Atticus:

Nothing in [Pompey's] *conduct seemed to deserve that I should join him as his companion in flight. But now my affection comes to the surface, the sense of loss is unbearable, books, writing, philosophy are all to no purpose.*

While others made their decisions whether to stay or go, Quintus at least stayed loyal – it would have been understandable had he gone to Rome to join with Caesar who now convened a much reduced in size Senate – and Caesar tried to attract them both to join him there. Cicero had great propaganda value to him and could assist him in representing his actions as legitimate and moral in line with the *auctoritas* that all Romans understood. His was a war for justice against injustice and Cicero could be a major architect of his image in this respect and possibly undermine Pompey's forces without the need to actually fight. This was something Cicero wanted to achieve as well, it was just a question of whether Caesar wanted to fight and win or not fight and win – whereas a score draw was what Cicero wanted.

Caesar was determined to see Cicero before he left for Spain having decided to eliminate Pompey's legions there before heading for Greece. There was a flurry of correspondence from Cicero in anticipation of this meeting and he responded to Caesar on 19 or 20 March still trying to play the moderate neutral card when Caesar only wanted his presence at the Senate meeting scheduled for 1 April and therefore his endorsement:

When I read your letter received from our friend Furnius in which you urge me to come to Rome. I was not so much surprised by your wish to 'avail yourself of my advice and standing', but I did ask myself what you meant by 'influence' and 'help'.

When arms were taken up, I had nothing to do with the war, and I judged you therein to be an injured party in that your enemies and those jealous of your success were striving to deprive you of a mark of favour.

The mark of favour was to be able to stand for the consulship in absentia and it was this denial that Cicero marks as the crucial issue. Their meeting on 28 March at Cicero's home at Formiae was pivotal. Caesar pressed Cicero to come to Rome and stand for him, but Cicero, to his great credit, stood firm and, according to his explanation to Atticus, stated that he would speak out against any expedition to Spain or to Greece and ask for a coming together with Pompey. Caesar apparently showed Cicero a new side to his, up to now, benevolent character and told him that he should think the matter over carefully – and more menacingly – came the Parthian Shot, that he could get good advice just as easily elsewhere. In closing, Cicero described Caesar's entourage – with memories of Catiline in his mind he saw an 'underworld' and 'a gang of desperadoes'.

Caesar spent April and part of May in Rome trying to pretend that all was normal and that he was standing firm until matters were resolved, but in reality everyone knew Italy was now divided and at war. Any pretence at Caesar acting democratically was washed away when his men ransacked the treasury in the Temple of Saturn and stole 15,000 bars of gold along with 30,000 of silver and 30 million sestertii.

At some point in May the Caesarean G. Scribonius Curio decided to drop in to visit Cicero. He held long discussions before setting off on his mission for Caesar to Sicily to take over the vital corn supply. Cicero refers to having 'gained Curio' in a letter to Atticus dated 28 March after Caesar had left, but we have no more information other than that Curio continued on his mission and thence to Africa where he was to die in battle.

During early April, Cicero decided to visit his collection of properties in the area – for what might be the last time. On the roads he described to Atticus how everyone at Arpinum was depressed and the roads full of levies of men being recruited and taken off for training. 'You may be sure that every disreputable character in Italy is with Caesar.' Then to the Bay of Naples and his villa at Cumae and a short visit to Pompeii in mid-May. The stay in Pompeii was to mask the preparations being made elsewhere for his departure. While he was there, three centurions from local cohorts stationed nearby came to see him and asked if they and their men could be placed in his hands. The matter of loyalties in any civil war are extremely difficult to appreciate and understand. For the ordinary soldier the new war was just a matter of money, for others, perhaps the majority, the war was inextricably linked to their loyalty to their commander, while for some it clearly was loyalty to the Republic that was the gap between themselves and their comrades in arms. Cicero had to let them down – they were not great enough in number to do much and he needed to get to safety.

The weather was too unstable to travel by sea on his arrival so the smoke screen of remaining was maintained and a steady flow of correspondence to many of the big hitters emanated from Formiae, Cumae or Pompeii. Cicero was also receiving letters daily and not just from Caesar and Pompey but Dolabella (his new son-in-law and a Caesarian), Caelius and Sulpicius all enquiring as to his intentions. It was as if Quintus did not exist, but they may have been deliberately allowing his father to deal with the emotional and behavioural problems exhibited by Quintus Junior; things were pretty bad it seems and the young man wanted to leave to join Caesar or at least not go to Greece. Possibly he felt guilty as if this move by his uncle looked like cowardice or had he been got at in some way?

> *As for the young man, I cannot help but feel affection for him but I plainly see he has none for us.*

One of the letters he received was from Marcus Antonius – now left in charge of Rome in Caesar's place as he headed north to deal with Pompey's Spanish legions. Antony's letter was a mailed fist within a velvet glove of plain speaking:

> *I cannot believe that you mean to go abroad, considering how fond you are of Dolabella* [not necessarily accurate] *and that most admirable young lady your daughter and how fond we all are of you.... I have specially sent Calpurnius, my intimate friend, so that you may know how deeply I care for your personal safety and position.*

Some advised him to await events in Spain – and Cicero pondered for a moment whether to pause, perhaps Caesar would be defeated and then he could be seen as not having wavered in his neutrality as this extract from a letter to Atticus on 5 May 49 shows:

> *'I must sail off on the sly then, and creep secretly on board some freighter.... If only things go right in Spain! Though as regards Sicily too I only hope it may be true, but so far we have had no luck – there's a report that the people have rallied to Cato, begged him to put up a fight, promised everything, and that he was sufficiently impressed to start raising troops...from Spain we shall soon have news.*

He was right about Cato at least. The dispersal of commands saw Cato trying to cut off grain to Rome, requisitioning ships and repairing old ones to defend Sicily, but Caesar was ahead of him and a force under the command of Asinius Pollio landed at Messana and Cato ultimately made the decision that without help from Pompey, which again was not forthcoming, he should withdraw and he also departed for Dyrrhachium, leaving Sicily and Sardinia with the grain and the ports to Caesar – another critical mistake on Pompey's part, but for which Cicero was to blame Cato.

By early June, and knowing that he was being constantly watched by Caesar's spies, Cicero, Quintus, Marcus and Quintus Junior slipped away one night from Pompeii and, yet again, took a ship for Greece to join up with Pompey. From the ship on 7 June Cicero wrote to Terentia about how sorry he was for the apparent 'miseries and cares' with which he plagued her on the night before he left. It seems Tullia was there too, who had recently lost a child. Cicero had been suffering from bouts of insomnia and a stomach condition – perhaps all the stress and anxiety had been too much to bear – and he apologized:

All the miseries and cares with which I plagued you to desperation (and very sorry I am for it) and Tulliola too, who is sweeter to me than my life, are dismissed and ejected.... I trust we have a very good ship – I am writing this directly after coming aboard [Cicero took his ship from the small post of Caieta – modern day Gaita to the north of the Bay of Naples]. *I shall next write many letters to our friends, commending you and our Tulliola most earnestly in their care.... The farm at Arpinum with the servants we have in town will be a good place for you if food prices go up.*

Chapter 27

Pharsalus 9 August 48

There is a large gap of several months in the correspondence from Cicero spanning the point where he left Caieta and when we pick his correspondence up again in early 48. In the early months of June, July and August, Cicero and his small retinue which included his son, brother and nephew landed at Dyrrachium and once more made contact with familiar senatorial faces, including Cato at some point. The forces were gathered to Pompey, but only slowly and by the time he was camped in Thessalonica, where he established his main army, Pompey is said to have created nine legions – five had been brought over from Italy and Cicero's old two legions in Cilicia were merged into one. Pompey had also gathered a large 7,000 strong force of cavalry.

Caesar spent little time dealing with Spain and in a brilliant operation lasting less than forty days, with no main battle, he outmanoeuvred Pompey's seven legions commanded by Marcus Petrius, Lucius Afranius and Marcus Varro. Leaving Cassius Longinus in command of Spain, Caesar had praetor Marcus Aemillius Lepidus appoint him dictator – this meant that he no longer had to worry about giving up his *imperium*, his legions or his provinces. Once he was back in Rome and in a sham façade of democratic process, Caesar quickly passed laws restoring the rights of those condemned under Pompey's courts in 52, and surprisingly enough, he held elections and was himself elected consul for the second time – he resigned the dictatorship after only eleven days and immediately left Antony still in charge of Rome and headed for Greece.

Caesar was ready to sail by the late autumn of 49, but given the size of his new army, swelled by many of the Spanish legions who had joined him, there were not enough ships in Brundisium to transport them all so this meant a shuttle service across the Adriatic. Here we come to an interesting episode unheard of in modern warfare. As *Pontifex Maximus*, Caesar was responsible for updating the Roman calendar but, due to his many campaigns and service in Gaul, the calendar had been allowed to drift, Bibulus had been placed in command of the fleet Pompey had presided over in order to prevent Caesar from crossing unhindered; he thought that it was winter, took his ships into port at Corcyra to the south and prepared to wait for spring – but Caesar well knew it was still autumn and therefore also knew that the weather would probably be fair enough to cross. His crossings went ahead until Bibulus heard what was happening and quickly got moving, eventually arriving to disrupt the flow of men, which left Caesar with seven legions on the Greek mainland and few supplies. Bibulus further blockaded Brundisium, preventing the other part of Caesar's army from crossing. Sending Rufus, a Pompeian captured twice by Caesar, east from the coast to discuss terms with Pompey might suggest that Caesar was worried, he was effectively isolated, had only half his army and Pompey would soon come.

Caesar must have known it was a risk sending Rufus and he was right, as he immediately defected to Pompey and thus, by forced march, Pompey arrived, although he lost many men to exhaustion on the journey. A stand-off continued for weeks on either side of a river near Dyrrachium. Meanwhile, more of Caesar's men were arriving, playing cat and mouse with Bibulus' ships; Antony was now in command and in January 48 he managed to get three whole legions across to the north of Pompey – helped substantially by the unexpected death of Bibulus. Extensive fortifications, trenches and ditches were dug on both sides and siege warfare followed and eventually a serious number of battles between forts and trenches resulted in Caesar almost losing his life, the death of over thirty officers and thousands of men and the retreat of Caesar's army. Apparently, many men who had been captured from Caesar's legions were executed – not on Pompey's orders, but those of Labienus and this was both unexpected and harsh. Dyrrachium was a serous reverse for Caesar, but a lost battle does not mean a lost war. Caesar started to garrison the southern areas and refit and replenish his forces and, like a chess game, both sides raced to reach their allied forces further inland, but Pompey was still wary of a pitched battle with Caesar's far more experienced and lethal legions. But numerous senior figures were pressing Pompey for a decisive battle, their force was larger and they had the support of locals for supplies and they suffered from the crippling military illness of over-confidence and hubris borne of the victory at Dyrrachium.

In May 48 Cicero received a letter from his son-in-law Dolabella who was present in Caesar's camp, now in Thessaly. Dolabella wrote that Tullia had recovered her health. The main thrust of his letter, however, was to try to convince Cicero that all was lost and that he should listen to and heed his warnings and advice:

You did me an injustice if at any time you suspected that in advising you to throw in your lot with Caesar and with me, or at least to retire into private life, I was thinking of party interests rather than of yours. But now, when the scales are coming down on our side, I imagine that only one thing can be thought of me, namely, that I am proffering advice to you which it would be contrary to my duty as your son-in-law to withhold.

You see Cn. Pompeius' situation. Neither the glory of his name and past nor yet the kings and nations of whose dependence he used so often to boast can protect him. Even the door of an honourable retreat, which humble folk hold open, is closed to him. Driven out of Italy, Spain lost, his veteran army taken prisoner, he is now to crown all blockaded in his camp.

What was Cicero to make of this plea? It could, of course, have been inspired by Caesar and thus Dolabella was just fulfilling his request, but the tone has a feel of genuine concern. Towards the end of the letter 'dearest Cicero' is asked

'You carry Caesar and Caesar's fortune' – Julius Caesar and all he became was dependent on his Legions.

to retire to Athens and let Pompey ensure his own fate and even promises that Caesar will look kindly on him even now. We cannot know how Cicero responded, but respond he certainly would have. What we do know is that as the two great armies with their great commanders consolidated their forces near a place called Pharsalus, that two months later, Cicero is still in Pompey's camp writing to Atticus about how little he has to do and how he has been given no command 'in a manner appropriate to me and my past career.' Finally, Pompey relented against the constant pressure to fight, and lost.

The battle was brutal, but neither Cato nor Cicero was there to see the slaughter of Pompey's army. Despite being outsized two to one, Caesar's veteran legions such as the IX and XIII, cut their way into the newly formed legions that Pompey had quickly assembled – with five years of fighting in Gaul under their shields, Caesar's troops were in their element in the traditional battle that Pompey offered them. Many senators and heirs to senatorial houses were cut down, including Ahenobarbus, finally meeting his end near an eagle of his legion. Pompey was disorientated, distraught and disconnected from events, overwhelmed by what he saw, as his army was enveloped on the flank and collapsed before him. He rode to camp, changed into civilian clothes and quit the battlefield. News spread fast.

As men, families, wounded and the hunted ran in all directions, groups of senior officials and distraught commanders fled either on foot or on horseback through the Greek hills back towards Dyrrachium where Cato was still in command and many took boats south down the coast to Corcyra where there was a Republican naval base and port and where part of Bibulus' fleet was still anchored. During September the survivors were able to take in the size of the calamity that had just taken place. A meeting was called by Cato, assuming leadership of what *optimates* were still there, to decide what they should do and thus send out messages to all who still supported the Republican cause. Pompey was missing, many leaders had fled or worse and the discussion ranged on whether they should surrender or fight on. Cato even offered command of the army to Cicero who refused – much to the obvious anger and disgust of some officers present. For Cicero the war had been doomed from the start, but this may have been the result of months of living in difficult conditions in the field, long exhausting journeys, dislocation yet again from Rome and normal life – or what passed for normal life these days. How long ago it must have seemed that he was all powerful, speaking to adoring crowds in the sunshine of the forum or in the bright marbled halls of the Senate and temples of Rome. How had it come to this and what was he to do now?

The pivotal moment

For October Cicero mostly resided in Patrae, further inland from the coast to the east and stayed at a house belonging to his friend Manius Curius. Here he had time to consider the present situation and the future. Cicero said many goodbyes over these days as Republican leaders mainly fled or left quietly for north Africa – Afranius and Petrius who had been defeated in Spain, Labienus who had survived Pharsalus, Cato and Pompey's two sons who had no idea where their father was, but not Cicero, he was done with war.

By 4 November 48, Cicero is no longer writing from Patrae, but he too had left Greece and sailed the long journey, probably at night, across the Ionian Sea once more to Brundisium. Having thought matters through, Cicero had decided to return to Italy. How might we interpret this decision, for it could be that this moment has been ignored by history and the way in which we reflect on the character of the man? For historians who can be rightfully critical of Cicero – for example Theodor Momsen who labelled him 'a short-sighted egotist' or D R Shackleton Bailey who referred to Cicero variously as being a 'windbag', 'humbug' and 'spiteful', or the more recent comment from Richard Alston who remarked that immodesty was 'a trait with which Cicero should have been abundantly familiar' then perhaps this decision carried little relevance compared to the immense universe of his other contributions. But in this seemingly simple decision, Cicero relaunched his entire life in the face of tremendous self-doubt and depression. Every ego has as its antonym disgrace and dishonour, the fear of infamy and shame. In writing to Atticus, Cicero refers to his own lack of reflection in the past, confused as he was by loyalty to state and friendship and he felt the pain:

> *It would be intensely painful for me to tell you in writing of the causes – bitter, grave, and strange as they are – which have influenced me, driving me to follow impulse rather than reflection. They were powerful enough at any rate to bring about the result you see....*

The opposite side of Cicero's admittedly huge ego, but then he had much to be grateful for, reverberates in the next lines from the same letter, the feelings of dishonour, disrepute and shame:

> *You say you think I ought to draw nearer, travelling through the towns at night. I don't quite see how that is to be done. I don't have stopping places so suitably spaced that I can spend all the daylight hours in them; and so far as your object is concerned, it doesn't make much difference whether people see me in a town or on the road.*

Cicero would have reflected in Patrae on his options and knew full well that if he came back to Italy any egotistical traits he still harboured would be themselves put to the sword and lost in the complexity of emotions of feeling ashamed to have returned while his comrades fought on. He may not have been on the battlefield, but he was still a Pompeian. The contention here is that the decision to return to Italy was not borne out of cowardice but courage, it was not inevitable that he returned – he chose to do it, the *opprobrium* he would receive was predictable, but Cicero chose to be attacked from all sides and the reason for this was that he still felt that he had a role to play in the healing of the rift between tyranny and democracy. His skills were those needed in the forum, he knew he was no general and had admitted as much many times, but his weapons of choice were still *contra arma verbis* (with words against arms) so using the spoken and written word was how he intended to continue the civil war, fighting his battles regardless of the risks and ridicules that his return could bring.

After requesting Atticus to write to anyone of authority that might extend a hand of friendship to him, he finished by saying:

> *Quintus was most unamiably disposed towards me at Patrae. His son joined him there from Corcyra. I imagine they left with the rest.*

Quintus and Quintus Junior had left to join Caesar. Without any documentary evidence to make an assessment of their reasoning we can but deduce that defeat at Pharsalus felt like disgrace and disgust at the side they had chosen. As far as we can tell, Quintus was given no military command by Pompey, although this might be unfair, and we already know that his son was no doubt telling him every day that his choice to support the Republic and his brother was wrong. There was little love lost between Cicero and his nephew from this point and there had not been a great deal for a while.

Chapter 28

How to Survive

Bad officials are elected by good citizens who do not vote.

George Jean

It was by no means certain how the Caesarian faction would react to the news of Cicero's return to Brundisium and when a letter arrived from Mark Antony in Rome stating that Caesar would determine the future of any Pompeian who returned to Italy, Cicero must have felt a chill wind of uncertainty.

It was while Cicero waited in Brundisium to hear his own fate that news of Pompey arrived. The great man had decided that his best hope of survival and fighting on lay in Egypt where he was still the Senate's choice to look after the boy Pharoah and he felt he could rely on his protection. Sailing in one of the ships that remained of his fleet, Pompey left Larissa on the eastern coast of Thessaly and headed south, stopping at Mytilene on the island of Lesbos where he received on board his wife Cornelia and his son Sextus Pompeius – Cornelia we may recall had been the wife of Publius Crassus who was slain at Carrhae. This is relevant because it was from a boat off the Egyptian shore that she watched her husband take a boat and land – to be met by officers of Ptolemy XIII, who took Pompey in hand and cut his throat while his wife and son watched helplessly. The same men then cut off Pompey's head. The shock and awe of this moment we cannot even begin to appreciate and Cornelia and Sextus had to sail away leaving the body of their father and husband, one of the greatest men in the history of Rome, lying bleeding on the sand of Egypt. Not many weeks later when Caesar arrived in Alexandria, he was shocked to learn of Pompey's execution by a Pharoah trying to get Caesar's affection. Caesar sent Pompey's ashes and signet ring back to Rome to be handed on to Cornelia.

Cicero heard the news in November, but does not seem to have taken it badly – it was almost expected, he wrote to Atticus. News also arrived of how Quintus Junior had been spreading despicable and shameful news about Cicero. This came as a shock, especially as young Quintus was spreading rumours that Cicero was scandalizing the name of Caesar, which was of course a total lie, as Cicero write to Atticus in December 48:

Wherever he is he never stops heaping all manner of abuse on me. It is the most unbelievable thing that has ever happened to me.

This news was very unwelcome at a time when his future was so uncertain. Relations with his brother Quintus would never be close again, as with all arguments, those within families can be the most acidic. As if the activities of Quintus Junior were not bad enough, matters were further magnified by the actions of his overzealous son-in-law Dolabella, now a tribune in Rome, who was actively pushing for the cancellation of debts – which was currently against the Senate's wishes. Antony managed to get affairs back under control, but Dolabella was a marked man and now of little comfort to Cicero.

Meanwhile in Egypt, Caesar was fighting for his new paramour, the young Cleopatra. He had arrived chasing Pompey in October 48 and his eyes became fixed on the Egyptian campaign and the body of Cleopatra – both of which at times seemed likely to end his own future. Early in 47, and lacking in numbers, Caesar had decided to take on the Egyptian army of the Pharoah, which he defeated at the Battle of the Nile and install Cleopatra as Queen Cleopatra VII. Fleeing from the battle against only 4,000 legionaries, Ptolemy's ship capsized and he was drowned. Undoubtedly more than smitten, Caesar's eyes had been taken off the ball of the civil war – Antony was struggling in Italy with volatility in Rome; remaining ships of the Republican fleet which were dominating the Adriatic; to his west Cato and the Republican forces were gathering; to the east, Mithridates' son Pharnaces had defeated a Roman army sent out to crush him, which now threatened the whole eastern coastal provinces. The luxury of Alexandria had come at a cost. Just before the birth of his son Caesarion, Caesar gave orders for his army to march northeast and, on 2 August 47, he met Pharnaces at the Battle of Zela where he uttered his famous words 'I came, I saw, I conquered.'

Meanwhile back in Brundisium, Cicero had continued to lay low. He despatched letters regularly of course, but only very carefully, always worried that they would fall into the wrong hands and be used against him. In June, Tullia came to see him regarding her marriage which was more than under strain – Dolabella was living up to his playboy image – and with Terentia moving between Arpinum and Rome; Cicero wrote her a rather curt letter on 14 June explaining his distress that his actions had played a part in her current unhappiness.

By October 47 Caesar was hurrying back to Rome, but diverted his journey to visit Cicero. It would have been a momentous meeting as Caesar arrived at Cicero's temporary home either in or on the outskirts of Brundisium and where he had been waiting for almost a year. With an embrace, Cicero realized that he was not only safe but useful. We have no idea what was discussed, but the regard that both men had for each other, despite the way they saw the world, was obvious. Caesar regarded Cicero well – not just as a political asset but as a genius of the spoken and written word and he held him in high regard compared to those many whom he mistrusted.

Caesar left Cicero to return to Rome where there were many pressing issues and a backlog of people to see and deal with. His immediate need was to restore the Senate to a pretence of democratic functioning – with numerous faces missing either through being killed in battle or self-imposed exile – he appointed hundreds of new senators all of whom were, on the surface at least, loyal to him. This loyalty was tested many times not least by Caesar instructing them to bestow numerous honours upon him such as the title *Pater Patriae* and naturally *imperator*. Quite what Caesar had saved the country from no one was brave enough to ask. Mythical and imagined enemies had been vanquished, the power of Rome would be opened up to achieve its true potential, enemies of the state would be crushed, all problems solved and so on and on. If this sounds a familiar refrain then that was how he chose to 'spin' his position of absolute power and we will witness an attempt by the Republican Party to do the same in the USA during the elections of 2024. Caesar had millions of coins minted with his image, he gave himself the right to speak first before his enemies and gave out rewards to those most loyal and unquestioning.

There was only one real threat to his position in 46 and that was the mutiny by a large section of his army. Stationed in Campania to the south of Rome, his legions were stationary and therefore had time and energy to complain. Many wanted to retire and be fully paid off. Caesar simply did not have enough money to pay the arrears and, as the army started to pack up their tents ready for a move towards Rome, Caesar decided to meet them face to face. By a combination of bluff and temptations of greater rewards in Africa when they defeated the Republicans, he was able to calm events and live to fight another day. He was lucky that no general like himself existed and had been able to challenge him – the blessing of synchronicity shined upon Caesar.

The correspondence with Varro and Paetus 46

During early 46, while Caesar was dealing with the remnants of Republican resistance in Africa and Spain, Cicero divorced Terentia, his wife of thirty years. We are very limited in detail about how their relationship came to an end, there were worries of financial irregularity on Cicero's side and concerns over the ability of Cicero to control his spending on Terentia's and as in all things there are at least two sides to this story. Spending years apart, the stress of dealing with constant worry over their safety, more anxiety over Tullia – all would have played their part and Cicero's intention to return to Rome yet again rather than retiring peacefully may have been the final straw. Later, Terentia is thought to have remarried, this time to a certain Caius Sallustius Crispus – known to history as Sallust with his many important writings and it is possible, if not indeed likely, that he was able to draw on his new wife's recollections of events to which she was a perfect observer and participant herself.

There were signs that Cicero was reigniting his political engines. A steady stream of letters covers the year 46 and notably his intellectual pursuits were recovering after the shock of civil war. In a number of letters to Varro and Paetus, we can detect Cicero thirsting for debate, ready to emerge from his self-imposed literary and rhetorical exile – especially as Caesar was too busy either to care or find out. Written from either Rome or Tusculum, we can deduce that Cicero was back in his homes surrounded by a no doubt relieved staff, though minus a wife. What a relief it must have been to be home, but there was to be no rest – despite his constant protestations that that is what he desired most.

Marcus Terentius Varro was himself a prolific author, polymath and scholar described by Petrarch as 'the third great light of Rome' after Virgil and Cicero himself. Varro had supported the Republican cause and even been in Spain, but with the result at Pharsalus he was one of many who, like Cicero, knew that a military victory was now out of the question and it was a matter of how to handle Caesar. After all, Cicero had been in the same position with Pompey all those years earlier, working out a way to remain relevant.

Of L. Papirius Paetus we know nothing more than what is said by Cicero in his letters. Both men were, however, significant figures in their own right, both wealthy and hospitable and both had remained aloof from the troubles in recent years so Cicero seems to reach out to rebuild his connections and network and at the same time portray himself once more as the genius of the written word and the sculptor of a treatise. There is a sense that he protests too much about how he enjoys his free time, his reading and his literary pursuits and that, perhaps, something greater once more looms. To Varro in June 46:

We live, it may be said, in a state that has been turned upside down [and followed this with an extended hand in friendship to a fellow scholar of Rome]. *I have always thought you a great man and I think you so now, because in this stormy weather you almost alone are safe in harbour. You reap the most precious fruits of learning, devoting your thoughts and energies to pursuits which yield a profit and a delight for transcending the exploits and pleasures of these worldlings.*

To Paetus in November 46:

> *You may advise me to spend my life in literary work. Surely you realise that this is my only occupation, that if I did not spend my life in that way I could not live at all. But even literary work has, I won't say its saturation-point, but it's due limit.*

In Rome, Cicero had to work with and in between many new faces – some of them he did not much like. Under Caesar's authority many less than able men were in positions of power and many of the old heads of families were dead or disappeared. Mind you, there were also plenty of old enemies but, given that Cicero and Caesar had made terms, he was generally left alone to build fences, enjoy dinner parties, write and play the new role of benevolent past servant of Rome.

The suicide of Cato the Younger 46

News from Africa in the summer cemented the fait accompli that Caesar was now dominant in every sphere. In December 47 Caesar had left Rome and joined with his legions in the south and transported them by sea to Egypt where Cato had managed to muster ten legions and many of the survivors from Pharsalus. Plutarch relates how Cato had maintained his steadfast resistance to comfort – often training with his men and never resting when he could be with them at the front of a column. Observing the *mos maiorum*, Cato deferred command to Scipio who had the greater experience and because Cato had only reached the rank of *praetor* in Rome. Arguments were, however, frequent when it came to strategy and the inevitable onslaught from Caesar with the certainty of death should they lose – Caesar's famed clemency would surely not extend to them now. After much initial manoeuvring, with Scipio and Cato operating two independent commands rather than one concentrated force, battle came at Thapsus on 6 April 46 between Scipio and Caesar. It was another brutal affair with no quarter given on either side and when Caesar's legions knew they would be victorious, they embarked on the complete slaughter of Scipio's forces. Again Plutarch related how Scipio escaped and wrote despatches to Cato asking what he planned to do now from his stronghold of Utica.

There are many references to how Cato handled the next few days. Some say he allowed and helped many Roman citizens to flee the city in a display of magnanimity that was typical of his noble sense of duty. One of the Republican supporters with Cato was a relative of Caesar – Lucius. Cato discussed sending an embassy to Caesar led by Lucius and taking Cato's own son with him, they left the city and rode to Caesar's camp. It was while they were gone that Cato made his final preparations, not for the battle, but for his suicide. He had no intention of being any sort of beneficiary of Caesar's tarnished and false clemency – this was something Caesar only ever gave to those he had defeated. The death of Cato ranks in history and literature alongside that of Catiline and indeed Cicero as a turning point, a demonstration of something much more important than the individual – belief in values worth dying for. After discussing with his friends the Stoic idea that only the good man is truly free and bad men live as slaves, it was clear to them that he was preparing to die. He embraced those around him and decided to read Plato's *Phaedo*, which concerns the final hours of Socrates' life. Later finding his sword had been removed from his room, he angrily shouted and screamed until his slaves and friends returned begging him not to end his life. He calmed them, read *Phaedo* once more and this time reached for his sword and fell on it through his stomach. Accounts vary, but he was still alive though in terrible pain and a doctor was called and began repairing the wound at which point Cato awoke and screamed, tearing at his skin and organs until he passed out and died of blood loss.

Caesar arrived the next day. He had hoped to take Cato alive, it was not in his interests that Cato should die a martyr, but Cato was victorious over Caesar in death. To history he is known as either Cato the Younger or 'Cato Uticensis' – a mark of what Drogula calls 'the defining action of his life'.

It would have taken a little over three weeks for news of what had happened at Utica to reach Cicero. No matter how you viewed Cato's suicide, it was a defining moment for Caesar, whose real intentions were becoming clearer even to those without a political perspective. Events had moved from a battle for supremacy between two heavyweight giants that would eventually reach an agreement. Thoughts of the injustices done to Caesar's *auctoritas* were replaced by the realization that tens of thousands of young Roman soldiers and their families had died, been executed, raped and tortured; respected political leaders shamed and committed suicide rather than accept what was now and always had been a bare-faced lust for total power. Cato's shadow would walk wherever Caesar went from now on.

A return to the stage

During 46, Cicero was increasingly busy. He was dining with Hirtius, a close friend to Caesar and even Dolabella – who could have thought that Cicero could have extended his once broken network to such a point where he could write:

Hirtius and Dolabella are my pupils in oratory but my masters in gastronomy.

It was possibly due to the fact that he was now in demand teaching oratory to the next generation of would-be senatorial leaders, even to his daughter's playboy husband, that Cicero embarked on his next philosophical work. Written at some point in 46, *De Claris Oratoribus* also known as *Brutus* was another of the dialogues so loved by Cicero – that enabled him to get points across in writing, but deny that they were his own thoughts instead they were those of the participants in a play – a dangerous game – and one that was designed to highlight his knowledge of Roman history through the medium of its greatest orators. The three characters of Atticus, Brutus and Cicero discuss the qualities that make a great orator, naturally Cicero himself leads this debate and, naturally, has all these qualities. The current situation had robbed Rome of its eloquence and he then refers to many great orators of the past but, interestingly, not all and misses out Marius, Sulla, Catiline and Clodius Pulcher, all of whom were regarded as excellent speakers. *Brutus* has been endlessly assessed by literary critics and historians, but it might just be that Cicero was doing what he needed to do if he wanted to publicise and remind people of his oratorial prowess – and bring himself back into the life of Rome under Caesar and at the same time draw himself closer to Marcus Brutus, friend to Caesar.

It was a good time to be seen as part of the new regime – Caesar himself returned in July 46 to maintain a tight hold on power, seek out rats at the core of the Senate and enjoy his Triumphs in September. Caesar would certainly want to eclipse memories of Pompey's extraordinary triumphal display on his return to Rome in 61 – that had only been fifteen years earlier. Naturally, Pompey having had three Triumphs meant that Caesar granted himself four. Pompey's amazing Triumph in 61 lasted two whole days, Caesar's four lasted a total of eleven so if evidence of ego was needed in ancient Rome, then Caesar quite eclipsed every great man in the history of the city – and that is what he wanted. There was no end to the largesse – some of it as distasteful as only a Roman could do. A gladiatorial display with all the blood, guts, pain and torment was held to celebrate the life of Caesar's cultured and gentle daughter Julia while one of the processions contained images of the vanquished and executed Republican leaders – even the crowd was said to have groaned in disgust when an effigy of Cato was seen as part of the display – apparently pulling at his bloodstained organs. But it was not all good news for the would-be emperor, and Caesar's spin doctors would have been aghast at the sight of a small number of legionary veterans taking exception to the amount of blood on show – images that reminded them of their dead comrades – and Caesar was forced to act to contain matters and executions followed to stamp his authority over his troops.

In the year of 46 Cicero also saw Caesar enjoy a renaissance with Brutus. This was not, apparently the Brutus of his recent philosophic sojourn but Marcus Junius Brutus, a former supporter of Caesar until his conscience would not allow Caesar's excesses to continue and he joined the Republican army of Pompey and survived Pharsalus. Now reconciled, as was Cicero, to Caesar's dominance, Brutus received a pardon from the tyrant and formed a good relationship with Cicero and we know that Cicero was teaching Brutus oratory in Rome at this time. It may have been due to Brutus that Cicero was able to get closer, and then almost free access, to Caesar. Brutus had a reputation for being honest and open with Caesar, who may have even loved him more than a brother, theirs was a sincere friendship and Caesar trusted him as far as he trusted anyone. The relationship between Brutus and Cicero was so strong that Brutus asked Cicero to write a book by way of tribute to his Uncle Cato. Cicero did this and comments to Atticus in the summer of 46 'I am pleased with my Cato'. However, it may be that Brutus was not so pleased as he wrote his own the following year. Possibly Cicero was just not able to rid himself of the irritations that Cato caused him even in death – we will never know, as Cicero's Cato has not survived.

The Caesarean Speeches 46

It is also possible that Brutus and Cicero worked together in Cicero's attempts to reconcile others to Caesar. This was done in a series of orations now referred to as the Caesarean Speeches. In his 1993 book, Harold Gotoff dissected each of the three and it is possible to see the old Ciceronian sentence structure, dynamics and flair had returned. Each speech was given in front of Caesar, who gave up time to listen to this most celebrated of all orators as if listening to a performance – which of course is exactly what the speeches were. The Pro Marcello was in defence of Marcus Claudius Marcellus. Descended from an illustrious family, Marcellus was a die-hard opponent of Caesar, he had been consul in 51 and tried to deprive Caesar of his commands and was also present at Pharsalus – he was now in exile in Lesbos but desired a return. Cicero had the Senate on its feet pleading for mercy from Caesar who relented to great acclaim and thanks – Caesar liked his leniency to be seen in public or in the Senate. Sadly, Marcellus was murdered at a dinner party before he could return. The details are not clear, but it may have been by design, but this is pure guesswork as to how Caesar may have worked out how to get his own way after all.

With *Pro Ligario* we have an entirely different result. Ligarius was in exile and facing charges not only of being a Pompeian, therefore needing Caesar's clemency, but he was also charged with collusion with a foreign king. Cicero had written to Caesar in late November, but it is probable that Caesar wanted Cicero to defend Ligarius in the forum so that the crowd could call for leniency and Caesar could be seen to grant this – the PR spin doctors were hard at work to take any opportunity they could to show Caesar in a softer light. In an article by Holly Montague from 1992, there is a discussion regarding just how brilliantly Cicero dealt with the dual problem of apparently needing to mount a legal defence but not so convincingly that there was no role for Caesar to be able to grant clemency. The real genius of Cicero is displayed, as he was once again able to display his expert skills as a jurist combined with those of the orator and not allow the two to blur into each other. *Pro Ligario* was a mixture of a plea for clemency wrapped up in a legal format and structure. Cicero hardly mentioned the facts of the case at all, let alone argued reasons for their existence, instead it has the feel of a staged event to display both Caesar and Cicero in a positive light – had there been a deal between the two? Thus, it has been debated whether this speech should fall into the ranks of his legal defences or his orations. Ligarius was acquitted and allowed to return home after the praise of the people had echoed around the forum. The final element of the three Caesarian Speeches was *Pro Rege Deiotaro* and was given by Cicero in the home of Caesar in defence of King Deiotarus, whom Cicero had known well and regarded highly from his time in Cilicia. The ruler had lost part of his kingdom and was accused of trying to assassinate Caesar. With the death of Caesar, no decision was made for some years.

No doubt now from the safety of his home on the Palatine, which was well preserved while he was away – Caesar had no interest in destroying houses – Cicero was again engaged by Brutus to write an extension piece on *Brutus* that had been published earlier in 46. Titled *Orator* (not to be confused with *De Oratore),* and again dedicated to Brutus, Cicero describes in detail the perfect orator. The world of Rome was changing and the younger elements of what might be termed new Roman society – that of the Caesarian period – were already frowning on the stylistic paradigms of Cicero and his predecessors. They wanted a new type of literary music to listen to; Cicero felt that he was being relegated to the position of an anachronism. Thus, *Orator* is a bit of a battleground to stay relevant and to convince Brutus to practise and preach the main pillars of traditional oratory.

After this prolonged period in Rome, Caesar left for Spain at the end of 46 where the two sons of Pompey, Sextus and Gnaeus, had been building up yet another army for the Republican resistance with the support of his former friend Titus Labienus, and Publius Varrus. Caesar managed to get his force of three hard bitten legions – V, VI and X – over the 1,500 miles to southern Spain in under a month (writing a short poem about this feat called *Iter*) and he was accompanied by his great-nephew Octavian. After a series of short preliminary engagements at the Battle of Munda in March 45, Caesar had been joined by a further five legions and in a day-long fight, which could have gone to either side, Caesar was victorious; both Labienus and Varus were killed on the battlefield and Gnaeus was killed a few days later, while Sextus escaped. Caesar's position was now unassailable and he was the undoubted master of the known world at that time.

Domestic bliss and grief

Cicero found himself at something of a loose end without Caesar. His natural habitat had always been within the orbit of a great man whether this had been Hortensius, Crassus, Pompey or Caesar but now he had no obvious anchor. The business of the Senate, which used to be his daily bread of activity, had little business to conduct as nothing of note could be concluded without the presence of the tyrant. There were fewer political events in Cicero's diary than he could remember and even Caesar had ignored the normal precedents of elections and made himself consul for 45 before he left for Spain and put his deputy Lepidus in charge of Rome in his absence. Cicero wondered about what to do next and whether he should indeed retire from public life to read and write as he wrote to Papirius:

> You say you are not dissuading me from buying a house in Naples, but encouraging me to spend my time in Rome. That is what I took you to mean, but I also understood as I understand from this later letter, that you thought I do not have the right to abandon metropolitan life, as I conceive myself entitled to do, not altogether, but to a great extent.

Cicero tried to think of reasons to communicate with Caesar, writing to him from either Rome or one of his country houses over the winter of 46/45 encouraging him to take on the freedman of Publius Crassus whose services Cicero had been using himself. Cicero lamented the death of the young Publius as he wrote to Caesar in ever more informal terms:

> 'Young P. Crassus was my favourite among the whole range of our aristocracy. From his earliest youth I had good hopes of him (not for his son Marcus then?), but he rose really high in my estimation when I saw how well you thought of him.'

Perhaps to fill a void in his life, Cicero did not exactly cover himself in glory by marrying his ward, a young girl named Pubilia. Little is known of her except that she came from a wealthy background and that he was perhaps infatuated with her. When ridiculed for this move on the grounds that Pubilia was so young, Cicero compounded his error by stating, on the eve of his wedding, that 'She'll be a woman tomorrow', and it is sad that this throwaway comment, perhaps made with a glass or three of wine consumed, should have made it through the millennia. But happy though he might be revelling in memories of love and infatuation, a happy marriage was not to be, a far more treacherous period of Cicero's life came when the ship of his life crashed upon the rocks in the February of 45.

The death of Tullia 45

If there was one weakness that trumped all of the others exhibited by Cicero during his very mortal lifetime – despite his many great gifts of genius he was still just a man – it was his love for Tullia. It can be referred to as a weakness because in Cicero's life so much was dependent on display, passion, confidence and arrogance and it is especially these things that are largely destroyed when any parent loses a child. If the years after Pharsalus are characterized in this book as years of how to survive, then this was a crunch point for Cicero.

The prelude to Tullia's death was that she was pregnant with the child of Dolabella, whom she had recently divorced, and Cicero himself was happily visiting as many of his properties as he could before the birth. Cicero described to Atticus in happy, glowing terms how his newly acquired Villa at Astura was beautiful, peaceful (apart from regular visitors), surrounded by the sea and how Cumae and Tusculum excited his senses before returning to his palace on the Palatine for the birth of his grandchild which came in January 45. But Tullia had not enjoyed an easy birth and for reasons of convalescence they relocated to Tusculum where, despite every doctor, nursemaid and help, Tullia passed away – shortly followed by the child. Death affected Cicero terribly, but these two deaths took away his own life.

The funeral most likely took place in Rome and a very recent discovery may serve to support this. In 1896 Rodolfo Lanciani published a book on the tombs found along the Appian Way – mostly those on the final few miles into Rome. Amongst the many beautiful sketches and drawings was a section on Tullia. In 1540 a tomb was opened, inside which a lamp was still burning 1,500 years after the burial of what was identified then as the body of a young woman named Tullia – the flame expired when it met the air outside, but both the lamp and the body were floating in a container of a mystery liquid that

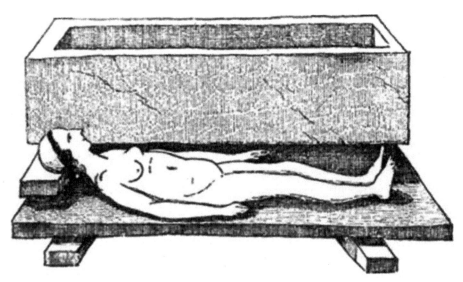

The fully preserved body of Tullia as it was captured in a fourteenth century drawing which was subsequently shown to the Pope.

had sucked all the oxygen and yet still allowed, what become known as the eternal flame, to keep burning. The body was so well preserved that it seemed to onlookers as if it had only very recently been buried and a sketch was made.

Fantastical though this may seem, observers were convinced it was Tullia, Cicero's daughter, and the Pope was informed accordingly. If indeed this was Tullia's tomb then we can capture a fleeting image in our minds of the scene as she was laid to rest in these most amazing of mysterious liquids that her father had procured to keep her body intact for eternity.

Cicero left Tusculum for respite with Atticus in Rome. No doubt many tears were shed and many emotions unleashed. In March Cicero left for isolation and wrote and received many letters of condolence, for example in March 45 from Servius Sulpicius Rufus who was in Athens. Sulpicius had been consul in 51, a supporter of Pompey and although he and Cicero had seen many differences in their legal careers, Sulpicius was also a great orator in his own right and his long letter is a model of compassion for all who experience grief:

When the report reached me of the death of your daughter Tullia, I was indeed duly and deeply and grievously sorry and felt that the blow had struck us both. Had I been in Rome, I should have been with you and shown you my grief in person. And yet that is a melancholy and bitter sort of comfort. Those who should offer it, relations and friends, are themselves no less afflicted. They cannot make the attempt without many tears, and rather seem themselves to stand in need of comfort.

How should not any heart practised in such experience have grown less sensitive and count all else as of relatively little consequence?

The loss of children is a calamity, sure enough – except that it is a worse calamity to bear our present lot and endure.

She saw you, her father, praetor, consul and augur. She was married to young men of distinction. Almost all that life can give, she enjoyed; and she left when freedom died.

Throughout March, Cicero wrote nearly every day to Atticus:

In this lonely place I do not talk to a soul. Early in the day I hide myself in thick, thorny wood, and don't emerge till evening. Next to yourself, solitude is my best friend.

During April Cicero was back staying with Atticus and trying to recover his shape as a person and wrote at length to both Dolabella and of course Rufus and both letters survive as testament to Cicero's warmth towards them both and a rekindled spirit of acceptance of his daughter's death. By May Cicero was able once more to walk the corridors and rooms of Tusculum. Thereafter, Tullia is rarely mentioned, she was locked away in a father's treasured and secret place that only they know.

Chapter 29

The Final Flurry

The fault dear Brutus, is not in our stars, but in ourselves.
William Shakespeare, Julius Caesar

The last meeting between Caesar and Cicero as far as we know, was at a dinner held at Cumae as Caesar happened to be travelling nearby. The date was 19 December 45 and there was much to discuss and reflect on in what had been a tumultuous year, amongst many others of its kind. Cicero wrote that the day before, Caesar had arrived at the nearby home of an acquaintance accompanied by 2,000 soldiers and there were so many people surrounding him that there was hardly anywhere for Caesar to sit. At Cicero's the camp was pitched away from the house and instead sentries were posted all around while Caesar took a walk on the shore, had a bath in the early afternoon and appeared later for dinner. News was constantly arriving and today a report included a letter telling Caesar that one of his closest lieutenants in Gaul, Mamurra, had died. According to Cicero, there was no change of expression on Caesar's face, indeed it seems to have been merely a pleasant, non-political evening:

I entertained in style. In a word, I showed I knew how to live.

Towards the end of the same month, Cicero told Atticus that he had received an unexpected visit at Tusculum from Quintus Junior who was on his way to join a legion preparing for the Parthian campaign that Caesar had planned for the coming year. Cicero writes that Quintus Junior was 'down in the mouth' and short of money, but his main gripe was with his Uncle Atticus – apparently young Quintus was uncertain of who to marry before he left and this had attracted the anger of his mother and therefore his uncle too. The discussion seems not to have been as acrimonious as it might and Quintus left on the best of terms he had been with his uncle for many years.

But a few miles to the north, the plot to assassinate Caesar was gathering pace. Whether Caesar's spies had informed him of the brewing attempt or not, Cicero seems to have been unaware and his letter writing was perhaps

'All honest men killed Caesar... some lacked design, some courage, some opportunity; none lacked the will' – Marcus Tullius Cicero on the death of Julius Caesar.

perceived as a risk too much to take. In any event, Cicero was now playing the part of the elder statesman, too neutral to be of any use.

Whatever warnings Caesar may have had, even on the morning of his assassination, which Cicero witnessed, he ignored them, perhaps believing that his self-belief was stronger than the assassin's self-doubt. On the morning of the Ides of March (the 15th) he had been at a meeting at the senate house and was due to attend another at Pompey's great theatre and rumours of what was developing started to leak out. Caesar was warned but carried on, possibly his keen sense of political smell even warned him that something might happen, nevertheless he pressed on, as senators awaited him in a marble columned hall halfway along the 300-metre length of the arena. What was a bloody, painful and violent death was celebrated as each dagger was thrust into the body of a man so many hated, all revered and few loved – this perhaps is what greatness has to mean. Amid screams and senators and clerks running for the doors, Brutus is said to have held up his bloodstained arm and dagger and looked at Cicero, shouting to him that freedom had been returned to Rome. The reaction of the crowd was mixed, but the majority set out to attack the assassins who had to cover their heads with whatever they could find; while trying to speak to the crowd in the forum, they were chased up on to the Capitol. Meanwhile below, quietly and nobly carrying Caesar's litter, were slaves who had not run away and took Caesar's blood covered body across the forum for all to see, to scream, to wail and lament and on to Calpurnia and his household waiting for it to arrive. Sometime later, Brutus, Cassius and the other plotters had decided to surround themselves with armed gladiators. Brutus would have paid them for their service and, as praetor he was responsible for them anyway, and they were due to be fighting that afternoon in Pompey's theatre. No doubt the discussions were frank and Brutus would have asked for Cassius' opinion on what they should do. Gaius Cassius Longinus we may recall, had been at the side of Crassus in the Parthian campaign, he knew no fear and also knew how to fight a rear-guard action as he had had to do in Syria nearly ten years earlier – Cassius was brave, bloodstained and regarded well by all.

The result of their discussion was that the plotters returned to the forum to speak to the people. Dolabella, dressed in a consular toga (he was not officially consul until the following year) also came to try to exploit the situation – followed by his lictors. It did not go well. Confusion reigned.

For Cicero the plotters had made two cardinal errors. Firstly, they seemed to have no plan to follow Caesar's death. They were taken by surprise by the violent and negative reaction of the Roman citizenry and they left his deputy Mark Antony alive. The time to act was straight away and in the evening of the 15th, Cicero arrived. His sadness for the death of his much-admired friend Caesar – if we are to believe his letters – did not seem to last much longer than a few minutes. Cicero advised not waiting for the consul Antony's reaction (Antony was missing for a few hours no doubt wondering if he was next on the list), but as praetors, Cassius and Brutus should convene the Senate in the morning and take steps to secure Rome and the situation. However, while they were doing this, Antony was already ahead of them. He visited Calpurnia in secret and took many of Caesar's papers and a large sum of money before he himself as consul called a meeting of the Senate and regained control – Cicero never forgave Brutus and Cassius for this error.

In May, Cicero wrote to Atticus:

That affair was handled with the courage of brave men and the policy of children. Anyone could see that an heir to the throne was left behind.

He wrote at greater length on 7 June:

A deal of talk followed, in which they complained, Cassius especially, about the opportunities that had been let slip, and Decimus came in for severe criticism. To that I said it was no use crying over spilt milk, but I agreed all the same. And when I began to give my views on what should have been done (nothing original, only what everyone is saying all the time), not however touching on the point that someone else ought to have been dealt with, only that they should have summoned the Senate, urged the popular enthusiasm to action with greater vigour, assumed leadership of the whole commonwealth.

Antony regained control when the Senate met and decreed that all Caesar's decisions had been legal – to do otherwise invalidated all their positions, new senators, consuls, Dolabella – so naturally, and in a huge irony perhaps unmatched in history, there was unanimous support for what Caesar had done. This was followed by amnesty for all the assassins and a very uneasy Senate dispersed, uncertain of whether the Republic was restored or just another successor appointed. The will of Caesar was then read out in public. Caesar's private gardens on the western side of the Tiber, many acres in a city overcrowded, were given as a public park and every Roman citizen was left 300 sestertii. But the surprise came for everyone when his heir was named as the 18-year-old grand-nephew Caius Octavius – who was now to be known as Caius Julius Caesar Octavianus – and later Caesar Augustus, first Emperor of Rome.

The journey that led to the Philippics

The events that led to Cicero's drafting and presenting his series of fourteen speeches across 44 and 43 condemning Mark Antony are well known. The reaction of the people of Rome to Caesar's funeral disgusted Cicero, as did the actions of the post Caesarean faction – especially Mark Antony and his wife Fulvia – she reappears in this story even if in reality she had never left Cicero, always watching him, calculating her revenge and plotting his downfall.

The homes of the conspirators were attacked, despite efforts to accommodate what they had done by supposedly freeing Rome to allow it to return to a Republic, all they had done was replace one tyrant with another. Many left, only just saving their lives, raised armies that were loyal to them and a whole new power struggle began. Mark Antony, claiming he had Caesar's written directions in his hands, and now with the Senate's blessing that they were legitimate, wasted no time in passing bills for – example to grant Roman citizenship to the people of Sicily. Cicero wrote to Atticus about this on 5 April:

> Atticus, I fear the Ides of March have brought us nothing except joy and a satisfaction for our hatred and pain. The things I hear from Rome! And the things I see here! 'Twas a fine deed, but half done! You know how warm a feeling I have for the Sicilians.... Well here is Antony posting up (in return for a massive bribe) a law allegedly carried by the Dictator in the Assembly under which Sicilians become Roman citizens.

In another cutting but so precise a remark Cicero commented 'We could not bear Caesar as master, but we bow down before his notebooks' and he was right because Antony continued to claim that he was governing in the name and written legacy of Caesar throughout 44. The relationship between Antony and Cicero was shallow and riddled with pretence and not helped by Antony's choice of wife. Fulvia was as politically active as ever and no doubt Antony's ears were frequently bent by her hatred of Cicero – she had seen her first husband Clodius destroyed by Cicero and she intended to use her second to destroy him in turn. It was therefore expedient for Cicero to at least metaphorically bend the knee, if not physically, as his correspondence shows. To Antony in April 44:

> For one reason and one only I would rather you had raised this matter with me in person than by letter. You could then have seen my affection for you not only in my words but in my eyes, written as the saying goes, all over my face.
>
> At the present time the national interest has commended you to my regard, so much so that no one is dearer to me. And now your affectionate and flattering letter has made me feel that I am not conferring a favour upon you, but receiving one at your hands.

Cicero was responding to a letter from Antony of earlier in April where he had asked Cicero for his support in recalling Sextus Cloelius from exile. Sextus had been a rioting supporter of Clodius after his murder and was no doubt well known to Fulvia – although this again is just guesswork as to why Antony wanted him back. Cicero claims he can think of nothing better than for wounds to be healed and even goes as far as responding that had Clodius still been alive there would be no animosity between them – they were just political adversaries. We can only wonder if Cicero's response was shown to Fulvia – one can almost hear the screams of anger down the centuries. Hardly able to bear what he had written, Cicero in a way purges his conscience by writing to Atticus:

> *I return to our unhappy, or rather non-existent, commonwealth. Mark Antony has written to me about the recall of Sextus Cloelius, in how complimentary of style so far as concerns me personally you will see from his own letter, of which I enclose a copy; how unscrupulously, disgracefully, mischievously, so that one is sometimes tempted to wish Caesar back, you will readily appreciate. Things that Caesar neither did nor ever would have done or permitted to be done are now brought out from his forged memoranda. As for me, I have shown myself all compliance to Antony. After all, having once made up his mind that he had a right to do what he pleased, he would have done it just the same if I had opposed. So I enclose a copy of my letter too.*

Cicero, the great composer of sonatas to individual ears, had no knowledge that his jigsaw of relationships would be pored over, interpreted, misinterpreted, criticized, praised or condemned. Had he done so then we can but wonder if he would have burnt every letter. What needed to be done had to be done and, as Rome's central statesman of words if not politics, Cicero wanted to be involved, though even he must have wondered about the impact of some of his letters and whether the layered and textured terms could be taken in more than one way. Maintaining his status quo with sides now so diametrically opposed was an impossibility and he seemed likely to fall into a crevasse in the middle, and then Octavian arrived on his way to Rome to claim his totally unexpected inheritance. On the way, he was met by Cicero – two men at opposite ends of their lives, each with an immediate affection, one for the vitality of youth, the other for the legend in his own lifetime.

Octavian was in Apollonia on the western coast of Greece where Caesar had asked him to wait for him as he planned to begin a great campaign against the Parthians in 44 – what a campaign that would have been. As a junior officer in one of Caesar's legions, when the death of their commander arrived along with news that he was Caesar's heir, the legion protected him as one of their own – he was certainly now a target from all directions. In effect, his military links were already vital for his future as he had the immediate loyalty of men loyal to Caesar. Apollonia was at the start of the great road that led eastwards across from the Adriatic coast to eastern Thrace, a road that Cicero and thousands of Romans had travelled and while he was stationed there, he studied under the tutelage of Athenodorus of Tarsus. Octavian immediately wished to be known as Caesar to cement his heritage with the army. Arriving in Brundisium, the young Octavian felt a great warmth in his reception. His advisors would have enlightened him as to the political dynamics that faced him and he very rapidly formed a strategic view that surprised many around him – but was why his Great Uncle had chosen him. He was indeed special.

As Octavian arrived in Puteoli amongst the olive trees and flowers, the smell of the wafting ocean, the great villas with their colonnades and fresh running water, old met new. Only the previous year Philippus and Cicero had dined with the old dictator and now they were dining with, potentially, the new one. But Cicero was concerned about the advisors – these were a new breed of 'enablers', the men that feed off power, create the openings and bring structures down rather than work within them and Cicero sensed their ambitions had already exponentially expanded in the light of their new relationship with the former 18-year-old student who now had immense opportunity.

As if to recharge his batteries for the battle that lay ahead, a battle that was to be his final foray into the Senate, Cicero decided to get away from Rome. Rome was confused and dangerous, Antony was butting heads with Octavian, who now laid claim to a political heritage that threatened them all and for Cicero, discretion rather than valour (*virtus*) proved to be a wise move. Before he went, Cicero represented Atticus, who had cause to complain that his estate and lands in and around Buthrotum had been given by the dictator Julius Caesar to many of his veterans from the Civil War and so Cicero wrote to Brutus asking if he could intervene and reduce the numbers planned to go there.

Apart from keeping his head down away from Rome, possibly thinking of going to see Marcus in Athens, Cicero seems also to have wandered, perhaps wondering as he went about what to do with what was left of his life, possibly toying with putting down final roots and he wrote variously from Astura, Puteoli, Pompeii, Tusculum and by July he was in Vibo in the toe of Italy writing about waiting for gales and stormy weather – he should have been in Rome if he wanted that – another letter followed from nearby Regium. But Cicero was not alone either in writing or receiving lengthy correspondence. Tiro had recovered and in August 44 he too received a letter from Cicero – though this time from Marcus who was beginning his own journey with correspondence. Marcus relayed his love for his father, his studies in Athens and his love for Tiro who had now bought his own property – quite a journey from slave to scribe, to friend of a consul, private biographer and now landowner. 'You are now a Roman squire', Marcus joked with him. During May, June and July 44 Cicero too had been extensively corresponding with Atticus on the progress

Marcus was making in his studies in Athens, remarking on how he wanted him to want for nothing and praising his classical writing style and expression.

Octavian (Caesar)

Two letters from Octavian in one day! Now he wants me to return to Rome at once, says he wants to work through the Senate...in short, he presses and I play for time. I don't trust his age and I don't know what he's after.

This is how Cicero wrote to Atticus from Puteoli on 4 November 44. He had been offered a chance to join Dolabella, currently consul after Caesar, but looking ahead to his proconsular appointment in Syria the following year – was this another portent just as Caesar had offered him a chance to escape Rome prior to his fights with Clodius and ultimate exile? It certainly rang familiar bells, but Cicero only toyed with the idea – it would be, under the new legislation, a five-year posting and Cicero mentioned to Atticus something along the lines that the sands of time would not grant him that long to complete the mission. So, still in Italy and sensing he was needed or that he needed Rome like an addict needs a drug, Cicero returned to the city at the very end of August 44 to what Plutarch described as quite a reception. The crowd possibly hoped that his return may help restore Rome to some sort of normality in the Senate. The thought of becoming a mentor to the young pretender to the throne was also a lure for Cicero, and Octavian did not have to work too hard to make himself an attractive proposition in a cocktail of homoerotic tendencies mixed with the potential of power.

The complex games of cat and mouse had continued all summer with the young Octavian displaying all the clever manoeuvring that only a natural cold hearted and ruthless successor to his great uncle could be. Antony, more of a playboy than a politician thought that he was managing Octavian well, they both vied for the loyalty of their legions like gunfighters in the wild west touching the handles of their pistols to see who would flinch first. Cassius and Brutus struggled to gain traction and they may have sensed that, ultimately, Octavian would track them to the ends of the earth for their murder of his uncle. They were right and they retreated to Syria and Athens respectively to heal their wounds. Into this cauldron of intrigue, power and politics, Cicero stepped as one of the few surviving statesmen of the 'old' Republic.

Many books and papers remark that from this time on Cicero displayed a new resilience, what Anthony Everitt describes as 'ruthlessness and clarity', saying, 'the sensitive ditherer had disappeared.' Perhaps freed from his fears by age or ties to anything he loved, Cicero was a born-again orator of the first degree.

On 1 September 44, Antony convened a meeting at his palatial residence to pass a decree honouring Caesar's memory. It was as much a test of loyalty as a testament to the dictator. Cicero feigned exhaustion and did not attend and out of Antony's mouth spewed (Antony could often be sick through anxiety before speaking) bile, invective, castigation and denunciation at Cicero's duplicity and cowardice. The pent-up frustrations of months of reading Cicero's fawning letters, the continual vituperations of his wife day and night regarding Cicero, the anxiety of the times and the embarrassment that Rome's leading statesman had snubbed him combined to create an explosion that was to change history and lead to perhaps Cicero's finest hour. The journey to the Philippics was finished, it was time for the main event.

Chapter 30

The Philippics 44

There are so many moments in the lives of men that are worth recording for history and this was certainly one for Cicero. Only the day after, not even twenty-four hours had passed since Antony's condemnation, and Cicero was on his feet on the marble floors of the senate house delivering the first of what would become known as the Philippics in a nod to the critical speeches given by Demosthenes against Philip of Macedon – these were Cicero's equivalent.

Antony was not present to hear the first oration and this probably saved Cicero from possible arrest straight away, as it was left to Antony to respond in a similar way and the battle of rhetoric had begun. Cicero laid out the tone and position he was now willing to take. He was buoyed by the relationship of many of his peers in the Senate who saw Cicero as the ideal foil against Antony and that Cassius and Brutus had within them the makings of two new Republican heroes. Then there was Octavian and, although he never betrayed his inner ambitions or feelings, he said and did enough for Cicero to feel that he was listening to his advice, and guiding him did not seem difficult. Thus, all seemed set fair for Cicero to resume his former garb of litigator in the case of Antony, illegitimate usurper of the Republic. A moderate start saw Cicero take Antony to task for his actions over the previous summer months and to tell him he needed to change his approach or suffer the fate of his predecessor. No doubt many in the Senate were shocked, but equally others were inspired that someone of Cicero's renown was willing to start the turn of the tide.

Antony kept away from Rome until he was ready and two weeks later and, after much burning of midnight oil no doubt irritating what may have been an ulcer and undoubtedly with input from Fulvia, he delivered his response, also in the Senate, on 19 September. This was a no holds barred assault on Cicero, his character, faults, mistakes, murderer of Catiline and his supporters and disingenuous friend. Cicero wrote to Cornificius in the autumn of 44 who was governor of Africa and a correspondent of Cicero. Quintus Cornificius had been a supporter of Caesar and defended Illyricum from Pompey and his fleet, as a well thought of general, noble and cultured man, the Senate had appointed him to Africa after the assassination of Caesar, but Antony tried to relieve him of his post on the grounds that Cornificius was acting illegitimately. Ultimately, he was to be proscribed by the coming 'New' or 'Second' Triumvirate and to die in battle near the site of Cato's death at Utica:

> *Here I have a fight on my hands with a most rascally sort of gladiator, our colleague Anthony.*
>
> *The whole country is under heel. The boni have no leader, our tyrannicides [Cassius and Brutus] are at the other ends of the earth.... What will come of it I simply don't know.... I at any rate shall not fail the commonwealth, and shall bear with courage whatever will befall, provided I am not to blame for it.*

From the first Philippic in September 44 through to the last, which was given in April 43, Cicero had to speak against a background of constantly changing events. The details of the events of this period are well known and revolve around the gradual usurpation of the Republic by Octavian, the aim here is to focus on Cicero's speeches rather than the other main players in this complex and ever-changing drama.

Having heard Antony's response, Cicero could have changed course, but he was relishing the challenge and of course the opportunity to perform and, without his normal nervousness and timidity which always sat beside him when speaking, Cicero felt freer than he had ever done. Even if it led to his own death, which it would, Cicero was embarked on the final journey of his life. The second speech was conceived in October 44, written but never given – it may be that Atticus and others advised against it, but it was preserved and published after Cicero's death. It stands as one of his most vitriolic attacks on Antony and is the longest of the *Philippics*. At the same time, Cicero wrote his On Duties, to which this book referred earlier, and was dedicated to his son Marcus and perhaps now we can see that the context in which it was written could suggest, and very likely does, that this was a father's final testament to his son, embarked as he was on a course of action that could lead to his death.

It is during November that Cicero's last extant letter to Atticus was written and, although we have more correspondence to others after this date, Atticus and Tiro, for whatever reason, did not preserve any more of Cicero's letters to his closest ally and friend. Cicero remarks to Atticus about many things including:

> *The boy [Octavian] is taking the steam out of Antony, but we had best wait and see the issue. But what a speech! – a copy was sent to me. Swears 'by his hopes of rising to his father's honours,' stretching out his hand towards the statue! Sooner destruction for me than a rescuer such as this!*

Cicero emphasises here the talents that the young Octavian displays. Much to everyone's surprise he is already a powerful speaker with a talent for visual display in reaching out towards his 'father's' [Caesar's] memory and legacy. The obvious concern here is that the veil of uncertainty is slowly being dropped as Octavian sensed the growing volume of support behind him, he has to become Caesar himself – all he has to do is deal with his enemies at the head of armies – Antony, Brutus and Cassius. With a final note regarding his financial worries, or even bankruptcy, Cicero ends this, the last letter we have from him to Atticus.

The recalcitrant nephew returns

Smouldering in the background of these national events were family matters which continued to vex (*vexare*) Cicero and his brother. Quintus Junior, having left to fight for Caesar in Parthia, his uncle Atticus now referred to him as 'Antony's right-hand boy.' But Quintus Junior was nothing if not unreliable and in June 44 he had changed sides again and from Pompey to Caesar to Antony he now moved to Brutus and Crassus – anywhere that he could gain promotion, glory and money. His father may have lamented over how his son's loyalties were as solid as dead leaves in the wind, but he could not argue with the results, given that he had accrued a small fortune of 400,000 sestertii and he was making overtures for a return to his father. Cicero was as distant as ever from his nephew, who seems to have been as confused as to whom to support in recent years as many young men in similar positions would have been. We should cut Quintus Junior a little slack and not judge him by the standards that his elders would have judged him by. In a world turned upside down it was difficult indeed for even the eldest statesmen to know what to do. But young Quintus had indeed caught the eye enough for even Antony to include him in his invective, accusing him of plotting to kill his father and uncle – as Cicero remarked – he really had arrived if the likes of Antony sought to belittle him.

By December, events had progressed further and two new moderate consuls now took up office, Hirtius and Pansa. Aulus Hirtius was a loyal Caesarean whose loyalty was stretched too far by Antony. An experienced general, Hirtius had served Caesar in Spain and Gaul and became consul for 43 based on the still 'legitimate' decisions of Caesar which Antony had tried to uphold. However, he was turning towards the Senate – Cicero helped him in this decision – and ultimately opposed Antony in the coming events of early 43. Gaius Pansa Caetronianus was an equally moderate and well thought of senator of great experience and, while he had also been a supporter of Caesar, he too was vocal about wishing to see a return to the Republic.

Antony, aware that his consulship was ending and that Hirtius was waiting in the wings, had ordered the Parthian legions home to Italy and took command over them and began to move them from north towards Gaul. Antony had been able to see the reaction of the Senate to Cicero's speech in September and realized that to survive he needed to fight. Octavian too had been acting illegally and raised his own loyal force of some 3,000 men while Brutus and Cassius were quickly seizing the provinces in the east.

The third Philippic came at a meeting of the Senate on 20 December 44 and here Cicero asks the Senate to display solidarity with Octavian and to act against Antony. That same day, Cicero maintained his assault on Antony, but this time in the forum where a huge crowd gathered to hear the great statesman speak his fourth Philippic. For many this would have been a nostalgic experience, hearing Cicero's voice boom out from the rostra where he had created so much history in the past and led the city in some of its darkest hours. For others, this was a novel experience and all listened to his further denunciation of Antony, calling him a public enemy with whom a peaceful settlement was not going to be possible. Cicero even raised a comparison between Antony and some of the phantoms of the past comparing him to Spartacus in the threat that he posed as an outlaw and illegitimate leader of an army without *imperium*. Around the same time, Cicero despatched a letter to Brutus encouraging him to act in defence of a Senate not yet in command of itself:

> *The main point, which I want you to thoroughly grasp and remember in the future, is that in safeguarding the liberty and welfare of the Roman People you must not wait to be authorized by a Senate which is not yet free.*

This advice needs careful attention because Cicero is asking Decimus Brutus to act independently of the Senate – why is he doing this? It can only be that Cicero well knows that the Senate, in its current state of disunity was not able to act for its own survival. Not all the Senate agreed with the direction of Cicero's arguments and there were some who remained loyal to the Caesarean cause – although their ranks had diminished – and there were others who did not wish to see another civil war. For Cicero, the stakes were high. His attacks on Antony meant that he had crossed his own Rubicon some time back and any survival of Antony meant the certainty of his own demise. Therefore, in his fifth Philippic, Cicero tried to ramp up the rhetoric, again cataloguing Antony's crimes and, trying to create a new breed of heroes, proposing a statue to honour Brutus. Cicero also proposed Octavian be given pro-praetor status and be co-opted to the Senate – the Senate agreed and Octavian was inducted to the Senate on 1 January 43 and with *fasces* and *lictors* on 7 January – the start of his formal career in the history of Rome. Cicero even going so far as to vouch for his loyalty:

Members of the Senate, I promise, I undertake, I solemnly swear, that Caius Caesar will always be such a citizen as he is today and as we should especially wish and pray he should be.

We can interpret this statement in a number of ways, but all are guesswork as there is not a shred of evidence to explain why and how Cicero miscalculated so badly – because this is what it was – perhaps the major miscalculation of his life. Theories include that a deal was done with Octavian's advisors or that Cicero was 'inebriated with the exuberance of his own verbosity' to, possibly, quote Disraeli on Gladstone, or was it that he allowed himself to believe that he could manipulate and control Octavian – and that Octavian had played a clever game all along of using Cicero's needy personality to serve Octavian's purposes?

The Senate went along with most of this, but still hoped for a resolution to avoid war and a mission was sent to Antony which included Piso, Philippus and Servius Sulpicius. They did not have far to travel as Antony was illegally laying siege to Brutus at the city of Mutina in the northern centre of the neck of Italy. They were to take the Senate's instructions with them that Antony should obey the Senate and People of Rome (SPQR), not come closer than 200 miles of Rome and move his troops away from Mutina. The news of this decision was given to the people in Cicero's sixth Philippic in the forum, but with the addendum that he did not believe Antony would listen.

In his seventh Philippic, Cicero takes the opportunity of adding the current situation to a meeting of the Senate stating that the most pressing matter facing Rome should not be avoided, that Antony had moved the situation to tumult – the final stage before war and that the Senate must act. By February, Antony had responded with a compromise, he was prepared to give up his claim to Italian Gaul, where he was camped for now, but in return wished to be granted Long-haired Gaul (essentially modern-day France) for a five-year command, thus freeing him from threats of prosecution and retaining his *dignitas*.

The Senate reacted by declaring the Final Act and Cicero gave his eighth Philippic where he now used the word *bellum*, to indicate that the Republic was once more at war with an insurgent. Standing in military uniform, Cicero must have looked an inspiring sight amongst so many other senior figures both young and old all in military garb and he had done his best to position all the chess pieces on the board with or without the authority of the Senate and via his secret correspondence with all the major players – there were at least five players in this game of chess that only one could win.

The ninth Philippic was a speech in the Senate on 4 February asking for an honour to Servius Sulpicius Rufus who had died on the mission to Antony which was agreed and then in the middle of the same month, the crucial tenth and eleventh Philippics came. In these two speeches, Cicero changes strategy. Up to this point his was a campaign of attrition, but not with Antony, instead with the Senate. His choice of rhetorical strategies was based on the need for building up the confidence to resist Antony, to bring the people of Rome with the Senate together under his leadership and to outlaw Antony. Now it was necessary to legitimize the assassins – the men Everitt refers to as the freedom fighters or what others call the Liberators – despite the obvious opposition that would come from Octavius and the Caesarian faction in the Senate. To this end Cicero wants the military successes of both celebrated especially because he sees Brutus as the natural successor to the future, the man to whom he had taught rhetoric by way of preparation for the role and his confidante in correspondence whom he hoped to guide to the very top. Cicero succeeded and Brutus was granted command of the provinces of Greece, Macedonia and Illyria and he did this by use of his, by now, familiar legal approach of not dealing with the complaints of those in opposition, such as Calenus, but by focussing on Calenus and his motives and that Brutus was acting to protect the *res publica* not control it, ready to hand it back when asked. Philippic ten is a model speech for Brutus, his perfect character, his courage in executing a friend to save the Republic, his assiduous attention to his roles in the state, as a magistrate – in short, the perfect model of *auctoritas* and the *mos maiorum* in one.

At the end of March, Philippic eleven was stimulated by news from the east that his former son-in-law Dolabella had yet again made a strategic error. He had been offered the province of Syria in return for his loyalty by Antony and on a campaign marked by plundering and extortion he also executed Gaius Trebonius – but not before he had tortured him and put him on trial for treason – by beheading him. Trebonius, one of Caesar's assassins but also currently governor of Asia – was a leading figure in the Senate with a far more distinguished history than Dolabella and the Senate agreed with Cicero that Dolabella should be relieved and brought back to Rome. This Philippic sees Cicero using Dolabella as an example of what a return to the rule of Antony would mean, the poor duality of his supporters, the inadequate men trying to feed off the carcass of an empire that they would destroy, the imagery was perfect. For anyone who has been on the receiving end of prosecuting oratory then the use of praise for the client and invective against the accused is deliberate and an accepted strategy – the facts do not need to be correct, it is all about achieving the desired effect.

The final two Philippics come in March and April before the Republican victory at Mutina, where Antony was forced to retire north and lick his wounds. The fourteenth and last was especially pleasing for Cicero as he was, at last, able to celebrate a victory at the Forum Gallorum over Antony by the Senate's forces led by the two consuls Pansa and Hirtius, who had been ordered by the Senate to meet Antony and defeat him. The battle took place on 14 April, but it took seven days for news to reach Rome and for Cicero to give his speech – the very same day that a second battle was fought and this one was decisive. This was another brutal face to face confrontation between men of the same army, ordered by their respective commanders to kill each other, that is civil war. The legions were experienced, they knew how to kill and they did it without enthusiasm but with loyalty. Octavian was present, although he did not take much part in the battle. He led three legions and commanded well and was proclaimed *imperator* by his troops. But here we see synchronicity come into play. Had Octavian not been there, then he could not have played his part in gaining the glory that flowed from it. Had Pansa not been wounded and then died tragically only a few days later – to the surprise of his officers and doctors – then Octavian would not have benefitted from his death – or been there to order his poisoning which is the rumour that immediately spread. Had Octavian not been present at the next battle only seven days later on the 24th then he would not have also been there to witness the death of Hirtius, and Octavian as propraetor assumed command of his legions too. So, at the very same time as Cicero was giving his triumphalist speech in the Senate celebrating the victory at Forum Gallorum, Octavian was walking to his tent. Bloodied, victorious, the only surviving commander of the three and now in command of a huge army of eight legions. Whenever we look at the causes of the collapse of democracy, or wonder if it is happening in our own world, never underestimate the value of synchronicity.

Rumours also spread that in the melee of the battle at Mutina, where Octavian was found to be fighting – celebrated fighting bravely by future Augustan historians keen to retain their heads – beside Hirtius, that he had the consul killed. There is not a shred of proof to this, but when stories were told of how Octavian saved the Eagle standard and how he brought the body of Hirtius from the field of battle under the swords of the enemy, one has to wonder what on earth was he doing there – two key commanders within feet of each other. It was a grand plan and it worked, or it was synchronicity if it was not.

Between the two key engagements, Cicero had received a despatch from Galba dated 15 April, the day after the first battle, he had been an eye witness to the slaughter and bloodshed at Forum Gallorum. At the end of the letter Cicero would have read:

> *So Antony has lost the greater part of his veteran troops; but this result was achieved at the cost of some losses in the praetorian cohorts and the Martian Legion. Two eagles and sixty standards of Anthony's have been brought in. It is a victory.*

Can we imagine the deep and long intake of breath from Cicero that may have followed those words? In such confidence that abounded after Mutina, the Senate and Cicero rushed to rain honours down on the victors, Brutus was voted a Triumph, Cassius was confirmed governor in Asia, and even Sextus Pompeius, the son who had watched his father's head cut from his body, was received back into the Republican fold with a naval command. The only victor ignored was Octavian – another major error. Cicero recognized this, but understood why, the general feeling was that Antony was finished and even Cicero allowed himself to say in a passing remark that found its way back to Octavian *'laudandum, ornandum, tollendum'* – Octavian must receive the praises due, the honours due and the elevation due.

The greatest mistake was thinking that Mark Antony was defeated. He was in fact far from finished, and both he and Octavian shared a vituperative hatred of Cicero and all that he and the Senate stood for. Within weeks he had amassed a new force in the north and Octavian had turned south to march on and take Rome. On 19 August Octavian, we may now call him Caesar for ease, was made (made himself) consul. For Cicero, the entire world had once more turned on its head. There were no more speeches, no more Philippics and there was no more Republic. There were many more communications to fly back and forth between Cicero and Brutus or anyone else that could possibly save the situation. As the summer gave way to autumn it was wise to leave Rome and some did, but Cicero was not among them.

In Bologna in October 43, Mark Antony, the survivor Lepidus, and Caesar met. The Second Triumvirate was formed between these three men, each with their army camped nearby, each having a body search each day for the three days of their conference, each mistrusting each other and each after the glory of the Dictatorship of Rome. They knew that whatever they agreed would not last, and they were right, but with one exception. Before they again tried to destroy each other and before Caesar became the first emperor of a new Imperial age, they agreed to proscribe not just their enemies, but anyone that might become an enemy, anyone whose name had been mentioned to them as worthy of proscription, anyone with substantial fortunes that would enable them to find, fight, and kill Cassius and Brutus (they read letters and reports with increasing acceptance that their life was coming to an end) and anyone who had ever set out to hurt them. Amongst the hundreds of names that then started to be dictated down onto a list for their *scribae* to record, there was one name that fitted almost all of the categories.

In fact, all four Ciceros were proscribed, so were between 150 and 300 senators, thousands of others, and vengeance was not just limited to contemporaries. If we reach back into the pages of this book to Verres, the scourge that we can perhaps regard as the first case that Cicero tried in the court of public opinion, the man whom Cicero made his name in prosecuting was still alive! The news reached him that Antony wanted his art collection – as Cicero had always said stolen from the provinces and where Cicero established that very important principle of governance without exploitation – but Verres would not let it go. He was proscribed, murdered, and it was Antony that had the pleasure of viewing his stolen property – at least for a while.

We don't know exactly when Cicero said goodbye to Tiro or where, nor what final letters he wrote or to whom – no doubt there were many, but news that their own names, and those of their sons were on the list came to Quintus and Marcus at Tusculum and they immediately left for Astura with the intention of taking a boat for Greece and the protection of Brutus. Carried by their retainers and slaves on litters, Plutarch relates that their journey south was punctuated by stops where they consoled each other. At one point Quintus needed to rush back to the villa with his son to get more money – this was fatal. The great attraction of proscription was that anyone could legally kill you for a reward – or even betray you for a share of the reward and what were in fact gangs of professional killers, retired soldiers, soldiers on leave, thieves, thugs and anyone with a grudge was on the lookout for you. Quintus, the story goes, found men already at his home to kill him but Quintus Junior, the prodigal son, was with him and found a place for him to hide and even under torture would not give up his father's hiding place until he could stand no more. Father and son were executed separately, but at the same time.

Cicero himself must have known that something had gone seriously wrong. He was able to reach the boat and sailed a good way further down the coast before coming ashore – he should have kept going, even though he hated the sea. He walked for a time in the direction of Rome, some say ten or even twelve miles, but then he came back. What was in his mind 2,000 years of conjecture has never been able to resolve, we might ask what would have been in ours under similar circumstances. Perhaps he knew that the next strangers he saw on the horizon would be his own murderers. They sailed on further nearly to Formiae where they again disembarked and this time for the final part of his story. Plutarch says that Cicero remarked to those around him 'I will die in the country I have so often saved', and he did. A while later he rested at a villa before being taken on again in his litter along a coastal path in sight of the sea with green fields all around and a wind blowing in from a December afternoon. Some say he got out of the litter and began walking northwards, back towards Rome – towards the city that had been the centre of his life and was now to be instrumental in his death.

At the villa a group of men arrived on horseback, Cicero was betrayed by Philologus, a freedman of Quintus, perhaps under threat of death, who told them the direction and route Cicero was taking and, running down the path, they caught up with him – perhaps to Cicero's great relief. They were led by a tribune named Popillius Laenus who had no doubt been given precise orders that Cicero was his to kill and they must have come from Rome directly. Cicero may have recognized him, as Laenus had once been defended by Cicero in a civil matter and with him was a centurion – a man named Herennius – certainly used to killing and doing it quickly and well.

There are any number of descriptions of what happened next. The truth, like so much of Cicero's life, is somewhere between educated guesswork and contaminated source material. Amongst the hundreds of biographies written about Cicero, most are unable to capture what we need most, the truth.

Chapter 31

The Beginning of History

Death is dreadful to the man whose all is extinguished with his life; but not to him whose glory never can die.

Marcus Tullius Cicero

It is with the murder of Cicero, probably on 7 December 43, that debates on how he died began and have continued ever since. All the renowned Roman historians of the time and after differ in the details of an event that shocked the people of Rome and the nation. Plutarch proves perhaps the most convincing account, but to his we can also add that of Appian and Dio and therefore the consensus starts to fragment. They were followed by those giants of the Augustan age – Livy and Pollio. Altogether, the patchwork of information provides history with a text book dilemma. No single event in the history of the Republic has been focussed on so intensely, and Cicero's death draws everyone, whether first time reader on Roman history, schoolchild, student or professor of Classics. We are all interested to know how this event may have unfolded. Why is this? Why are we so attracted to this final moment in this one life? The answer, if we can bring one to life, might then enlighten us to the greatness and majesty of this one man. It was and is not so much the gory narratives that appeal to us, but the manner in which Cicero is supposed to have died. If we are constantly in awe of what Cicero was able to write, achieve and enlighten us to in his lifetime then we also want to know what his last lesson was to us – as if desperate for the very last drop of wisdom from one of the wisest human beings who ever lived. Of course, Cicero had frailties, we all do, and we can recoil from many of those that Cicero left us to reflect upon in his letters – because that is where the real Cicero exists, not in the epic speeches or works on philosophy. If this book shows nothing else then it should demonstrate that Cicero was a performer and his scripts were his speeches, he was a Shakespeare performing his own plays to his own public. Consequently, the correspondence of Cicero takes us beyond what he intended to leave to posterity and to Tiro and Atticus we owe a huge debt of gratitude, for they allow us to understand a man in a way that is possible of no other Roman.

We do not know if Tiro witnessed his friend's death, but we do know that Plutarch at least tried to verify what happened. The story had a well-established and vivid structure a few years later across the world of Emperor Augustus as W. C. MacDermott pointed out in his 1972 book on Cicero and Tiro. Had Tiro's lost biography still existed then we would almost certainly have been in possession of the facts rather than speculation because that is what all accounts are – over time we have to be aware of contamination of what evidence there is both from the pro- and anti-Ciceronian writers. Ultimately, we can be left to read in modern historical accounts a mixture of second-hand accounts and fantasy to which this book does not intend to add. Essentially, Cicero was killed by either the tribune Gaius Popillius Laenas or the centurion Herenius. The man most skilled in dealing with copious amounts of blood and hacking off the head of a man was Herenius – but Appian's account, which tells us that it took three attempts to saw through the bone and muscle of Cicero's neck might suggest that the less experienced tribune did the deed. The nearly contemporary historian Bassus states that Cicero reproached his killer for being too timid – having come face to face with the legend that was Cicero – even if he was as Everitt reiterates dusty, tired and worn – would have caused a pause in anyone so we cannot see from this range whom Cicero may have been ticking off. Whether Cicero sat in his litter and had to have his head pulled out past the curtains, if indeed there were any, or if he willingly leant out to allow the killer to cut his throat then hack off his head we will never know. It makes for a grand gesture to have offered his neck, but he could equally have reclined as he spoke and then been pulled forward in a final act of defiance. Finally, accepting that Cicero was dead, was one or both of his hands cut off at the wrist with a single blow from the heavy, sharp and deadly *gladius*? That certainly would have been quick and easy, probably holding the fingers and gold rings of the man who had held Rome with these same hands in 63, the sword severed at least one hand on the orders of his superiors. This at least seems like strong circumstantial evidence that Antony and Fulvia knew what they were going to do with Cicero's body parts – a premeditated and sadistic order to bring back his head and hand or hands.

History usually stops at this point, as we have no information regarding what Cicero's slaves or freedmen did with his body. Was the headless and handless body taken back to the villa in the litter bleeding profusely, was he buried nearby or cremated? What happened to his ashes? How must his attendants have felt as they took Cicero down from the litter and wrapped him, probably, in his toga – one can see how easy it is to add to the fantasy. We do not know, but every detail adds to the lustre of the story of how perhaps Rome's greatest man met his end that day.

The ride back to Rome would have been swift, a matter of a few hours by fast military horse taking parts of Cicero back along a route he had often travelled – Popillius was keen to deliver his gifts to Antony so it is unlikely that he would not have stopped on the way. For Popillius this was a glorious moment, able to fulfil the wishes and desires of his own hero and to be celebrated with his own statue with laurel leaves and, of course, a sizable reward.

The reactions of Antony and Fulvia, when a dusty and tired Popillius arrived at their mansion are again only for the imagination, but no doubt both lusted to see the head of the man that each of them so hated. Did Fulvia pull out her hair pins and stab the tongue of Cicero for the words he had spoken against them both in their lifetime? Was Cicero's head and hand or hands then nailed to the wooden rostra in the forum – nailed to his own stage and the scene of so much history and where he had condemned Antony so completely in the Philippics? We will never know for sure, but it would have made for a fitting gesture from two such vengeance riddled individuals. But by the standards of the time, punishments were only limited to what could be imagined. Even Pomponia, the mother of Quintus Junior, divorced from his father, is said to have asked Antony to hand over the freedman Philologus to her, which he happily did, and she is reported to have ordered him to cut off his own flesh piece by piece, roast it and eat it.

Just as the debate surrounding the death of Cicero does not allow his glory to die, something so vital to the purpose he saw for his life, so do the many legacies he has left the world to consider. Cicero provides us with natural law as the basis of legal systems around the world – his notion that a body of universally accepted moral codes are inherent to every individual and are not conferred by legislation. Throughout his life and in many trials, Cicero argued that harmony with nature means that there is no evolution, but an unchanging set of compass directions by which we can all travel:

> *There will not be one such law in Rome and another in Athens, one now and another in the future, but all peoples at all times will be embraced by a single and eternal unchangeable law.*

Cicero lives on not just in law but in our concepts of democracy and how fragile a hold we have on freedom. As a man determined to uphold freedom, even if that meant bending truth, operating outside of government or outright lies, Cicero demonstrated, and we look back and see, that democracy has to be fought for – to become complacent is for democracy to die. Everyone has a role to play in fighting and even dying for, if necessary, freedom:

Though liberty is established by law, we must be vigilant, for liberty to enslave us is always present under that very liberty.

As the modern world and the future moves through the eternal cycle of retreating democracy, advancing popularism and tyranny and back through to democracy we would do well for all the world to be aware that Cicero saw the entire cycle in one lifetime and to read and understand how easy it is for people to give up their freedom:

Do not blame Caesar, blame the people of Rome who have so enthusiastically acclaimed and adored him and rejoiced in their loss of freedom and danced in his path and gave him triumphal processions.

Replace the name of Caesar with Trump and Rome with Washington and we can see how close we are to a similar point in our own time.

It is Cicero that also lives on today in his views of greed and happiness. Though he himself displayed many of those features that he so despised in infecting the *mos maiorum* with greed and accumulation of material goods, Cicero continues to ask us difficult questions:

I don't understand what the man who is happy wants in order to be happier.

From over 2,000 years ago, Cicero remains like a radio transmitter out in deep space, pinging out the repeated philosophical messages that we want to hear and understand. Through the medium of his books and treatises we can study and try to understand the very real messages he was sending to posterity. Indeed, the genesis of this book was to provide another means of not only understanding more about the Roman Republican word, but also about ourselves through the life of Cicero and his works. Stoic idealism is growing in a world affected by a Covid pandemic, a reaction against capitalism through the fears of climate change and war. Although Cicero was not a devoted Stoic like Cato, he did use Stoic doctrines in his speeches and philosophical works – ideas of duty (*officium*), virtue (*virtus*), the good man as Cato said shortly before his death and utility (*utilitas*) – as he wrote in his final epistle to Marcus as long as it is morally right. In *De Officiis* Cicero talks to Marcus about finding the balance between utility, what needs to be done, and morality, what needs to happen to achieve the moral end result.

For those in government, who really ought to study a mandatory course in Ciceronian ethics before taking up their post as an MP – instead of the zero required of them at present, Cicero provides the essential basis for being a good leader – as well as a good speaker, and how we miss those in parliament today. Barely rising above the level of a GCSE debating society, the UK parliament long ago lost the eloquence of anything approaching even being one of Cicero's students let alone equalling his ability. Wisdom, justice, liberality, honour, these are the watchwords of a Ciceronian government and yet his language is all but invisible in the world of the twenty-first century democracy. There was a time when Ciceronian speech was a language of use – but no more. Even the ideals are misty, but Cicero is still sending out his messages through his probing writing, thought and speeches preserved for us if we would only read them.

Cicero had to fight his way to the top and, once he was there, spent his life fighting in the Senate – not so much a parliament as a gladiatorial arena – and he sacrificed his life to ideas and actions within the framework of his beliefs. Perhaps Mary Beard was right, when she wrote of a critical review of another biography on Cicero, that no such perfect book exists nor will it ever. This book is also far from a perfect effort, another attempt to capture the man, the lawyer, politician, father, statesman, orator, poet, philosopher, correspondent, general and husband, who was just as imperfect as we are and maybe that is why we are still drawn to Cicero. Not because of what he was, but because of what he is – one of us who achieved extraordinary things speaking to us across the centuries to a world where history is repeating itself.

If there is one major criticism of Cicero, it is that he strove to keep the world standing still. He had been raised at a time when instability under Sulla had been managed and the Republic had survived – he felt it could be done again and again. But the problems that had created Sulla remained and had not been either recognized or dealt with. Cicero was as much to blame for this as any other senator. The government of the Republic remained static whilst all around it the Roman world was changing.

Today President Biden exhibits the same crisis of identity. Biden is a product of the instability of the Cold War, he still sees the world in terms of good versus evil, democracy versus dictatorship with America as the great protector of all. But Biden misjudges the world just as Cicero did – he feels America can continue to save the world over and over again. Thus, democracy stands still while insidious, less obvious, more subtle and corrupt influences are well advanced which the death or removal of Putin will do nothing to stop. Like Cicero, many a US senator will wonder why they and the Republic they served is one day overwhelmed and they did nothing for the want of only doing a little.

The End.

Bibliography

Arena, V. *'Libertas' and the Practice of Politics in the late Roman Republic* (Cambridge: Cambridge University Press, 2012)

Babcock, C.L. 'The Early Career of Fulvia' *The American Journal of Philology* (Jan. 1965)

Batstone., Wiliam.W. (ed.) *Sallust: Catiline's Conspiracy, The Jurgurthine War, Histories.* (Oxford: Oxford University Press, 2010)

Beard, M. *The Roman Triumph* (Cambridge MA and London: Harvard University Press, 2007)

Beard, M. *SPQR A History of Ancient Rome* (London: Profile Books, 2016)

Brennan, T.C. *The Praetorship in the Roman Republic* (Oxford: Oxford University Press, 2000)

Claassen, J.M. 'Cicero's Banishment: "Tempora Et Mores"' *Acta Classica* (1992)

Dawes, T. 'Strategies of Persuasion in Philippics 10 and 11' *The Classical Quarterly* (May 2014)

De Selincourt, A. (trans.) *Livy, The Early History of Rome* (London: Penguin Books, 1971)

Drogula, Fred. K. *Cato the Younger. Life and Death at the End of the Roman Republic* (Oxford: Oxford University Press, 2019)

Drummond, A. *Law, Politics and Power: Sallust and the Execution of the Catilinarian Conspirators* (Stuttgart: Steiner, 1995)

Dyck, Andrew R. *Cicero Pro Marco Caelio* (Cambridge: Cambridge University Press, 2013)

Everitt, A. *Cicero A Turbulent Life* (London: John Murray, 2002)

Fantham, E. *Julia Augusti The Emperor's Daughter* (London and New York: Routledge, 2006)

Frier, B.W. 'Cicero's Management of His Urban Properties' *The Classical Journal* (Oct-Nov. 1978)

Freeman, Philip. *Commentariolum Petitionis by Quintus Tullius Cicero* (Princeton: Princeton University Press, 2012)

Gildenhard, I. & Hodgeson, L. *Cicero, On Pompey's Command* (*De Imperio*) (Cambridge: Open Book, 2014)

Goldsworthy, A. *The Complete Roman Army* (London: Thames & Hudson Ltd, 2018)

Grant, Michael. *Cicero: Selected Political Speeches* (London: Penguin Books, 1989)

Hales, S. 'At Home with Cicero' *Greece & Rome* (April, 2000)

Harrer, G.A. 'The Site of Cicero's Villa at Arpinum' *Studies in Philology* (October 1924)

Hartmann, B. *The Scribes of Rome* (Cambridge: Cambridge University Press, 2020)

Hughes, J.J. 'Invective and Comedie Allusion: Cicero, *In Pisonem*' *Latomus* (July-September 1998)

Keaveney, A. *Sulla: The Last Republican* (London and New York: Routledge, 2005)

Leach, E.W. 'Cicero's Cilician Correspondence: Space and Auctoritas' *Arethusa* (2016)

McCracken, G. 'Cicero's Tusculan Villa' *The Classical Journal* (February 1935)

McCracken, G. 'The Villa and Tomb of Lucullus at Tusculum' *American Journal of*

Archaeology (July-September 1942)

MacDonald, C. (ed.) *Cicero Orations In Catilinam, Pro Murena, Pro Sulla, Pro Flacco* (Cambridge MA: Harvard University Press, 1977)

Millar, Fergus. 'The Aerarium and its officials under the Empire' *The Journal of Roman Studies* (1963)

Mitchell, T.N. 'Cicero on the moral crisis of the late Republic' *Hermathena* (Summer 1984)

Montague, H.W. 'Advocacy and Politics: The Paradox of Cicero's *Pro Ligario*' *The American Journal of Philology* (Winter 1992)

Phillips, E.J. 'Catiline's Conspiracy' *Historia: Zeitschrift fur Alte Geschichte* (4th Qtr 1976)

Robb, M.A. *Beyond 'Populares' and 'Optimates': Political Language in the Late Republic* (Stuttgart: Steiner, 2010)

Root, M.V. 'A Visit to Cicero's Tusculum' *The Classical Journal* (October 1920)

Rowen, C. 'The Profits of War and Cultural Capital. Silver and Society in Republican Rome' *Historia: Zeitschrift fur Alta Geschichte* (2013)

Saller, Richard. P. *Personal Patronage under the Early Empire* (Cambridge: Cambridge University Press, 1982)

Scullard, H.H. *From the Gracchi to Nero. A History of Rome from 133 BCE to CE 68* (London and New York: Routledge, 1982)

Seager, R. 'Clodius, Pompeius and the Exile of Cicero' *Latomus* (July-September 1965)

Shackleton Bailey D.R. *Cicero: Selected Letters* (London: Penguin Books, 1982)

Shackleton Bailey D.R., *Cicero, Classical Life & Letters* (London: Duckworth, 1971)

Shackleton Bailey D.R. *Cicero Letters to Atticus, Vol.IV* (Cambridge MA: Harvard University Press, 1999)

Smethurst, S.E. 'Politics and Morality in Cicero' *Phoenix* (Autumn, 1955)

Smith, R.E. *Cicero the Statesman* (Cambridge: Cambridge University Press, 1966)

Stanton, G.R. 'Why did Caesar cross the Rubicon?' *Historia* 52 (2003)

Stockton, D. *Cicero: A Political Biography* (Oxford: Oxford University Press, 1971)

Sumi, G.S. 'Power and Ritual: The Crowd at Clodius' Funeral' *Historia: Zeitschrift fur Alte Geschichte* (1st Qtr 1997)

Taylor, L.R. 'The Election of the Pontifex Maximus in the Late Republic' *Classical Philology* (October 1942)

Treggiari, S. 'Home and Forum: Cicero between "Public" and "Private"' *Transactions of the American Philological Society* (1998)

Wright. Andrew. 'The Death of Cicero. Forming a Tradition: The Contamination of History' *Historia: Zeitschrift fur Alta Geschichte* (4th Qtr. 2001)

Index